ABRAHAM
KUYPER

Collected Works in Public Theology

GENERAL EDITORS

JORDAN J. BALLOR
MELVIN FLIKKEMA

ABRAHAMKUYPER.COM

ON
BUSINESS &
ECONOMICS

ABRAHAM
KUYPER

Edited by Peter S. Heslam

LEXHAM PRESS

ACTONINSTITUTE
FOR THE STUDY OF RELIGION AND LIBERTY

On Business & Economics

Abraham Kuyper Collected Works in Public Theology

Copyright 2021 Acton Institute for the Study of Religion & Liberty

Lexham Press, 1313 Commercial St., Bellingham, WA 98225
LexhamPress.com

Print ISBN 9781577996767
Digital ISBN 9781683594505
Library of Congress Control Number 2020948473

Acton Editorial: Ingrid De Groot
Lexham Editorial: David Bomar, Claire Brubaker, Justin Marr, Abigail Stocker
Cover Design: Christine Christophersen
Typesetting: ProjectLuz.com

CONTENTS

FOREWORDS

In the hyperpaced, global marketplace of the twenty-first century, what can be gained from the writings of a theologian-philosopher who seems preoccupied with critiquing the French Revolution of 1789? And given the sophisticated tools of modern economic analysis, why should anybody care about this theologian-philosopher's analysis of labor unions, government subsidies, and pensions in the Netherlands over a century ago?

One reason is that this theologian-philosopher, Abraham Kuyper (1837–1920), understood the underlying dynamics of today's global economy better than almost all of today's leading academics, analysts, and marketplace leaders. In fact, over a century ago, Kuyper forecast one of the central paradoxes of contemporary economic and social life.

On the one hand, the spread of capitalist narratives, institutions, and practices from "the West to the rest" has resulted in unprecedented increases in income and in other dimensions of human and cultural flourishing. Particularly encouraging has been the impact on poverty.[1] Indeed, since 1990 the number of people living on less than $1.90 per day—the

---

1. Richard Bluhm, Denis de Crombrugghe, and Adam Szirmai, "Poor Trends: The Pace of Poverty Reduction after the Millenium Development Agenda," UNU-MERIT working paper series, IPD WP19, February 2014; Aart Kraay, "When Is Growth Pro-Poor? Evidence from a Panel of Countries," *Journal of Development Economics* 80, no. 1 (June 2006): 198–227.

World Bank's poverty line—has declined by more than half, largely due to the benefits of economic growth.[2] Furthermore, many global leaders believe that, should these trends continue, it may be possible to lift the entire world above the $1.90 poverty line by the year 2030.[3] This massive reduction in global poverty is one of the greatest accomplishments of human history and should give pause to the critics of globalization.

On the other hand, there is a gnawing sense that something has gone terribly wrong in the West. Families are disintegrating, communities are fragmented, and political processes are in disarray. Our minds and bodies can feel it.[4] As leading social psychologist Jean Twenge laments:

> I think the research tells us that modern life is not good for mental health. ... Obviously, there's a lot of good things about societal and technological progress, and in a lot of ways our lives are much easier than, say, our grandparents' or great-grandparents' lives. But there's a paradox here that we seem to have so much ease and relative economic prosperity compared to previous centuries, yet there's this dissatisfaction, there's this unhappiness, there are these mental health issues in terms of depression and anxiety.[5]

The West is not alone in these disturbing trends. As market expansion has spread economic growth to the rest of the world, similar results have been found for transitional economies, resulting in what some economists are calling the "paradox of unhappy growth."[6]

---

2. United Nations, *The Millennium Development Goals Report 2015* (New York: United Nations, 2015), 4.

3. United Nations, *Sustainable Development Goals* (New York: United Nations), available at http://www.un.org/sustainabledevelopment/poverty/.

4. Brian Fikkert and Kelly M. Kapic, *Becoming Whole: Why the Opposite of Poverty Isn't the American Dream* (Chicago: Moody, 2019); Brian Fikkert and Michael Rhodes, "Homo Economicus vs. Homo Imago Dei," *Journal of Markets & Morality* 20, no. 1 (Spring 2017): 101–40.

5. Jean Twenge, as quoted in Jesse Singal, "For 80 Years, Young Americans Have Been Getting More Anxious and Depressed, and No One Is Quite Sure Why," *Science of Us*, March 13, 2016, available at www.nymag.com/scienceofus/2016/03/for-80-years-young-americans-have-been-getting-more-anxious-and-depressed.html.

6. Richard A. Easterlin, "Paradox Lost?" IZA discussion paper series no. 9676 (January 2016): 7; William Tov and Evelyn W. M. Au, "Comparing Well-Being across Nations: Conceptual and Empirical Issues," in *The Oxford Handbook of Happiness*, ed. Susan A. David, Ilona Boniwell, and Amanda Conley Ayers (Oxford: Oxford University Press,

How can Kuyper help us explain the paradox of the contemporary global economy? On the one hand, he would not have been surprised by the benefits of globalization, and he would have been particularly delighted by its impacts on poverty. Unlike many who have viewed the marketplace as outside God's domain, Kuyper understood economic exchange, business, and technological progress to be rooted in the created order, making them intrinsically good gifts from our creator.[7] Although Kuyper was not naïve about the cosmic scope of the fall, his belief in common grace recognized Jesus Christ as the creator, sustainer, and redeemer of the entire cosmos, including the economic domain (Col 1:15–20). In this light, Kuyper viewed business and economics not as something to avoid, but rather as one of many spheres in which human beings are to fulfill their calling to steward God's creation.[8]

At the same time, Kuyper would not be at all surprised by the ills that characterize the current economic and social order. In fact, he predicted them. Although Kuyper believed in common grace, he also saw the cosmos as contested terrain in which King Jesus is in "mortal combat" with all would-be usurpers of his throne.[9] This fundamental antithesis between warring kingdoms expresses itself in cultural endeavors, as human beings with differing worldviews shape culture in the image of the god they worship, however secular they may claim to be.[10]

At the dawn of the twentieth century, Kuyper believed the primary conflict in the West was between King Jesus and the god that had emerged from the French Revolution: the modern human being, an autonomous, rational, material creature whose flourishing depends solely on consumption.[11] Kuyper saw this as a grotesque distortion of the true nature of human beings; as image bearers of the Triune God, they are inherently relational

---

2013), 448–64; Bruno S. Frey, *Happiness: A Revolution in Economics* (Cambridge: MIT Press, 2010); Carol Graham, *Happiness around the World: The Paradox of Happy Peasants and Miserable Millionaires* (New York: Oxford University Press, 2009), especially 146.

7. See the appendix in this volume.

8. See Peter S. Heslam, "Editor's Introduction: Calvinism in Business—an Enlightened Enterprise?" in this volume.

9. *LC*, 11.

10. *LC*, 23–32.

11. *LC*, 11. See also "Money Is the Answer for Everything" and "The Love of Money Is the Root of All Kinds of Evil" in this volume.

and only truly flourish when they are in deep communion with God, others, and the world.[12]

According to Kuyper, the elevation of human beings and their insatiable desire for material prosperity was having devastating impacts on individuals and society:

> For the God of heaven is a God of compassion, but the money-god on earth is a god of boundless cruelty. Love of money abases you, dishonors you, robs you of spirit and backbone, and extinguishes in your soul the impulse for high and holy things. Money deprives you of your dignity, even when it gilds your life, your status, your position in society. It is not you that are rich, but it is money that makes you rich. If tomorrow your money is gone, gone is your glory. That is the lie that enters the world through love of money, corrupting everything. Since everything can be bought for money, the love of money won't stop until it has corrupted everything—through family feuds, usury practices, theft and robbery, breach of trust and deception, and in the end through suicide. What a frightful contrast! Those who choose the Lord as their God receive all lasting good for eternity; but those who put their faith in the god of money are heading for all manner of sorrows. Poor century! This then is your glory, that you have unleashed love of money. You promised us freedom, yet you shackle us in the chains of contempt.[13]

Now fast-forward one hundred years. Despite its adamant claims to being morally neutral, the neoclassical school of thought that has come to dominate Western economics and business has an implicit ethical standard and a god that it is worshipping. Indeed, neoclassical economics takes it as given that the goal of economic life is to serve *homo economicus*, an autonomous, rational, material creature whose flourishing depends solely on its consumption.

As an increasing number of scholars are noting, the goal of serving *homo economics* has come to dominate the narratives, institutions, and practices

---

12. *LC*, 23–32.
13. From "The Love of Money Is the Root of All Kinds of Evil," in this volume.

of the global economy.[14] Moreover, even noneconomic spheres are being shaped by the demands of *homo economicus*, including prisons, hospitals, libraries, schools, churches, and families.[15]

Of course, *homo economicus* is none other than the modern human being, the false god that Kuyper denounced over one hundred years ago. And as he predicted, this god would prove to be very cruel. For although the worship of *homo economicus* has resulted in unprecedented increases in economic growth and consumption, there is very strong reason to be believe that human beings are being transformed into the image of this horrible god.[16] Indeed, there is considerable evidence that Americans have become more individualistic and materialistic throughout the postwar era, resulting in lower self-reported happiness, poorer interpersonal relationships, higher levels of anxiety and depression, greater antisocial behavior, and lower health.[17] Moreover, there is evidence that globalization is spreading this deformation to other countries.[18]

---

14. Fikkert and Rhodes, "Homo Economicus"; Daniel Cohen, *Homo Economicus: The (Lost) Prophet of Modern Times* (Malden, MA: Polity, 2014); F. S. Michaels, *Monoculture: How One Story Is Changing Everything* (Kamloops, BC: Red Clover, 2011); Michael W. Goheen and Erin Glanville, eds., *The Gospel and Globalization: Exploring the Religious Roots of a Globalized World* (Vancouver, BC: Regent College Publishing, 2009); Bob Goudzwaard, Mark Vander Vennen, and David Van Heemst, *Hope in Troubled Times: A New Vision for Confronting Global Crisis* (Grand Rapids: Baker Academic, 2007).

15. Cohen, *Homo Economicus*; Michael Sandel, *What Money Can't Buy: The Moral Limits of Markets* (New York: Farrar, Straus, & Giroux, 2012); Michaels, *Monoculture*; Stephen A. Marglin, *The Dismal Science: How Thinking like an Economist Undermines Community* (Cambridge: Harvard University Press, 2008).

16. Fikkert and Rhodes, "Homo Economicus."

17. Jia Wei Zhang, Ryan T. Howell, and Colleen J. Howell, "Living in Wealthy Neighborhoods Increases Material Desires and Maladaptive Consumption," *Journal of Consumer Culture* 16, no. 1 (2016): 297–316; Tim Kasser et al., "Changes in Materialism, Changes in Psychological Well-Being: Evidence from Three Longitudinal Studies and an Intervention Experiment," *Motivation and Emotion* 38 (2014): 1–22; Aaron Ahuvia and Elif Izberk-Bilgin, "Well-Being in Consumer Societies," in David, Boniwell, and Ayers, *Oxford Handbook of Happiness*, 482–97; Richard Eckersley, "Is Modern Western Culture a Health Hazard," *International Journal of Epidemiology* 35 (2006): 252–58; Tim Kasser, *The High Price of Materialism* (Cambridge: MIT Press, 2002).

18. Carol Graham, Shaojie Zhou, and Junyi Zhang, "Happiness and Health in China: The Paradox of Progress," working paper 89 (Washington, DC: Brookings Institution, June 2015); Zhilin Tang, "They Are Richer, but Are They Happier: Subjective Well-Being of Chinese Citizens across the Reform Era," *Social Indicators Research* 117, no. 1 (2014): 145–64; Graham, *Happiness*.

At the start of this foreword I suggested that a key reason to read Kuyper's works on economics and business is that he understood the paradoxes of the current global economy better than most of us do. As he was a social activist and prime minister, not merely a theologian-philosopher, we can observe how he moves between theory and practice. We can see how he wrestles with such nitty-gritty things as operating hours for bakeries, railroad strikes, the role of tariffs, and the plight of the poor. It provides an example of what it means to improvise faithfully the economy of the kingdom of God, which is slowly but surely replacing the kingdoms of this world. *Homo economicus's* days are numbered. May we be found faithful when the one true King appears.

Brian Fikkert

***

Where does Kuyper fit in the dialogue between theologians, economists, and business? His world of the late nineteenth-century Netherlands was of course a very different one from ours. Theology and the church had authority and respect. Economics as an academic discipline was still taking shape and separating itself from theology—a process that was much more advanced in Britain than in continental Europe.[19] Business and management disciplines did not yet exist.

Kuyper picks up some of the longstanding themes of Christian engagement with the world of economics. There is great concern about poverty, which is especially scandalous in the Christian community, and about the spiritual dangers of wealth. In his late nineteenth-century context, the "social question" raised by the advance of commercial society and international finance absorbed his attention, as it did that of many other Christian leaders. This was the context of Pope Leo XII's encyclical *Rerum Novarum* and the development of modern Catholic social teaching. Peter Heslam and Jordan Ballor have written elsewhere on this shared context.

Two particular concerns evident from this collection of Kuyper's writing on economics were the doctrine of *laissez-faire*, which he associated with liberalism, and the French Revolution. Judging by the citations in

---

19. As described in Paul Oslington, *Political Economy as Natural Theology: Smith, Malthus and Their Followers* (London: Routledge, 2018).

this anthology, he seems to have read some of the English political economists such as Adam Smith. But his engagement with political economy was not deep, and his views were shaped by the fear of liberal and revolutionary ideas. Kuyper's comments about Manchesterism are revealing in this respect. This fear was shared by those who influenced the modern Catholic social encyclicals. Indeed, a suspicion of political economy persisted in Catholic circles for at least another century. Another of Kuyper's key concerns was the development of international finance and capital accumulation, which in several places in this collection he connects with the biblical critiques of mammon. While he does not offer much in the way of economic analysis, he is clearly an astute observer of the spiritual dangers connected with these developments.

As Peter Heslam discusses in his editorial introduction, the theological tools Kuyper brings to economics are common grace and antithesis. Common grace, in contrast to particular grace, is enjoyed by all, not just the elect. It flows from God's creative and providential activity, and it connects with Kuyper's doctrine of the Holy Spirit. As this anthology shows in many places, common grace for Kuyper is expressed in entrepreneurial activity, and commerce more generally. His engagement with Adam Smith does not seem to have included grasping his fellow Calvinist's idea of divine providence working self-interest toward the general good. I suspect, however, that it is an idea that Kuyper could have embraced if he had seen beyond his European prejudices about English political economy. Common grace in Kuyper must always be balanced against his doctrine of antithesis, his version of the familiar Christian doctrine of sin. This too was a doctrine emphasized by Smith in his treatment of economics. For instance, human sin and ignorance lies behind Smith's famous parody of the "man of system" who believes he can arrange economic matters as one arranges pieces on a chessboard. Our sinful nature also suggests to Smith that decentralization of economic power is preferable, as it restrains the damage flowing from human sin. I suspect Kuyper would have found this idea congenial to his own doctrine of antithesis in the economic sphere. It would also have sat well with his affection for the hard-pressed "little folk" (*kleine luyden*) of the Netherlands.

Heslam notes Kuyper's unusually positive approach to business for a theologian. How much does this flow from his theology, and how much from his friendships with Christian business leaders, including those who provided funds for projects such as his Free University? How much from proud memory of the commercial glories of the Dutch republic? I wonder even if the lack of explicit writing on economic matters reflects Kuyper's respect for a field he knew he had not mastered. Whatever the sources of Kuyper's appreciation of business, it sets an example to contemporary theologians.

Let me commend this volume of Kuyper's writings on business and economics put together by two fine scholars, Peter Heslam and Jordan Ballor, who have contributed much already to our understanding of Kuyper. In Peter's case, he has also contributed to working out Kuyper's ideas in practical business ventures around the world that are helping to tackle poverty, corruption, and other social ills. Though I have been critical of certain strands of "Kuyperian Christian economics,"[20] I retain a deep respect for Kuyper. If this volume makes his writing on business and economics more accessible, then we are all in the contributors' debt. Kuyper's writings are vast and must be read in the context Heslam and Ballor so helpfully provide. I hope most of all that this volume will encourage those who do not consider themselves Kuyperians to engage more deeply with his work.

Paul Oslington

***

Tertullian, the early church theologian and sometime Montanist, posed the now-famous question: "What indeed has Athens to do with Jerusalem? What concord is there between the Academy and the Church? what between heretics and Christians?"[21]

This was a reasonable question to pose, as many people both then and now perceived a deep dichotomy between things secular and things sacred. Tertullian maintained that dialectic and rhetoric served no useful purpose in the pursuit of truth, and he assigned an epistemological monopoly to the Scriptures. Not so his predecessor, Justin Martyr. Although his apologetic acknowledged the limitations of philosophical enquiry, Justin provided for the possibility that truth may indeed come from what appears to

---

20. Paul Oslington, "The Kuyperian Dream: Reconstructing Economics on Christian Foundations," *Faith & Economics* 75 (Spring 2020): 7–36.

21. Tertullian, *The Prescription against Heretics*, in *The Ante-Nicene Fathers*, ed. Alexander Roberts, James Donaldson, and A. Cleveland Coxe, trans. Peter Holmes (Buffalo, NY: Christian Literature, 1885), 3:246.

be nonreligious sources, but are in fact derived from the divine *logos* and therefore "are the property of us Christians."[22]

The idea that God's revelation of himself and his truth may, at least in part, be available to those outside the community of the elect is not a novel idea. But the widely accepted construct of "common grace" is a relatively recent phenomenon, largely accredited to the subject of this book, the late nineteenth- and early twentieth-century Dutch polymath Abraham Kuyper.

Kuyper is known worldwide as the theologian of common grace, and much has been written about his uncompromising *coram Deo* (also known as sphere sovereignty). However, as this book's editor, Peter Heslam, notes, little if any scholarship exists that relates the great man's theology to the areas of business and economics. It is a lacuna this tome is designed to address. Heslam admits this is a challenging task, as Kuyper himself did not connect theology and business in the sustained and systematic way he connected theology with other social spheres, such as education, politics, and science. However, Kuyper's vast codex, theological eclecticism, and Weber-like belief in a "this-worldly asceticism" gives Heslam and Jordan Ballor ample material from which to mine the treasures of his thinking on economic issues.

The book avoids the pitfalls of eisegesis and allows Kuyper's work speak for itself, including those areas in his thinking that appear to pull in different directions. For instance, he clearly has an Adam Smith–like appreciation for both the division of labor and the critical role of private enterprise; yet he lays his criticism of capitalism's *laissez faire, laissez passer* shortcomings squarely at Smith's feet. Similarly, while a critic of socialism, Kuyper nonetheless believed in the role of a strong and stable central government in the regulation of commerce and the restraint of economic activity marred by the fall. Indeed, in the metanarrative of creation, fall, redemption, and consummation that pervades these writings, Kuyper provides a very helpful framework for developing a theology of business and economics.

In this regard, Kuyper makes fascinating use of the Heidelberg Catechism. This confessional standard, representing the theology associated with sixteenth-century reformer John Calvin, was never intended to be used as an economic textbook or policy paper. But it was Calvin who influenced Kuyper more than any other theologian, as reflected in Kuyper's

---

22. Justin Martyr, *The Second Apology of Justin*, in Roberts, Donaldson, and Coxe, *Ante-Nicene Fathers*, 1:193.

famous Stone Lectures on Calvinism, delivered at Princeton University in 1898, which solidified his status as the preeminent neo-Calvinist of his day. What better prism could there be to view Kuyper's thinking on business and economics than the standard by which he calibrated his own beliefs?

Inspired by Kuyper's use of theology to address business and economics, Ballor offers in his introductory essay a tour de force through Kuyper's application of the tenets of the catechism in every area of life, including the economic interactions human beings have with each other, their stewardship of creation, and ultimately their duty to God.

Throughout these pages, readers will see the uncompromising nature of Kuyper's belief in the sovereignty of God and the constant tensions inherent in the "already but not yet" nature of human existence. He addresses head-on the telos of our economic activity and the idolatry of greed, the blessings of abundance and the curse of scarcity, the benefits of hard work and the need for Sabbath rest, the right to private property and concern for the common good. He addresses the nature and the use of money and in prescient fashion considers the pros and cons of what we would call globalization today. Yet in every instance, he views these issues as more than questions of political economy; he views them as issues of spiritual well-being and moral duty.

Were Tertullian to reframe his questions and ask Kuyper: "What has Jerusalem to do with *Wall Street*, the church with the *economy*, the Christian with the *capitalist*?" it is likely that Kuyper would say "Much," or perhaps as he states so eloquently in his reflection on Ecclesiastes 10:19:

> Whichever way you look at it, for God's child it always comes down to this choice. Whereas the power of money is the idol of the age, the Lord our Righteousness needs to be our God. This means our money must be made subject to the power, the commandment, the service and the honor of God.[23]

That is the underlying theme of this book. We are invited to gaze into the mind of a man whose superior intellect and commitment to the common good were surpassed only by his deep religious convictions and his commitment to the faithful service of God in every area of life. The result is a book that presents a fascinating, and at times complex, maze of traditional and

---

23. Abraham Kuyper, "Money is the Answer for Everything," in *On Business & Economics*, 361.

progressive ideas. Seasoned with Kuyper's penetrating insight and foresight, it sheds new light on the intricate and sometimes confounding relationship between faith, business, and economics. This anthology will be warmly welcomed and widely read, as its message is timeless and its wisdom is sorely needed to meet the economic challenges of the twenty-first century.

Kenneth Barnes

CALVINISM IN BUSINESS—AN ENLIGHTENED ENTERPRISE?

ABRAHAM KUYPER, COMMON GRACE, AND THE POTENTIAL OF BUSINESS

PETER S. HESLAM

INTRODUCTION

Common grace in business: putting these four words together implies a link between theology and enterprise, the existence of which is barely evident from the output of most theologians and business writers. The long-standing paucity of engagement between these groups reinforces the widespread perception that trying to mix commerce and religion is like trying to mix oil and water. This is reflected in the world of research and writing on Abraham Kuyper (1837–1920). In part due to more of his work appearing in English through this series of collected works, this world is rapidly expanding. Nevertheless, it is still the case that, among the countless studies that have been made of Kuyper for over a century, none deal with his views on business.[1] The closest are treatments of his engagement with poverty, working conditions, and pensions—generally referred to as the so-called social question. Kuyper's engagement with this question cannot, however, be taken as a proxy for his engagement with business itself.

Against such a bleak background, it is timely for an anthology on business and economics to appear made up of writings by Kuyper. This is especially the case given that he is increasingly known around the world as the theologian of common grace. In an era in which the sphere of business has risen in significance for human beings worldwide, this reputation raises the question of how Kuyper saw that grace at work in business. Before the appearance of this anthology, the material from which that question could be addressed lay too dispersed throughout Kuyper's huge legacy of writings to attract much attention. Add to that the traditional reluctance of theologians and other academics to engage with business, and the business lacuna in Kuyper studies becomes understandable. Another key reason for this lacuna, however, is that he failed to give much dedicated attention to business compared to other spheres of society. An example is his famous and influential Stone Lectures, which he delivered at Princeton in 1898.[2] Seeking to sketch out in those lectures the contours of a Christian worldview that engaged with every area of life, he dealt at some length with a

---

1. The only exception is Peter S. Heslam, "The Spirit of Enterprise: Abraham Kuyper and Common Grace in Business," *Journal of Markets & Morality* 18, no. 1 (Spring 2015): 7–20, on which this introductory chapter is based. A recent study with the promising title *Engaging the World with Abraham Kuyper*, by Michael P. Wagenman (Bellingham, WA: Lexham Press, 2019), has chapters on education, politics, society, and the church but not on business. A book that is slightly less recent but has an equally promising title, *For a Better Worldliness: Abraham Kuyper, Dietrich Bonhoeffer, and Discipleship for the Common Good*, by Brant M. Himes (Eugene, OR: Pickwick, 2018), also bypasses business.
2. *LC*. For an accessible yet comprehensive study of these lectures, see Peter S. Heslam, *Creating a Christian Worldview: Abraham Kuyper's Lectures on Calvinism* (Grand Rapids: Eerdmans, 1998).

number of spheres including politics, science, and the arts. But he gave no sustained attention to business.

A discussion of the many historical factors that help account for this void cannot be included here, though three can briefly be noted. First, business and economics had not yet been fully established when Kuyper was writing, either as professions or as academic disciplines, in the modern sense of those terms. Second, Kuyper and many of his antirevolutionary colleagues were children of the manse, with degrees in theology or law, rather than with trade backgrounds. Accordingly, their interests and commitments lay more naturally with the spheres of education and politics, the two spheres that were most central to the antirevolutionary cause.[3] Third, the industrial revolution occurred relatively late in the Netherlands, getting underway only in the final third of the nineteenth century. Consequently, the emergence of the large and complex organizations of industrial capitalism that set in motion the pens of moral philosophers in more industrially advanced economies were less within Kuyper's sights than more imminent perceived dangers inherent in other spheres.

Historical reasons aside, it is not without irony that a key impetus to the small but growing engagement between business and theology is the vision that animates Kuyper's works (including his *Lectures on Calvinism*)— an articulation of Christian faith that is discerning and critical yet world affirming. Indeed, Kuyper's legacy in the business world is greater than might be expected when judged by the range of social spheres with which he most engaged or by the produce of Kuyper scholarship.

Although this anthology (and to a lesser extent, this introductory essay) is a modest attempt to help supply the missing piece in Kuyper's intellectual legacy, it does so by providing a selection of his writings that do not necessarily deal with business and economics head-on but have important implications for those spheres. It may, indeed, be somewhat surprising that an anthology on business and economics should include reflections on a classic statement of ecclesiastical doctrine (the Heidelberg Catechism), biblical meditations, op-eds, occasional speeches, and travel memories. That it does use such sources is a mark of the breath of Kuyper's career. Here at work is a pastor, theologian, journalist, travel writer, philosopher, social reformer, spiritual writer, political party leader, and statesman. It is also

---

3. Education and politics were also central the Catholic cause, not only in the Netherlands but in many other Western democracies, during Kuyper's lifetime.

a mark of the *integral* nature of Kuyper's thought. For him, the boundaries between theology, spirituality, ethics, politics, business, and economics were permeable because they all operated under the sovereignty of God and embodied God's transcendence, immanence, and grace.

The integral nature of Kuyper's thought and action is offered in this anthology not merely as a model of interdisciplinary and practice-orientated thinking. It is also offered in the hope that it will spur a much richer theology-business engagement in the many parts of the world where Kuyper's name is known, and where he has hitherto been locked behind a language barrier for readers of English. This engagement will need to be made relevant, however, not only to business theorists but to business practitioners. For Kuyper, after all, Christian engagement with contemporary culture was not to be confined to ivory towers but needed to instigate tangible change that would help shape the social order.

Given that, when theology and business do at times engage, that engagement tends to be characterized by mutual hostility and suspicion, this introductory essay will provide an overview of what Kuyper regarded as the positive potential of business. This is not to imply that business, and economic issues in general, escaped Kuyper's criticism. The contents of this anthology provide plenty of evidence to the contrary. Indeed, his application of the theme of the "antithesis" gave him a more than adequate intellectual platform from which to mount severe critiques of these fields. This doctrine was, in fact, as central to Kuyper's thought as the doctrine of common grace. It held that the fall of humankind into sin constituted a radical disruption whereby the curse of sin infected and affected all existence. The innocence, freedom, and order of paradise constituted the "normal" state of things because it was in alignment with God's will. The postfall condition was "abnormal" in being at odds with divine intentions and subject to all manner of sin and evil and their ugly consequences—a predicament that ultimately could only be addressed through God's redemption.

From the vantage point of the twenty-first century, many of Kuyper's antithesis-inspired critiques of commercial activity have a poignant and prophetic feel. As readers of this anthology will see, he spoke out (to name just a few issues) against highly commoditized and speculative activity in finance, burgeoning consumerism, and the prioritization of wealth above all other concerns. Moreover, he often framed his critiques with characterizations of economic globalization that have a contemporary ring for later generations, even though they stem from the early years of the twentieth century. In one example, Kuyper writes,

> Money's power has thus become a world power that ignores the borders of land and nation, spreads its wings out over all of human life, lays claim to everything, and increasingly pene-trates into some of the most unknown corners of the world. It makes everything dependent on it, imposes its law on all lives, and consolidates in the great world cities in order to give life a bewitching glow, to have a temple there in its honor, and to rule the entire world from that base.[4]

Such imagery also finds expression in two important addresses Kuyper delivered. One is included in this anthology as the chapter titled "Sacred Order." The other he gave as prime minister to the Dutch Retailers Association. In the latter speech he claimed that big capital, international competition, and rapid developments in communication were producing a situation in which national industries hardly existed anymore.[5]

These examples, while drawn from the later part of Kuyper's career, when global capital markets were beginning the rise that would hit the buffers in the Wall Street crash of 1929, echo sentiments found earlier in his career in his writings on social issues. One of his most famous speeches, "The Social Question and the Christian Religion," delivered in 1891 and included in this anthology, provides particularly striking example. There he declares, "Christ himself, just as his apostles after him and the prophets before him, invariably took the side of the suffering and the oppressed against the rich and the mighty of this world." While avoiding the trap many theologians fail to avoid, of romanticizing the poor, Kuyper argued that "when Scripture corrects the poor it does so much more tenderly and gently; and, by contrast, when it rebukes the rich it uses much harsher language."[6]

All these examples serve as evidence that, on issues of socioeconomic justice, Kuyper was a strident critic and campaigner with indignation and

---

4. *PR* 1.I.10.5:88.
5. A transcription of the speech is available in *Vijf en twintig jaren middenstandsbeweging: gedenkboek van de Nederlandse Middenstandsbond, uitgegeven ter gelegenheid van zijn 25-jarig bestaan. Bewerked door A Ingenool* ('s Gravenhage: Vereeniging De Nederlandse Middenstandsbond, 1927), 29–31, here 30.
6. See "The Social Question and the Christian Religion," in this volume, pp. 185–91.

zeal comparable to that of the so-called liberation theologians of the later twentieth century.

Nevertheless, the common-grace theme of this introductory essay invites an inquiry into what Kuyper saw as the positive contribution that business makes to human and social flourishing. This inquiry assumes, rather than overlooks, Kuyper's countervailing doctrine of the antithesis. This is because common grace only makes sense when held together with the antithesis, as the former is in the first place an attempt to answer the question of how, *given the reality of the antithesis*, it is possible that non-Christian culture can exemplify great virtue. Particular grace, or "special grace," was, for Kuyper, the grace by which people turn from their sins, put their trust in Christ, receive the regenerating work of his spirit, and inherit the gift of eternal life. Common grace, in contrast, was grace at work in the world at large, by which God holds back the forces of evil, restrains the effects of the fall, and allows civility and human culture to flourish.[7] Against the background of this doctrinal framework, Kuyper's positive appraisal of the potential of business—as indeed of any sphere— is the other side of the coin to his denouncements of errors within that sphere. Disregarding this positive appraisal fails to do justice to Kuyper as a cultural critic with a sharp eye not only for pitfalls but also for potential.[8]

Common grace was, in fact, a means Kuyper used to break the stranglehold that was keeping business and theology separate. Judging by his critiques, this bifurcation was as much a feature of the late nineteenth- and

---

7. For a summary of Kuyper's doctrine of common grace, see Heslam, *Creating a Christian Worldview*, 117–23.

8. James Bratt's otherwise excellent biography is an example of scholarly writing that systematically overlooks Kuyper's positive attitude to the potential of business, focusing instead on his critiques of dogmatic *laissez-faire* and his warnings to the rich. The oversight allows Bratt to exclaim in his discussion of Kuyper's economic perspective, "For economic conservatives (that is, neoliberals) and American evangelicals, who assume an automatic affinity between their respective positions, Kuyper's deliverances will be bewildering at best, outrageous at worst." If Bratt is right, it is because "neoliberals" and evangelicals share Bratt's own blind spot regarding Kuyper's work. My hope is that this introductory essay, based largely on sources not included in this anthology, will help create some balance for the ideological constituency Bratt delineates, as well as for his own constituency (left-leaning academia). Kuyper cannot fully be captured by either camp, as he stands for elements championed by both. See James D. Bratt, *Abraham Kuyper: Modern Calvinist, Christian Democrat* (Grand Rapids: Eerdmans, 2013), especially 221–28 (the citation above is from 224).

early twentieth-century Netherlands as it is today in many parts of the world.[9] He railed against forms of Christianity that made no difference to the way people operated in the workplace, leaving the work of Christians indistinguishable from that of non-Christians.[10] Misconduct in business and in the handling of money served only to show believers to be hypocrites.[11]

For Christians to restrict their faith to matters of the soul allowed business to be regarded as an unholy distraction rather than as a dignified profession.[12]

Kuyper's positive view of business includes his ideas about economic freedom and the role of regulation, organized labor and the role of guilds, the eternal value of earthly work, stewardship and philanthropy, economic globalization, business as a "mediating institution" between the individual and the state, the workings of God's grace in business, the social function of money, and the calling of business. While all these matters deserve exploration, the confines of this article only allow a brief overview of the final three.

COMMON GRACE AT WORK

Biblical history and archaeology, Kuyper claimed, attest to the fact that crafts and practical skills were more prolific in the pagan cultures of Israel's neighbors, such as Egypt, Assyria, Babylon, and Persia, than in Israel itself.[13] For Kuyper, this was evidence that the spirit of God gifts human beings with talents and skills without regard to merit or piety. Whether or not the recipient recognizes the origin of their gifts, they have the potential to enrich all people and societies. Kuyper appealed to the accounts of the artisans Bezalel and Oholiab in Exodus 31:1-6 and 35:30-35 and of arable production in Isaiah 28:23-29 in support of his claim that God is the source of all artistic craft and skill and of all knowledge and insight in agriculture.[14]

---

9. See Peter S. Heslam, "Christianity and the Prospects for Development in the Global South," in *The Oxford Handbook of Christianity and Economics*, ed. Paul Oslington (Oxford: Oxford University Press, 2014), 359–83. See also Peter S. Heslam and Eric A. S. Wood, "Faith and Business Practice amongst Christian Entrepreneurs in Developing and Emerging Markets," *Koers: Bulletin for Christian Scholarship* 79, no. 2 (2014): 1–7.
10. See CG 2.39.2:338–39.
11. CG 2.44.4:382–83.
12. CG 1.30.3:267–69; 1.63.2:554; 2.31.3:268–69.
13. CG 1.38.4:337–38; 56.5:497–99; 57.5:506–8; PR 1.II.8.3:166–68.
14. CG 2.68.3:584; PR 3.IV.4.1:27–29.

In business, Kuyper explained, this giftedness works as God raises up exceptional leaders who grow their operations in accordance with their talents and with the opportunities they perceive. Such people stand out from their contemporaries in having "clearer insight, a greater practicality, a more powerful will, and a greater degree of entrepreneurial courage."[15] In exercising these gifts, they help others flourish and ensure that their ideas and inventions outlive them in society.[16] All this, Kuyper insisted, is the result of common grace, which works in a specific way in the sphere of commerce, just as it works in a specific way in other spheres: "Common grace extends over our entire human life, in all its manifestations. ... There is a common grace that shines in the development of science and art; there is a common grace that enriches a nation through inventiveness in enterprise and commerce."[17] As these forms of common grace take effect, they raise the standard of social life; enrich human knowledge and skill; and make life "easier, more enjoyable, freer, and through all this our power and dominion over nature keeps increasing."[18] While these developments inevitably provide additional opportunities for sin, common grace has raised human achievement to new heights through the invention of tools and machines, the division of labor, and the harnessing of nature to generate steam power and electricity.[19]

In the light of what is now known about the impact of carbon-intensive industrialization on the natural environment, Kuyper's appreciation of human power over nature appears to be insufficiently nuanced, revealing him as a child of his times. It is clear from the context of his words, however, that foremost in his mind is the centuries-long progress human beings have made in procuring such basic goods as food, shelter, energy, transport, and health. In terms, by contrast, that sound well ahead of his times, he averred that the potency of common grace to foster such progress, and the cultural development it facilitates, lay in the fact that humans are made in the image of a God whose essence, as Father, Son, and Holy Spirit, is diverse and relational. This *imago Dei* acts as a "seed" within diverse human beings that only germinates through their social relationships. It

---

15. *PR* 3.IV.10.3:83.
16. See *OP* 2II.20:20–21. See also *PR* 3.IV.4.3:31–33; *LC*, 95.
17. *CG* 1.56.5:497.
18. *CG* 1.56.5:497.
19. *CG* 1.67.6:594; *CG* 3:437–38.

thereby permeates culture, including "all kinds of business undertakings and industry."[20] Clearly, for Kuyper, business joined all other aspects of culture in reflecting God's creation of human beings in the divine likeness, an act that fills these beings with awesome potential.

PARTICULAR GRACE AT WORK

If the image of God in human beings is not restricted to Christians, and one of its effects is that it helps business flourish, what role did Kuyper reserve for particular grace within the commercial sphere? Here the distinction he made between the church as *institution* and the church as *organism* is of special relevance.

Kuyper taught that the institutional form of the church is found in its statutes, laws, offices, and registers, all of which facilitate the ministry of the Word, the sacraments, and acts of charity. Closely associated to this form of church is its rich organic form that finds expression in wider society, including in families, businesses, science, and the arts as believers live and work in those spheres. A Christian, he taught, is not merely a church member but a parent, a citizen, an employer, or an employee. As such, they "bring to bear the powers of the kingdom in their family life, in their education, in their business, in all dealings with people, and also as citizens in society." Whereas the church as institution is distinct from society, the church as organism "impacts the life of the world, changes it, gives it a different form, elevates it and sanctifies it."[21] This is especially the case when the life of the institutional church is most vibrant. As Kuyper put it, using a vivid metaphor:

> Even though the lamp of the Christian religion burns only within the walls of that institution [the church], its light shines through the windows far beyond it and shines upon all those aspects and connections of our human life. ...
>
> Jurisprudence, law, family, business, occupation, public opinion and literature, art and science, and so forth—the light shines upon all of this, and that illumination will be all the more powerful and penetrating the more clearly and purely

---

20. *CG* 2.83.4:716.
21. *CG* 3:421.

the lamp of the gospel is allowed to burn within the institution of the church.[22]

As an example of this occurring in practice, Kuyper highlighted the Dutch Republic (1581–1795), a period in the history of the Netherlands often associated with the heyday both of Calvinism and of commerce. Not only were Dutch farmers at this time the most advanced in Europe, Kuyper maintained, but Dutch merchants were renowned for their honesty and integrity. He attributed these characteristics to the power of the Word of God and of divine ordinances that were widely preached and shared in their midst.[23]

This power put Christian nations at an advantage and helped account for the contribution they had made to human development: "a rich development of the life of the soul arising from regeneration joined with a rich development proceeding from the life of common grace."[24] The potency of this mix of graces was not only demonstrated in these nations by their high level of care for the poor and the elevation of women but also by a highly developed business sphere.[25] The attributes of such countries derive from particular grace but operate in the sphere of common grace. Despite his readiness to admit that impressive business development had been achieved outside the influence of the Judeo-Christian tradition, Kuyper was clearly of the view that business' best prospects were served when the workings of particular grace and common grace converge.

MONEY AS A SOCIAL BLESSING

Despite Kuyper's many jeremiads against the dangers and abuses of wealth, he insisted that money was a gift of God. The appearance and development of money in world history "did not come from the Evil One, but was fully in line with the design of God. It was not intended as a curse, but a blessing."[26] Only when sin attacked it did money acquire a sinister omnipotence: it

---

22. *CG* 2.35.3:304.
23. *CG* 2.68.3:586; Abraham Kuyper, *Gomer voor den Sabbath* (Amsterdam: Wormser, 1889), 21 (see the chapter in this anthology titled "Do Not Withhold Good from Those to Whom It Is Due").
24. *CG* 1.67.6:594.
25. *CG* 2.88.4:756–57. Kuyper did not reserve the workings of common grace to nonbelievers. Common grace also operated in and through Christians, who were simultaneously recipients of particular grace. See *CG* 2.25.5:220–21.
26. *PR* 3.IV.12.3:99.

is in the human heart and not in money itself wherein lie the origins of mammon—the idolization of money. While mammon is allied to greed and dishonesty, money itself is "one of God's gifts for society so that it might develop more highly and richly."[27]

The uplifting and cohesive impact of money in society derives primarily from the ability it gives to the thrifty to save and from the stimulus this gives to commercial enterprise.[28] This blessing, Kuyper maintained, "is evident in the quiet, normal life of citizens whose activity in trading and commerce has been unbelievably enriched and simplified by money."[29] The positive potential of money was also evident in the charitable sector, where it facilitates care for the needy; and in the church, where it not only supports buildings but also clergy, missions, seminaries, and the practical help for the disadvantaged provided by the diaconate.[30] In the end, whether money works as a blessing or curse is a spiritual matter:

> It can be turned to the good, or to evil. The choice between the two depends only on the disposition of the human heart. Those who bow down to mammon use it for corruption; those who bow their knee before Christ as their King can use it to increase the luster of Christ's kingship.[31]

Kuyper's notion that money can provide sound foundations for a developed and unified society suggests he was influenced by the notion of the "commercial society," associated in particular with French intellectual Alexis de Tocqueville (1805–59), who visited the United States in 1831 and recorded his observations in *Democracy in America*. As early in his career as 1873, Kuyper acknowledged the influence of this thinker on his ideas; in a sermon he published that year, he held up the United States as a "golden land" that provided a model of freedom.[32] A quarter of a century later, he reechoed this theme several times when he visited America in 1898. There he argued, in somewhat rhapsodic tones, that the origins of the United States'

---

27. *PR* 3.IV.12.3:100.
28. *PR* 3.IV.12.2:98.
29. *PR* 3.IV.12.4:101.
30. *PR* 3.IV.12.4:101.
31. *PR* 3.IV.12.4:101.
32. Abraham Kuyper, *Vrijheid: Rede, ter bevestiging van Dr Ph.S. van Ronkel, gehouden den 23 maart 1873, in de Nieuwe Kerk te Amsterdam* (Amsterdam: De Hoog, 1873).

enterprise society lay in the Calvinism practiced by ordinary tradespeople in the Old World:

> Calvinism sprang from the hearts of the people themselves, with weavers and farmers, with tradesmen and servants, with women and young maidens.[33]

> With this there went out from Western Europe that mighty movement which promoted the revival of science and art, opened new avenues to commerce and trade, beautified domestic and social life, exalted the middle classes to positions of honor, caused philanthropy to abound.[34]

> There was a rustling of life in all directions, and an indomitable energy was fermenting in every department of human activity, and their commerce and trade, their handicrafts and industry, their agriculture and horticulture, their art and science, flourished with a brilliancy previously unknown, and imparted a new impulse for an entirely new development of life, to the whole of Western Europe.[35]

The flowering of Calvinism and commerce went hand in hand, Kuyper argued, with the division of labor. As this division increased, the scope and quality of production rose, and sufficient capital could be accumulated to develop large enterprises.[36] In turn, these stimulated "all kinds of inventions and the enrichment of our power over nature."[37]

While Kuyper was eager to admit that sin affects all such positive development, he was adamant that the abuse of money must not be allowed to overshadow its proper use. History demonstrates, he argued, that money facilitates the economic development necessary for social flourishing.

BUSINESS AS A CALLING

The positive social potential inherent in the creation of material wealth reflected, for Kuyper, that business is an honorable calling for an individual

---

33. *LC*, 24.
34. *LC*, 39–40.
35. *LC*, 73.
36. *PR* 3.IV.6.3:48.
37. *CG* 3:432.

to pursue and that business has an honorable calling to fulfill in society. Christians must be prepared, he argued, to counteract the corrupting effects of sin in business life by setting a good example in the production, processing, and distribution of goods and services. In so doing, they honor the workings of common grace in society and uphold the ordinances of God for commercial life. Christians should reject, therefore, the attitude of those who consider business to be a field in which Christians should allow others to take the lead because there can be no valid calling to commerce. Not least because of the financial requirements of churches, schools, and charities, Christians in business need to be competent in generating profit. God's children, Kuyper taught, should "take pride in not falling behind others in this realm, because also in this area of life it is God who gives us wisdom, God who prepares the means for us, and God who guides the development of societal life through his common grace."[38]

In making this argument, Kuyper appealed to Petrus Plancius (1552–1622), a Flemish astronomer, cartographer, theologian, and a founder-director of the Dutch East India Company. Based in Amsterdam during the Dutch Golden Age, this devout and impassioned preacher encouraged Calvinists to excel in commerce and used his expertise in geography to give navigational assistance to seafaring merchants. His example, Kuyper maintained, challenged the contemporary tendency "to view agriculture, industry and commerce as worldly side issues." Bringing the best goods to market, making wise acquisitions, and conducting sound commerce was the pathway to the prosperity that societies needed, and Christians needed to be in the vanguard.[39]

It was, moreover, from God that people receive the intuition, imagination, and skills—plus their delight in utilizing them—that cause them to excel in the commercial sphere. From God also comes their "spirit of enterprise," and "the desire and inclination people have to occupy themselves with a certain trade over another." What people chose to do with their lives, accordingly, is not a matter of coincidence but was a matter of what God has implanted within them. It is ultimately this divine orientation, rather than money or argument, that convinces them to pursue a particular career.[40] Entrepreneurs are given the rare talent, persistence, resources,

---

38. *CG* 3:433.
39. *CG* 3:433.
40. *PR* 3.IV.4.4:33.

and leadership qualities to grow their businesses from employing only their immediate family to employing hundreds of workers. All this involves an art that God gives to certain individuals, who eventually hand it on to those in the next generation who have a similar orientation. Here, too, Kuyper appealed to the account of the Israelite craftsmen noted earlier who were equipped in their work by God's spirit.[41]

Kuyper's defense of business as a valid vocation for an individual to pursue was inextricably tied to his idea that business itself had a vocation. In keeping with the calling of all other social spheres, its vocation was to glorify God through following God's ordinances for that sphere. These ordinances, he maintained, permeate all creation and human culture, and they provide the organic connections that hold the various social spheres together. They are connections that human beings find rather than create. Although human beings exert some influence on these connections, these connections exert a stronger influence on human beings.[42]

In the economic sphere, the workings of God's ordinances can be found in particular in the historical process, noted earlier, to which Kuyper attached great importance: the division of labor.[43] As this process unfolded, trade and industry flourished, thereby stimulating higher and richer forms of culture and society.[44] Despite threats imposed by human sinfulness, this development "brings to light treasures that were once hidden, increases man's power over nature, fosters interaction among people, and brings together nations. ... [It] counteracts much suffering, turns aside much danger, and in numerous ways makes life much richer."[45] All this is reflected in the expansion of local markets into national and international ones.[46] Clothing once made by tailors at home with the help of their spouses and children was now made in "a large garment factory, which wants to bring tens of thousands of pieces of clothing to the market all at once."[47] In such developments and in the power of steam and electricity that enables them, ordinances of God lay hidden for centuries. Only at the appointed time

---

41. *PR* 3.IV.4.1:27–28.
42. *CG* 3:431–33.
43. *PR* 3.IV.4.2–5:29–35.
44. *PR* 3.IV.3.1–4:19–26.
45. *PR* 3.IV.2.4:18.
46. *PR* 3.IV.6.1:45.
47. *PR* 3.IV.6.1:48.

did God raise up people to make the necessary discoveries.[48] Accordingly, the human task is not to devise theories and then to try to press reality to fit them. It is, rather, to trace the laws and relationships inherent in reality—regardless of whether or not God is recognized as their source.[49] As this quest is fulfilled in the commercial sphere, business flourishes and strengthens human culture.[50]

The idea that every sphere of society, including business, is charged with the ordinances of God and has the task of discerning them and acting on them was fundamental to Kuyper's social vision. It meant that society was not a random aggregate of individuals but an integrated and purposeful whole:

> Families and kinships, towns and villages, businesses and industries, morals, manners, and legal customs are not mechanically assembled but, like groups of cells in a human body, are organically formed by a natural urge that, even when degenerate or deviant, is generally obedient to a higher impulse.[51]

Because of this, each sphere of society has a fundamental moral purpose: "The various entities—human persons first of all—which God called into being by his creative powers and to which he apportioned power, are almost all, in whole or in part, of a moral nature."[52] From its divinely endowed moral purpose, rather than from any dictate from the state, each sphere of society develops a free life of its own:

> There is a distinctive life of science; a distinctive life of art; a distinctive life of the church; a distinctive life of the family; a distinctive life of town or village; a distinctive life of agriculture; a distinctive life of industry; a distinctive life of commerce; a distinctive life of works of mercy; and the list goes on.[53]

The sphere of the state stands alongside, rather than above, these social spheres, though it does have the right and duty to intervene when conflict

---

48. *PR* 3.IV.4.4:34; *OP* 3.I.28:31–32.
49. *OP* 2.II.20:20–21; 3.I.27:29–31.
50. *PR* 3.IV.6.4:51.
51. *OP* 4.I.39:44.
52. *OP* 5.IV.59:70.
53. *OP* 5.IV.59:70.

arises among them; to defend the weak; and to ensure (coercively if necessary) that citizens give sacrificially, in financial and nonfinancial ways, to maintain the "natural unity of the state."[54]

This is a core tenet of Kuyper's sphere-sovereignty doctrine, which has attracted a great deal of scholarly attention from around the world. Whilst this doctrine cannot be expounded here, an interesting example of Kuyper seeking to apply his idea of sectoral autonomy to a specific industry is that of bakeries. On the initiative of the Catholic Employers' Association for Bakers and Confectioners, the first Congress for the Abolition of Night work in the Baking Industry was held September 24–26, 1907. Kuyper delivered a speech in which he supported the proposal of a bill to ensure proper night rest for bakers. He did so on the basis that the ordinances of God are reflected in the way the rhythm of work and rest corresponds with the division of day and night. He argued, however, that family-owned bakeries should be made exempt from the proposed law, otherwise the state would be contravening the autonomy of the family. Ten days after the congress, Kuyper published a reflection on this issue in a meditation based on Hosea 7:6, which in the *Statenvertaling*, the Dutch translation of the Bible that was used in his time, includes a phrase that also appears in the King James Version but not in more recent Dutch and English translations: "Their baker sleepeth all the night."[55] When the draft law was rejected in 1912, Antirevolutionary cabinet minister Syb Talma, who introduced it, was (understandably) disappointed with Kuyper for not giving it his support. Clearly there were differences among members of Kuyper's own party as to how the principle of sphere sovereignty should be applied in practice. But it has remained a central concept among many of Kuyper's followers right up until the present day.

Representing an unusual form of sociopolitical pluralism, sphere sovereignty is often associated among scholars in the Netherlands with "pillarization" (*verzuiling*), a process of ideological group formation in Dutch history

---

54. Presumably the latter refers in particular to the paying of taxes, and to civic service (military of otherwise). See *LC*, 97; *OP* 2.II.21.

55. See *De Heraut*, no. 1553, October 6, 1907. Although Tjitze Kuipers claims Kuyper's meditation was based on faulty exegesis, it is more a question (at least with this particular meditation) of the alternative text traditions used by biblical translators. See *AKB*, 1907.17, p. 389.

on which Kuyper exerted significant influence.[56] The complex particulars of Dutch social pillarization fall outside this introduction. What matters in terms of Kuyper's approach to economic life is the idea, central to his notion of sphere sovereignty, that every sphere of society (business included) enjoys a certain freedom because its authority comes from God rather than from the state. This provided Kuyper with a key part of the intellectual framework with which to make the case that business—along with every other sphere of society—has a calling. As with those other spheres, business has the freedom and responsibility to discern and follow that calling for itself. As it does so, it helps human beings and the social spheres they inhabit to flourish to the glory of God.

BUSINESS AND LEADERSHIP

Kuyper was not a business leader, but he shared some of the traits associated with such leaders, including those he identified above in terms of practical insight, determination, and courage. He was also the key driver of many new ventures, including a newspaper, a university, and a political party, all of which had requirements familiar to the founders of commercial enterprises, such as the management of investments, budgets, cash flows, accounts, targets, delivery channels, marketing, publicity, and accountability to stakeholders. Using contemporary language, he could legitimately be referred to as a social entrepreneur.

The entrepreneurial instincts appear to have run deep. According to anecdotal evidence from his family, as a child he distributed cigars to local seamen in exchange for their giving audience to his mini homilies. In his first parish, he followed another Reformed clergyman—Henry Duncan (1774-1846), the Scottish founder of the world's first savings bank—in establishing a local bank for small savers. His endeavors clearly commanded respect and support, especially among business leaders. An ally of Kuyper for almost half a century was successful beer entrepreneur and social reformer Willem Hovy (1840-1915), who was the key financial backer of the fledgling Free University and played a founding role in the Christian trade union Patrimonium and of the Christian employers association Boaz, both of which Kuyper writes about in this anthology.

---

56. For a discussion of the link between sphere sovereignty and *verzuiling*, see Heslam, *Creating a Christian Worldview*, 158-60.

When Hovy died, Kuyper was his most long-standing friend and the only person the family invited to give a graveside address. In a subsequent obituary, he paid tribute to Hovy's generosity, his practical mindedness, his "almost unbelievable" knowledge of Scripture, his "unconditional attachment" to the Bible as the basis for all his actions, and his commitment to living out his faith in everyday life.

Kuyper also praised Hovy for two things he explicitly condones in writings included in this anthology: making money in order to support the work of Christ, and for being an employer for whom the well-being of his workers was paramount.[57] Hovy's aim to see Christ at work in people's souls gave him, Kuyper claimed, "that warmth, that inspiration and that fervor, which so ignited others and replaced so much stiffness and dryness with new life." Kuyper declared that whereas many Christians demonstrated the tendency to stay in their own tent, for Hovy it was about getting out from the tent to bear witness and to engage with contemporary society. His activities, including his promotion of the draining of the Zuidezee, reflected his "double employment of spiritual freedom and public involvement." He went to his brewery, "not as a capitalist checking up on his workers but as a brother who held his factory workers in a bond of respect and trust." He even, Kuyper continued, held daily times of worship and Scripture reading for his workers. This for Kuyper was an example of the ways in which Hovy helped bring down barriers between employers and employees. Concerned about the whole person, he shared in the ups and downs of his workers' lives; visited them when they were ill; helped provide them with accommodation, pensions, and paid leave on Sundays and feast days; and met with their families at Christmas. Standing at his graveside, Kuyper was struck, he recalled, by how much loss the second half of the nineteenth century would have suffered without Hovy. With unmatched certainty, Kuyper concluded, Hovy stood for his beliefs and principles, while always seeking to maintain unity between people of different outlooks. He felt at one even with his fiercest opponents, for they too were citizens and fellow

---

57. Regarding generosity in the support of Christian activity, see "Protectionism and Materialism," the extract in this anthology from *Varia Americana*. Regarding the treatment of employees by their employers, see the extracts from "Social Organizations under Our Own Banner" and "Draft Pension Scheme for Wage Earners."

human beings. In every area of their lives, Hovy had shown other people empathy and commitment.[58]

Kuyper's friendship with Hovy provides an important historical clue to why Kuyper is exceptional among theologians for appreciating the positive potential of business. Although they had some serious disagreements, the friendship they forged as young men remained until death separated them in their old age. In Hovy, Kuyper had a close friend, colleague, and supporter who was known both for his godly character and for being one of the country's leading Christian business leaders. This would have made it difficult for Kuyper to display the naïve dismissiveness toward business that has characterized the attitude of theologians down through the centuries.

A second reason for Kuyper's unusually positive approach to business was that he was opposed to the conservatism of the landed gentry and those of noble birth. Whether they were involved in some form of commercial activity or not, they were often out of touch with ordinary people working people and demonstrated little concern for their welfare. Kuyper, on the other hand, was the leader of the so-called *kleine luyden* ("little folk")— the small-scale entrepreneurs, tradespeople, shopkeepers, farmers, and leaders of family firms. He was aware that, for them, business was their livelihood—a way of life not to be looked down upon with the aristocratic snugness of the intellectual elite.

Third, while Kuyper was unquestionably a champion for the poor, he was also vociferously opposed the socialism that was rapidly on the rise during his career. Adamant that all those who follow Christ will defend the interests of the vulnerable and the weak, they are to be as opposed to the

---

58. Abraham Kuyper, "Bij de nagedachtenis van Willem Hovy," in *De Amsterdammer: Weekblad voor Nederland*, March 14, 1915, pp. 1-2, repr. in J. C. Rullman, *Kuyper-bibliografie* (Kampen: Kok, 1923-40), 3:411-15. In this obituary, Kuyper notes that Hovy's gift of 25,000 guilders to help launch the Free University was "in true American style" ("Bij de nagedacthenis," 1). Some of Kuyper's admiration for the "princely liberality" with which Americans supported their social institutions is expressed in the extract in this anthology from his American memoires *Varia Americana*. There he writes of "a level of generosity in charitable giving that is unknown elsewhere." See "Protectionism and Materialism," 255-60. Two notable accounts of Hovy's career are by Rolf van der Woude: "Willem Hovy (1840-1915): Bewogen christelijk-sociaal ondernemer," in *Geloof in eigen zaak: Markante protestantse werkgevers in de negentiende en twintigste eeuw*, ed. Paul Werkman and Rolf van der Woude (Hilversum: Verloren, 2006), 129-60; and *Geloof in de brouwerij: Opkomst, bloei en ondergang van bierbrouwerij De Gekroonde Valk* (Amsterdam: Lubberhuizen, 2009).

socialistic tendencies of those who claim to represent those interests as they are to be opposed to attempts to defend special privileges for the rich.

Fourth, Kuyper's belief in the inherent goodness of business (despite its fallenness) was determined in part by his concern for the welfare of the indigenous people of the Dutch colonies, especially in the Dutch East Indies (present-day Indonesia). The speech from the throne given at the opening of the Dutch parliament is, to this day, written by the prime minister. In 1901, at the start of Kuyper's term in that office, Queen Wilhelmina announced in her speech a new departure in Dutch colonial policy:

> As a Christian power, the Netherlands is obliged ... to imbue government policy with the understanding that the Netherlands has a moral calling to fulfil towards the people of the East Indian Archipelago. The low living standard of the native population in Java attracts my special attention. I wish to conduct an inquiry into its causes.[59]

This was the launch of the so-called Dutch ethical policy, which stressed the moral duty the Netherlands had regarding the well-being of its colonial subjects and remained in place until its colonies gained independence following the Second World War.[60] Although the ethical policy was not solely his achievement, Kuyper goes down in history as the person who made it official government policy. He sought to give form to this policy by putting entrepreneurship at the heart of the government's strategy for the economic betterment of the colonial peoples. Convinced that agriculture alone could not support their burgeoning population, he argued that the only way to help them escape the clutches of poverty was to assist them in starting new businesses.[61] One outcome of his policy was the creation of credit banks that made microloans available to indigenous entrepreneurs. While this echoed Kuyper's attempts noted earlier in this chapter to help his impoverished parishioners as a young clergyman, it was long before microfinance played a central role in the international development policy

---

59. Queen Wilhelmina, "Troonrede van 17 September 1901," in *Troonredes, Openingsredes, Inhuldigingsredes 1814–1963*, ed. Ersnt van Raalte ('s-Gravenhage: Staatsuitgeverij, 1964).
60. On Kuyper's colonial policy, see Peter S. Heslam, "Ethical Policy towards an Islamic People: The Colonial Politics of Abraham Kuyper," *Journal of Markets & Morality* (2020).
61. *Handelingen van de Eerste en Tweede Kamer der Staten-Generaal*, 1901–1902, Bijlage B, Begroting voor Nederlandsch-Indië voor 1901.

of the Netherlands and many other Western powers. Kuyper can, therefore, be considered well ahead of his time in terms of enterprise solutions to poverty. This is unlikely to have been the case had Kuyper been skeptical about the potential of business as a force for good.

Fifth, Kuyper's attempt to think positively and creatively about the calling and positive potential of business was a natural consequence, as we have seen, of his doctrine of common grace but also of two related ideas that are foundational to his thought and actions. In keeping with God's common grace, Christ shines not only in great works of art, philosophy, and science but also in the worlds of business and economics. Therefore, Calvinism in business is, quite literally, an en*light*ened enterprise (to recall the question posed in the title of this essay). That being the case, the vocation of a Christian in the contemporary world is to "think God's thoughts after him." Or, as he put it in his famous speech on sphere sovereignty, "Thinking God's thoughts after him, grasping what he has thought prior to us and about us and in us."[62] Alongside this is the idea, which Kuyper often repeated using the Latin phrase *coram Deo*, that human beings live their lives "before the face of God." Kuyper's attempts to address the world of business, modest as they are compared to his treatments of other fields, should be understood as an attempt to shun explicatory ideologies, whether from the right or from the left, in order both to think God's thoughts after God and to render business (along with every other sphere of human existence) before the face of God.

As suggested at the outset of this introduction, the "marketplace Christianity" for which Hovy and Kuyper stood has long been ignored by theology and religion scholars. While Kuyper gave relatively little undivided attention to it, his ideas about business are fresh, keen, and insightful. That they have been overlooked in Kuyper scholarship reflects the relative youth of business studies as an academic discipline. It also reflects a tendency among academics with socioeconomic interests to assume that they have engaged with business if they have provided critiques of such issues as inequality, individualism, indebtedness, greed, and consumerism. It is perhaps no wonder, in this context, that many business leaders today feel

---

62. Abraham Kuyper, *Souvereiniteit in eigen kring: rede ter inwijding van de vrije Universiteit, den 20sten October 1880 gehouden, in het Koor der Nieuwe Kerk te Amsterdam* (Amsterdam: Kruyt, 1880); ET: "Sphere Sovereignty," in Abraham Kuyper, *On Charity and Justice*, ed. Matthew J. Tuininga (Bellingham, WA: Lexham Press, forthcoming).

their vocation is misunderstood and undervalued in religious and academic circles.[63]

As also noted at the beginning of this article, many business leaders who do seek to integrate their faith with their workplace are influenced by neo-Calvinism and the "Protestant work ethic" with which it is often disparagingly associated. This serves as testimony to the ongoing appeal and pertinence of Kuyperian worldview thinking within which common grace is central. In Kuyper's hands and in those of Kuyperian business leaders today, this doctrine provides a tool for dismantling the sacred/secular divide between theology and business. In so doing, to use Kuyper's terminology, particular grace mixes with common grace—a convergence he believed to have strong transformative potential. Its impact in the commercial sphere, in Kuyper's estimation, helped business develop culture to a higher level and to make life easier and freer. It had done so by helping God's image bearers steward creation more effectively. Accordingly, for Kuyper, this reflected the fact that, while mammon posed an ever-present hazard, money itself was a blessing. Its proper use undergirded flourishing societies and helped elucidate the call *to* business and the calling *of* business. Putting the four words "common grace in business" together again at the end of this brief exposition of Kuyper's thought suggests, therefore, the following conclusion: at the core of Kuyper's ideas on the workings of God's grace in business is the notion that business to the glory of God is business that, like the common grace it embodies, restrains evil and promotes flourishing.

---

63. Antibusiness sentiment in academia has a long history but reached a peak in the 1930s interbellum. See Peter S. Heslam, "The Role of Business in the Fight against Poverty," in *Christian Theology and Market Economics*, ed. Ian R. Harper and Samuel Gregg (Cheltenham: Edward Elgar, 2008), 164–80.

ABRAHAM KUYPER AND THE ECONOMIC TEACHINGS OF THE HEIDELBERG CATECHISM

JORDAN J. BALLOR

INTRODUCTION

Franciscan missionary Bernardino of Siena (1380–1444) tells the story of an interaction between Francis of Assisi (1181/1182–1226) and a demon-possessed man. When Francis contends that murder is the worst sin, the demon-possessed man responds instead that "keeping other people's property is worse than murder, for more sinners go to hell for that than for anything else."[1] This narrative exchange well illustrates the significance

---

1. This anecdote appears in Bernardino's preaching and is recounted in A. G. Ferrers Howell, *S. Bernardino of Siena* (London: Methuen, 1913), 272. See also Alejandro A.

of economic matters for Christian discipleship. From Ahab's seizure of Naboth's vineyard (1 Kgs 21) to the punishment of Ananias and Sapphira (Acts 5:1–11), throughout Scripture we encounter narratives that demonstrate the moral and spiritual importance of faithfulness in matters relating to money, property, commerce, lending, alms, and wealth. The right or wrong use of temporal goods has eternal and spiritual significance.

The purpose of this introduction is to explore the economic teachings of the Heidelberg Catechism (1563), a key confessional document in the Reformed tradition, from a particularly Kuyperian perspective.[2] As a summary of the Christian faith, the Heidelberg Catechism is not an economic textbook or a manual for economic policy. It does, however, have much to say about the fundamental categories of discipleship in economic matters, and what it says provides a helpful normative framework for thinking about economics, understood more generally as that which involves economic realities, phenomena, and human action rather than understood more narrowly as an academic discipline. Within the context of this study, economic phenomena are understood to particularly involve the production, exchange, consumption, and distribution of temporal goods and services.[3] The catechism speaks directly to the origins of our material existence in divine creation and the consequences for human action and stewardship in the world.

The argument in this essay is at the same time both historical as well as constructive. This study is focused on the biblical teaching as presented in the Heidelberg Catechism as it has been understood and expounded

---

Chafuen, *Faith and Liberty: The Economic Thought of the Late Scholastics* (Lanham, MD: Lexington, 2003), 31.

2. Text of the Heidelberg Catechism in this essay is taken from James T. Dennison Jr., *Reformed Confessions of the 16th and 17th Centuries in English Translation: 1523–1693*, vol. 2 (Grand Rapids: Reformation Heritage Books, 2010). On the historical context and theological significance of the catechism, see Lyle D. Bierma, *An Introduction to the Heidelberg Catechism: Sources, History, and Theology* (Grand Rapids: Baker Academic, 2005).

3. For this basic framework, see, for example, John D. Mueller, *Redeeming Economics: Rediscovering the Missing Element* (Wilmington, DE: ISI Books, 2010). For more on the relationship between economics and theology, see also Jordan J. Ballor, "The Economies of Divine and Human Love," *Research in the History of Economic Thought & Methodology* 31, no. 1 (2013): 157–64; and Ballor, "Theology and Economics: A Match Made in Heaven?," *Journal of Interdisciplinary Studies* 26 (2014): 115–34.

by interpreters within the Reformed tradition.[4] Moreover, the thought of Dutch Reformed theologian Abraham Kuyper (1837–1920) provides the lens through which the economic teachings of the Heidelberg Catechism are organized and expounded. Although Reformed theologians and pastors from the early generations of the Reformation down to present day have many valuable and timelessly instructive insights, Kuyper's proximity to modernity, and particularly his historical context after the dawning of the industrial revolution, allow his insights to map more easily onto contemporary economic realities in the twenty-first century. And although Kuyper himself never wrote an extended treatise on economics as such, his writings on the Heidelberg Catechism as well as other work bear directly on questions of faithfulness in economic matters.[5]

---

4. The commentaries of Zacharius Ursinus and Jeremias Bastingius form significant points of departure for this study. Ursinus's role in authoring the catechism provides enough rationale for including him among the most significant historical interpreters of the document. The connection between Bastingius and Kuyper is explored in more detail in the following discussion related to the theme of stewardship. See Zacharius Ursinus, *Explicationum Catecheticarum D. Zachariae Ursini* (Heidelberg: Johannis Halbey, 1607); ET: *The Commentary of Dr. Zacharias Ursinus, on the Heidelberg Catechism*, trans. G. W. Willard (Cincinnati: Elm Street, 1888); and Jeremias Bastingius, *In Catechesin Religionis Christianae* (Dordrecht: Canin, 1588); ET: *An Exposition or Commentarie Upon the Catechisme of Christian Religion* (Cambridge: Legatt, 1589).

5. Notable treatments include Abraham Kuyper, *Ons Program*, 2nd ed. (Amsterdam: J. H. Kruyt, 1880), which appears in translation in this series as *OP*; Kuyper, *Het Sociale Vraagstuk en de Christelijke Religie: Rede bij de opening van het Sociaal Congres op 9 November 1891 gehouden* (Amsterdam: J. A. Wormser, 1891); and Kuyper, *De Christus en de Sociale nooden en Democratische Klippen* (Amsterdam: J. A. Wormser, 1895). The first of these appears in this volume; the contents of the latter two appear in this series in the volume *On Charity and Justice*. On the Heidelberg Catechism, see Abraham Kuyper, *E Voto Dordraceno: Toelichting op den Heidelbergschen Catechismus*, 4 vols. (Amsterdam: Wormser, 1892–95). This present anthology, *On Business and Economics*, part of the Abraham Kuyper Collected Works in Public Theology, is intended to be a comprehensive primary-source introduction to these topics in Kuyper's thought. On the early attempts to develop neo-Calvinist economics, see Joost W. Hengstmengel, "The Reformation of Economic Thought: Dutch Calvinist Economics, 1880–1948," *Philosophia Reformata* 78, no. 2 (2013): 124–43. See also Harry Van Dyke, "Kuyper's Early Critique of Unchecked Capitalism," *Philosophia Reformata* 78, no. 2 (2013): 115–23; Heslam, "Spirit of Enterprise"; Peter S. Heslam, "Prophet of a Third Way: The Shape of Kuyper's Socio-political Vision," *Journal of Markets & Morality* 5, no. 1 (Spring 2002): 11–33; and James D. Bratt, "Passionate about the Poor: The Social Attitudes of Abraham Kuyper," *Journal of Markets & Morality* 5, no. 1 (Spring 2002): 35–44. On later neo-Calvinist thinking in economics, see Joost

This essay is thus a kind of Kuyperian exposition of the economic teachings of the Heidelberg Catechism, which can hopefully serve as a constructive introduction to Kuyper's commercial and economic thought. A standard neo-Calvinist approach to a topic is to identify the origin, essence, and goal of the issue under examination.[6] This kind of modified scholastic method sometimes identified with a "worldview" approach[7] can be fruitfully applied to identify the economic teachings of the Heidelberg Catechism. The result is that we can identify the *origin, essence,* and *goal* of economic realities

Hengstmengel, "Dooyeweerd's Philosophy of Economics," *Journal of Markets & Morality* 15, no. 2 (Fall 2012): 415–29; A. Zeegers, *Van Kuyper tot Keynes: De A.R.-partij op de dirigistische doolweg* (Amsterdam: Stichting Johannes Althusius, 1958); Rolf van der Woude, "Taming the Beast: The Long and Hard Road to the Christian Social Conference of 1952," *Journal of Markets & Morality* 14, no. 2 (Fall 2011): 419–44; Bram Mellink, "Towards the Centre: Early Neoliberals in the Netherlands and the Rise of the Welfare State, 1945–1958," *Contemporary European History* 20, no. 1 (February 2020): 30–43; and Paul Oslington, "The Kuyperian Dream: Reconstructing Economics on Christian Foundations," *Faith & Economics* 75 (Spring 2020): 7–36.

6. This formula (*oorsprong, wezen, bestemming*) with variations appears numerous times in the works of Kuyper and Herman Bavinck. See, for instance, Herman Bavinck, *Magnalia Dei: Onderwijzing in de christelijke religie naar Gereformeerde Belijdenis* (Kampen: Kok, 1909), 196–240; Bavinck, *Essays on Religion, Science, and Society*, ed. John Bolt, trans. Harry Boonstra and Gerrit Sheeres (Grand Rapids: Baker Academic, 2008), 205, 253, 263; Bavinck, *Reformed Dogmatics*, ed. John Bolt (Grand Rapids: Baker Academic, 2003–8), 1:52, 67, 258; 4:100, 435; Bavinck, *The Christian Family*, ed. Stephen J. Grabill, trans. Nelson D. Kloosterman (Grand Rapids: Christian's Library, 2012), 160; *On the Church*, 136; James D. Bratt, ed., *Abraham Kuyper: A Centennial Reader* (Grand Rapids: Eerdmans, 1998), 383; *PR* 1.II.1.3:110.

7. See James Orr, *The Christian View of God and the World*, 2nd ed. (Edinburgh: Andrew Elliot, 1893); Herman Bavinck, *Christelijke wetenschap* (Kampen: J. H. Kok, 1904); Bavinck, *Christelijke wereldbeschouwing* (Kampen: J. H. Kok, 1904); ET: *Christian Worldview*, trans. and ed. Nathaniel Gray Sutanto, James Eglinton, and Cory C. Brock (Wheaton, IL: Crossway, 2019); Bavinck, *Wijsbegeerte der Openbaring* (Kampen: J. H. Kok, 1908); ET: *Philosophy of Revelation: A New Annotated Edition*, ed. Cory Brock and Nathaniel Gray Sutanto (Peabody, MA: Hendrickson, 2018). See also Heslam, *Creating a Christian Worldview*; David K. Naugle Jr., *Worldview: The History of a Concept* (Grand Rapids: Eerdmans, 2002); Michael W. Goheen and Craig G. Bartholomew, *Living at the Crossroads: An Introduction to Christian Worldview* (Grand Rapids: Baker Academic, 2008); James Eglinton, *Trinity and Organism: Towards a New Reading of Herman Bavinck's Organic Motif* (London: T&T Clark, 2012), 128–30; Ab Flipse, *Christelijke wetenschap: Nederlandse rooms-katholieken en gereformeerden over de natuurwetenschap, 1880–1940* (Hilversum: Verloren, 2014); and Craig G. Bartholomew, *Contours of the Kuyperian Tradition: A Systematic Introduction* (Downers Grove, IL: IVP Academic, 2017), 101–30.

with the concepts of *superabundance, stewardship*, and *Sabbath*, respectively. The theme of superabundance is related to the fourth petition of the Lord's Prayer, "Give us this day our daily bread." The themes of stewardship and Sabbath relate to the eighth ("Thou shalt not steal") and fourth ("Remember the Sabbath day") commandments, respectively. Kuyper's own exposition of these three sections of the Heidelberg Catechism are the opening chapters in this anthology, providing a foundation for understanding and engaging Kuyper's insights into business and enterprise.

After exploring these three basic themes as formative of the economic teachings of the Heidelberg Catechism, this introduction concludes with some observations about implications for economics with particular attention for the way in which economic realities relate to a proper understanding of shalom and human flourishing.

SUPERABUNDANCE AND THE ORIGINS OF ECONOMICS

It is appropriate to open the discussion of economic issues with the fourth petition of the Lord's Prayer as presented in the Heidelberg Catechism, as this petition has traditionally been understood to refer to "temporal blessings," or those things necessary "for all our bodily need," as the catechism puts it. This petition of the Lord's Prayer teaches at least three basic things important for the foundation and origin of economic activity: (1) the intrinsic goodness of temporal blessings, (2) the eternal or spiritual orientation of all these good gifts, and (3) the divine source of all these blessings.[8] In addition to these teachings, the framework of superabundance must be contextualized within the context of the fall into sin and consequences for human labor and the concept of scarcity.

> Lord's Day 50
>
> *125. What is the fourth petition?*
>
> *"Give us this day our daily bread"; that is, be pleased to provide for all our bodily need (Ps. 104:27–28; 145:15–16; Matt. 6:25–26), so that we may thereby acknowledge that Thou art the only fountain of all good (Acts 14:1; 17:27–28), and that without Thy blessing neither our care and labor, nor Thy gifts, can profit us (1 Cor. 15:58; Deut. 8:3;*

---

8. See Bastingius, *Exposition or Commentarie*, 182v.

Ps. 37:3–7, 16–17); that we may therefore withdraw our trust from
all creatures and place it alone in Thee (Ps. 55:22; 62:10).

TEMPORAL AND SPIRITUAL GOODS

As Zacharius Ursinus (1534–83) makes clear, the instruction to pray for temporal goods includes not only bread as such, but everything needed for survival and flourishing. Thus the term "bread" represents everything "necessary for the support of life." Understood in this way, writes Ursinus, "It is, however, certainly right and proper to desire riches, if we remove all ambiguity from the word."[9] By this Ursinus means that temporal goods or "riches" are those things that human beings need, not just individually, but also socially, and not just to survive but also to flourish and thrive. In this way Ursinus observes that these goods are to be prayed for not only as good in themselves, but particularly as they might be put to human use: "Nor did Christ merely comprehend under the term bread things necessary for the sustenance of life, but he also comprises such a use of these things as is profitable; for bread, apart from such a use, is no better than a stone."[10] And the uses that these goods are to be put toward are not individualistic or selfish but instead are directed toward the good of others as well as ourselves.

Each person has a particular office or calling, and Ursinus speaks of goods "acquired by lawful labor in some honest and proper calling, pleasing to God and profitable to society at large."[11] This petition therefore asks God to provide those resources that are necessary to rightly discharge the responsibilities of such a position. "If we, therefore, understand the term riches as just defined," writes Ursinus, "they are certainly to be sought and prayed for at the hands of God, inasmuch as we are to desire such things as are necessary for nature, and for the position and office which God has assigned us in life."[12] Another way of understanding this petition, Ursinus observes, is to ask God: "Give us so much of what is necessary for

---

9. Ursinus, *Commentary on the Heidelberg Catechism*, 645.
10. Ursinus, *Commentary on the Heidelberg Catechism*, 644.
11. Ursinus, *Commentary on the Heidelberg Catechism*, 644.
12. Ursinus, *Commentary on the Heidelberg Catechism*, 645–46. For more on positive historic Reformed teachings concerning riches and temporal goods, see Jordan J. Ballor and Cornelis van der Kooi, "The Moral Status of Wealth Creation in Early-Modern Reformed Confessions," *Reformation & Renaissance Review* 21, no. 3 (2019): 188–202.

the support of life as every one of us needs, to serve thee and our neighbor in our several callings in life."[13]

If temporal and material blessings are understood to be goods that are conducive for human survival and flourishing, they are also understood to be supportive for spiritual and eternal realities. Ursinus writes, "In this fourth petition we are taught to pray for temporal blessings," and he explains its placement in the middle of the Lord's Prayer as a way of relating temporal to spiritual or eternal goods. "Christ having regard to our infirmities," writes Ursinus, "placed this fourth petition respecting our daily bread, as it were in the middle of the prayer which he prescribed, that we might both commence and end our prayers with petitions for spiritual blessings as being most important."[14]

This relationship between material and spiritual realities as taught in the Lord's Prayer underscores the broader dynamic between created nature and special grace. As Kuyper writes, "You must first live before you can live for God. Your life as a human being on earth depends, after all, on God providing you with your bread."[15] In this way we are to regard temporal goods as truly good and necessary, understood within the context of and oriented to the greater good of spiritual and eternal blessings. Kuyper notes that the Lord's Prayer provides a model for all human prayer, and this is true also with respect to the relationship between material and spiritual needs. He writes, "But when the prayer now turns to ourselves, all prayer must take our physical needs as its point of departure. This is not in order to stay there—this petition is followed by two petitions concerning our spiritual needs—but to start there."[16]

THE DIVINE SOURCE OF ALL GOOD GIFTS

The central teaching of this petition in the Heidelberg Catechism comes in the phrase which appears in the answer acknowledging God as "the only fountain of all good." This phrase connects the catechism's response with the long Christian tradition confessing God to be the *fons omnium bonorum*.

---

13. Ursinus, *Commentary on the Heidelberg Catechism*, 645.

14. Ursinus, *Commentary on the Heidelberg Catechism*, 641. See also Bastingius, *Exposition or Commentarie*, 182v: "For when God abaseth him selfe to feed our bodies, it is not to be doubted, but that he is much more careful of our Spirituall life: therfore his so bountifull goodnes, lifteth up our affiance higher."

15. Kuyper, *E Voto Dordraceno*, LD 50, §1.

16. Kuyper, *E Voto Dordraceno*, LD 50, §1.

The image here is of a source or fountain, as in the case of water, and the goodness of God that overflows to creation. All good things that exist come from God and continue to exist on the basis of his beneficent grace. Understood as the source of everything good, the blessings human beings experience can be well understood to come from God's *superabundance*, the overflow of his grace. God is, as Bastingius describes, the one "who so aboundeth in all store of good things, that he is content with him selfe, and hath sufficient for him selfe, so that whosoever hath him can want nothing besides, as possessing the very fountaine of all good things [*fontem omnium bonorum*]."[17] For Kuyper, God as the fountain of all good things is "the profound thought that underlies this fourth petition."[18] Acknowledging God as the divine source of all good gifts has consequences for the Christian's understanding of providence. As Ursinus puts it, "God desires that this praise should be given to him, inasmuch as he is the source of all good things, and that we may not suppose these things to come by mere chance."[19] The temporal blessings that we receive come from God according to his providential care.

If God's superabundance is the source of all our blessings, including temporal goods, then the means and purposes of his distribution is also significant. A primary image for God's role in provision is that of an owner of an estate or house. Thus, writes Ursinus, "God, as a householder, distributes to every one his own portion, or that which we deserve at his hands."[20]

If we take bread, for example, the good mentioned explicitly in the petition, we have record of God providing bread in two basic ways. First, God can provide bread immediately and miraculously, as in the case of the manna in the wilderness (Exod 16) and Jesus' feeding of crowds of people (Matt 14:13–21; 15:29–39). Kuyper specifically invokes the exodus narrative to illustrate this possibility: "The history of manna in the wilderness teaches without a doubt that God lacks neither the power nor the capability to feed an entire nation on a barren expanse of sand."[21] This is a special and unusual means of provision. The second, more common way of provision is by the

---

17. Bastingius, *Exposition or Commentarie*, 183v.
18. Kuyper, *E Voto Dordraceno*, LD 50, §2.
19. Ursinus, *Commentary on the Heidelberg Catechism*, 642. See also Bastingius, *Exposition or Commentarie*, 184v: "It is God, who with a bountifull hand imparteth unto us the treasures of his goodnes and liberalitie."
20. Ursinus, *Commentary on the Heidelberg Catechism*, 644.
21. Kuyper, *E Voto Dordraceno*, LD 50, §3.

divine gift of an abundant and fertile world with which humans are able to grow and produce the materials necessary for making, giving, selling, and eating bread. God deigns to use human beings as the regular means for the provision of temporal goods that we all need to survive. Kuyper contrasts these two methods: "God can feed us in the usual way, but also in an unusual way. He can feed us through the common means which he chooses as the vehicle of his divine power, or without those common means. God does this by letting his divine power work apart from any means or through uncommon means—by a miracle."[22]

For Kuyper the common means of provision are latent in the created order and are discovered by human activity. He likens the means of farming grain and baking bread to divine laws or ordinances. Thus, he writes, "The ordinary means are neither our invention nor our fabrication; they are ordinances of God instituted at the time of creation for the sake of his creation. And even there where the means underwent some modification as a consequence of the fall into sin—like nourishment, since the fruits of paradise were replaced after the Fall by nourishment through bread—the means of nourishment are and remain his divine ordinance."[23] Elsewhere Kuyper discusses the regular, human means of production on the basis of God's created order and writes of the first farmer that

> God gave him the soil, a head to think with, hands to work with, and (besides these) a basic *hunger*. God stimulated him by means of this drive. God taught him to think about things. And thus he had to try things. First one thing, and when that did not work, something else, until finally one person found this and the other that, with the results confirming that this was the right solution. Subsequently, the one imitated the other, and it was passed on from father to son, and in this way agriculture expanded.[24]

It is very tempting to focus on the proximate means of the production of human goods and services and neglect to appreciate the divine origins of all good gifts. Of this danger Kuyper writes, "The knowledgeable person knows quite well that all power in the created thing is only derivative power

---

22. Kuyper, *E Voto Dordraceno*, LD 50, §3.
23. Kuyper, *E Voto Dordraceno*, LD 50, §3.
24. CG 2.68.3:585.

and that all this ability is only derivative ability, the source and wellspring of which lies in God and God alone. He is the Almighty, which means that neither in heaven nor on earth any power exists or works other than the power that was in God and came to us from him."[25]

The consequence of God's superabundant provision of the material and the means for meeting human temporal needs is that there is a corresponding human responsibility to put this material and these means to proper use. Ursinus, Bastingius, and Kuyper all invoke the concept of stewardship in this regard. Ursinus writes,

> We should regard ourselves as stewards of God [*oeconomos Dei*], who has committed these riches to our charge for the purpose of being properly expended, and has imposed upon us the duty of administering them so as to promote his glory, and that we shall at some time be required to render and account to God for our stewardship [*dispensationis*] and administration [*administrationis*].[26]

Bastingius contends that in this petition God "meant also to put us in minde to love our neighbor: for therefore it is called our bread, that we should not eat it alone, but distribute it to the poore, as being appointed Gods stewardes [*Deo oeconomi*], that is, dispensers of his bread [*illus panis dispensatores*]."[27] Kuyper observes that God's purpose for his people in this portion of the Lord's Prayer is that "after such a prayer they may perhaps have a better sense of their calling to be stewards of their possessions on God's behalf. They may also then be more willing than they might otherwise have been to stretch out their hand as servants of God in distributing daily bread to *those who have no bread*."[28] The concept of stewardship relates to the essence or nature of economic faithfulness and is more fully explored in the Catechism's treatment of the eighth commandment.

Sin and Scarcity

In his discussion of the relationship between proximate causes of material production as related to divine origins, Kuyper discusses the changed

---

25. Kuyper, *E Voto Dordraceno*, LD 50, §3.
26. Ursinus, *Commentary on the Heidelberg Catechism*, 646.
27. Bastingius, *Exposition or Commentarie*, 183r.
28. Kuyper, *E Voto Dordraceno*, LD 50, §1.

situation following the fall into sin. The inherent fruitfulness of the created order has been altered at least insofar as it relates to human productivity. Human work is now marked by struggle and suffering. At the same time, observes Kuyper, God has promised to continue to uphold the basic ordinance connecting human work to productive provision. Faced with death and destruction as a consequence of sin, human beings must depend on God's faithfulness and provision of forbearance and grace for survival. As Kuyper puts it, "Over against death stands life; and for life two things are necessary, namely, the emergence of life and the maintenance of life."[29] In this way God's promises in the midst of the curses after the fall into sin in Genesis 3 provide assurance that human life will continue through procreation ("you shall bring forth children," v. 16) and material provision ("you shall eat bread," v. 19). What is remarkably new in this situation is the challenge and opposition that characterizes these elements necessary for provision. Procreation and cocreative labor are both marked by "pain" (vv. 16, 17).

Sin is the reason for this changed situation, but there is a fundamental continuity in God's promises of provision and preservation. Kuyper writes of the curses and promises, "These words contain a double prophecy that, combined into one, says, 'I, your God, restrain death and in spite of the fact that you invoked death and brought it upon yourself, I, your God, will to the contrary cause *life* to be born and *life* to be maintained.'"[30] Sin also has consequences for how bread is to be obtained; it is more difficult not only in a physical sense but also as relates to human cognitive capacities. Human beings observe things differently than they did or would have continued to do without encountering the noetic effects of sin. In the primal state in paradise, writes Kuyper, "Adam immediately perceived the nature of these animals in such a way that he immediately gave them names."[31] After the corruption of our capacities, however, human beings must operate in the world differently. "If we want to learn to understand a plant or an animal," for example, Kuyper contends, "then we must observe that animal and that plant carefully for a long time, and from what we observe gradually draw conclusions about their nature. This occurs apart from us ever learning

---

29. *CG* 1.31.2:273.
30. *CG* 1.31.2:273.
31. *CG* 3.63.4.

to understand their essence."[32] The fall into sin thus adds difficulty and complexity to the challenges of human provision and preservation, even as common grace provides the basis for God's continuing care and maintenance of the created order.

A common critique of mainstream economic thought has to do with the economic idea of scarcity. From a theological perspective that affirms divine superabundance, an assumption of scarcity as foundational of economic thought can seem deeply mistaken. As D. Stephen Long has concluded, for instance, "Theologians must deny this narrative of scarcity for it forces our language and actions into the inevitable embrace of death."[33] As such a judgment is grounded in the understandings of God's fundamental superabundance and gracious overflowing, it must be agreed that there is no scarcity in God. As a judgment about the relevance of scarcity for human life and economic thought, however, a simple juxtaposition of superabundance and scarcity is inadequate.[34] Even in the midst of abundant divine blessing there are limits to human activity. Moreover, scarcity ought to be considered not only in terms of material realities, as for example the possible fruitfulness of a piece of land or a tree, but also in moral and temporal terms. Human concupiscence has given rise to unrestrained desire.[35] There is a deep disconnect between what humans desire from creation and what it is designed by God to offer. There is thus a basic limitation both in spiritual terms and moral and material terms on human expectation and interaction with the rest of creation. Further temporal implications of scarcity will be explored in more detail in the discussion related to the fourth commandment, concerning the Sabbath. Even in the midst of sin, God has preserved the possibility and reality of abundance of his creatures. But there are nevertheless unavoidable and intrinsic limitations related to

---

32. *CG* 3.63.4.

33. D. Stephen Long, *Divine Economy: Theology and the Market* (New York: Routledge, 2000), 146.

34. For more detail on the inadequacy of this juxtaposition, see Jordan J. Ballor, "Interdisciplinary Dialogue and Scarcity in Economic Terminology," *Journal of Markets & Morality* 23, no. 1 (Spring 2020): 131–37.

35. See Daniel M. Bell Jr., *The Economy of Desire: Christianity and Capitalism in a Postmodern World* (Grand Rapids: Brazos, 2012). See also Jordan J. Ballor and Victor V. Claar, "Envy in the Market Economy: Sin, Fairness, and Spontaneous (Dis)Order," *Faith & Economics* 61–62 (Spring/Fall 2013): 33–53.

human finitude and causality that require economic responsibility, economizing, and the exercise of prudent stewardship.

STEWARDSHIP AND THE ESSENCE OF ECONOMICS

It is common in the Reformed treatment of the Decalogue to identify both the positive obligations and duties as well as the negative prohibitions that attend to each commandment. As J. Douma has observed, the prohibitions of this commandment have to do with property and material goods, but these material realities are also to be understood morally and spiritually. Christians are to avoid unjust and unrighteous attachments to material things, which has to do not only with acquisition but also with loyalty and love. Thus, writes Douma, "this commandment is designed to protect us from every new form of slavery."[36] This includes actual slavery, oppression, and manipulation as well as idolatry. But the "roots of the eighth commandment" are also to be found positively in the reality of stewardship, which means that "everything man has received from God to manage must be cared for and used not according to man's wishes, but according to God's will."[37]

> Lord's Day 42
>
> *110. What does God forbid in the eighth Commandment?*
>
> *God forbids not only such theft (1 Cor. 6:10) and robbery (1 Cor. 5:10) as are punished by the government, but God views as theft also all wicked tricks and devices, whereby we seek to get our neighbor's goods, whether by force or by deceit (Luke 3:14; 1 Thess. 4:6), such as unjust weights (Prov. 11:1; 16:11), lengths, measures (Ezek. 45:9–10; Deut. 25:13–15), goods, coins, usury (Ps. 15:5; Luke 6:35), or by any means forbidden of God; also all covetousness (1 Cor. 6:10) and the misuse and waste of His gifts (Prov. 5:10).*
>
> *111. But what does God require of you in this Commandment?*
>
> *That I further my neighbor's good where I can and may, deal with him as I would have others deal with me (Matt. 7:12), and labor*

---

36. J. Douma, *The Ten Commandments: Manual for the Christian Life*, trans. Nelson D. Kloosterman (Phillipsburg, NJ: P&R, 1996), 295.

37. Douma, *Ten Commandments*, 295, 298.

faithfully, so that I may be able to help the poor in their need (Eph. 4:28).

The idea of stewardship has a rich history in the Christian tradition. In many ways it is a basic image of Christian discipleship, particularly within the context of material goods. As A. Troost puts it,

> Stewardship does not mean individualism. On the contrary, it emphasizes that in each and all of his relationships man has a particular responsibility to God, free from the domination of church or state, or family or an economic power organization. To be a steward, to administer the goods of Another, is a *religious* relationship of man to God, a relationship which ought to govern the spirit of all the functional human activities.[38]

Stewardship must be oriented to both God and neighbor.

In his analysis of the stewardship idea, Nicolaas H. Gootjes points particularly to Abraham Kuyper as the figure who popularized this image in modern theological discourse in this context.[39] Gootjes observes that the image of stewardship is used by Bastingius in connection with the eighth commandment, but only in passing, and it is left to Kuyper to turn this into a central model for understanding the right use of property.

Gootjes is correct that Bastingius's mention of stewardship in connection with the eighth commandment is not central. In fact, the term only really is treated substantively in the Dutch edition of his commentary on the catechism, which is an amplification of the Latin original, and which, as Gootjes observes, was being prepared for publication in a new Dutch edition in Kuyper's own time.[40] For Bastingius, the mark of a true steward is the

---

38. A. Troost, "Property Rights and the Eighth Commandment," *International Reformed Bulletin* 24/25 (1966): 31.

39. Nicolaas H. Gootjes, "De mens als Gods rentmeester," *Radix* 6 (1980): 20–26; ET: "Man as God's Steward," trans. S. Carl Van Dam, in Nicolaas H. Gootjes, *Teaching and Preaching the Word: Studies in Dogmatics and Homiletics*, ed. Cornelis Van Dam (Winnipeg: Premier, 2010), 249–55.

40. Jeremias Bastingius, *Verclaringe op den catechisme der Christelicker religie* (Dordrecht: Canin, 1591). The Dutch version is significantly longer than the original Latin, owing, it seems, to amplification by the translator Henricus Corputius, done with the blessing of Bastingius himself. See the foreword by F. L. Rutgers to the Bibliotheca Reformata edition, *Verclaringe op den catechisme der Christelicker religie* (Amsterdam: J. A. Wormser, 1893), vii.

willingness to distribute the goods he has been entrusted with to others.[41] This is an obligation of human nature as well as the divine commandment: "Therefore he that loveth not, and by the Law of love seeketh not the profite of his neighbor, is rebellious against God and fighteth with nature, beeing unworthie to injoy the goods of nature."[42] But as we have seen, Bastingius as well as Ursinus before him and Kuyper after him also explicitly invoke the stewardship idea as a corollary to an understanding of God as the source of all good gifts in their discussion of the fourth petition of the Lord's Prayer.

PROPERTY RIGHTS

The role of stewardship arises from the responsibilities attending to property. As Ursinus writes, "This commandment sanctions and authorises a distinction in property or possessions."[43] The first relevant distinction for property is between the owner of something in an absolute sense and the steward or owner of something in a relative sense. God, as Creator and sustainer of all things, is the owner and sovereign of everything in an absolute sense. Only in light of God's primary ownership in this regard can proper appreciation of human ownership and stewardship be achieved. Kuyper puts it this way:

> What Scripture says about the owner as steward points us in the one and only safe direction, and Christ's Church abandons her calling if she does not constantly and ceaselessly preach and imprint on humankind the sacred truth that the Lord God is the only lawful owner, and that no person ever is or can be anything but a steward over a part of that which belongs to God alone.[44]

The reality of God as the source of all good things and as the Creator and sustainer of all reality entails the absolute sovereignty of God over all of creation: "The Lord our God is the owner of all that is, the sole and complete owner—he and no one else."[45] This understanding of God's absolute claim

---

41. For Bastingius's discussion of stewardship in connection with this commandment, see p. 633 of the 1893 edition.
42. Bastingius, *Exposition or Commentarie*, 158r.
43. Ursinus, *Commentary on the Heidelberg Catechism*, 595.
44. Kuyper, *E Voto Dordraceno*, LD 42, §1.
45. Kuyper, *E Voto Dordraceno*, LD 42, §2.

to ownership is the background for any proper understanding of human property rights.

For Kuyper this means that there are really only two possibilities of human ownership. Property is either held in accord with God's law or in violation of it. Because God is the Creator and the first cause of all things, "Absolute right of ownership can for that reason only be conceived of in God. He who created everything does with everything as he pleases. He alone has total control over all that exists." With this in view, "no one can own anything except insofar as he has received or stolen it from God, always either in dependence on or else in rebellion against him who created it."[46] God's ownership rights provide the normative framework and ontological basis for human property rights and stewardship responsibilities.

Referring back to the fourth petition of the Lord's Prayer, Kuyper observes, "What a rich sentence this is, in language with golden simplicity: *Father ... give us this day our daily bread!* It is a petition of only six words, but if you could bring all patriotic sons of our country to pray those six words with convicted hearts, would not suddenly all false concepts of ownership, all plutocracy, all worship of the golden calf, and all socialism not suddenly disappear from the face of the earth?"[47] A proper understanding of the divine origin of temporal blessings would rule out of bounds mistaken attitudes, customs, and legal arrangements with respect to the distribution and use of these goods.

Another distinction follows this basic distinction between absolute and relative property rights, and it has to do with the distribution of property among human beings. Ursinus writes that the goal or telos of this commandment is "the preservation of the property or possessions which God has given to every one for the support of life."[48] For Kuyper this basic distinction or division of property is part of God's creational design and not merely a consequence of sin. Thus, writes Kuyper, "When God created man, he also created in him an awareness of the distinction between one person and another, and consequently also between the belongings of one and those of another." After the fall, "Sin attempted to destroy this awareness altogether and would indeed have succeeded had the Lord God not checked this destruction by his common grace and left in us a certain awareness

---

46. Kuyper, *E Voto Dordraceno*, LD 42, §2.
47. Kuyper, *E Voto Dordraceno*, LD 42, §1.
48. Ursinus, *Commentary on the Heidelberg Catechism*, 595.

of the respect we must show for someone else's possessions."[49] That some distinction in property between individual persons is a feature of creation does not mean, however, that all subsequent arrangements of property and distribution of wealth are justified. As we have seen, the reality of sin and the fall mean that there are two basic ways human beings can possess property, either in accordance with God's law or in rebellion against it. In this way the reality of property rights leads directly into an understanding of the corresponding stewardship responsibilities.

STEWARDSHIP RESPONSIBILITIES

As the apostle Paul describes the basic responsibilities of stewardship, "it is required of stewards that they be found faithful" (1 Cor 4:2). The catechism provides both negative prohibitions and positive mandates in its exposition of the eighth commandment, things that a faithful steward is to avoid and things that a faithful steward must do. Ursinus and Bastingius describe those things that are to be done as virtues and those things to be avoided as vices.[50] Ursinus outlines seven virtues of faithful stewardship that are enjoined by this commandment: (1) commutative justice, (2) contentment, (3) fidelity, (4) liberality, (5) hospitality, (6) parsimony, and (7) frugality.[51] These are the general virtues that positively attach to the commandment "Do not steal."

---

49. Kuyper, *E Voto Dordraceno*, LD 42, §1.

50. See Bastingius, *Exposition or Commentarie*, 158r. This basic fact, that it was common for Protestant theologians to exposit the Decalogue in connection with attendant virtues and vices, belies the sharp dichotomy between Roman Catholic virtue-ethical approaches and Protestant biblicist approaches that focus on rules and commands. As Brad S. Gregory puts it, Protestants rejected the traditional medieval perspective in which "virtuous actions were rational because they simultaneously fostered individual and communal flourishing; they were also actions consonant with God's natural law, if it were understood to mean that good must always be sought and evil avoided." See Gregory, *The Unintended Reformation: How a Religious Revolution Secularized Society* (Cambridge: Belknap, 2012), 192–93. Both Reformed and Lutheran theologians connected the Decalogue, the moral and natural law, and virtue ethics in the early modern period. For a Lutheran perspective, see Niels Hemmingsen, *On the Law of Nature: A Demonstrative Method*, trans. and ed. E. M. Hutchinson (Grand Rapids: CLP Academic, 2018), 91–163. See also Sebastian Rehnman, "Virtue and Grace," *Studies in Christian Ethics* 25, no. 4 (2012): 472–93. On the typology of Protestant and Roman Catholic approaches, see James M. Gustafson, *Protestant and Roman Catholic Ethics: Prospects for Rapprochement* (Chicago: University of Chicago Press, 1978).

51. Ursinus, *Commentary on the Heidelberg Catechism*, 596–600.

Stewardship is an individual and personal matter as well. People are placed into different circumstances and have different responsibilities. They have different roles in different times and places. Therefore, the temporal blessings they need to fulfill their stewardship responsibilities differ as well. Bastingius writes that it is part of the requirements of this commandment "that every one diligently and faithfully goe bout his owne worke, and doe that which belongeth to his calling."[52] For Kuyper the divine orientation of the stewardship calling is definitive. The social order regulates the relationship between human beings and between human beings and the created order. But as Kuyper puts it, "Whether you think of the object or of the person, you must always take your point of departure in the Lord our God, because both object and person exist only by his grace. He created both the object and the person." This means that there is an objective divine standard for executing stewardship responsibilities: "the parties whose right of ownership you seek to regulate are also not free to act as they wish, but in the regulation of ownership both are bound to submit themselves in obedience to God."[53] Stewardship responsibilities are a corollary of relative property rights. Thus, writes Kuyper, "all your belongings are immediately placed under a higher rule, are subjected to a moral order, and are made not to elevate you in your pride but to raise your responsibility before God."[54]

Human beings are therefore never free to do whatever they might wish with their possessions or, indeed, with the creation itself. This is true for inanimate objects, land, and animals as well as in our relationships (contractual, covenantal, and otherwise) with human beings. Nothing in this world is simply value-free or outside the mandate of God's moral order: "Nothing exists by virtue of a power residing within it, but every single object is maintained by the Lord's omnipresent power."[55] God therefore has a purpose for everything, and all of creation is called to act and exist in harmony with that purpose.

Indeed, the responsibility of human stewardship is only one aspect of any particular element of the created order. Kuyper outlines four basic relationships that govern all created things. First, the thing "is related to

---

52. Bastingius, *Exposition or Commentarie*, 158v.
53. Kuyper, *E Voto Dordraceno*, LD 42, §2.
54. Kuyper, *E Voto Dordraceno*, LD 42, §2.
55. Kuyper, *E Voto Dordraceno*, LD 42, §2.

itself, because it is handled in accordance with the nature God has established in it." Everything that is created has a nature that God has given to it and which must be respected.[56] Second, each good "is related to God, who created and maintains it, and who is its absolute Sovereign." Third, the thing "is related to its temporal stewards whom God has appointed over it." And finally, it "is related to our fellow creatures, that is, to our neighbors, to all stakeholders, to our community, our society and even our country as a whole."[57]

While the specific stewardship responsibilities of each person will differ to some extent depending on the nature of their callings, each "temporal steward" is bound to respect these four relationships and to manage the goods they have been entrusted with in light of these diverse realities. "Everything can be a spiritual calling," writes Kuyper, but this is true when stewardship responsibilities are exercised within the framework of the divinely created, ordered, and sustained reality.[58] As we shall see in considering the goal or telos of economics, this includes pursuing temporal stewardship in light of eternity and the "everlasting Sabbath."

FAITHFUL LABOR AND ENTREPRENEURSHIP

Specific stewardship responsibilities include the mandate to be productive and fruitful. Work and labor are in this way understood as forms of fruitful service.[59] The catechism outlines an explicit use of material wealth: we are to "labor faithfully, so that I may be able to help the poor in their need." The Christian is called to work productively so that there is a surplus beyond what an individual person needs and so that there is plenty to share with one's own family and with those in need.

This positive injunction implies that there is thus a prior responsibility to be generative of material goods in labor.[60] To "labor faithfully" is to

---

56. See *CG* 3.62.3: "A thought of God constitutes the core of the essence of things, and it was primarily this thought of God that prescribes for created things their manner of existence, their form, their principle of life, their destiny, and their progress."

57. Kuyper, *E Voto Dordraceno*, LD 42, §4.

58. Kuyper, *E Voto Dordraceno*, LD 42, §5.

59. See Lester DeKoster, *Work: The Meaning of Your Life—A Christian Perspective* (Grand Rapids: Christian's Library, 2015).

60. The Heidelberg Catechism occupies an important place within the broader spectrum of Reformed confessional expositions of the eighth commandment and the degree to which the positive moral status of the creation of wealth is made explicit. See Ballor and van der Kooi, "Moral Status of Wealth Creation."

exercise responsible stewardship, and one aspect of this is that the labor is productive as relates to the good of other people. Out of this generative and fruitful work there is enough to fulfill the appropriate needs and requirements of each person and his or her own intimate communities, but also to care for the maintenance, preservation, and advancement of the needs of others and other institutions, including the government and church.

This stewardship responsibility to labor faithfully can be seen as a mandate for humans to exercise their creativity in response to the realities of divine superabundance and prior creative activity. For Kuyper, this is the basic dynamic of human responsiveness to God's gracious act of creation. Human causality operates as a derivative and responsive reality on the basis of what God has done and makes possible. All human learning and advancement are only realizable because of the latent possibilities that God has embedded in creation. Thus, writes Kuyper, "we may simply conclude that knowledge and learning are nothing but discovering and learning the mystery of the means of common grace that God has ordained and appointed for us."[61] This means that human beings learn not only on the basis of special revelation and Scripture, but also from nature and creation itself.

Productive human labor is thus made possible on the basis of divine creation, and sustained as possible by God's preserving grace. "In life after the fall," writes Kuyper, "everything needed to stave off death and distress had to be discovered or invented and employed by human beings themselves; this would occur under steady exertion, with much effort, by pondering and reflecting and then working."[62] Picking up on the basic biblical image of bread from the fourth petition of the Lord's Prayer, Kuyper applies this basic framework specifically to the case of agriculture: "God's instruction continues ceaselessly, and throughout the centuries he uncovers for us new forces, new means, new ways of doing things; the same applies to agriculture."[63] The result of days, months, years, and generations of working the land provides insights and continues to provide new knowledge about the interrelationship of soil, tools, air, water, seeds, and human effort in cooperating to produce a bountiful crop. Thus, observes Kuyper,

> All newly acquired knowledge then has its application in agriculture and in the preparation of agricultural products,

---

61. *CG* 2.68.2:583.
62. *CG* 2.68.3:584.
63. *CG* 2.68.3:585.

> in order to make the soil produce more, to simplify the work, and to better prepare the particular crop. And in all this, the common grace of God is at work, which increases our power over nature, gives us a more bountiful and better harvest, and makes us enjoy the fruits of the earth in even greater ways.[64]

In this way, productive and faithful human labor, as in the case of farming and agriculture, requires the application of human creativity and ingenuity to discover and make actual the latent possibilities embedded by God in the creation order.

We might therefore understand the economic phenomenon of entrepreneurship in light of these important distinctions between divine and human causality.[65] Entrepreneurship is a form of human creativity and discovery, particularly as relates to economic life.[66] Because of their diligence in discovering and applying new techniques, Kuyper notes, "In the sixteenth century, Dutch farmers really were the teachers of Europe. We were the most advanced, and our products garnered the highest prices." Similarly it is a corollary of the mandate to labor faithfully for all Christians to be good stewards and exercise their gifts, talents, and abilities to develop human culture and society. Kuyper thus calls for Christians to "allow ourselves to be instructed in more and better ways by our God—not only in the Heidelberg Catechism but also in the catechism of agriculture, in the catechism of industry, and in the catechism of commerce."[67]

SABBATH AND THE GOAL OF ECONOMICS

If the focus of the eighth commandment has to do with liberation and stewardship, the fourth commandment is focused on time. Reflecting on Revelation 14:13, " 'Blessed indeed,' says the Spirit, 'that they may rest from their labors, for their deeds follow them,' " Kuyper writes of the blessed dead who die in the Lord that there are two key teachings here. "The Spirit is saying, first, that the effort is ended at death, for they will rest from

---

64. *CG* 2.68.3:585.

65. See Jordan J. Ballor and Victor V. Claar, "Creativity, Innovation, and the Historicity of Entrepreneurship," *Journal of Entrepreneurship and Public Policy* 8, no. 4 (2019): 512–22.

66. See Jordan J. Ballor and Victor V. Claar, "The Soul of the Entrepreneur: A Christian Anthropology of Creativity, Innovation, and Liberty," *Journal of Ethics & Entrepreneurship* 6, no. 1 (Spring 2016): 115–29.

67. *CG* 2.68.3:586.

their labor. The eternal Sabbath dawns for them." And second, "their work, that is, the fruit of their labor, the profit obtained, does not remain behind, but goes with them and follows them."[68] In this way Kuyper introduces the key dynamic relating human work in time to the Sabbath in eternity.

> Lord's Day 38
>
> *103. What does God require in the fourth Commandment?*
>
> *In the first place, God wills that the ministry of the Gospel and schools be maintained (Titus 1:5; 1 Tim. 3:14–15; 4:13–14; 5:17; 1 Cor. 9:11, 13–14), and that I, especially on the day of rest, diligently attend church (2 Tim. 2:2.; 2:15; Ps. 40:10–11; 68:26; Acts 2:42, 46) to learn the Word of God (1 Cor. 14:19, 29, 31), to use the holy sacraments (1 Cor. 11:33), to call publicly upon the Lord (1 Tim. 2:1–2; 2:8–10; 1 Cor. 14:16), and to give Christian alms (1 Cor. 16:2). In the second place, that all the days of my life I rest from my evil works, allow the Lord to work in me by His Spirit, and thus begin in this life the everlasting Sabbath (Isa. 66:23).*

Sabbath is the end or goal of temporal work in this age. Out of God's superabundance we are given the task of stewardship, which is to be directed to God's everlasting Sabbath. Our daily work in this life ends in a real sense in restful observance of the weekly Sabbath. This is a rhythm that is ingrained in creation itself. But it also is a type or image of what is to come in the consummation of creation. The everlasting Sabbath, which we begin to observe spiritually in this life, will be the end of our temporal stewardship in the consummation of the age to come.

A key distinction in understanding the relevance of the fourth commandment in the era of the Christian church is between the moral and ceremonial aspects of the law.[69] For Ursinus, there is a creational, moral, and spiritual aspect of the Sabbath commandment that pertains in all times and places and to all peoples. But there are also ceremonial and external elements that are particular to the Jewish people of the Mosaic dispensation.[70]

---

68. *CG* 1.63.1:553.
69. See Lyle D. Bierma, "Remembering the Sabbath Day: Ursinus's Exposition of Exodus 20:8–11," in *Biblical Interpretation in the Era of the Reformation*, ed. Richard A. Muller and John L. Thompson (Grand Rapids: Eerdmans, 1996), 272–91.
70. A chart with further subdivisions of this basic distinction appears in Ursinus, *Commentary on the Heidelberg Catechism*, 563.

This in part helps to explain how the day on which the Sabbath rest is observed was able to change from the seventh day to the first day of the week. For Kuyper, the key principle of the fourth commandment comes in its connection to the account of creation and God's resting on the seventh day. As Kuyper puts it, "This deepest life principle lies in this, that you as a human being are created in the image of God and that for that reason the nature of the divine life must be the rule for your human life."[71] There are two elements of this imitation of God that is ingrained in human nature that are of special significance for the Sabbath as the end or goal of economic activity. First, human beings are called to rest from evil works in this life, and second, in so doing, begin to participate in the eternal and everlasting Sabbath rest in God.[72]

Rest from Evil

On Ursinus's understanding, the prohibition against work on the Sabbath is not to be understood as absolute, in the sense that all work is forbidden. Rather, "When God forbids us to work on the Sabbath day, he does not forbid every kind of work, but only such works as are *servile* — such as hinder the worship of God, and the design and use of the ministry of the church."[73] Kuyper puts it even more strongly: "Read and reread what the Catechism says about the fourth commandment and you will not be able to reach any other conclusion than that (apart from the name "day of rest") it contains not one letter about abstaining from work."[74] Instead, what is prohibited is the work that distracts us from God, that which is intrinsically sinful, or that aspect of work which remains tainted by imperfection and sin in this life.

This means, as Bastingius puts it, the Lord's command to rest from labor is in this sense a recognition that human beings are "by nature ... corrupt and prone to all vice."[75] Our life, including but not limited to its economic elements, is lived in the time between redemption and consummation. "Here on earth we still live our sinful life," writes Kuyper, "and what is sinful in our life consists precisely in this, that our life does not follow the

---

71. Kuyper, *E Voto Dordraceno*, LD 38, §2.1.
72. Kuyper, *E Voto Dordraceno*, LD 38, §4.4: "For the people of God this resting is in part resting from something and in part resting in something."
73. Ursinus, *Commentary on the Heidelberg Catechism*, 558.
74. Kuyper, *E Voto Dordraceno*, LD 38, §2.1.
75. Bastingius, *Exposition or Commentarie*, 144v.

rule of God's life."[76] This commandment is in this way a call to continually work against evil and strive for goodness and faithfulness. It is thus part of what the catechism identifies as conversion, that is, mortification or the putting to death of the old man (Lord's Day 33). As Ursinus writes, the Sabbath may in this spiritual sense be understood as "a ceasing from sin, and a giving of ourselves to God to do such works as he requires from us. The Sabbath, although it ought to be perpetual in those who are converted, is nevertheless only begun in this life."[77]

The dying away of the old self points to the coming to life of the new self.[78] When the "everlasting Sabbath" is fully realized, on that day, "when sin will no longer be, things will be altogether different. Then the life of God's elect will proceed uninterrupted according to the standard and rule of the life of the Lord."[79] But Kuyper highlights two reasons that this perfect state cannot yet be realized: "First, because the consequence of sin is still at work and because God's children must still work in the sweat of their face. And second, because prior to our death God's work of grace does not bring about a complete check on sin."[80] In this way resting from our evil works is the beginning of what it means to positively enjoy the everlasting Sabbath in this life. It is a foretaste of the coming kingdom.

Rest in God

The everlasting Sabbath is thus to be understood as resting in God. As human beings created in God's image, our nature is to imitate him. "What God does must be the rule of life for us humans," writes Kuyper, at least as such is appropriate to our nature as creatures.[81] The rhythm of work and rest that God enacts and exemplifies in the work of creation (Gen 2:1–3) is to be manifest in the life of his creation, particularly those creatures who are made in his very image.

Even while in the fallen and not yet consummated world there is a distinction and antithesis between the spiritual and the worldly, the Sabbath

---

76. Kuyper, *E Voto Dordraceno*, LD 38, §2.2.

77. Ursinus, *Commentary on the Heidelberg Catechism*, 562.

78. See Kuyper, *E Voto Dordraceno*, LD 38, §3.4: "For this letting go of our evil works is nothing other than the dying off of the old man, and that letting God work in us is in fact nothing other than the resurrection of the new man."

79. Kuyper, *E Voto Dordraceno*, LD 38, §2.2.

80. Kuyper, *E Voto Dordraceno*, LD 38, §2.2.

81. Kuyper, *E Voto Dordraceno*, LD 38, §2.1.

commandment is not to be understood as creating a sacred/secular divide between the first day of the week and the six that follow. Rather, given the nature of human beings as material as well as spiritual beings, there is a rhythm of rest and worship, work and labor that should be mutually reinforcing. As Kuyper describes it, the purpose of this commandment "is therefore not a spiritual life on one day and then a spiritless life for six days in the world. Rather the reverse: to enrich us with spiritual provisions and spiritual weapons on the Sabbath, in order to be able to continue the six days that follow with less danger on our pilgrimage through this hazardous life."[82]

All of the elements that are specifically enjoined in the exposition of this commandment—ministry of the gospel, schools, public corporate worship, administration of the sacraments, almsgiving—are indispensable elements in beginning to inaugurate the everlasting Sabbath in this world, not only on one day of the week but every day. Just as dying to self and rising to Christ, mortification and vivification, is a daily reality, so too is this call to rest from evil works and rest in God. But this resting in God is not to be understood in merely a passive sense. Resting in God actually includes Sabbath work.

SABBATH WORK

The work required by Sabbath observance can be understood in two senses, just as there is a kind of typical meaning of the Sabbath and a spiritual, eternal reality to which that type points. In the first, ordinary or typical sense, the work of the Sabbath is precisely that which the catechism outlines. It is the work of the ordained ministry in public corporate worship. It is the work of Christian charity as well as moral and spiritual formation and education. In this way the commandment to observe the Sabbath and keep it holy actually requires human work. Thus, writes Ursinus,

> Such works as do not hinder or interfere with the proper use
> of the Sabbath, but which, on the other hand, rather carry
> out its true intention and so establish it, as all those works
> do which so pertain to the worship of God or religious cere-
> monies, or to the duty of love towards our neighbor, or to the
> saving of our own or the life of another, as that necessity will

---

82. Kuyper, *E Voto Dordraceno*, LD 38, §2.2.

not allow them to be deferred to another time, do not violate the Sabbath, but are especially required in order that we may properly observe it.[83]

But even this temporal Sabbath observance is not really to be limited to a single day of the week. As we have seen, there is a deep connection between Sabbath observance on a particular day and the spiritual consequences throughout the rest of the week. One example may suffice to illustrate this connection.

Proper Sabbath observance requires the giving of alms and the practices of Christian charity. And as we have seen above, the proper exercise of Christian stewardship enjoined in the eighth commandment requires, among other things, productive labor and the creation of wealth so that there might be goods to share with the poor. The Sabbath is the ordinary manifestation of charity and almsgiving in the church, and so the ordinary work of the Christian in the world comes to its fulfillment in one way in the generosity of the Christian church.

In this same way Kuyper observes that all of the work required by the fourth commandment requires financial means. "Where can this money be found?" he wonders. The answer is, of course, that it must ordinarily "come from the annual incomes of the members of the congregation. The money must be earned and acquired in civil society."[84] Kuyper proceeds to outline the connection between worship and work in this way:

> Through her preaching the church is to elevate and inspire her members also in carrying out their God given occupation. Your members should, as good Calvinists, earn more than others through the faithful execution of their duties, through greater zeal, through putting more of their heart into their work. And it is precisely from these extra earnings that the money should come for maintaining the ministry of your church and all that comes with it.[85]

All of this has to do with the temporal observance of the Sabbath in this life. But this observance, even as it is spiritual in comparison with the

---

83. Ursinus, *Commentary on the Heidelberg Catechism*, 559.
84. Kuyper, *E Voto Dordraceno*, LD 38, §5.2.
85. Kuyper, *E Voto Dordraceno*, LD 38, §5.2.

requirements of the Sabbath in the Mosaic dispensation, points still yet to the everlasting Sabbath. And even here, says Kuyper, there is a kind of Sabbath work. "The resting from our sin, our vain works, and our misery must be immediately filled with a resting in something positive, a resting in the rest of God," writes Kuyper. Indeed, this resting in God "is not a doing nothing but an ever deeper immersion in his work, so also will this rest of God not be a sitting still and doing nothing, but an ever greater immersion in and therefore richer enjoyment of all that God has accomplished. This then shall be the eternal Sabbath, when everything is finished and the eternal enjoyment will begin."[86] This will be, in other words, the ultimate consummation of work and worship, the harmony of which we strive for in this life.

CONCLUSION

Twentieth-century economist John Maynard Keynes famously observed, "In the long run we are all dead."[87] His point had to do with the importance of time horizons for economic calculation and policy making. In the economic teachings of the Heidelberg Catechism, however, death has a similarly formative significance. If the origin of our economic activity is God's superabundance, and the essence of that activity is stewardship, then the goal or telos of economic activity is Sabbath rest. This Sabbath involves both resting from our evil works and resting in God, now as we are able and fully in eternity. But as the Heidelberg Catechism also teaches, our temporal death is "a dying to sin and an entering into eternal life."[88] The economic teachings of the Heidelberg Catechism thus prepare us both for grateful and faithful stewardship in this life and for patient and hopeful expectation in the world to come.

This survey of the basic economic teachings of the Heidelberg Catechism opens up important lines of future inquiry and application. We have seen that the foundation of economic life in divine superabundance does not remove all dimensions of scarcity, which is best understood as a feature of finite, creaturely existence. Certainly after the fall into sin there are new

---

86. Kuyper, *E Voto Dordraceno*, LD 38, §4.4.
87. John Maynard Keynes, *A Tract on Monetary Reform* (London: Macmillan, 1923), 80. On the moral consequences of the Keynesian perspective, see Victor V. Claar and Greg Forster, *The Keynesian Revolution and Our Empty Economy: We're All Dead* (New York: Palgrave Macmillan, 2019).
88. Heidelberg Catechism, LD 16, A 42.

forms of scarcity and suffering, and it is on the basis of God's abundance and preserving grace that human action can be taken to alleviate and address material inequities and poverty. This involves not only institutional, structural, and social action but also individual virtue.

The relationship between virtue and Christian discipleship, especially in the context of economic stewardship, is ripe for interdisciplinary investigation. Ursinus's exposition of the virtues of the Christian steward is noteworthy as an example of Reformed theological reflection on economic ethics. Greater attention to the early-modern relationship between Reformed theology and virtue ethics can help reorient contemporary applications of theological perspectives to economics.[89] Areas of important concern include the virtues of a faithful Christian steward as well as the virtues of Christian entrepreneurs, particularly as approached from a comprehensive and robust doctrine of Christian vocation. Similarly the dangers and temptations, and characteristic vices, of economic endeavors in an increasingly complex and diverse landscape warrant sustained reflection.

More particular topics and areas of inquiry are likewise worthy of sustained attention. The phenomenon of Sabbath observance, not only from a theological and practical religious perspective but also as an economic and social phenomenon, is one obvious area where greater work needs to be done. Better understanding of the rhythms and dynamics of work and worship, labor and rest, as well as prayer and practice hold the promise to help correct pathologies characteristic of modern economic life, including job dissatisfaction, alienation, and workaholism.[90]

The relationship of Sabbath to daily life underscores the deeper relationship between economic realities and human flourishing. The biblical

---

89. For a comprehensive survey of the bibliographic sources, see Manfred Svensson, "Aristotelian Practical Philosophy from Melanchthon to Eisenhart: Protestant Commentaries on the *Nicomachean Ethics* 1529–1682," *Reformation & Renaissance Review* 21, no. 3 (2019): 218–38. See also Luigino Bruni and Robert Sugden, "Reclaiming Virtue Ethics for Economics," *Journal of Economic Perspectives* 27, no. 4 (Fall 2013): 141–64.

90. On the recurring theme of agriculture in this essay, see Britney Rosburg, Terry W. Griffin, and Brian Coffey, "The Cost of Being Faithful: What Do Farmers Give Up to Keep the Sabbath?," *Faith & Economics* 73 (Spring 2019). See also Justo L. Gonzáles, *A Brief History of Sunday: From the New Testament to the New Creation* (Grand Rapids: Eerdmans, 2017); and Edward O'Flaherty and Rodney L. Peterson with Timothy A. Norton, eds., *Sunday, Sabbath, and the Weekend: Managing Time in a Global Culture* (Grand Rapids: Eerdmans, 2010).

and theological notion of shalom, understood as ultimate peace and our participation in it within this world, can help us to better frame the relationship between created nature and saving grace, between material and eternal goods. Nicholas Wolsterstorff describes shalom in connection with peace, rest, and right relationship: "Shalom is the human being dwelling at peace in all his or her relationships: with God, with self, with fellows, with nature." He continues, "But the peace which is shalom is not merely the absence of hostility, not merely being in right relationship. Shalom at its highest is *enjoyment* in one's relationships."[91] Ultimate reality infuses penultimate realities with meaning and significance. Shalom involves not only right relationships in themselves but relations put right in terms of relative significance and valuation.

As Richard Baxter (1615–91) puts it, "We pray for our daily bread before pardon and spiritual blessings, not as if it were better, but that nature is supposed before grace, and we cannot be Christians if we are not men."[92] Or as Kuyper articulates the dynamic between life in this world and the next:

> Re-creation brings to us that which is eternal, finished, perfected, completed; far above the succession of moments, the course of years, and the development of circumstances. Here lies the difficulty. This *eternal* work must be brought to a *temporal* world, to a race which is in process of development; hence that work must *make* history, increasing like a plant, growing, blossoming, and bearing fruit. And this history must include a time of *preparation, revelation*, and lastly of filling the earth with the streams of grace, salvation, and blessing.[93]

In this way the temporal economic life of faithful stewardship is to be properly oriented and related to the reality of eternity. Far from evacuating this life of significance, the Christian life of stewardship is hereby infused with proper meaning and perspective. It is neither worthless nor of ultimate value. Rather, it is penultimate, an appropriate valuation given to us already in the words of Jesus: "But seek first the kingdom of God and his righteousness, and all these things will be added to you" (Matt 6:33).

---

91. Nicholas Wolterstorff, *Until Justice and Peace Embrace* (Grand Rapids: Eerdmans, 1983), 69.

92. Richard Baxter, *How to Do Good to Many: The Public Good Is the Christian's Life*, ed. Jordan J. Ballor (Grand Rapids: Christian's Library, 2018 [1682]), 31.

93. Abraham Kuyper, *The Work of the Holy Spirit* (New York: Funk & Wagnalls, 1900), 50–51.

ABBREVIATIONS

AKB	*Abraham Kuyper: An Annotated Bibliography 1857–2010.* Tjitze Kuipers. Translated by Clifford Anderson and Dagmare Houniet. Brill's Series in Church History 55. Leiden: Brill, 2011
AKCR	*Abraham Kuyper: A Centennial Reader.* Edited by James D. Bratt. Grand Rapids: Eerdmans, 1998
ARP	Antirevolutionary Party
CCS	*Calvin's Commentaries Series.* Edited by John King. 45 vols. Edinburgh: Calvin Translation Society, 1844–56
CG	Kuyper, Abraham. *Common Grace.* Edited by Jordan J. Ballor and Stephen J. Grabill. Translated by Nelson D. Kloosterman and Ed M. van der Maas. 3 vols. Bellingham, WA: Lexham Press, 2016–
ET	English translation
LC	Kuyper, Abraham. *Lectures on Calvinism.* Grand Rapids: Eerdmans, 1931
LD	Lord's Day
LW	Luther, Martin. *Luther's Works.* 55 vols. American ed. Edited by Jaroslav Pelikan and Helmut T. Lehmann. St. Louis: Concordia; Philadelphia: Fortress, 1955–86
OP	Kuyper, Abraham. *Our Program: A Christian Political Manifesto.* Translated and edited by Harry Van Dyke. Bellingham, WA: Lexham Press, 2015

On Education Kuyper, Abraham. *On Education*. Edited by Wendy Naylor and Harry Van Dyke. Bellingham, WA: Lexham Press, 2019.

OT Old Testament

PR Kuyper, Abraham. *Pro Rege: Living under Christ's Kingship*. Edited by John Kok with Nelson D. Koosterman. Translated by Albert Gootjes. 3 vols. Bellingham, WA: Lexham Press, 2016–

SV *Statenvertaling* ("States translation," or Authorized Version of the Dutch Bible, 1637)

GIVE US THIS DAY OUR DAILY BREAD

COMMENTARY ON LORD'S DAY 50 OF THE HEIDELBERG CATECHISM

TEXT INTRODUCTION

The Heidelberg Catechism is a manual for basic instruction in Christian doctrine. Published in 1563, the catechism consists of 129 questions and answers and quickly proved useful for faith formation of children and adults alike. Divided into 52 parts, each "Lord's Day" enables the entirety of the teachings of the catechism to be covered in weekly sermons throughout the year.

At the Synod of Dort, in its 146th session of April 30, 1619, delegates of the participating churches from abroad exhorted the Dutch church "to persevere in the Reformed faith, to pass it on to posterity, and to preserve it until the return of Christ." In reply, the delegates from the Dutch church made a solemn vow, pledging to preach and preserve the Reformed faith, pure and undiluted.

When Kuyper started his commentary on the Heidelberg Catechism in fall 1886 in the Sunday paper *De Heraut*, he recalled this vow and subsequently titled his series *E voto Dordraceno*: "from the vow made at Dort." The title is usually shortened, at Kuyper's own directive—"for ease of citing," he said—to *E Voto*.

As detailed in the Heidelberg Catechism, the Lord's Prayer contains six petitions, or requests, of which "Give us this day our daily bread" is the fourth. Lord's Day 50 covers this petition in Question and Answer 125, and Kuyper's exposition of the fourth petition addresses the topic of the *origin* or *source* of material blessings, that is, God's superabundant blessings and

God himself as "the only fountain of all good." The chapter on Lord's Day 50 first appeared in three installments in *De Heraut* of March 3, 11, and 18, 1894.

Source: Abraham Kuyper, *E voto Dordraceno* (Amsterdam: J. A. Wormser, 1892–95), 4:506–28. Translated by Ed M. van der Maas. Edited and annotated by Harry Van Dyke.

COMMENTARY ON LORD'S DAY 50 OF THE HEIDELBERG CATECHISM

Question 125: *What is the fourth petition?*
Answer: *"Give us this day our daily bread"; that is, be pleased to provide for all our bodily need, so that we may thereby acknowledge that Thou art the only fountain of all good, and that without Thy blessing neither our care and labor, nor Thy gifts, can profit us; that we may therefore withdraw our trust from all creatures and place it alone in Thee.*

> *And he humbled you and let you hunger and fed you with manna,* §1
> *which you did not know, nor did your fathers know, that he might*
> *make you know that man does not live by bread alone, but man*
> *lives by every word that comes from the mouth of the LORD.*
> Deuteronomy 8:3

The fourth petition is the first one of the final triad. In the first triad, the petitions focused on the longing of the soul for the glory of God; they therefore say, "Hallowed be *your* name; *your* kingdom come; *your* will be done." But in the fourth petition there is a change: "Give *us* bread; forgive *us* our debts; and lead *us* not into temptation."

We must pay close attention to this, since otherwise the praying soul does not get sufficient insight into itself. For the Lord's Prayer shows and teaches us that it is well with our soul only when, spontaneously and naturally, the petition for God's *name*, *kingdom*, and *will* arises in our soul from an ardent impulse of love for our God.

Conversely, it is not well with us if this threefold petition is either omitted or included as an afterthought. Also in our prayers, the first and highest commandment applies: "You shall love the Lord your God with all your heart and with all your soul and with all your might" [Deut 6:5]. The fact that for this purpose the Lord's Prayer places exactly three petitions on our lips does not mean, of course, that we must always have exactly *three* petitions arise from our love for God. But it *does* mean that the petition for the glory of our God must constitute a separate element in our prayer. It must not be added merely incidentally but must be a distinct component of our prayer.

Therefore, in our prayer our thoughts must begin by drawing back from our own needs, by forgetting ourselves and our neighbor, by denying ourselves entirely before our God, in order to allow our *whole* thought world to be filled by love for our God. When we do this we will notice how our petitions automatically move through a certain cycle, and how after having gone through this cycle they come to a point of rest. It is this cycle of our prayers for the glory of our God that is indicated by this triad. By first calling upon "our Father in heaven" our soul must free itself from earthly things—from our house and home, from ourselves, from our own persons—in order to climb upward and lift itself up to the God of our life. As we encounter him when lifting up our soul and finding in the blood of the Mediator access to the throne of grace, and as we are drawn by his virtues and perfections, we cannot but long for the honor of his *name*, the coming of his *kingdom*, and the rule of his *will*. Only then are we to come down again to earth, to our home, our self, our cares, in order to enter an entirely different group of petitions, and to invoke the grace of our God also for our physical and spiritual needs.

This second group of petitions, in turn, also constitutes a triad, and so likewise a complete unit. Here also the intent is not that we should always stammer exactly these three petitions, but rather that our prayers and entreaties for ourselves should always have a certain unity, a certain completeness, and should not get stuck halfway. It should not be a praying only for being rescued from physical distress but must always be at the same time a praying for being saved from our spiritual needs. Conversely, we should not just pray for our spiritual needs but also bring our material needs before God.

In the second place, our spiritual needs should not only refer back to our sinful past but must always include our spiritual future as well: not only "forgive me my guilt of past sins," but in addition, "lead me not into temptation" in the hours to come. Not only, therefore, a prayer for atonement for the past but equally a petition for sanctification for the future.

Third, there should also be this order, that we begin with our physical needs in the *present*, then move on to our spiritual needs of the *past*, and only then express our need for grace for the *future*. When we pray we kneel down in the *present*, look back at the *past*, and look ahead to the *future*. And it is precisely in this order that Jesus puts the three petitions in the second triad. First: "Give us *this day* our daily bread." Next: "Forgive us our debts in the *past*." And finally: "Help us against Satan in the *future*." Note also that among all these needs our neighbor should be able to find in our petitions the same love for him as we bear toward ourselves as we pray. In all three of these petitions it is not *me* but always *us*. He who prays appears in a priestly function before his God, laying before him his *own* need, the need of *his nearest and dearest*, and the need of all *humanity*.

If we have sufficiently indicated what guidance has been given in the Lord's Prayer for the content, the order sequence, and the comprehensiveness of our prayer, then we must now take a closer look at the first petition of this second triad. First a brief comment about the text of this fourth petition. In our Bible version it reads, "Give us this day our daily bread." The only problem here is the word "daily," a translation we have become used to after it was brought into vogue by Luther. Calvin already noted, however, that the word *epiousios* in the original Greek text literally means something different. It is, unfortunately, a word that is found only here and probably means "as much bread as is *adequate* for us," in contrast to *periousios*, which means *abundant*. The meaning is then the same as what believers in the Old Testament prayed: "Give me neither poverty nor riches;

feed me with the food that is *needful for me*" [Prov 30:8].[1] Since the word "daily" expresses approximately the same thought: "the bread I need for this day," there would seem to be no pressing reason to replace "daily" with another word, especially not in a prayer that everyone knows by heart and the wording of which we have been familiar with since childhood. (This comment is inserted here only to keep believers from becoming upset by a pedantic display of learning on the part of some preachers who like to refer to "the original text.")

Let it be very clear, first and foremost, that any spiritualization of this petition is misplaced and improper. This prayer should not be applied, for example, to the bread of the Lord's Supper, nor to "the bread come down from heaven" [see John 6:51]. This has been done repeatedly, and some still do so. But no matter how it is done, it is always contrary to the purport and the order of the Lord's Prayer. In the order of the prayer that Jesus taught us, this petition is intended to ensure a proper place in our prayers for our physical needs. Those who nevertheless spiritualize this petition assault the Word of the Lord and take away from the Lord's Prayer that which Christ has intentionally included.

Conversely, we must note that our physical needs are covered by only one petition in the Lord's Prayer, as compared to five petitions with a spiritual import. This contains a clear indication that he prays wrongly who turns this order around and sends up many petitions for his physical needs but limits his spiritual needs to a single petition. Nor should we lose sight of the fact that the petition for our physical needs comes first in this triad. That corresponds perfectly to our human condition. You must first live before you can live for God. Your life as a human being on earth depends, after all, on God providing you with your bread. This does not contradict what Jesus says elsewhere: "But seek first the kingdom of God and his righteousness, and all these things will be added to you" [Matt 6:33]. For in the Lord's Prayer the petition for bread is preceded by three petitions for the kingdom of God: the petition that the name of the *King* be hallowed, that his *kingdom* come, and that his *subjects* may fulfill his will. But when the

---

1. The authorized Dutch version of the Bible, the *Statenvertaling* of 1637, uses the word *daaglijks* ("daily") to translate the Greek *epiousion* in the Lord's Prayer in Matt 6:11 and Luke 11:3. But the OT passage Kuyper refers to here is Prov 30:8, where the SV uses the word *bescheiden* ("modest") in its rendering of the Hebrew *lechem choq'qi* (often translated "daily bread"). Literally the Dutch reads "feed me with the bread of my modest portion."

prayer now turns to ourselves, all prayer must take our physical needs as its point of departure. This is not in order to stay there—this petition is followed by two petitions concerning our spiritual needs—but to start there.

In this connection, the addition of the word "this day" is very effective. Generally, people praying the Lord's Prayer do not limit themselves to the present. In the three preceding petitions their prayer extends *into eternity*. This is felt most clearly in the petition "Your kingdom come," in which the *Maranatha* and the longing for the return of Christ are so clearly implicit. Likewise, the fifth and the sixth petition do not stay with the present but look back to the past and forward to the future. The emphatic addition of "this day" is therefore intentional, rather than superfluous or incidental. With this word our Savior has fully introduced our praying soul to what he expresses elsewhere as follows: "Do not be anxious about your life" [Matt 6:25]. The expression *about your life* points not only to today but encompasses our entire future. And that future we shall not take into our own hands but entrust quietly to our God. Each day constitutes its own, distinct unit. Our sleep at night separates today's day from tomorrow. When the sun sets, the day ends; and when the sun later emerges from its tent again, a new day has dawned. God the Lord has made the division into day and night, and they shall be signs to us. We shall therefore not allow the boundary between one day and the next either to fade or to be erased, but we shall respect it. The day of tomorrow will take care of itself: sufficient unto the day is the evil thereof [Matt 6:34]. The strength of our soul is not equal to bearing the cares of more than one day at a time. The cares of the day we now experience are already more than sufficient. *This* day we received from our God. Whether *tomorrow* shall also be ours is God's mystery. We do not know. And if it pleases God to grant us tomorrow, then tomorrow there will also be access to the throne of grace, to petition God for *that* day.

For that reason, the prayer for our physical needs must be focused on and limited to "this day." Otherwise we move from God to mammon and become entangled in the many details and cares of life. Even as the Sabbath divides our weeks and we cannot disregard this division without robbing ourselves of our rest and the peace of our soul, so also does the day divide up the hours of our life. If we fail to do justice to *this* division we needlessly unsettle our hearts and we bypass God, who took it upon himself to take care of us. Finally, the words "this day" indicate that we should pray anew each day and not skip the Lord's Prayer for a single day. For it is in those very words "this day" that Jesus indicated that he was giving us a prayer for *each and every day*.

The petition asks for *bread*—for nothing more, for nothing to go with that bread. In paradise, fallen humanity was told, "By the sweat of your face you shall eat bread" [Gen 3:19]. It is this ordinary, dry bread that every human being has to ask from his God every day. The fact that it pleases God often to give us *more* than bread is beside the point. If need be, *bread* and *water* are sufficient to sustain life. But we cannot do without *bread*. Our body has been created by God so that it digests and metabolizes the substances it takes in. Eating is therefore in fact nothing but replenishing the digested intake with new intake, to renew what has been used. But strictly speaking bread and water are sufficient for this purpose. The reason why only bread is mentioned here is that, especially in the mountainous regions where Jesus walked, brooks of fresh and delicious water gurgled everywhere, so that water was always present. It was not the water but only the bread that required time and effort. Nowadays we have, in addition to bread, all kinds of other foods and side dishes at our disposal, and in addition to water all kinds of other means to quench our thirst. This is the consequence of the superabundant goodness of God, who let all kinds of fruit grow, ordained meat for us to eat, and made the grape vine, the coffee tree, and the tea bush grow. But we do not have a right to anything, and by limiting all petitions concerning physical needs in the Lord's Prayer to the single petition for bread, Jesus wants to evoke a twofold attitude in our praying soul.

First, that we shall not claim anything more than bread; and second, that we realize daily what great goodness we experience when God the Lord gives us something else in addition. There is an old Dutch saying about people being "unable to bear prosperity well," meaning that they have all manner of pretensions to lead a comfortable life, while looking down on precious bread with a measure of disdain as being beneath them.[2] This is the height of ungodliness. We should rather honor the wonderful food God has given us in bread. Bread is actually a food entirely intended for and suited to man, which, together with water, contains almost everything we need for the sustenance of our body. Everybody needs bread—our body cannot do with less, and it is therefore harsh and merciless to withhold bread from any human being. But bread as such is sufficient. The many

---

2. The obscure Dutch saying Kuyper refers to here is (in his words) *Iemand de brood-kruimels steken*.

people among us who sit down at the table and look discontented when they see that there is nothing but bread, and nothing to accompany the bread, or to use on the bread, are guilty of ingratitude. As long as God gives us each day sufficient bread to feed our body, we have nothing to complain about. For anything we receive in addition we should be *doubly* grateful. We must remember that everything additional is surplus goodness of our God toward us. We may therefore use and enjoy this surplus if God gives it to us. But we must banish any thought that, should God give us nothing but bread, he would actually do us an injustice. Parents also would do well not to foster any false notions in this regard in their children. It is a splendid preparation for a better understanding of the Lord's Prayer to eat nothing but bread and drink nothing but water for a day while abstaining from anything else.

Jesus teaches us to pray for bread, whether we be poor or rich. But it goes without saying that those who are poor learn to pray this petition much more readily and earnestly than those who are better off. Those who live amid rich abundance, who always have more than enough bread in their pantries and even consider bread a secondary concern among all their other foods, do not easily arrive at an attitude in which they pray for bread from the inner urging of their soul, for bread for this one day, and for nothing but bread. Those who are poor, by contrast, and especially those who are truly poverty stricken, who have no bread in the house for themselves and their children when they wake up in the morning, and who do not know where they might find it, such people automatically come to this prayer. What is more natural than that they pray, "Father, give me our bread for today"? But those who are rich and have a well-filled pantry and cellar, and who let anything they might want to eat be bought for them, who get anything they want delivered at their house each morning by the baker and the butcher, such people will never spontaneously come to this prayer. They must first be enabled by the Holy Spirit to pray this prayer.

Rich people may be capable of giving thanks spontaneously when they think of all their riches and wealth and may then say to themselves, "What makes me so different that I am Dives and not poor Lazarus?" But praying for bread, which they barely value and which lies abundantly on their table and will later mostly be taken from the table again without having been used—this they can learn only through the Holy Spirit. Indeed, even those who are not rich but nevertheless enjoy a measure of prosperity and who, while not disdaining bread, still always put butter and even toppings on it, and who enjoy a hot meal every day, never come spontaneously to an attitude in which they pray to God from a sense of need for a piece of bread for this particular day. They may feel anxious when their business does not generate enough profit, or when they have difficulty paying their bills, and therefore they pray to God for help in their temporal concerns. But what Jesus puts on our lips here, to pray every day for *a piece of bread* from a gracious God, does not occur to them spontaneously. Rather, they must be taught to pray this through the Word, by its light and under the influence of the Holy Spirit. There are therefore few people who pray the Lord's Prayer, and therefore also this petition, each day anew from an ardent need of their soul.

In this context, also pay attention to the word *us*: give *us* this day our daily bread. Let that little word set the rich and the more well-to-do at least on the right path. Even though they themselves have bread in abundance, they know that there are thousands living in their surroundings who face each new day with distress, in part for lack of bread. Even though they themselves have everything their heart desires, let them begin by allowing their thoughts in this prayer to also go out to the many who live in worry and distress and barely know how they can get from one day to the next. Then at least they will immediately sense that the prayer "Give *us* this day our daily bread" reflects a reality rather than a fiction. And if they then, rising from prayer, look at their own abundance and think of the terrible need in which others find themselves, and if they are then cut to the heart by the fearful word "hunger," which they never knew themselves, then after such a prayer they may perhaps have a better sense of their calling to be stewards of their possessions on God's behalf. They may also then be more willing than they might otherwise have been to stretch out their hand as servants of God in distributing daily bread to *those who have no bread*.

§2
Beware lest you say in your heart, "My power and the might of my hand have gotten me this wealth." You shall remember the Lord *your God, for it is he who gives you power to get wealth.*
Deuteronomy 8:17–18

The petition for simply a morsel of bread contains the affirmation of our absolute *dependency*, and as such embodies *the root of all true piety*. It is not that there is piety in asking bread from God because you are really hungry and there is nothing but an empty breadbasket on your table, but rather because most human beings do *not* find themselves in this kind of emergency situation. Sadly, even in Christian countries there are still a few families who upon waking face the unanswered question whether they will see any bread that day, and if so, where this bread will come from. But that is not the situation in which Jesus puts the petition for daily bread on the lips of his disciples. The disciples were not *that* poor! Jesus' intention is that this prayer for the fulfillment of our daily needs would spring from our heart, even when we at least have bread. And since this petition confines itself to the *present*, that is, to the bread for this one day, it is also clear that it is Jesus' intention that this petition shall not spring from acute lack of bread but shall be prayed by all of us, even though we can very well get by this day with what we have on hand.

We emphasize this because even among God's children the petition for daily bread so easily flags as long as the need is not urgent. We notice this most clearly in meetings of Christian organizations. As long as the treasurer has money on hand, we rarely hear in such meetings petitions for the daily bread of the organization. This petition begins to cross our lips only when the Lord God makes us face disturbing deficits. It is true: need teaches us to pray. We even concede that need exists in order that we may learn to pray. But he who just *learns* to pray does not yet know how to pray *as he should*.

Where prayer is as it should be, the petition "Give us this day our daily bread" is not inspired by fear that we will otherwise die of hunger, but is meant to give God the glory. Even in the absence of prayer our Father in heaven provides; and thousands upon thousands who never pray are fed every day, sometimes even sumptuously. In fact, there are cases where there are two people, one of whom prays and scarcely receives bread, while the other does *not* pray yet bathes in luxury. That poor Lazarus, who had to live off the crumbs, probably did pray, but even though Dives, that rich man, still uttered formal prayers, he certainly did not pray from the heart. And this is how it still is. Morning after morning, noon upon noon, a rich, well-supplied table is laid out in many homes where prayer is either entirely abolished or formal prayer has been retained but has long since lost its essence. There is then a moment of silence, the eyes are halfway or three-quarters closed, the hands are not quite folded, something is mumbled, then comes the *Amen* and it is over. This is the kind of prayer of which the Lord said to Israel in the days of Isaiah: "When you spread out your hands, I will hide my eyes from you; even though you make many prayers, I will not listen" [Isa 1:15].

This evil not only is certainly found in the homes of the godless but is also well-known among Christians when the routines of life extinguish the Spirit, or when at festive meals heads and hearts are filled with earthly thoughts and virtually no one seeks access to the throne of grace when someone is "saying grace." We do not conclude from this that it is better not to pray in that case, for even formal habits have a power for good. Rather, we point this out in order that Christians may realize their guilt before God and at least pay such attention to their prayers that these prayers no longer indict them before God's merciful throne. Note that Jesus links this petition for our daily bread to the petition for forgiveness of our debts: believers are sure of the forgiveness of their sins, know they are reconciled through their Savior, and yet the Lord wants them to implore that forgiveness daily. That is also how things stand with this petition. Children of God know full well that their heavenly Father has already taken care of them or will take care of them. But they must nevertheless ask their God every day anew for their morsel of bread, in order that they may be mindful each day, and may express before their God, how also this day they have life, well-being, and all things only through the favor and grace of God.

This is of profound import. Those who live without God fancy that they have their life and prosperity in their own hands, and that the enjoyment of the sun that lights up the sky and of the air that they breathe and of the water that they drink is their natural due. They use their brains every day, they see with their eyes, they hear with their ears, they move on their feet, imagining that all this is theirs as a matter of course. Only when insanity threatens, or blindness sets in, or deafness comes to plague them, or gout ties them to their chair, only then does it begin to dawn on them that all these commonplace functions can be taken away from them. And then they pray to God that the use of their heads, their senses, and their feet may be restored, and when God does indeed answer their prayer they thank God for it.

But this is of course a wrong way of thinking. For all this is not only God's gift when the use of any of their senses is restored to them; it was God's gift all the days of their life, from their youth onward, and it was nothing but extreme superficiality and thoughtlessness on their part to fancy that they possessed and enjoyed all of this automatically, without God receiving the glory for it. If then such culpable thoughtlessness and smugness in God's children has to be systematically broken and conquered by faith, the implication is that children of God must think of God in all these things, even when enjoying the light and warmth of the sun, since it is God who "makes his sun rise on the evil and on the good" [Matt 5:45]. Where evildoers are silent, the good at least shall give honor and glory to God for his works.

We do not mean this, of course, in an unnatural sense. We humans are much too limited to be continually conscious of all these God-given gifts, and to fully appreciate the blessing they bring, and to thank him for them with heartfelt conviction. That would be simply *impossible*. But what is possible, and therefore must happen, is that God's children praise the goodness of God in all these common blessings and praise his Name for them. Only now and then do the petition and thankfulness for the light in our eyes, the flow of our blood, the swiftness of our feet, and so much more bring us to giving thanks. But Jesus has ordained that we praise our God at least once every day for the food with which he nourishes us. He also feeds the young ravens and the birds of the forest, although these cannot thank him. But we humans have this double gift: (1) that God feeds us and (2) that we know that he does this. And because we are the only creatures who have this knowledge it is our duty to pray and give thanks. The honor of all that glorious work of feeding and sustaining all his creatures accrues to God in the prayer and thanksgiving of his children.

Even though you may sit down to a copious meal with an abundance of bread and so much more, nevertheless that bread before you is *not yet yours*. As it lies there, that bread still belongs to your God. Our petition *Give us this bread* is therefore neither an idle sound nor an inner pretense, but it is meant literally even as the bread is laid out in front of you. It is meant to say: "Lord my God, all this is yours. You are therefore, this morning and this noon hour, my host. Come and give it to me, and distribute it to me and my wife and children, and let us thus live together by your grace."

To be sure, you earned this bread yourself, through your work. But your work too was not yours. All the strength you applied to get that bread was strength from God at work in you. It was in his service that you did this work. And that which the work yielded is not your property but remains the property of God. Poor people know that very well, and many a godly person among the poor certainly thanks his God when he returns home Saturday evening with his wages. The godlessness that almost never gives thanks is found much more frequently among those who are more richly endowed, who collect their salary every other month or every quarter, and who receive their dividends. Truly, if you were to add up the men and women who are in the habit of thanking God when their salary or dividends arrive, you would find the group to be very small. There are those who do indeed give thanks, but they are few. You cannot determine this for each person individually, but you can notice it in the self-assured way they speak about their salary and their money. It is as if everything *bypasses* God.

Yet here lies the fundamental error. Unless we look upon the wages for our labor or upon our financial possessions or upon our investments as things that belong to God and therefore not to us, we will never come to the right attitude in praying "Give us this day our daily bread." We have money; we use it to buy our bread and so much else. If we have more than enough bread, why then would we still pray first for the bread that is already ours? This is then also related to the inability of many people to give generously. They do not recognize that their money is God's, and so they think that they are already godly if they set apart a trifle of their own money for the poor or for God's church. Especially the well-to-do middle class is trapped in this evil. Members of this class do give, but they give ever so little—so much less than they could and should give. And this springs only from the false notion that the money in their purse is their money rather than God's. Above all things, those who want to walk in godliness before God must banish this false notion. *All* your money is God's money, even though you may have slaved and labored for it in his service. Therefore, all you buy with this money belongs and continues to belong to God, until he hands it over and gives it to you. Once you are firmly convinced of this, it is natural that you will also acknowledge this when it comes to the bread on your table: "This bread too belongs to God," and that before partaking of it you will ask in prayer, "Give me this bread, which is yours, that I may receive it from your hand." This then automatically subdues the discontent which so easily makes us grumble when the food does not suit our taste or is not served in what we consider sufficient quantities.

After all, we have no right to anything, not even to the smallest piece of bread. Rather, we have forfeited everything, and it is from sheer goodness that we are granted, when it pleases God, the necessities of life.

But there is more in this petition: it also points *the blessing*. This blessing does not mean that we are to think: "I've got my bread; now if only God will add his blessing." Rather, the blessing must work *in* the bread, because this bread does not exist without God having created it and maintaining it as bread. He created it. He ordained that the earth should bring forth, along with many other herbaceous plants, the fruitful and nourishing grain— wheat, rye, corn, and so much more. He ordained that the earth should bring forth this grain in such a way that it contained precisely those components that are necessary for nourishing the human body.

But God's actions are not limited to this. When the earth, at his command, brings forth the grain, and it is threshed and ground into flour and baked into bread, God does not abandon this bread. It does not lie on your table apart from your God while your God is in heaven, but in the very moment that you take that bread it is the omnipotent and omnipresent power of God that sustains that bread and maintains its nutritious powers. That which nourishes you and sustains your life is therefore not that bread but the power of God at work in this bread—or, as Moses put it to Israel in Deuteronomy 8:3, and Jesus repeated to Satan, "Man does not live by bread alone, but man lives by every word that comes from the mouth of the LORD." This statement has been grossly misconstrued and misused, and is still repeatedly interpreted, even by orthodox preachers, as though it meant: "You should not just provide bread for your body, but it is far more important that you feed your soul with the Scriptures." But the misuse of this verse is gradually decreasing, since there is a growing realization that verse 3 is explained and elucidated in verses 17 and 18 of the same chapter, where Moses says explicitly to Israel: "Beware lest you say in your heart, 'My power and the might of my hand have gotten me this wealth.' You shall remember the LORD your God, for it is he who gives you power to get wealth." The statement "Man does not live by bread alone, but man lives by every word that comes from the mouth of the LORD" referred to the manna. At that point Israel had no bread, and yet it stayed alive because a word went out from God that manna should descend; Israel then lived from this word of God, without bread, by manna alone.

Applied to us, this means that day after day a word of God goes out to this earth that this earth will nourish us. And it is this creating and sustaining word of our God by which our life is maintained. There is therefore no reference here to a *spiritual* word, to the word of Scripture, nor to the word of grace. This fourth petition refers to the body and to the body alone, and Deuteronomy 8:3 only points to God's word of power from which we gain *the blessing* in the nourishment and sustenance of our body. The catechism therefore says quite accurately that in this fourth petition lies the affirmation "without Thy blessing neither our care and labor, nor Thy gifts, can profit us." This blessing is therefore not something *added* to the bread, but God works the blessing *in* our bread. If he does not let his omnipotent and omnipresent word work in this bread, it is of no benefit to us. And if he, after we have eaten the bread, does not (we say this reverently) also support it in our stomach through his power, and let it have the effect there to which he has ordained bread, our blood will remain poor and our strength will falter. There is undoubtedly a blessing in it when God lets the oil in the jug and the flour in the jar not get used up, but it is very wrong to see the blessing only in such an event; for what happened at Zarephath was a miracle that God does not repeat in our day [1 Kgs 17:8–16]. If we look for the blessing only in miracles, we can only come to the conclusion that God's blessing is highly exceptional, and we will cease to pray for a daily blessing, since a blessing in this sense will not return.

Thus it is important to see clearly that the blessing lies in the omnipotent and omnipresent power with which God the Lord sustains the bread that lies on our table and soon will go down into our body, where he lets it be bread. Certainly, God is in heaven, and therefore we call upon him as our Father in heaven; nevertheless he is and remains omnipresent. In him we live, we move, and we have our being [see Acts 17:28]. There is never a piece of bread, however small, on our table but that it is at the same moment God's power that sustains it. A person who lives close to God therefore sees in his bread not only the love of God which gives it to him, but also evidence as well as the very picture of God's omnipotent power. And when he then prays for *the blessing* he wants to show that even the gift of this bread does not help him if God the Lord withholds his power. He therefore prays that it may please God to continue to work with his power in the bread, not only when it lies on his table but also afterward in his body, where it must be converted into nourishment. God's blessing begins on the field and accompanies the wheat when it is ground into flour, the flour when you bake it into bread, and that bread when you consume it and it is digested into the components of your own blood. All other views seek God only in the extraordinary, but fail to see him also in *all* aspects of *ordinary* life. And this was precisely the intent of the Reformed, that they would learn from Scripture to honor God's work and the revelation of his power in *all* things, and to let all things, without exception, depend on his divine blessing.

God is "the only fountain of all good" that comes our way, as the catechism puts it so perfectly. This is the profound thought that underlies this fourth petition. It is not so that your daily bread is God's but the marvelous gastric juices that convert bread into nourishment are yours. No, everything is *his* gift—everything without exception, everything outside your body and inside your body, working together to nourish and sustain you, working in accordance with *his* ordinances and through *his* divine power. Viewed in this way, the fourth petition thus contains a daily instruction which invites and compels us every morning to confess the omnipotent power of our God and to acknowledge that in ourselves we are not able to do anything, also not for our body, unless God works his power in us. This must be acknowledged and confessed not only in days of illness, when our appetite deserts us, when we leave the bread on our plate, when we experience how bread does not help us. It must not only be acknowledged when God does not let the bread prosper and does not accompany it in our body with the power of his holy ordinance. No, not only then. It must also be affirmed and expressed each day in which we are granted strength and well-being. Health, it is said, is a great good, but people begin to pray for it only when they are sick, and they begin to give thanks for it when they are restored from illness. And yet, what is well-being, what is health, other than *the blessing of God on your body*? We are healthy and feel well when the ordinance of God over the human body functions normally in our body. Each day of our life is, also with that well-being, a precious gift that comes to us from the Source of every good thing, a gift that we do not have from ourselves and for which we therefore have to petition every day and give thanks every evening.

Accordingly, our entire external existence is covered in this fourth petition—our whole bodily life. Those who pray this petition acknowledge that not only their soul but equally their body exists from moment to moment only through the favor of God. And they therefore ask each morning anew that the favor of God in their bodily existence may be granted them for this day; and when the day is over and God's goodness has been enjoyed again, they give thanks every evening for what came their way in their bodily existence from the favor of God. For it goes without saying that every petition calls for a thanksgiving. In the morning: "*Give* us this day our daily bread," and in the evening: "I thank you, Lord, that you *have given* me bread for this day."

The eyes of all look to you, and you give them their food in due season.   §3
Psalm 145:15

The fourth petition does not bypass the *use of means* but rather incorporates it. He who believes in "God the Father, the Almighty, Creator of heaven and earth" acknowledges and confesses that God the Lord can feed and preserve him *also without bread*. But the petition "Give us this day our daily bread" shows that the praying soul must seek God's help in the first place along the path of ordinary means. The history of manna in the wilderness teaches without a doubt that God lacks neither the power nor the capability to feed an entire nation on a barren expanse of sand. It was precisely by looking back on the miracle of manna that Moses taught the people in the name of the Lord that "man does not live by bread alone" [Deut 8:3]. That is, man can stay alive also without bread. But what he cannot do without, lest he die, is the almighty word that proceeds from the mouth of God. If God speaks blessing we do not die but stay alive, even if we don't have bread. But if God's blessing ceases we perish, even if we were to sit among tables laden with bread. We live and survive, not at one time by the word of God's omnipotence that proceeds from his mouth and at another time by bread. Rather, no one ever survived or survives except through the word of power that proceeds from the mouth of God. The difference is only that God's omnipotence usually works through the bread, but when Jesus was in the wilderness for forty days and forty nights it worked *apart from bread*. That is why Jesus then took up the word of Moses and threw it back at Satan: a person can continue to live without bread as long as the power that comes through God's command sustains them and keeps them alive.

The correct contrast here is that God's power works through ordinary means as well as without means. For when the ordinary means are absent, two things are possible: either extraordinary means come into play, or no means at all. Extraordinary means were used when God caused manna to descend in the wilderness, or when he fed the widow at Zarephath through the flour in the jar that did not diminish, or when Jesus fed the five thousand with a few loaves and some fish. On the other hand, no means whatsoever were used when Jesus was led into the wilderness and for 40 days and 40 nights received neither bread nor manna. It is true that at Zarephath, and in the miraculous feeding of the five thousand, the normal means of bread and flour availed. But this only seemed to be so because the actual feeding of the five thousand did not come from the five loaves, and bread was therefore distributed to all but not bread in the usual sense. The flour itself at Zarephath and the bread which the apostles distributed was, like the manna in the wilderness, miracle bread. The contrast therefore remains as we stated: God can feed us in the usual way, but also in an unusual way. He can feed us through the common means which he chooses as the vehicle of his divine power, or without those common means. God does this by letting his divine power work apart from any means or through uncommon means—by a miracle.

It is undeniable that a pious mind is inclined to consider it more glorious when it happens *without* means or through *uncommon* means. If it were appointed that someone who prayed fervently and earnestly would stay alive without bread, or if, as in the case of manna, someone saw a kind of miraculous bread come down to him, then the first impulse of piety might well tempt *us* to set aside the common bread and to wait for the revelation of such a miracle. We sinners have the impression that an immediate revelation of God's omnipotence stands on a higher plane than a mediated one. It offends our feelings somehow when we begin to think that God is tied to means. We think that tying himself to means somehow degrades God's omnipotence. We would rather banish the notion of a God that uses means. In the case of human beings, we consider the use of means only natural, but the use of means seems to us to be in conflict with God's majesty. If the Lord our God is so omnipotent that he could equally well do *without* means as *with* means, why then, our soul ponders, does God the Lord not spurn the means and demonstrate his omnipotence directly and straightforwardly?

But look, with the fourth petition Jesus goes against this seemingly pious, but in fact very impious, consideration. For this petition does not say, "Support us today through your omnipotence" but "Give us today our daily *bread*." This petition therefore directs itself *to the means*. It does not set aside the means. It does not even leave undecided whether it may please God to sustain us without bread or through bread, but it attaches itself to the means and desires humbly that it may please God to give the means ordained by him, that is, the bread for this one day. If we had thought up this petition ourselves, we could not draw any other conclusion from it except to say, "That's how we humans are. We live superficially, so we think in the first place of bread, we forget God's omnipotence and so we pray that God will give us bread. But anyone who is more pious thinks more profoundly; he does not care about the bread and goes beyond it, looking only at God's omnipotence." But now that it is *Jesus* who places this petition on our lips and *commands* us to pray this, the matter stands quite differently. Now the fourth petition makes clear that Jesus rejects looking for the exceptional and wants us, rather, to turn our eyes in prayer to the *ordinary* means ordained by God. And only in this way can it be understood in a godly manner.

Only this reading is truly pious. Remember, he who looks past the common, ordinary means and does not honor the path of using means offends

God the Lord in his majesty as Creator. The ordinary means are neither our invention nor our fabrication; they are ordinances of God instituted at the time of creation for the sake of his creation. And even there where the means underwent some modification as a consequence of the fall into sin—like nourishment, since the fruits of paradise were replaced after the fall by nourishment through bread—the means of nourishment are and remain his divine ordinance. Thus, once a sinner is born again and now prefers to bypass the use of means, he is exhibiting a trait that springs not from piety but from sin. His sin alone has made miracles necessary; only on account of his sin have miracles made an entrance. And the whole miracle of Christ and his work, together with what preceded and came after, served only to annihilate sin and death. If there had been no sins, there would never have been a single miracle. In paradise there were no miracles, and in the kingdom of glory there will no longer be room for miracles. Our thirst for miracles stems from our nature, which is still bound. It is due to our habit *not* to see the common means used by God that we long for the manifestation of his power in uncommon ways. By contrast, the more our soul is initiated in the omnipresent and omnipotent working of God's power in *all* things, the less we thirst for miracles. Whoever still thirsts for miracles shows that he still ignores the working of God in ordinary life or simply has no eye for it. And because he does *not* see God's omnipotence in the ordinary, he longs for an *extraordinary* revelation in which that omnipotence may show itself to him.

It must therefore rather be the rule that we apply ourselves to be ever more aware how we live and move and have our being in God and that we more and more seek the glorification of his holy name in his use of means. The disposition of our heart is not good if we still always seek to go outside his use of means. The disposition of our heart in prayer is pure only if we follow Jesus' command and learn to pray for what has been ordained for us by way of ordinary means, and hence if we learn to pray for our daily bread.

Admittedly, by far the majority of people acknowledge this, at least in relation to *bread*, and there is no disagreement about this, at least not among Reformed people. But the same applies to our earthly needs as a whole, including those associated with illness or accident. Illness also comes to us in accordance with God's ordinance, but it is—under God's permission and ordinance—an *evil force* which would not exist apart from sin. It is something of an effect in advance of death and is therefore ultimately *satanic* in origin. We may not feel it in this manner in the case of common illnesses, but when pestilence strikes, or toxic smallpox manifests itself, or typhus threatens to kill its victim, we certainly do feel it. Pathogens were absent in paradise; they all came into being only after the fall, as part of the curse that came on the earth, together with thorns and thistles that gradually covered the earth, and along with death that visited human beings. God had said, "You will certainly die," and as a prelude to the death of the body came the scourge of illness. Here we therefore see the same contrast. God could also heal this illness without means. Many healings mentioned in Scripture show us this.

Nevertheless, the experience among all peoples teaches that this is *not* the way ordained by God. On the contrary, the ordained way is that God allows all kinds of herbs against illness to grow; that he then has one people after another discover the working of these herbs; and that he blesses the application of these herbs. It is striking how even among the simplest peoples a rich knowledge of all kinds of herbs is found, and how the mortality rate among people who seek healing in such a primitive way is but a little higher and sometimes even lower than among us. On Java, with a population five times than that of the Netherlands, there are virtually no physicians in the sense in which we understand the word; the natives still almost exclusively make use of their common herbs. Nevertheless, the mortality rate on Java compares quite favorably with that in our country. Even in Europe, high up in the mountains, there are still remote valleys which are almost never visited by a physician but where common herbs are generally effective. We do not point this out to undervalue medical science but to emphasize that in the herbs of the earth God has given us an antidote against the power of death which resides in all plagues and diseases. Even as it is a divine ordinance that we shall take bread to feed ourselves, so it also is an ordinance that in the case of illnesses and epidemics we shall resort to the means God gave us for combating them. Precisely because all illnesses and infectious diseases are the fruits of death and thus of satanic origin, they must not be *coddled* but *combated*.

Meanwhile, human beings are generally much less godly when it comes to medicine than when it comes to their daily nourishment. People don't begin to eat without saying grace, at least not in those circles where the fear of God dwells. But it is an impious phenomenon, observable even in the most devout families, that when we are ill and take medicine day after day we do so without praying about it or giving thanks for it. There are those who pray that God may *bless* the medicine, but it is extremely rare for people realize that God let the herbs grow and allows us to discover them and use them, and that therefore the glory belongs to him. The consequence is that, instead of looking at all medicines as gifts of God's grace, some people live under the mistaken impression that medicines come *from man* and that they represent some kind of attempt by proud man to conquer illness apart from God. In reaction, the more spiritual souls develop a certain phobia about medicines and prefer to turn away from physicians in order to fall into the hand of the Lord.

It cannot be denied that doctors often feed this false notion. We could almost say that most doctors have broken with all faith in God, and when they come to visit an ill person who still speaks of God's help, they adopt an attitude as if to say, "Just leave it to me; I can do much better than your God." And this attitude irritates, of course. It hurts. It annoys. Doctors too cannot do without God, and if they want to be anything more than an instrument of God's grace to take away the infectious disease, they have already received their reward. But should this sin of medical doctors become a rule for our behavior? Just because so many physicians in a sense of their own importance imagine they can do without God, is this a license for us not to give God the glory for his work, also in medical science? Shall the unbelief of a physician determine the faith of God's child?

This cannot and should not be. Just because I have an unbelieving baker who does not think of God when he bakes his bread, should I therefore disdain his bread? And likewise, just because the physician who treats me writes his prescription without considering God, should I therefore declare the medicine that God has prepared to be worthless, or sinful? In the fourth petition, our Savior gives an answer also to this question. For when you are ill and have no appetite, when the mere thought of bread gives you nausea and the illness torments you, then the fourth petition does *not* become "Give me today my daily bread," but something quite different: "Give me today the medicine against my illness."

We could easily enlarge upon this, since the needs of the body, in addition to bread and medicine, encompass so much more. You also need a place to live to protect your body against inclement weather; you need clothes to cover your nakedness, a bed to sleep on, some household goods to prepare your food, a source of light for when it gets dark, a fire against the cold, and so on. These too are all part of the common means that God uses to sustain your body and protect it from all kinds of influences of death. All this is therefore also included in the fourth petition for our daily bread. All this your God gives you as well. You should also pray to him for all these things. And for all this you should thank him, even as you should thank him for your daily bread. Even though your wardrobe is overly full and your linens pile up on the shelves, and you only have to turn on a tap to get water or gas; even though your cellar is filled with coal and you live in your own house—nevertheless that house, as well as the gas and the water and the linens and the clothes and the fuel, are not yours but are the loving provisions *of your God*, given to you by grace to take care of the needs of your body. A poor man knows all too well what it is to pray for a roof over his head when he is evicted, what it is to pray for clothing and coverage when poverty has forced him to take so many things to the pawnbroker. The godly poor therefore *pray* for these things and *thank* their God when on occasion they are privileged to have all these things. But your average citizen and the rich almost never think of it. They usually view these things as theirs, as things that belong to them as their own. What God gave them by grace keeps them away from God, and it is precisely for this reason that Jesus said so emphatically that it is hard for a rich person to enter into the kingdom of heaven.

And with that we automatically come to what the catechism summarizes at the end as the quintessence of this fourth petition: "that we may therefore withdraw our trust from all creatures and place it alone in Thee." For this is the end of all wisdom: all creatures *nothing*, God alone *everything*.[3] He is our life force, our light, our strength, our refuge, our rock, and the shield of our hope. Read and reread the Psalms and see how these lofty hymns of piety never tire of rousing us to this frame of mind. Time and again our difficulty is to see in the *creature* a real creature, and nothing but *a created thing*. We imagine over and over that something created is something of its own right, something with its own indwelling power, something with its own native ability, so that we see it as existing apart from God, indeed over against God, and now live in the conceit that there are two powers which we must take into account, on the one hand the *creature*, on the other hand *God*. We then oscillate between these two. One time we turn to the

---

3. From here until the end of this commentary, Kuyper makes much use of the word "creatures," in keeping with the use of that term in Lord's Day 50 of the Heidelberg Catechism. In doing so, he refers not only to living organisms but to all things that exist, including things made by human beings. He returns to his discussion of God's ownership of all such creatures in his commentary on the Lord's Day 42, which is also included in this volume.

power of the creature, but when the creature falls short and fails we seek our refuge in God. As long as we are healthy and all goes well and there is money in the bank, we often lean on our physical strength, our wisdom, and on our money and possessions. Only when we get sick, when everything goes wrong, when the money runs out, only then do we seek out the God we forgot. Even as a seafarer who for many days drifts along, propelled by wind and waves, and laughs and mocks and curses, but when the storms rise and the ship is in distress and the rudder no longer functions, suddenly his *curse* turns into a *prayer*: O God, help me!

This sinful way of life must be opposed. It must not be tolerated. And they who know God must wrestle against it in the power of the Holy Spirit until they are delivered from this false illusion. No, your money is *nothing*, your physical strength is *nothing*, and all your wisdom is *nothing* except to the degree to which God is at work in them and is using these means to guide you. A creature is *never* anything *of* itself, nor *in* itself, nor on its *own*. A creature should never be considered as anything other than an instrument and a means that God the Lord makes use of in order to let his power operate. There can therefore never be such a contrast between God and the creature. Leaning and relying on the creature as if it were something separate from God is idolatry. It is assigning to the creature something that is due only to God, and consequently it is placing a trust in the creature that may only be put in God. Even though the wind blows into the sails and not below deck, and although I am moving forward as I sit below deck, I nevertheless know quite well that it is not the ship but the wind that moves me forward. Even though I am not sitting in the locomotive as I speed along the rails, I know quite well that the motive power comes not from the carriage in which I sit but only from the steam of the locomotive that pulls me forward. Even though I have no gas power plant in my home that allows me ignite the gas as soon as I merely turn on the tap, I nevertheless know that the light-giving gas comes not from the gas tap itself but from the gas power plant.

And thus it is with all creatures. All created things harbor a certain power, a certain capability that I notice as soon as I make use of a created thing. But the knowledgeable person knows quite well that all power in the created thing is only derivative power and that all this ability is only derivative ability, the source and wellspring of which lies in God and God alone. He is the Almighty, which means that neither in heaven nor on earth any power exists or works other than the power that was in God and came to us from him. It is therefore pure absurdity for the sinner to lean on the created thing and not to look up to the God who brought forth and sustains that created thing. A sinner is like a dog that bites on the stick that was thrown to him yet ignores the thrower. Sinners are mesmerized by the movement of a saw but do not notice that there is someone pulling the saw. They do not realize that this earthly house rests on foundations, and thus in their folly and foolhardiness they come to ignore completely the Foundation of all things, thus surrendering the only certainty—the only security that remains eternally and stands firm forever.

YOU SHALL NOT STEAL

COMMENTARY ON LORD'S DAY 42 OF THE HEIDELBERG CATECHISM

TEXT INTRODUCTION

The Heidelberg Catechism is a manual for basic instruction in Christian doctrine. Published in 1563, the catechism consists of 129 questions and answers and quickly proved useful for faith formation of children and adults alike. Divided into 52 parts, each "Lord's Day" enables the entirety of the teachings of the catechism to be covered in weekly sermons throughout the year.

At the Synod of Dort, in its 146th session of April 30, 1619, delegates of the participating churches from abroad exhorted the Dutch church "to persevere in the Reformed faith, to pass it on to posterity, and to preserve it until the return of Christ." In reply, the delegates from the Dutch church made a solemn vow, pledging to preach and preserve the Reformed faith, pure and undiluted.

When Kuyper started his commentary on the Heidelberg Catechism in fall 1886 in the Sunday paper *De Heraut*, he recalled this vow and subsequently entitled his series *E voto Dordraceno*: "from the vow made at Dort." The title is usually shortened, at Kuyper's own directive—"for ease of citing," he said—to *E Voto*.

The treatment of the Ten Commandments in the Heidelberg Catechism typically follows the pattern of expositing both those things that are forbidden by each commandment and those things that are required. The Eighth Commandment, "You shall not steal," similarly has both positive duties and negative prohibitions. Lord's Day 42 covers this petition in Questions and Answers 110 and 111, and Kuyper's exposition of this commandment addresses the topic of the *essence* or *nature* of human responsibility with respect to material blessings, that is, the role of stewardship in the Christian life. The chapter on Lord's Day 42 first appeared as five installments in *De Heraut* of March 5, 12, 19, 26, and April 9, 1893.

Source: Abraham Kuyper, *E voto Dordraceno* (Amsterdam: J. A. Wormser, 1892–95), 4:184–227. Translated by Albert Gootjes. Edited and annotated by Harry Van Dyke.

COMMENTARY ON LORD'S DAY 42 OF THE HEIDELBERG CATECHISM

Question 110: *What does God forbid in the eighth Commandment?*
Answer: *God forbids not only such theft and robbery as are punished by the government, but God views as theft also all wicked tricks and devices, whereby we seek to get our neighbor's goods, whether by force or by deceit, such as unjust weights, lengths, measures, goods, coins, usury, or by any means forbidden of God; also all covetousness and the misuse and waste of His gifts.*

Question 111: *But what does God require of you in this Commandment?*
Answer: *That I further my neighbor's good where I can and may, deal with him as I would have others deal with me, and labor faithfully, so that I may be able to help the poor in their need.*

You shall not steal.
Exodus 20:15

§1

From the seventh commandment[1] we move on to the eighth[2], and with that from a person's *body* to his *belongings*. As we noted in our treatment of the division of the law, you can sin against your neighbor in his *person*, his *world*, and his *name*. When you break the sixth commandment[3] you sin against your neighbor in his *person*, with the ninth commandment[4] in his *name*, and with the seventh and eighth commandments in his *world*. Our soul is related in two ways to the sensible, visible world: first, in a very close sense through our body; and second, in a wider sense through the clothes that cover our body, the food that sustains our body, the dwelling in which our body finds protection against the cold—in short, through all the earthly goods that in some sense enter into a relationship with us. Thus it is hardly surprising that the issue of injuring one's neighbor in his world is not addressed in one commandment but is divided over two commandments. For while our body does belong to our being, our belongings do not. All the same, our being is designed to enjoy the good things this world has to offer, and so we have the promise of eternal bliss in which we will not only have a glorified body but also a glorified world—a most beautiful paradise, a Jerusalem filled with glory. Yet that great distinction between our body and our belongings still remains; our body is *part of* us, our belongings are *with* us.

Thus, the seventh and eighth commandments together form one commandment if we take body and belongings together under the one concept of the visible, in distinction from our person and our name. But the moment we pay attention to the profound difference that exists between what belongs to us and what is part of us, the two commandments divide and separate. Of course, in the commandments that concern not our neighbor but God, this distinction falls away entirely because God is a spirit and has no body. For that reason we can indeed sin against God in his person (that is, as God), in his world, and in his name—but because the entire world belongs to God, there is no division into different commandments, as is the case with the commandments relating to offenses against one's neighbor in his world. The parallel as we had set it up at the outset of our discussion of the Ten Commandments therefore remains.

You shall not sin against (1) God or (2) your neighbor:

---

1. That is, "You shall not commit adultery" (Exod 20:14).
2. "You shall not steal" (Exod 20:15).
3. "You shall not murder" (Exod 20:13).
4. "You shall not bear false witness against your neighbour" (Exod 20:16).

	God	Neighbor
1. in his *person*:	first commandment	sixth commandment
2. in his *world*:	second commandment	seventh and eighth commandments
3. in his *name*:	third commandment	ninth commandment

The special import of the fourth and fifth commandments[5] we have already treated in our commentary and for that reason does not need to be discussed further. We only bring the above to our readers' attention again so that they may be reminded of the context in which these commandments must be placed as they pass from the seventh to the eighth and to understand from what perspective the eighth commandment ought to be approached.

This immediately makes it clear that it is most incorrect the way many people have appealed to the eighth commandment in order to defend today's distribution of wealth as well as current rights of ownership and property. Beginning in 1840, when Proudhon with his *Qu'est-ce que la propriété?* suggested that all ownership is in fact grounded in theft, people have consistently (and most correctly) pointed to the eighth commandment as a fixed point for men's conscience.[6] Without such a fixed point, people can twist things in such a way that in the end everything is reduced to the same thing, and every distinction between truth and falsehood, between justice and injustice, and so also between ownership and theft, falls away. Insofar as the eighth commandment is appealed to in order to make this point, we agree with it: it indeed gives us a fixed point for the question of ownership. In that sense, the eighth commandment is one of the foundations for the very structure of society. Those who believe in the Word of

---

5. The fourth commandment is "Remember the Sabbath day, to keep it holy" (Exod 20:8); the fifth is "Honor your father and your mother" (Exod 20:12).

6. Proudhon's book of this title was translated from the original French and published as Pierre-Joseph Proudhon, *What Is Property? An Inquiry into the Principle of Right and of Government*, trans. Benjamin R. Tucker (New York: Humboldt, 1890). Kuyper also refers to Proudhon in two of his most significant addresses: "The Social Question and the Christian Religion," appearing in this volume, and "Modernism: A Fata Morgana in the Christian Domain," in *AKCR*, 101.

God should never allow themselves to contribute to a society that pushes that commandment aside.

However, if rich owners push their appeal to it further and show their concern to be more for their own treasure than with the "earth's foundations," and so try to deduce from the eighth commandment that all they have is their lawful property and that God has given them the freedom to do with it as they please, then Christian ethics has the duty and calling to break down all such false notions. A simple reading of the Heidelberg Catechism's explanation of the eighth commandment would have sufficed for this purpose. It states that this commandment is transgressed (1) by all who have in their possession something that was obtained by a scheme, by deception, by usury, and so forth; (2) by all who are greedy or who squander what they have; and finally (3) by all who do not use their possessions in order to promote their neighbor's utmost good and to help the poor. Thus it is immediately clear that the transgressors of the eighth commandment are largely found precisely among the owners, and that their number is greater outside the prison walls than inside them.[7] Proudhon's claim that *all* property comes from theft is certainly untrue. On closer examination, however, it is true that *a very large part* of people's belongings in this world is stolen property—yet it was not Proudhon who discovered this, for as early as 1563 this awareness could already be found in the Heidelberg Catechism.

Nevertheless, we shall not halt at this more or less superficial line of reasoning. The catechism is there to explain the Word to us, but in itself it is never a rule for our actions. We need to go back to Scripture—not, however, as if God's words *You shall not steal* are the deepest foundation on which respect for our neighbor's right of ownership rests. This can never be the case, for an *external* commandment always has less force than a commandment written by the Lord himself on the table of our hearts. In fact, had the Lord not written his law on our hearts we would not understand what he meant with the external commandment. An external commandment that does not depend on an *internal* commandment is always one that needs a full definition describing in detail what you may and may not do. As an example, we can think of the command given in paradise about a *specific* tree and God's word to Adam and Eve about precisely what they were to do with respect to it. However, a general commandment such as "you shall not steal" which extends to all people in every aspect of their lives would neither be

---

7. Kuyper's refers here to those serving custodial sentences for theft.

understood nor grasped did not an internal commandment matching this eighth commandment rule in the heart of man.

This, then, is how things went: When God created man, he also created in him an awareness of the distinction between one person and another, and consequently also between the belongings of one and those of another, between mine and thine. Sin attempted to destroy this awareness altogether and would indeed have succeeded had the Lord God not checked this destruction by his common grace and left in us a certain awareness of the respect we must show for someone else's possessions. That is why this awareness still functions among the Gentiles, even apart from the Sinaitic law. For as Paul says in Romans 2:14: the Gentiles "who do not have the law, by nature do what the law requires." The apostle could say this with truth because in his time people lived under Roman law that was developed in great detail on the specific issue of property. At the same time, it was only with the declaration of the eighth commandment on Mount Sinai that the broken sound of this commandment in the heart of man was externally restored and made to penetrate deep into his conscience in the form of an external voice. If the eighth commandment is understood in this way—as reestablishing the fading awareness of the distinction between the possessions of one man and those of another, and (when property was inevitably attacked by theft) as reaffirming the foundation on which social order rests—then we too can agree fully with the appeal to the eighth commandment as a fixed point, provided that one does not attempt to make it say more than it does and take it out of the context of the other things God's Word reveals concerning ownership and possession.

Consequently, serious protests should be raised against any form of the idea that the eighth commandment requires all things on earth to belong personally to some individual, and as if for that reason it excludes communal ownership. It neither says nor implies this. A society in which all pastures, fields, and so forth are communal property and where personal property does not exist with the exception of clothing, household goods, and tools is not at all in conflict with the eighth commandment. But even then, much of the earth's goods would be *personal property*—possessions that at one point in time belong to one person and not to another. Moreover, because the strong are inclined by sin to take away from others what is theirs, the commandment "you shall not steal" would still be fully in force. Consequently, the eighth commandment says nothing about the nature of the distribution of earthly goods and leaves room for different forms of the distribution of wealth. One would only come into conflict with this commandment if one were to try to organize a society where no one would have anything that he could call his own, and where all property without exception would be communal. When it is said of the first New Testament church in Jerusalem, for example, that they shared everything they had [see Acts 4:32], we should not understand by this that they also gave up their clothes, household goods, tools, and the like. Rather, it applies only to their money, land, or rental houses.

We insist on this so strongly and clearly because many have now become used to appealing to the eighth commandment in their battle against socialism as if the society envisioned by the majority of social democrats would inevitably come into conflict with the eighth commandment. This is simply *not* the case. Most academically trained social democrats do not envision a society where *all* property is abolished but only where the *greater part* of personal property is abolished. When it comes to clothing, jewelry, household goods, hand tools, and so forth, they maintain that these and the like must remain personal property. Particularly in times such as these, we should be most careful when we draw consequences from the Word of God. If it is decreed that all that is now personal property is simply to be taken away from its owners, the situation would of course be completely different. If a person considers (in light of or even on the basis of) the eighth commandment that a society where property is largely communal is forbidden by God, he or she is entirely mistaken. This becomes even more evident once we realize that this commandment was given to Israel in the desert when there was no land ownership, when no trade could be carried out, and when personal possessions were limited almost exclusively to the clothes the people had taken with them, along with some household goods, cattle, jewelry, and hand tools.

A second misunderstanding we wish to clear up is the conclusion some have drawn from Matthew 20:14-15, where Jesus in a parable tells of a landowner who hired workers for his vineyard and paid those who had put in a few hours of work the same as those who had labored the entire day. When those, Jesus continues, who had worked longer grumbled about this, the landowner replied: "Take what belongs to you and go. I choose to give to this last worker as I give to you. Am I not allowed to do what I choose with what belongs to me? Or do you begrudge my generosity?" Some have concluded from this that Jesus sanctioned with his divine authority the concept of absolute ownership as it has come down to us especially by way of Roman law, and that consequently all who follow Jesus must acknowledge that *every owner can do with his possessions as he pleases*. That this is *not* the case will become clear when we take a somewhat closer look at Matthew 20:15.

There are three things we wish to point out. First, it is not Jesus himself who says these words, but he rather places them in the mouth of a character he presents in his parable. The parables of Jesus are not pictures of virtue depicting people in their ideal so that every act and word of the characters he places on stage is to be to us as a rule; rather, his parables are taken from real life. He depicts people for us as they really are with their virtues and vices. In the parable of the lost son [Luke 15:11–32], the lost son is a miserable wretch; the man who hires him and gives him pig slop to eat is a greedy farmer whose treatment of his slaves is a shame; the prostitutes on whom he wastes his possessions and who clean him out are women of the worst kind; and the older brother is a self-satisfied man who lacks any kind of noble impulse. Only the father emerges from this parable "clean." The same applies to all of Jesus' parables—especially the parable of the unjust judge [Luke 18:1–8]. In the parable of the workers in the vineyard [Matt 20:1–16], Jesus places the landowner center stage. But the fact that the landowner speaks in this manner in no way means that things really are as he says they are. It means only that a man from Jesus' time was accustomed to thinking about the issue in this way rather than in any other way.

Furthermore, the words Jesus places in the mouth of the landowner in no way constitute a wickedly whimsical utterance, as if he meant: "I'm free to do with my belongings as I please." The character the Lord gives him in this parable is much too noble for that. Rather, it is a matter of the landowner's having free disposal over his belongings *for the purpose of doing good*. Jesus says that the landowner had come to an agreement with the workers he had hired first to pay them a certain amount per day. They had supplied the labor, and the landowner paid them the wages they had coming to them. When there remained "unemployed" men in the market-place—that is, healthy and robust men who had been willing to work but unable to find employment—he also took them into his service late in the afternoon. Proportionally, this latter group should have received only one tenth of what the others were given; if the men in the first group received one guilder, the latter would have gone home with a dime. This stirred something in the landowner's heart, and he could not bear to see it. These men were without fault, for they had been willing to work but unable to find any. They, too, had to live, and perhaps even had a family. As result, a feeling of mercy came over him and he thought: *These men, too, cannot do with less than a guilder*. Here, a guilder for you, too! At this point those who had worked the entire day challenged his right to do that, saying, "You *may* not do this. If you give them one guilder, you owe us ten." It is to this charge that the landowner responded that he was not being unfair to them because they had agreed to work for one guilder and that he had the freedom to give to those other men more than what they, strictly speaking, deserved.

Finally, we point out that this interpretation is fully confirmed by the last words, where the landowner adds: "Or do you begrudge my generosity?" This question of course is not redundant but clarifies what he had just said. What else could he mean by it if not this: You challenge my right to do good with what is mine, and this stems from the fact that I am good while you are envious. Accordingly, every appeal to these words of Jesus as if he places an official stamp of approval on the absolute concept of private ownership will have to be abandoned. Furthermore, the owners of today who are so ready to appeal to the landowner in this parable for confirming their absolute rights would perhaps be of more benefit to themselves and to society if they asked themselves whether they are using their freedom to do good with their money as liberally as did the owner of this vineyard.

God's Holy Word has been misused for so long that with the increasing seriousness of the times we should reflect seriously on how we can make room for the conviction that absolute ownership of all natural goods cannot belong to anyone but the Lord our God. What Scripture says about the owner as steward points us in the one and only safe direction, and Christ's church abandons her calling if she does not constantly and ceaselessly preach and imprint on humankind the sacred truth that the Lord God is the only lawful owner, and that no person ever is or can be anything but a steward over a part of that which belongs to God alone. All Christians confess this in prayer, but *outside* prayer they neither think nor act according to it. In order to know what Jesus himself thought of ownership, just look at him as he walked on earth and proclaimed, "Foxes have holes and birds of the air have nests, but the Son of Man has no place to lay his head" [Matt 8:20]. Ever since the beginning of his public ministry, Jesus lived from things that were *given* to him, and he blessed not the rich man but the poor man Lazarus.

Along these lines, our Savior gave us in the fourth petition of the Lord's Prayer the true maxim for all property when he taught every person, rich or poor, to pray every day again: *Our Father … give us this day our daily bread.*

Here more than anywhere else it is clear that Jesus wants you to consider all that is yours as the property of your Father in heaven. After all, a child lives with his father, and it is not the child but the father who owns all. It is clear that you are to do this even when your food is waiting on the table, and that you are to do this not only for a lavish meal but even for a *morsel of bread*. Even that piece of bread on the table in front of you is not yours, but is the property of your Father in heaven. It is also clear that you should ask for your *daily* food from your God who is its owner, not once a month or once a week but every day again. Above all, it is clear that you should never ask for that food for yourself without at the same time asking for it for all people who need it as much as you do. What a rich sentence this is, in language with golden simplicity: *Father ... give us this day our daily bread!* It is a petition of only six words, but if you could bring all patriotic sons of our country to pray those six words with convicted hearts, would not suddenly all false concepts of ownership, all plutocracy, all worship of the golden calf, and all socialism not suddenly disappear from the face of the earth?[8]

We add to our exposition one last saying from Jesus: "You always have the poor with you" [Matt 26:11]. People also appeal to these words to prove that Jesus willed that there should always be rich and poor people, and infer from this that we would in fact act against Jesus' will if we were to try to eliminate poverty in our country. Such misuse of Jesus' words always arouses our indignation. What was Jesus' end goal in his struggle? Was it not to make *each and every one* without distinction overflow with heavenly affluence in his kingdom, to give them *all* a place to sit at the wedding feast of the Lamb, and to invite them to a "a feast of well-aged wine, of rich food full of marrow" [Isa 25:6]? These people would now picture this same merciful Jesus, who was always so deeply moved by human misery, as rising up in anger over you if you were to try to make crying poverty disappear from the earth. Does this not tend to blasphemy? Is it not an insult to Jesus' holy name?

If the poor appeal to these words in order to comfort themselves—so be it. But those who have received a rich portion from God should take care never to use Jesus' words in order to excuse the hardness of their

---

8. Kuyper reflects extensively on the petition "Give us this day our daily bread" (Matt 6:11) in his Commentary on Lord's Day 50 of the Heidelberg Catechism, contained in this volume.

hearts. If you do this, you only sin against your own soul. Nothing is easier than to show that Jesus' words do *not* intend what some infer from them. Had Jesus said, "You will to the very end of time always have people who commit suicide," would people conclude that we should make no effort to combat suicide? If that were indeed the case it would be as if there were no difference between saying *how things will always be*, given human nature and its implications, and saying *how things must be* by instituting a rule or promulgating an ordinance.

The same distinction applies to Jesus' words in Matthew 26. Some take them as if Jesus were instituting a rule as to how things *must be* until the end of time, so that if there were no longer any poor we would have to try to *make sure that there were*. Yet, what Jesus said was nothing of the sort. It was a prophecy. He who knows the hearts of humankind and knows what consequences sin would continue to bring along with it to the very end said to Judas: "You always have the poor with you." If, in contrast, it were indeed a rule for how things ought to be, we suggest that today's fortunate owners trade places for a year by making rich those who are now poor and to take upon themselves the role of a poor person for an entire year. Would that not likewise be a way to fulfill the ordinance that they assume these words of Jesus contain?

This, however, is not how they would want things to be, and for that reason it is so cruel, heartless, un-Christian, and offensive to the name of Jesus when those with great possessions but little compassion appeal to this saying of our Savior.

§2

> *O Lord, how manifold are your works!*
> *In wisdom have you made them all;*
> *the earth is full of your creatures.*
> Psalm 104:24

The Lord our God is the owner of all that is, the sole and complete owner—he and no one else. Those in authority who continually tried to preach to everybody that God Almighty is the *Sovereign over all people*, yet almost systematically suppressed the fact that the same God Almighty is also the owner *of all property*, made it all too clear that they were driven more by the desire to strengthen their own power than to honor their God. The Lord God then caused all winds of doctrine to arise as a punishment in order to rouse the unperturbed owners from their dreams. Further, only the church of Christ may claim that also on this issue she has throughout the centuries pointed to the only true and correct principle when she wrote down her confession that all that has been created belongs to God alone, and imprinted this on her mind. This principle is in direct conflict with the legal principle as we have inherited it from the world of Roman law, and the battle over property that continues to rage today is one between the Christian and the ancient Roman view. We put it this way on purpose, for while we are well aware that legal specialists are accustomed to speak of a contrast between the Roman and Germanic notions of property, the contrast with the Christian view runs still deeper and addresses us more directly as people who confess the Lord.

For this reason, with this commandment we may not take our point of departure from anywhere else than creation. God's creation was twofold in that he made *people* and *things*, and because both are his creatures he has both at his absolute disposal. Thus, one can say that God rules as sovereign over all people and over all things. In itself, sovereignty means nothing if not supreme authority, highest governance, greatest discretionary disposal, and this can apply to both people and things. Because it is common nowadays to speak of sovereignty only as a concept that extends over conscious creatures, which themselves act as secondary causes under God, we commonly label total disposition over all things not as "sovereignty" but as "possession." In its most complete sense, however, we understand "possession" to mean that someone has such great disposition over a thing that he alone has every say over it and that no one else has any say. An owner may in some way be dependent on a third party, but in the disposition over his property he must have absolute power. His right of ownership is complete if, and only if, he can himself choose to destroy it. Just as absolute owners claimed the right of life and death over their slaves, so every owner is supposed to have the right of life and death over everything he owns. This right is indeed exercised with respect to animals.

If the essence of the concept of absolute possession is as described above, it follows that ownership in that fullest sense can only arise by virtue of creation. Only that which I produce in an absolute sense is mine in the fullest sense of the word. Only I can decide to do with it as I want. If, on the other hand, something is not produced by me but by someone else and then given to me by the one who produced it, I am not free. This is so in the first place because receiving a gift always makes one dependent, and in the second place because I have to accept it as the original creator made it. Absolute right of ownership can for that reason only be conceived of in God. He who created everything does with everything as he pleases. He alone has total control over all that exists. Thus, no one can own anything except insofar as he has received or stolen it from God, always either in dependence on or else in rebellion against him who created it. The principle *that God is the owner of all that exists* may not for that reason be considered only a religious idea. It is at the same time a legal principle, given that as long as the absolute concept of ownership cannot be conceived of except in God, any concept of ownership among men loses its absolute character.

If God is indeed the sole and absolute owner of all things, it follows immediately that nobody, however unparalleled he may be in his riches, can claim an absolute right of ownership over even a single thing on earth. The Rothschilds or Goulds, regardless of the hundreds of millions they may have or have had, cannot say of even a single piece of bread on their table that they can do with it what they want.[9] They may think they can say this, as the vast majority of people including the poorest in fact do, but it is simply *not* true. As long as God is the Creator of all and no human being can ever own anything except what God created, no mortal creature can ever own even the smallest thing independently of God. This is true not only of those things that came into being apart from him and were brought to him, such as a person's cattle. It is equally true of that which human beings themselves makes or helps to produce. Human beings help bring grain forth from the field and fruit from the trees that they plant and cultivate. Here people appear only as helping hands, but when it comes to the houses they build, the linen they weave, and the weapons they forge, they function to a much greater degree as origin and producer.

In some cases, a person's role can be so decisive that he appears to be acting literally as a *creator*. As examples, one can think of a poem they sang, a canvas they painted, a piece of music they composed, or a book they wrote. All these are products where one hardly notices anything but human acts and where human dependence barely surfaces at all. Yet no matter how greatly man's role appears to be involved in all such products,

---

9. The Rothchild family descended from Mayer Amschel Rothschild (1744–1812), a German Jewish banker in Frankfurt. During the nineteenth century, the family possessed the largest private fortune in the world. Jason ("Jay") Gould (1836–92), an almost exact contemporary of Kuyper, was an American railroad magnate and financial speculator widely disliked for his unscrupulous business ethics.

here too man's freedom is merely an illusion. The farmer can sow, but only God can give the increase; the arborist can plant, but only God can cause the fruit on the branches to ripen. A man builds a house, but he is unable to produce a single stone or a single piece of wood or iron out of nothing, and, what is more, in working on that stone, wood, or iron, he is bound to the structure God has given them. It is the same with the wool that people spin and the linen that comes from their looms.

The same applies no less to the products of their mental labor. Those who write poetry or prose do so in a language that exists outside and independently of them. Those who compose music do so within a world of tones over which they have no say whatsoever, and they become greater masters only in the measure that they immerse themselves in and subject themselves to the laws governing that world. Further, even where those who have immersed themselves in that language, that world of tones, and that world of imagination show signs of brilliance and talent, that brilliance and that talent are not of their own creation but are given to them by God and are for that reason bound to the measure, the scope, and the design that God has given them.

The Word of God points to the potter time and again as the most free artisan because the clay he uses has almost no value, while he has the power to form it or not form it, to form it in this or another way, or even to break it into pieces afterward. The potter is and ever remains dependent on the clay God had to create for him, on the makeup of the clay, on the wheel he uses for his work, on the fire to harden the clay into pottery, and no less on the movement of his fingers and feet. If his feet and his fingers become stiff with arthritis, even the potter is powerless before the clay. While we do at times use the word *create* for people and speak of a human creation especially in the case of works of art, these remain figurative expressions. In the true sense of the word only the Lord is and remains Creator, because he alone has produced all matter on his own, he alone gave a law unto all things, he alone gives to each thing its nature, he alone has the power and capacity to do with his creatures as he pleases, and he alone in all freedom determines for each thing its purpose and end. Because humankind, inversely, can never produce matter but must accept it as given (that is, with the law it was given and the nature with which it was created), it is simply absurd to speak as though human beings have free, unrestricted disposal over anything, even when they call something their own "creation."

Thus, when we confess that God and God alone is the owner of all things, we do not do so just to appear pious, and even less because in Israel God was seen as the sole owner. Rather, we say this because it belongs to the nature of ownership and flows directly from our confession of God as Creator. Because God is the Creator of all things, there can be no other Creator aside from him or alongside him. The concept of Creator is exclusive. There can only be one Creator, and the fact that God was the one who created puts all those who work with what he created in a position of dependence. A creator cannot alienate his property. God cannot say: "I no longer want to be owner of that part of my creation." That would only be possible if God were to let something go after creating it and allow it to be controlled by some power residing within it. But that is not the way things are. Nothing exists by virtue of a power residing within it, but every single object is maintained by the Lord's omnipresent power. If God were to give an object away in the sense of withdrawing from it, that object would in that very instant be annihilated. God can give in no other way than by still holding on to that object. A thing cannot leave his hand for even a single moment.

As the Creator, God does not have some things that he keeps with him and others that he places at the fringes of his estate. Instead, every object is always present to him, and his divine power works in every object at each and every moment of time. Even when he gives certain earthly possessions to man, he never lets them leave his hand completely but forever sustains the things he created. No man can therefore hold onto them in any other way but as God holds onto them for him, and he can never own anything except on condition that God's power remains free and that the law God gave to that object is honored. On his horse, a rider may think that he is lord and master, but God and not he remains the creator of that noble animal. For that reason the rider cannot use the horse in any other way than as God willed it; he cannot make his horse do anything except that for which God gave the horse the abilities and skills. The moment God ceases to bear and sustain the life of that animal through his omnipotence, the rider loses his ability to keep that horse as his property. The animal dies and is lost to the rider.

Now someone might respond to the above and say that all this may be true, but that speaking of the right of ownership is not meant in that lofty sense but simply in terms of one person's rights over against another, with the tacit assumption, of course, that all goods are bound to their nature. Such a response would is no trouble at all. Even if I were to think of ownership exclusively in terms of the relationship it entails between one person over against another, the concept of sovereignty still brings me back again and again to the Lord God, because he has sovereign command over those two people whose right of ownership you are regulating. Whether you think of the object or of the person, you must always take your point of departure in the Lord our God, because both object and person exist only by his grace. He created both the object and the person. Accordingly, the parties whose right of ownership you seek to regulate are also not free to act as they wish, but in the regulation of ownership both are bound to submit themselves in obedience to God. The eighth commandment itself shows this. From Sinai, the Lord places himself between the two, involves himself directly in the issue of ownership, and says to all people of all nations: "You shall not steal." And a little later he adds: "You shall not covet your neighbor's house ... his ox, or his donkey" [Exod 20:17]. At the present time, these commandments are being set aside and ignored in order to come up with some definition of ownership apart from God. Many jurists today are working on it, but they will never succeed. It may have been possible for a particular time period, when thanks to respect for divine law there was at least some standard concept of ownership. But that is no longer the case, now that respect for this law is waning and the first principles for the right of ownership are no longer fixed.

This situation has also given rise to the socialist, communist, and nihilist theories, which are a just punishment from God for the pride of owners who imagined that they could safeguard their mammon rights apart from God. Those theories, absurd as they mostly are, do an excellent job of laying bare once again the foundations of society and of forcing humanity once more to reckon with primordial principles, also as they apply to ownership. If you, happy owners of the moment, try to base your right of ownership apart from God on nothing but your human insight and your tradition and on what you consider necessary and imperative, we will give you—as a consistent socialist will say—a taste of your own medicine. We, too, will regulate the right of ownership apart from God, this time according to our insight and distinct tradition and in light of what we judge historically necessary and inevitable. Be warned, however, that we will regulate it in a way that is entirely different from yours!

This may sound odd, but on the basis of that standpoint nothing can be said against it. One side's assertion is as good as the other's. What they call the "tradition of misery" has as great a claim to legitimacy as what others call the "tradition of the social order." When they point to the necessity to end the existing misery, they have as firm a standpoint as those who emphasize the necessity to maintain the stimulus of private ownership. If the discussion is set up in that way it remains a mere matter of one opinion over against another. No decision can then be made, and in the absence of a verdict from a higher judge, the only solution is for one person to fight another for ownership—a battle in which the strong will defeat the weak. If you dismiss all higher sanctions you can only end up with the right of force.

Does this mean that God in his Word gave us a firm law for how the earth's goods are to be divided among its 1.4 billion inhabitants? Not at all. Whoever sees the Mosaic law in this way misunderstands its meaning entirely. Yet it is undeniable that the whole issue of ownership appears in an entirely different light for those who recognize God as the supreme owner, as opposed to those who think only of people and the things they pursue. Don't forget that the stimulus in human nature to accumulate all kinds of goods is already very strong as it is. Hunger acts as a powerful sword, and every morning and evening our half-full stomachs let us know they are there. You are cold and need to be warmed; you are naked and need to be clothed; you are outdoors and need to be sheltered. None of these needs are of your own invention but are given in your very nature. They never leave you but follow you everywhere and control your entire life.

Further, even apart from these pressing needs the temptation and attraction to obtain for ourselves a large number of earthly goods is incredibly strong. Just mention the word "money"—money is a power that puts within your grasp all the pleasures and bliss that the world has to offer. Still more: not only do earthly goods satisfy your earthly needs, which you can temper and suppress to a certain degree, but so much of what you consider sacred depends on money. The first thing that Christ's church needs in order to be able to make her presence felt and exercise any influence, and the first thing that the advocacy of fundamental principles requires, is a *campaign fund*. Without money it is impossible in any part of life to make propaganda, and it costs money to organize even a meeting and to distribute literature. Never has there been an election where the victory did not to a considerable degree depend on money.

What shall we further say about how you raise your children and about many other interests that are even dearer to us and are most tightly tied to money? Was not the whole battle waged against us by unbelievers over the question of school funding fought with the superior strength of the state's money? Does that battle not continue to this today?[10] Does life not show how even the questions as to whether you will reach your destiny in your marriage or whether you will fulfill your true and full financial potential in this world are so often determined solely by the question as to whether you stand to inherit money? If you add the whole question of charity, you will have to ask yourself what delight you would have to deny your soul if you did not have extra money to give away, and how much joy escapes those who cannot afford the luxury of charity because they are themselves needy. It is thus no wonder at all that the battle over money rages in this world with such bitter cruelty and such lack of compromise. It *cannot* be otherwise, and *must* be so.

Toward the end of the eighteenth century, it had become quite popular to speak of "earthly mire," but that language was restricted almost exclusively to emotional hymns and sentimental sermons. Both preacher and parishioners knew better: the moment they left church they did not linger in their sentimentality but were down to earth enough to occupy themselves in filling their ledgers and squaring their accounts. This is the very reason why the way this prickly incentive will affect you depends entirely on the standpoint you take. Obviously, as soon as you know and confess that everything in this world belongs to God and that you depend on God in the fullest sense and are responsible to him when it comes to your belongings, the incentive for money will work in you in a different way. Even among people here on earth, the things that do not belong to you but have only been borrowed for use, or have been entrusted to you for a time, you treat in an entirely different way compared to those things for which you are accountable to no one on earth. This crucial distinction will fully determine your view of ownership as soon as you know and confess that nothing on earth belongs to you, but that everything is the Lord's; that you have only borrowed it for use; that it has been entrusted to you for a time and a specific purpose; and that the Lord will hold you accountable for what you have done with his property. In this way all your belongings are immediately placed under a higher rule, are subjected to a moral order, and are made not to elevate you in your pride but to raise your responsibility before God.

---

10. Full financial parity between government and free schools was not achieved until 1920. For more on the school struggle in the Netherlands, see *On Education*.

If someone who has thirty million or more knew what it meant to direct such an enormous sum for many years according to God's order and to his glory, the foolish and feverish thirst to increase that huge treasure even more would at once be quenched. Moreover, too great wealth would then turn out to be more of a burden than a delight, and knowing that such an enormous fortune can be had only because others lack what they need makes it something bitter rather than something to be desired. Of course, as for those who do not sense that their duties and responsibilities only increase as their possessions grow, they simply fix their eyes on the power it gives them and are only out to increase that power. But as for those who recognize that every added million raises their responsibility enormously and multiplies the weight of their duty, they acknowledge the great wisdom of what the prophet said: "Give me neither poverty nor riches; feed me with the food that is needful for me" [Prov 30:8].[11]

Once the realization that "*God is owner and we—great or small—are stewards*" penetrates us once and for all, the absurd notion that we can do with our property as we like can arise in no sound mind. What our fathers imprinted on their children, that it is sin to waste even a single piece of bread for which God had caused the grain to grow, expresses the general rule that we are first of all to inquire after God's will for all the possessions with which he has entrusted us. The growing animal-protection movement undoubtedly has an unhealthy side to it, and it is at times revolting to see how animals are given royal treatment while people are allowed to die of want. Insofar as the animal-protection movement has this tendency, it should be resisted. Yet, as the next chapter will show more clearly, this does not take away from the fact that it is also based on a profound truth: even when it comes to animals, human beings cannot do with them as they please. Animals have rights over against humans insofar as God has grounded those rights in their nature.

§3

The land shall not be sold in perpetuity, for the land is mine. For you are strangers and sojourners with me.

Leviticus 25:23

---

11. Kuyper discusses the meaning of this verse toward the start of his commentary on Lord's Day 50, which is included in this anthology.

From a biblical point of view, there can be no such thing as an unlimited and absolute right of ownership. It is a serious misunderstanding to take the phrase "God alone is owner, we are stewards" as nothing but a pious expression that imposes no rule and has no benefits. We would like to demonstrate on two levels that this is not at all the case: first, for the use we may make of our possessions; and, second, for the regulations imposed by the government.

In regard to the first point, you become most aware of it when you think of a slave or a beast of burden. Even though slavery has—formally, at least—been banished so completely from our society that we can hardly imagine how one person can ever be another's *property*, this does not undo the fact that until a few centuries ago slavery, serfdom, and other similar relationships existed all over the world, and that at present in more than one continent slavery still exists in one form or another. For those who regard God as the owner of all creatures, it is a foregone conclusion that slavery is *evil*. I would never be able to own "a person" in any other way than as a steward, and my ownership of that "person" would never be allowed to conflict with the relationship that exists between that person and God as his owner. Because this relationship demands that the person created after the image of his owner be morally free and directly responsible to God, it is unthinkable and nonsensical that one person could ever exercise right of ownership over another. If, on the other hand, the realization is lost that God alone is the owner of all creatures including humankind—if this should erode and disappear from the human mind—I would of course have no need to seek God's ordinance even in the case of a human being. The only thing I would need to ask myself about any other person is how I can overpower them and become their master. Consequently, there would be no fundamental difference between a slave I obtain in a slave hunt and a horse I capture on the open range. The only difference would be that a slave is usually much easier to catch and, once caught, much more profitable.

Not until the awareness returns that God alone disposes over man and that he cannot place one person at another's absolute disposal without at the same time coming into conflict with his creation ordinance do we cut the notion of slavery at its very root—even if the practice of slavery continues for a time after being cut off at its root as it was in Israel. The fact that people accepted its abolition only when forced follows from the fact that slave owners cannot acknowledge that their slaves belong to God unless they at the same time recognize and confess that God is the absolute owner not only of their slaves *but also of themselves*. Therefore, as long as their hearts remain unbroken and proud over against God, and as long as they refuse to place themselves in the hand of God as their owner, sinful people also cannot see their slaves as God's property.

It is just as clear that the teaching of the gospel that "my only comfort in life and death is that I am not my own but belong to my faithful Savior Jesus Christ" necessarily leads people to see themselves once again as God's property. And when they see *themselves* in this way the only outcome must be that in the end they see this also *of their slaves*. As result, biblical teaching had to lead eventually to the gradual undermining of the whole system of slavery. Slavery is a curse that had fallen on our human race. When we no longer wanted to be slaves to God—that is, when we no longer wanted to belong to him in full ownership as his creatures so that he could do with us entirely as he pleased—our punishment was that one man became the slave of another. And in cannibalism we sank merely one step deeper by placing humans on the same level as beasts of burden and as wild animals that are captured in order to be slaughtered and devoured. God had created humans according to his image, but people agreed to relinquish that great honor and consequently came to bear the image of an ox that pulls the plow or a deer that is caught and consumed for food.

God's right as the sole owner comes out, in the second place, when you think of animals. By nature, no one has the right to seize an animal and slaughter it for food. At least, Christians who hold to God's Word are not allowed to think so. They know that it was God who said first to Noah, and in Noah to us: "Every moving thing that lives shall be food for you. ... I give you everything" [Gen 9:3]. Only because God gives the animals to us and further grants us permission to slaughter and eat them do we human beings have the right to use animals in this way. It is absolutely not true that you have this right simply by virtue of being a human. The commonly accepted view that people may do with an animal just as they please "because it is only an animal" must for that reason be resisted by all Christians, because the animals are not ours but God's. We do not have the least right to them, because we did not create them. Only after God gives us a right of usufruct with regard to animals are we free to use and employ them in that way. Without God's permission we have no right to haul even one fish out of the water and kill it, to shoot down and pluck a single bird, or hunt and slay any game.

Animal-rights activists do good work in that they seek to regain acceptance for the conviction that humans' purported right over animals to do with them as they please is simply absurd. To this extent, these activists deserve our support. However, we should advise them no longer to base their case on a false standpoint. They try to defend animals by attributing rights to them by virtue of being animals, and in order to achieve this they come to the false thesis that animals have some kind of immortal soul just as we do. In this way they try to make people consider an animal as a kind of human being of a second order, with rights over against us who are humans of a higher order. This is simply absurd. They would have a much stronger case and find greater acceptance among Christians, and also receive more support in the public conscience, if they were to return to the Word of God and show from the Word that every animal finds its owner in God rather than in man and that humanity for that reason has no say over an animal at all except insofar as it has received the animal from God.

Everyone can decide for themselves whether they want to be vegetarians and abstain from eating meat. Nowhere has God commanded people that they must eat meat. However, if the animal-rights advocates want to forbid the eating of meat on the ground that we are not allowed to slaughter and eat animals, they negate the explicit statement of God's Word and thereby abolish God's right over animals. As a result, they actually fuel the cruelty to animals by people who know no higher principles and thus emancipate themselves from God's ordinances. The animal-rights advocates go to battle against the vivisectionists, but their false theory only fosters the cruelty of the latter.

Up to this point we have considered animal rights only from one perspective. However, we must also pay attention to the right, which is never anything but conditional, that we may exercise over animals when we use them as pack animals or draft animals. Here no one is allowed to say, "I do as I please with my horse or ox or donkey." No, also in this use of animals you are bound to God's ordinance concerning them. Much of this ordinance is already being respected at present by those who keep pack animals, because God has so ordained things that resistance against it means that the pack animal will decrease in value. If you do not feed your ox, horse, or donkey, it will waste away and die. If you do not help an animal when it is sick, you will lose it. If you do not protect it from the cold, it will wither away. The animals' natural needs, therefore, already prompt us to honor God's ordinance concerning them.

However, if things are left at that, this honoring of God's ordinances is merely a matter of self-interest. You can only speak of true fear of God in your relationship with your animals when you care for them because you want to be righteous—and "whoever is righteous has regard for the life of his beast" [Prov 12:10]. Then you listen to God's command not to muzzle an ox while it is treading grain, nor to take a bird that is sitting on her eggs, nor to ignore an animal that has fallen down but instead help lift it up again [Deut 25:4; 22:4, 6]. Then you enter imaginatively into the life of your animal, to learn something of its life and to be ready to treat your animal as God the owner desires of you as his steward. Only then will cruelty against animals be rooted out from the earth. It is incomprehensible that there are towns where year after year the catechism is taught, the Word is preached, and home visitations are made, without any serious instruction concerning the way in which the farmer is to honor the law of God Almighty as it extends to the treatment of animals.

It goes without saying that what applies to slaves and animals extends also to everything else that people call "mine" and for which God as the sole owner on earth has determined the nature and manner of the way we are to treat them. "Listen," the prophet Isaiah cries out,

> Give ear, and hear my voice;
>> give attention, and hear my speech.
> Does he who plows for sowing plow continually?
>> Does he continually open and harrow his ground?
> When he has leveled its surface,
>> does he not scatter dill, sow cumin,
> and put in wheat in rows
>> and barley in its proper place,
>> and emmer as the border?
> For he is rightly instructed;
>> his God teaches him.
> Dill is not threshed with a threshing sledge,
>> nor is a cart wheel rolled over cumin,
> but dill is beaten out with a stick,
>> and cumin with a rod.
> Does one crush grain for bread?
>> No, he does not thresh it forever;
> when he drives his cart wheel over it
>> with his horses, he does not crush it.
> This also comes from the LORD of hosts;

he is wonderful in counsel
and excellent in wisdom. [Isa 28:23–29][12]

There is nothing to add to these wonderful words of the prophet. It is entirely clear that no one can do with a tree or a plant as he wishes. People must sow at the time God has intended for sowing, and they must adjust themselves in everything to the ordinances that God has given for the plant and animal kingdoms. In the case of plants, people already obey God's ordinance of their own accord. Those who do not are looked upon as fools. In the end, the same also applies to metals, all kinds of stones, fire, and water. All of this has been given to you by the one and only Owner, but far from having these things freely at your disposal, you are quite strictly bound to the nature of each thing and to the laws to which each is subject. These are called the "the laws of nature," but what are they if not God's ordinances from which you cannot emancipate yourself in the use of your belongings?

This important theme could be extended much further if we were also to consider whether humans are free to take for themselves as much as they want from what is theirs. It would show that the Lord God also imposes a fixed ordinance on our bodies regarding our daily intake of protein, nitrogen, and so forth, and it would demonstrate that all excess is punished immediately by illness or nausea, or later on by other ailments. The same would be demonstrated in connection with alcoholism. But rather than going into greater detail on this, we wish to point out in passing that it is in particular by way of money, in its function as the measure of wealth and the means of exchange, that humankind has forgotten that God's ordinances govern all their belongings. This evil was allowed to progress even further when paper money came to replace hard cash, so that a kind of property was born that was subject to almost no natural power or ordinance. It was not ownership of land or animals, of iron or copper, but specifically of money that insinuated into people's minds the foolish notion of omnipotence and thus deluded them into thinking that they had an absolute right of disposition over all money and over all that has monetary value or can be obtained for money.

Particularly because money is free from all natural bonds and because the only thing that can restrain the power of money is a moral bond, ownership not of natural objects but of money has become the cause both of the false notions of ownership that have found acceptance, and of the

---

12. Kuyper provides sustained reflection on this passage in *CG* 3:59.

incredible abuses that have crept into the distribution of wealth. To this extent, there is a genuine basis of truth to the current reaction against what is called capital. Already among the Israelites, the Lord sought to restrain the terrible evil that comes from money by giving them laws. It goes without saying that money as such gains power especially when money becomes something productive and is accorded the power of reproduction that properly belongs to plants and animals only. Just as animals produce animals and plants produce plants, so money is made to produce money through interest.

It was with a view to this that the Lord commanded regarding one's brother in Leviticus 25:36–37: "Take no interest from him or profit, but fear your God, that your brother may live beside you. You shall not lend him your money at interest, nor give him your food for profit." Although these stipulations concerning interest have been relaxed by people who claim they refer only to usury, this interpretation actually conflicts with the real meaning of the text. The passage means that money should indeed be lent in return for repayment of the principal, but without increase. And it is a sign of the deep fall of today's Jews that they who claim to live under the Mosaic Torah have become the greatest nation of usurers in Europe and Asia. They justify this by saying that Leviticus 25:36 only forbids the practice of usury with their kin, and for that reason they double or triple the interest rate—sometimes as much as 20 percent more—from Christians.

Our Reformed theologians have also often considered how, on the basis of Leviticus 25:36, the limits that this commandment offers against the unholy aspect of the power of money can also be applied in our days in order to restrain evil. All our theologians from Calvin onward have warned against the corruption that would overtake society if the misuse of others' need and one's own financial power were allowed to continue and thus elevate money to a power in and of itself. They were entirely correct when they pointed out that Scripture not only forbids what we negatively call usury but without doubt also demands that money's reproductive power be kept as small as possible. They usually concluded that the only permissible rate of interest was equal to the productive power that a sum of money could realistically count on over a set period of time. It is thus entirely in the spirit of the Reformation to try to restrict, just as our economists are at present intent on doing, the procreating power of money. The more the interest rates rise, the further we distance ourselves from the ideal. The more they fall and the more it is made either impossible or else a punishable offense to surpass a particular interest rate, the closer we come to the ideal of Scripture. More careful attention to Leviticus 25:36–37 would have spared us a great deal of social misery, shameful dishonesty, and lost fortunes.

And so we have automatically made the transition to the second point of discussion: the duty of the government. This duty can be none other than that the government is to regulate all ownership rights. The assumption that the right of ownership is regulated on its own by social relationships is on the whole false, and to the degree that it does contain some truth it does not excuse the government. As God's minister, the government is charged with the responsibility to ensure that the regulation of the right of ownership does not lead to the ruin of society. This duty of the government is also indicated in the property laws that God gave Israel. These law were given to a particular nation in a particular land in a particular situation and therefore cannot be adopted as such into our constitutional arrangements. Nevertheless, they do have lasting value on two counts: (1) government is to give guidance to the distribution of wealth, and (2) there are basic principles that must govern this guidance. These basic principles are essentially twofold, the one pertaining to buying and selling, the other to the right of inheritance. Both, it should be added, have a particular regard to land as a special possession, which in the case of Israel was also their main possession. Israel began with an equal distribution of land so that every tribe, every clan of every tribe, every house of every clan, and indeed every family within every house first received from God a nearly equal piece of land as a loan. From land comes the bread and wine that delights the human soul, and it was the Lord's will that at the outset his people would be placed in a situation where all had equal enjoyment of the land.

This at the same time created the private and distinct right of ownership. This is evident especially in the fact that a person could become poor or rich as a lazy or careless Israelite lost his land through sale, while a clever and hardworking Israelite increased his land by acquisition. However, God gave provisions in his law so that the bitter consequences of this private right of ownership would not continue for impoverished families throughout their generations. If a father had been lazy and careless, his son—if he was hardworking—was not to be without a chance of regaining ownership. Conversely, an intelligent and hardworking man was indeed to profit personally from his diligence, but there was no reason why later his lazy son should end up being better off than the hardworking son of a lazy man. This was the reason behind the law which determined that, after a human life-span, all real estate that had been sold out of necessity was to return to its former owner. Laziness was punished with loss, but the loss would not extend to the following generations. Diligence was rewarded with increased possessions but only for a time. This is the profound meaning of the law of the Year of Jubilee, as well as of the law of redemption that we do not discuss here.

The above yields two far-reaching economic principles. The first is the principle that land must be governed by a different right of ownership than movable property. The second principle is that inequality of possession, which follows as a natural and necessary consequence from the difference between lazy people and squanderers on the one hand and industrious and moderate spenders on the other, should not exceed a certain limit but should always stay within certain bounds. Countries where the right of ownership of land and real estate had been regulated according to these principles would not have seen the alarming contrast between owners and nonowners and between the immensely rich and the utterly poor—a condition which today is a curse on all social relationships. At present the situation in Europe is such that if one family member long ago succeeded by his efforts in accumulating a large part of what was originally in the hands of others, then centuries later his descendants still retain these possessions—at times even without investing any energy at all. Conversely, if a family has once had a member who neglected and squandered everything, the curse of poverty continues to press down on that person's descendants so that they no longer have the chance by their own efforts to regain the property that was lost. The legal principles that God gave to the Israelites combat such a situation. It is a law which in a remarkable way produces harmony between contrasting pursuits—on the one hand, to concentrate all right of ownership in one person through unrestrained freedom, and on the other, to install a tyranny of equality that would rob human effort of all incentive.

Finally, we must pay attention to the right of inheritance that is clearly founded in the Word of God and cannot be abolished without violating the principles of God's Word. Scripture does not understand a nation as an aggregate of individuals but as a people that exists organically in its generations and families. In God's Word, the rule obtains that just as there is continuity from one generation to the next, there must also be continuity of possessions and property in the line of those generations. To own an estate is to have another body, and just as the generations continue bodily, so they must propagate themselves in the enjoyment of inherited property. The right of inheritance in Israel maintained the right of sons and daughters, of brothers and of father's brothers, and even of more distant blood relatives for as long as there was progeny within that family.

This far-reaching right of inheritance could thus function in Israel simply because through the law of the Year of Jubilee, together with the original equal distribution of land, and through the above right of inheritance, there could never be either sustained poverty or mass accumulation of possessions in any single family. The right of inheritance in Israel was not intended to allow fortunes to be amassed but rather to secure the bond between members of one family and to maintain the organic bond of the nation. Only from this point of view may one appeal to Israel's right of inheritance as a principle and as a revelation of God's will—and then preferably, just as in Israel, with the preferential right of the oldest son, who received a *double* portion, in order that primogeniture retain its role in strengthening the family bonds.

It need hardly be pointed out that our current laws of inheritance conflict with this, not only in that not the slightest consideration is given to the necessary division of land but especially in that monetary capital has become a power which, once accumulated, ends up flowing to people who may not even be blood relatives and have only the flimsiest link to the deceased. All rights have been taken away from the firstborn. The result is that the contrast is upheld between a class of those who own far too much and those who own far too little, so that the right of inheritance no longer serves to strengthen the moral notion of familial bonds and instead serves to do little else but maintain the contrast between owner and nonowner. The situation has now become so bad that consideration is already being given as to whether the law should prescribe a limit to all fortunes, whether inheritance laws should be restricted to closer degrees, and even whether the state should in some cases be able to inherit. This third idea aims at the very same goal as Israel's law did, namely, that overly amassed wealth flow back to those who have been overly robbed—albeit that achievement of this goal is currently sought through the wrong channels. For the state never can inherit, because it stands entirely outside of the idea of the family on which all rights of inheritance are based. Rather than allowing the state to inherit, it would be much better if the government were once again to regulate land ownership, interest rates, firstborn rights, and rights of inheritance. This should be done in such a way that the repulsive inequality between powerful capitalists and defenseless citizens stays within certain limits and continues only for a certain length of time.

§4
*Do not withhold good from those to whom it is
due, when it is in your power to do it.*
Proverbs 3:27

Scripture uses the word "ownership" exclusively for the Lord (see Exod
19:5; Deut 7:6; 14:2; 26:18; Ps 135:4; Mal 3:17).[13] In all these instances, Scripture
speaks of Israel *as the Lord's possession*. The translators of our Bible used the
word "ownership" nowhere else; in fact, they did not even use the expression "owner" in connection with earthly belongings, although, remarkably, they did use the word "master" ("meester"). Accordingly, we read in
Proverbs 3:27: "Do not withhold good from its masters when it is in your
power to act" [SV]. This is virtually the only place where the word "master"
is found in our Bible, but that is a question of translation. In the Hebrew
text, the word "master" is often found where our translators have opted
for "possessor."[14] In Hebrew, an owner is called a *ba'al*—the same word that
is used for that well-known god of the Canaanites. It was not the material
concept of "possession" and "property" that took center stage but rather
the concept of being *lord and master* of one's belongings and, in the same
vein, of being in a position as a *steward* on behalf of God.

Now, if you were to ask who under God is the *master of all goods* we
would answer unconditionally: the government of a country. This holds
true on two levels. First, the law of the land decides how one can become
the master of any good. Second, the government in its capacity as judge
decides who is the rightful master in cases of dispute. If someone takes
something away from you, we use the word "master" in saying that person
has *made themselves master* of what was yours. In that case you go to court,
that is, to the government, and you have to accept the judge's decision. Or
else, if you made yourself the master of something to which you thought
you had a right, but someone legally disputes your right and the judge's
decision goes in his favor, you are to return the goods. As far as the factual legal situation is concerned, neither party A nor party B is allowed to
decide; in questions of *mine* versus *thine*, this has to be the case. There must,
therefore, be a power above A and B that can decide. God has appointed the
government as this power.

---

13. The Dutch word Kuyper is using is *eigendom*, which can be translated as "possession"
or "ownership."
14. The Dutch word (translated here as "possessor") that Kuyper is citing is *bezitter*.

For this reason, you should not say (as does the pantheist) that the law instituted and proclaimed by the government is the only true law. That would make God a mindless God who did not determine laws but could only do so by appointing governments or legislators. This offends God's honor and cannot be reconciled with worship of the living God. Rather, those who worship God know that God alone establishes the true, pure, and complete law. Had there been no sin, this true law alone would have been obtained forever. But through our own fault, knowledge of this true law was lost, and it is by God's grace that he through the government still maintains the law partially in the form of the legal order.

The laws of the government, however, are not nearly so pure and true as God's law. But it is through our own fault that we cannot have a purer law. Sometimes the laws instituted and proclaimed by a government are only a hair's breadth away from being downright *unjust*. This happens especially in the East, but to a lesser degree also in the West. It happens regularly that the innocent are condemned and the guilty acquitted. And laws lay down property rules that are downright wrong. That is why we are always ready to revise and improve the law; people see how unjust a law actually is and set out to improve it. In all such cases you do need to bear the injustice and submit yourself to it because it is God's common punishment for our sin. However, you may—and indeed you must—raise your voice in protest. You are permitted to defend your lost rights. What is more, for the sake of God and your neighbor you are allowed to help get the law revised. In the meantime, however, you are to submit, for you do not live under God's pure law but under government law, which as a rule cannot be pure.

Consequently, the very fact that government law is and remains only an *imperfect* shadow of God's law obliges the government to strive for purer knowledge of God's law. This knowledge we must obtain from Scripture, as well as from natural life on which Scripture sheds its light. For that reason, it is necessary for us to eradicate completely from both government and its subjects the false notion that people are the gods of their possessions and can do with them as they please. Every good on earth is bound to four relationships: (1) it is related to itself, because it is handled in accordance with the nature God has established in it; (2) it is related to God, who created and maintains it, and who is its absolute Sovereign; (3) it is related to its temporal stewards whom God has appointed over it; and (4) it is related to our fellow creatures, that is, to our neighbors, to all stakeholders, to our community, our society and even our country as a whole. The situation concerning earthly possessions is only as it should be when justice is done to those four relationships.

Suppose we had a communist or socialist government. This government would undo two of the four relationships, retaining only the relationships to the nature of the goods and to society. You would have to submit yourself not only to it as the government, but you would also feel duty-bound to boldly resist such monstrous law and to promote better views. So far so good. However, mark how our present government barely does justice to even one of these relationships (namely, to the temporal stewards) and neglects the other three almost entirely! Is it then not likewise your bounden duty to push for the purification and improvement of the law?

You only delude yourself if you think that the right of ownership has always and everywhere been regulated as it is regulated among us today. It is true that we are used to this arrangement from childhood and that our parents, too, knew of no other law. However, if you look at history and consider how property rights were regulated among other nations, you will soon see that those rights passed through a variety of forms and that there is a great deal in those other regulations that comes closer to what is the ideal law in God's sight. One can hardly deny that there is currently a movement underfoot for a significant amendment to the regulation of property rights. Jurists and all others who love the Word of God have the high and noble calling in particular to fight for God's ordinances in this area and so be a blessing to the nations. This is true especially today, because the current regulations concerning land ownership, the power of capital, and the laws of succession have created situations that cry out for divine justice. We will not go further into this, for the solution lies not with theology but with jurisprudence.

What we are called to do as God's children instead is to point to the deeper, underlying meaning of God's law as it pertains to *our conscience*. There are many ways and means to acquire possessions which the law either does not prevent or does not have any power over yet are condemned by God and make us guilty before the Holy One. Whoever sins against the eighth commandment is a thief in the eyes of God even if he is not a thief in the judgment of a court. In fact, even when you have been acquitted by a judge you may still be returning home as a thief in God's eyes. For that reason we will not dwell too much on different forms of outright theft and fraud that are punished by the government. In those cases we are clear on what we are dealing with, and those who commit transgressions in that sense do so in most cases with full knowledge that they are sinning: they act with premeditation, deliberately, hoping they will not be caught, or else escape the consequences through cunning. What does this mean for the children of God? They are more concerned with the judge of heaven and earth than with an earthly judge. For them it is insufficient not to be guilty of what the catechism calls outright "theft and robbery," which is punished by the government. To them, "theft" includes the countless tricks and schemes by which people think they can acquire their neighbor's belongings.

Here we should not be weak, but we are to take a strong stand when we preach the Word and state clearly that whoever does such things is *a thief in God's eyes*. The world may find that terrible, but if people do not want to listen to this verdict of the Word of God, the Lord through Satan raises up the communist who points out to them that so much of the current distribution of wealth is based on theft and robbery. Indeed, if you were able to trace back to its very origin the way all of a current owner's possessions came to be his, you would begin to wonder whether there was a single significant piece of property that does not hide the sin of theft somewhere in its history. Christ's church therefore has the calling to awaken the conscience, to sanctify the notion of ownership through awareness of guilt, and to prevent Christians from continuing their participation in this sinful traffic.

Business and commerce do not enjoy the best of reputations. Whatever goods are being traded, all sectors have had practices which are at the very least dodgy and about which God's tender children have always decided, when they learned of them, that they could not pass the test of conscientious honesty. A number of such people have had to withdraw from their branch of commerce in order not to sin against their soul. Yet many Christians have been familiar with these practices from their youth and have gradually come to regard them as some kind of unwritten law that cannot involve sin because "everyone is doing it" and because refraining from such practices puts them in an impossible position businesswise. There is no doubt that this *cannot* be a good principle. The views and acts of fellow sinners *can* never be a rule for what to do or not do. For this reason we advise Christians not to give up on business and commerce, but with God to be bold and simply cut off all dealings, transactions, and practices which their conscience condemns. To do something against your conscience is *never* safe. In fact, the example of our fathers who cheated less than the other nations shows how God can bless such honesty. Over the last fifty years, many farmers thought they could cleverly tamper with their butter.

What was the outcome, if not that our entire butter trade caved in, and that (at least in the British market) Danish butter supplanted ours? As the proverb says, "Honesty is the best policy." May it long be the mindset of our business class.

Our catechism made a significant contribution to fostering this mind-set amongst our fathers. In the days when everyone attended church, including the afternoon service, they clearly heard God's will concerning "unjust weights, lengths, measures, goods, coins, usury" explained to them every year. The conscience of Dutch shopkeepers and merchants thereby remained keen on all these points, and by the power of preaching much injustice was eliminated or prevented.

The mere attempt to be clever or cunning in business can bring one into conflict with honesty. People may laugh together with their business buddies about how they managed to trick the fool or made use of his igno-rance of the market, of the merchandise, of the money, or of anything else, for the purpose of getting him to pay more or to receive less than was just. God, however, does not laugh. He curses you for having abandoned love and for having brought your neighbor to the point where he had to turn to God himself for justice. Such deception has become second nature to horse dealers, but it has also crept into nearly all branches of commerce. Especially in the stock market, it has become standard practice to try to pull a fast one on someone else, and these dirty practices have led to expressions such as "to palm something off on someone." A vendor knows that there is something wrong with his product and that its value is no higher than one hundred guilders, but some fool comes along and does not notice that the vendor with his lies manages to jack the price up to three hundred guilders. The vendor accepts the money, and by the time the poor soul notices that he has been cheated it is too late—cheated so badly that, to add insult to injury, he does not even dare to complain out of fear that he will become everyone's laughingstock.

The speculation practiced on a large scale in today's financial world like-wise incurs considerable guilt. First, the lottery was promoted, fostering the notion that is was possible to make not only a living but even an entire for-tune without working, simply by engaging in a game of chance on bended knees before "Lady Luck." People thought so little of it that the government to this day often encourages the lottery. In the past even churches saw the lottery as a source of income for building a new sanctuary or planting a new church. This evil continues in charity lotteries. People have thus become used to gambling, and the rule of Genesis 3 that humans shall eat by the sweat of their brow has been transformed into the rule that they shall gain a fortune by trying their luck. "Nothing ventured, nothing gained" takes the place of the apostolic rule that those who are unwilling to work shall not eat [2 Thess 3:10]. Although all scholars, even non-Christians, have concluded that games of chance ruin people and for that reason have also campaigned to have the state lottery banned, the city of Amsterdam still gives lottery loans, and members in society circles at times play with such shamefully high stakes that time and again people go broke in these games. In fact, such wicked games are part and parcel of what is often called the *high life*. If you want to see it done in public you only need to go to Monaco, or else have yourself introduced to the circles in The Hague where this is done behind closed doors.

Fanning the flames of this passion for gambling produced the speculation in both stocks and commodities such as grain, oil, zinc, and so forth. A price is set that determines the value of the stocks and commodities; one day it is set at this amount, and the next day it is either higher or lower. You buy the stocks and commodities when they are low—not to own them but rather to sell them the next day if their value has gone up, and so to pocket the earnings. The risk, of course, is that their value will drop and that you will need to invest more money. When this kind of speculation was adopted on a broader scale, people began to ask themselves what the purpose of buying actually was. After all, even without buying they could simply decide to wait and see how the market would look after ten days or more, and then make up the difference. With that, of course, speculation could really take off. As long as people actually bought in order to resell later, there was still some moderation. They could only buy a limited number of stocks or a certain amount of commodities because they had to pay up front, with insufficient reserves. There were also added costs for the transportation and storage of those commodities. But once the kind of speculation caught on where people could buy and sell without taking delivery, the natural limitation dropped away, and they were able to purchase one hundred times more than before. Therefore, they no longer paid the principal but only the difference and needed no storage. This led to an enormous level of speculation in all kinds of commodities that made some people immensely rich in a single day and reduced others to extreme poverty overnight. This cannot meet with approval in God's eyes, and those who confess the Lord and live according to God's ordinances will have nothing to do with it.

The large corporations that have appeared in particular since 1850 gave rise to a similar kind of evil. They placed into the hands of a few an unimaginable amount of capital belonging to thousands who could not exercise any control over it. These powerful conglomerates were thus able to speculate on an enormous scale. Thanks to their capital, they could determine the course of the market, take control of the media, and mislead the masses in a big way. The public scandals with the Panama Canal Company in France and with the Bank in Italy clearly demonstrate how far this can go. With the money of a trusting public, they simply bribed everyone and fattened their own wallets. These large banking establishments and financial institutions then lured several national governments into extending all kinds of risky loans, from which these companies earned fortunes. The masses were misled once again, turned over their savings, and were cheated. One country after another went bankrupt, and in one day, millions were lost—not, however, by the rich classes, but by the lower middle class. Think only of Portugal and more than one South American republic. None of those powerful corporations would ever have received this money had the large bankers not taken a lead in this and deceived the people in order to earn their premiums.

If governments, as God's servants, could declare bankruptcy, how much shame can there still be for individuals if they do the same? As a result, a new demon has been unleashed among the nations in the form of *bankruptcy*. You do business; through it you acquire another's goods; you make a mistake; things go against you; even without intentional deception you lose not only your own money but also that which others are entitled to receive from you; you declare bankruptcy, and you escape. Meanwhile, your bankruptcy means that through your actions your neighbor has lost their property. Admittedly, this *can* happen to even the best of businessmen, so for that very reason it has to be covered by some kind of regulation. The immoral part comes in when people no longer see any shame in it, and if they can just manage to come to an agreement at no more than 10 percent they start all over again and do not repay the other 90 percent to their former creditors once they become well-off again. This evil, too, was something that arose not from the ranks of the common people but rather from the wealthy class. And the government, which had itself declared bankrupt, led the way.

What more shall we say about the swindling that occurs on the stock exchange when bank drafts are offered and when money that is not actually there is created through "kite flying" or trading futures? The terrible financial debacles, one after another, that strike even the highest circles testify all too clearly to this. Hardly a week goes by without some corporation, here or abroad, coming to ruin, which means that thousands of common people have lost their money. To the shame of our society, it has happened on more than one occasion that notaries, who are regarded as holding a position of trust, were found to be accomplices in fraudulent transactions but managed to flee the country in the nick of time, thanks to telegraph and train. It is one great financial sin that has gripped all of Europe, especially among the Jewish population.[15] Everyone wants to climb higher and become richer, and to set their sights on money and more money. The only thing that matters is that you get more money, by whatever means. In the end you also see Christians give way to this widespread temptation, and you keep hearing of people in our circles who have lost their riches through all kinds of speculation. In the case of many it became clear that the loss of their fortune was the only way they could be cured of the money fever that coursed through their veins. Had they not lost their fortune, they would have bowed down even deeper in the dust before mammon. Only after their fortune was crippled were they checked and came to their senses. Whatever forms this money fever takes, whether it seeks satisfaction through usury, outright fraud, the lottery, or speculation, it has the demonic effect of drawing people away from God and toward mammon.

Preachers have guarded and warned against this evil from the pulpit, but they have not been concrete, persistent, and detailed enough. It seems that they are not sufficiently persuaded of the kind of evil spirit by which people are increasingly possessed. It cannot be emphasized enough that they need to address the people on this topic more directly, specify the issues, and so revive the awareness that one cannot serve both God and

---

15. The historic association rooted in specific social contexts of Jews with money has been occasion for anti-Semitic discrimination. The origins of this phenomenon and the stereotypically negative assessment of Jews by many Christians are to be found in the long history of Christian Europe. When combined with the legal prohibition against Jewish participation in many other professions, "the economic forces pushing Jews out of other occupations were matched by others pulling them into the money trade." See Derek J. Penslar, *Shylock's Children: Economics and Jewish Identity in Modern Europe* (Berkeley: University of California Press, 2001), 17.

mammon. To all this should also be added that Christians who are aware that they have money and possessions which they did not obtain in the ways of the Lord should return them to their masters in order to unburden their conscience or, where this is no longer possible, to return them to the Master of all—that is, to the service of the Lord, and to all that in his name is worthy of financial support.

§5

As each has received a gift, use it to serve one another, as
good stewards of God's varied grace.
1 Peter 4:10

As we have seen, what makes money evil and dangerous is that it is unchecked. All other possessions are of themselves bound to certain divine ordinances, as is evident especially with animals and plants, and with basic materials. All such objects through their nature limit our right of owner-ship when it comes to their use. However, money as such obeys only the rules established by human interrelationships. The relative value of gold and silver, which has considerable influence in this world, depends partly on the fluctuations in the amount of gold produced by the mines, but only partly. Further, if you consider money as a world power, that often in its fake paper form is free from nearly all restrictions, it soon becomes evident that this power is entirely different from that which resides in a parcel of land, a herd of cattle, a coal mine, or the like. With all other possessions you are de facto tied to a number of divine ordinances; it is only with money that you are not.

It would be a mistake, however, to conclude from the above that it would have been better had money never appeared at all and that if need be it should be abandoned again. For even if it is entirely true that the greatest danger lies in money, it cannot be disputed that the appearance of money as a means of exchange renders possible the noble use of money. Here, too, we meet the fixed law of human life: that society can only advance by being exposed to grave dangers. It is the very principle of moral freedom that comes into play. If you always let your children hang onto something for support, they may never walk away, but they will never learn to walk either. Without the temptation in the wilderness, there is no transfiguration on Mount Tabor. God placed the tree of the knowledge of good and evil in the middle of paradise. The same principle applies here as well. Those who have great possessions but cling to God and have truly turned to him in their wealth stand spiritually on a higher level than the poor man Lazarus who feared God but without ever really feeling the temptation of this world.

For those who are like Lazarus, the question of how they would have reacted had the rich man's fortune dropped into their laps will forever remain unanswered. If you have so few possessions that you have almost no freedom in the way you dispose of them, you will never have to make a choice, and for that reason never perform a moral act. If your possessions are such that you can do with them as you please, you can do both good and evil with them—what you choose to do depends on your personal moral formation. Money as the means of exchange plays a stimulating role precisely in this moral formation regarding your possessions. Unless you lease out or sell a piece of land, you can do nothing with it but cultivate it. Money that is freely at your disposal, however, can make you the master of all that your heart desires. We do not mean that land ownership cannot lead to terrible sins, but those sins usually emerge only in the context of inheritance, marriage, mortgage, lease, sale, and purchase—in other words, when the land is assessed in terms of its monetary value. This does not, however, take anything away from the rule that a field valued at one thousand guilders harbors less temptation than a one-thousand-guilder bill, and that ownership of such a field demands much less moral resilience than having one thousand guilders in cash.

This observation takes us by way of the catechism to consider in this final chapter how we are to make positive use of our possessions. As the catechism sees it, the eighth commandment has a positive side to it. Therefore, in this commandment God not only forbids but also commands. As the catechism remarks, the eighth commandment confronts greed and squander and demands that people use their money for their neighbor's good—always according to the rule of the apostle Peter: "As each has received a gift, use it to serve one another, as good stewards of God's varied grace" [1 Pet 4:10].

The effort you exercise determines what earthly goods you are entitled to. If you are not willing to work you shall not eat. This condemns the life led by those who do literally nothing, put in no effort, and still live in the lap of luxury. It reveals that such a phenomenon is impermissible and that there is something wrong with a society where this occurs. The fruit of people's labor does not extend merely to one day but to their entire lives, and not only to themselves but to all who are in any way related to them. There, too, however, one must always hold to the principle that the exercise of effort is the mother of ownership. It is impermissible that those who work should end up such that they have no bread if they become sick or advanced in age. God did not measure the application of human effort by the day but divided it unequally over the years of a person's entire life. First a person cannot work, then gradually a little; then he becomes an adult, and afterwards he begins his decline. God's ordinance is thus that people shall be certain of their daily bread throughout the days of their lives, provided that every day of their lives their effort was commensurate with their strength on that day. For that reason, the concept of daily wages in the strictest sense conflicts with the ordinance of God unless its context is such that it ensures the worker's sustenance from cradle to grave. This was why, in the second place, we pointed to the organic relationship in which people stand with respect for each other. A man who is a father must also earn the bread for his children, and when the children are grown up and their father has become old, they must support him to the end. This is the order of nature, and all provisions in this regard by way of pension funds and the like will all come down to the fundamental principle that a *day's wage* should be enough for people to support themselves and their families, including the elderly. We shall not enlarge upon the right of inheritance here, since we discussed it already in the previous chapter.

Ownership of property will always rest on the twin principles that "if anyone is not willing to work, let him not eat" [2 Thess 3:10] and that "the laborer deserves his wages" [1 Tim 5:18], provided they are *not taken individualistically and per day but calculated over the whole of life and in connection with the organic relationship* that exists between us and our offspring. At the same time, these principles determine that ownership cannot be equal. It matters little by what efforts people obtain their possessions. Some work with their vocal cords as singers, others with their eyes as inspectors, a third group with their ears as musical adjudicators, a fourth group with their hands as manual laborers, a fifth with their hearts as professional caregivers, a sixth with their minds as scholars. Humans are very complex beings. They can exert themselves in many different ways, and the rule "By the sweat of your face you shall eat bread" in no way implies that we must all work the land. Those who do make this claim understand little of either the human race or of the great variety of gifts that God has given to humankind. A man such as Marnix of Saint Aldegonde never touched a plow or spade, but he did more for his country and nation than all the farmers of the sixteenth century put together.[16] The question is not the sort of effort but the effort itself. Everything can be a spiritual calling. The only question for you is whether you in your divine calling apply and exert your strengths so as to accomplish a part of the greater task and so receive the right *to eat*—that is, to exist as a person and sustain your existence by consuming a portion of the goods intended for humans.

It is precisely in the division of tasks and goods, as described above, that money acquires a great deal of power—not only to distribute more accurately but also to lead astray. Take a rich Chinese person on Java who advances money to a Javanese person, sells him all kinds of trinkets, and is kindness itself to him ... until the amount he has advanced equals the value of the Javanese man's land. Then it is as if a new page has turned, as he ejects the Javanese off his property.

That's how it goes in life. When money functions as the means of exchange it is possible to measure out wages much more precisely, and to provide help and exercise benevolence in ways that are both great and small. However, that same money disrupts natural relationships, makes room for shrewdness and cunning. By the momentary application of this cunning, it serves to distribute property so unequally that no normal human effort can reverse the imbalance for years, at times even for centuries. In addition to the role it gives to such cunning, money also produces worship of mammon. That is, money begins to fascinate for its own sake and turns into a power all its own. This power takes a grip on our hearts to feed the sins of *love of money* and *squandering* as two shoots that sprout from the same trunk.

The Scriptures say, "For the love of money is a root of all kinds of evils" [1 Tim 6:10]. This does not refer to miserliness as in one who stows away their gold in a closet and cannot part with it. That is not the love of money referred to here. Rather, the *love of money* that Scripture speaks of here is *covetousness*. To love money is to covet it, to crave it for its own sake. It is an insatiable thirst for more and more money, to add to one's belongings, to become richer and richer, and to be able to call more and more capital one's own. This is the "love of money" that is the root of all evil. It is a result of the fact that money, precisely because it is the means of exchange for everything and can get you everything, resembles a *god*. *God* can give you

---

16. Philips of Marnix (1540–98), Lord of Saint-Aldegonde, was a sixteenth-century Dutch writer and statesman who studied theology under John Calvin and Theodore Beza in Geneva.

everything; *your money* can give you *almost* everything. It cannot provide inner peace or spiritual goods, but lovers of money do not thirst for that anyway. As long as they are doing well they can use their money to get all that they thirst after. In that sense, their money is indeed a god. But it also governs them as a god, takes away their freedom, and requires constant worship from them—the worship of mammon. For their daily bread and their future they trust not the living God but the god of money. All their contriving is directed toward that money-god; all the thoughts of their hearts extend to mammon. Lovers of money are not made happy by the Lord's favor but by the favor of fortune. If fortune fails or mammon is ill-disposed toward them, they reach for their poison or pistol, for their money was their life. This is why service to mammon—the lordship of money—cannot go together with service to Christ. You cannot serve two masters. Whoever serves mammon and loves money hates God. This is not a saying we ourselves have made up; it is a clear pronouncement made by the Lord Jesus. Those who confess the Lord but are known by others, and by their own hearts, as being "too tied to their money" should take heed lest they turn out to have fallen from grace for the sake of money.

This love of money diverges into two different streams: *miserliness* and *squandering*. Misers, the real lovers of money, are those who want to keep their money-god with them. They always want to save and save. Money is not a means for them but an end. They toil and slave away for money, and for it they cheat and lie. All their joy is found in money. What Psalm 42 says of the panting deer can be applied to them in the fullest sense: As the wounded and hunted deer pants for streams of water, so the miser thirsts for the stream of gold. Only it can quench their burning thirst. That sin of miserliness is found not just in those who hide their gold in socks and eat dry bread. No, misers can live the most proper of lives and eat and dress as they should. Before God, however, they are and remain guilty of the sin of greed if, instead of using their money and placing it in the service of the Lord as his stewards, they hoard it to make it grow and secure their future through the appreciation of its value.

What we say of course does not mean that there are no ways of saving up money that are commanded by God, nor that preparation for one's old age and for one's descendants after death is not a God-given duty. Each and every person knows in their own heart whether they are saving as God wills it, or hoarding and storing up their money against God's will, so as to make their money-god more and more powerful. Thousands, ten thousands, even millions have been stored away in that sinful way and taken out of circulation, only because some wretched mammon worshippers cannot separate themselves from their precious god. This money is of no use to them, to their family, or to the world. The golden idol only glitters in their house, and before it these wretches fall on their knees and, in rejecting God in favor of mammon, bring eternal condemnation upon their souls. Some of these sinners have come to repentance at the last moment and gladdened God's churches with generous gifts, but the hardened sinners could not even be brought to that. Their fearful pride was for people after their death to stand amazed at the capital they had amassed. They celebrated their last sweet but empty triumph on their deathbed as they thought about the sizable succession duties their estate would be subject to.

At first glance, the *squanderer* seems to be an entirely different person. In the end, however, they are guilty of the same sin. The heart's desire of squanderers is not to worship the power of their money-god in private, but to see, experience, and flaunt that power in life. If misers are the mammon mystics, squanderers are the mammon pietists. Squanderers are proud that mammon has chosen them as his servants, altar boys, or priests, and they love to show themselves to others in full priestly regalia, richly dressed and well fed. They are even generous. Throwing a guilder or two at the poor, why not? We call it charity, but at bottom it is nothing but mammonistic boasting. Mammon is all-powerful, and as mammon's prophets the squanderers too are powerful. It is in the gaps in their conscience that you notice the sham of their position. Squanderers have no problem making poor creditors wait long for their money. For them, the most important thing is to have money in their hand or wallet. Spending, displaying, and squandering money is all one and the same thing to them. For this reason, cutting down expenses so that creditors can receive their money goes against their rule of life. Squanderers are sloppy. They are not neat in keeping their books, and in fact they prefer not to keep any books at all. They will spend today what they are due to receive a few months down the road. It is beneath their priestly dignity to make careful calculations and then to check them. Owing to their squandering nature, their wives and children soon lack what they need; they get talked about, their futures are in danger, and yet there is almost never remorse. A smile forms around their lips and they play the lottery one more time in case fortune will look on them with favor. Thus squanderers, too, do not take God into account. They care for duty nor order. They do not feel themselves bound by any of God's ordinances.

They are the free and the mighty priests of mammon. With half a grin on their faces, they place the future and destiny of wife and children on the sacred table where mammon's fate will be decided.

Therefore, both miserliness and squandering render a person equally guilty before God. They are two different forms of one and the same sin, and whichever form it takes in any given person depends only on their constitution. A hot-tempered person is a born squanderer, while in the melancholic person is prone to miserliness. Yet whatever differences there may be between them, the point of departure for both is that effort does not produce a right to property, in order to spend it in the service of God, but to misuse in stroking their own ego. Miser and squanderer are both *godless* in the fullest sense of the word.

In contrast, those who do not act godlessly but follow God's will when it comes to their assets understand what the catechism says: *You must work for the poor*. I am to "labor faithfully, so that I may be able to help the poor in their need." This is a most beautiful expression and it contains a near sublime concept. You are to put in the effort. Once you have put in your best efforts so as to have enough for yourself and your family, you are to go back to work and carry on in order to earn more—so that you can help those who are in need. Oh, where are God's children who have had the courage to plumb the depths of this charity? To be sure, the children of God already give a lot, and many hands have become more generous. This was less the case in times past. Even half a century ago, their hands were not as open as they are now. Especially in the last quarter of this century, God's children from the two largest social classes have learned something of this art. This can be very touching at times, especially among the lower class. Still, we have not even come close to the peak of our giving. We give, it is true, when we have something left over, from our surplus, from what we can do without, but always with the thought that we can only give when we can afford it. This is the very issue that is addressed here. Simply as a human being, says the Heidelberger, it is your duty to give to the needy, just as it is your duty to care for your children. You never say, "I will give my children bread if I have something left over." No, you are only too aware of your duty to keep on working and working until you are sure to have bread for your children. You likewise have a duty from God to continue working until you have something to give to the needy.

The poor among us understand this all too well. Many workers put in extra hours in the evening in order to complete the tasks of a less competent worker. Many housewives who are themselves tired and worn out go to help the bed-ridden neighbor. There are poor widows who have almost no bread and yet give a penny to the poor person who knocks on their door. Not only your children but also the poor belong to your family. They belong with you. They do not stand outside you, and you may not say that they are none of your concern. Society may claim that it has completed its task only when enough work has been done that everyone including the poor has their bread.

This giving is an "art" that has to be learned. Half a century ago, someone with an income of fifty thousand guilders considered themselves quite generous if they gave five hundred guilders a year in charitable donations. Today it would be at least five thousand guilders. Even then, this is not really *generous* giving. On this point, too, we need to educate one another. That will take time; we have to be patient. The collections taken up in church have proved this. What is collected today in the free churches, and mostly from among common people, is already five times what used to be brought in when the gentlemen sat there in their furs. Thankfully, the days are gone when on Saturday evenings rich matrons eagerly needed a nickel to tie into a corner of their kerchief for Sunday morning's collection, and then they would make a mockery by sitting under the preaching of the gospel. There are now many families where you find stewards who give an account before God of the use of their possessions. They also do their bookkeeping not only to see whether they can make ends meet but to see whether they have been good and charitable stewards of God.

Little by little, some are beginning to see that they should raise their children for the exercise of that kind of stewardship. In the past, people had no grasp of this. At that time, children had to be raised above all as little mammon worshippers. The message they received was to save and save. A child who did not learn to save, it was thought, would later find no place in the world of mammon. Giving was also considered not to be good, as it only fed laziness and produced beggars and vagabonds. A child's bankbook, however, was as a patent of nobility. If children were interested in the state of their bank account, they surely had a promising future before them as adults. Yet here Christian education has produced change, and the free churches have made an excellent contribution. Children, too, should develop a mind for charity, a taste for the sweetness of giving. Helping, giving aid, doing something that contributes to the Lord's cause is completely different from being able to say, "I already have twenty or thirty guilders in my account." Even if children cannot give much, perhaps only pennies at a time—yet, as long as they give of their own money rather than what you just slipped into their hand, they are doing something—they are exercising moral strength and developing in themselves the ability to be dedicated and to give up something for others.

We need to guard against self-exaltation—the tendency to spiritual pride—and the reminder is hardly necessary that putting the names of children on a public list is a questionable practice. Money can also be gained by speculating on vanity. Then the Lord's judgment cannot be escaped that those who give in this way already have their reward. Children who learn to give this way do not seek God but themselves, and through their giving do not learn piety. Rather, they may in fact develop an ungodly attitude. For this reason one cannot emphasize enough that Christians should conduct themselves according to the Lord's demands, and learn the art of giving in secret. Then your right hand does not know what your left hand is doing. Then giving ennobles you, brings you closer to God, and turns you away from the world. Such giving creates true piety and is an exercise in devotion. For precisely this reason it is difficult to justify before the tribunal of the gospel the boisterous and bustling way in which many people attempt to collect funds through a charity party, a benefit concert, a public performance, a bazaar, a raffle, and so on. In the eyes of God, giving is first of all a matter of *the motivation of the heart*. If I move people to give something for the kingdom of God by showing them what they could get from a raffle, they have their reward and you have your blessing. Not to mention the dubious practice of young women at their booths as they try to get the men leaving the stock exchange to buy things from them. All these are motives and influences which, even if not sinful in themselves, are unholy and therefore cannot have a place in the service of the Lord.

We judge no one. We know very well that all kinds of institutions and foundations have a set budget for their expenditures irrespective of their revenue. So if not enough money comes in, what then? Yes, what then? They then resort to all kinds of extra means, and if money cannot be shaken loose from people without a bazaar or an organ concert, should we allow a useful institution to languish and die? This is a painful question, to which our only response for now is: If after the organ concert or bazaar you live in the realization that it is *a shame* that God's people were forced to have recourse to such means, then the danger is less. How acceptable can it be in the eyes of God if after the bazaar we hear Christians brag about how charitable they once again showed themselves to be? Can it be good to take pride in what is actually our shame? Let those who live close to the Lord decide.

What should always hold for us, and it continues to hold in increasing measure, is the golden rule that governs the eighth commandment in its entirety: that you are to live for a goal, for a life task, for a calling. And also that if you gain money or possessions as fruit of the exercise of your strength and talents, you are to lay everything you gained on the Lord's altar in order to take from it as much as you need for yourself and for your family, and then in his name to dedicate what remains to the cause of the Lord and to those whom he places on your path.

REMEMBER THE SABBATH DAY

COMMENTARY ON LORD'S DAY 38 OF THE HEIDELBERG CATECHISM

TEXT INTRODUCTION

The Heidelberg Catechism is a manual for basic instruction in Christian doctrine. Published in 1563, the catechism consists of 129 questions and answers and quickly proved useful for faith formation of children and adults alike. Divided into 52 parts, each "Lord's Day" enables the entirety of the teachings of the catechism to be covered in weekly sermons throughout the year.

At the Synod of Dort, in its 146th session of April 30, 1619, delegates of the participating churches from abroad exhorted the Dutch church "to persevere in the Reformed faith, to pass it on to posterity, and to preserve it until the return of Christ." In reply, the delegates from the Dutch church made a solemn vow, pledging to preach and preserve the Reformed faith, pure and undiluted.

When Kuyper started his commentary on the Heidelberg Catechism in fall 1886 in the Sunday paper *De Heraut*, he recalled this vow and subsequently titled his series *E voto Dordraceno*: "from the vow made at Dort." The title is usually shortened, at Kuyper's own directive—"for ease of citing," he said—to *E Voto*.

The treatment of the Ten Commandments in the Heidelberg Catechism typically follows the pattern of expositing both those things that are forbidden by each commandment and those things that are required. The fourth commandment, "Remember the Sabbath day, to keep it holy," similarly has both positive duties and negative prohibitions, but Kuyper takes the point of departure for his discussion in the limited treatment of what is forbidden by the commandment in the catechism. Lord's Day 38 covers this petition in Question and Answer 103, and Kuyper's exposition of this commandment addresses the dynamic between work and rest in the Christian life. The chapter on Lord's Day 38 first appeared as five installments in *De Heraut* of September 4, 11, 18, 25, and October 2, 1892.

SOURCE: Abraham Kuyper, *E voto Dordraceno* (Amsterdam: J. A. Wormser, 1892–95), 4:1–39. Translated by Ed M. van der Maas. Edited and annotated by Harry Van Dyke.

COMMENTARY ON LORD'S DAY 38 OF THE HEIDELBERG CATECHISM

Question 103: *What does God require in the fourth Commandment?*
Answer: *In the first place, God wills that the ministry of the Gospel and schools be maintained, and that I, especially on the day of rest, diligently attend church to learn the Word of God, to use the holy sacraments, to call publicly upon the Lord, and to give Christian alms. In the second place, that all the days of my life I rest from my evil works, allow the Lord to work in me by His Spirit, and thus begin in this life the everlasting sabbath.*

> *I gave them my Sabbaths, as a sign between me and them, that* §1
> *they might know that I am the* Lord *who sanctifies them.*
> Ezekiel 20:12

For the treatment of what is generally called "the Sabbath question" we refer here to our *Treatise on the Sabbath*.[1] To repeat in abridged form what was discussed there in more detail would not clarify but confuse the issue. Moreover, to present it in equal, or even greater detail, would be out of proportion to our treatment of the other commandments. Another consideration is that any exposition of the catechism regarding the fourth commandment should focus more specifically on the answer it gives to the question it poses. This provides us with a convenient opportunity to discuss what was not discussed, or only incidentally touched upon, in our *Treatise on the Sabbath*.

There is no disguising the fact, after a close reading of the answer, that if it were to be written today it would most likely turn out somewhat different. Today few people would be satisfied with the fact that the real Sabbath question was not touched upon. They would urge, not without cause, that the answer should deal more extensively, as it does in the case of the other commandments, with what this commandment *forbids*. Indeed, we dare say that many a godly person in our day who emphasizes Sabbath observance—or, as used to be said, who is overscrupulous about keeping the Sabbath—cannot on this point feel satisfied by the Heidelberg Catechism and must often have been annoyed by the fact that the catechism is entirely silent about what is called "breaking the Sabbath."

Let us therefore begin with a small attempt to reconcile these believers with the Heidelberg Catechism. They should keep in mind that everything that has been passed on to us from the days of the Reformation bears the imprint of the contrast with Rome. Salvation by works had caused untold evil. Not that the praxis of virtue was ungodly, or the doing of good works was not commanded, but rather because it virtually all ended up in penitential exercises or ceremonial performances which in themselves do not bear a holy character. What increasingly forced itself into the foreground as "good works" was not a quiet and tender life of godliness. It primarily consisted, instead, in faithfully observing all kinds of ecclesiastical ceremonies, bringing all kinds of ecclesiastical offerings, and performing all kinds of ecclesiastical penances. The soul suffocated under all this. The life of faith withered under this burden. And it was from such unbiblical

---

1. Abraham Kuyper, *Tractaat van den sabbath. Historische dogmatische studie* (Amsterdam: J. A. Wormser, 1890).

practice that sprang the spiritual tyranny of the priests and the corruption of the church's government.

It is not surprising that when, in the wake of Luther, the break was made with this evil practice of salvation by works, there was initially some movement to the other extreme. People, at least in some circles, became somewhat hyperspiritual. This found expression most strongly in the Anabaptists, who altered the customary practices related to baptism, civil government, the swearing of oaths, and so much more. In the end, they even came to compromise the authority of Scripture and the confession of Jesus' birth from the "flesh and blood of Mary." These devout people, who went astray, gradually eroded the natural foundation of life. Everything had to become spiritual. Following this train of thought, they also rejected the praxis of the Sabbath. Keeping the Sabbath, they said, was "observing a day," a sin against which Paul had warned so earnestly [see Gal 4:10]. Weighed down again under the ceremonial law, Sabbath observance meant reintroducing the Romish practice of works righteousness. It was making a distinction between today and tomorrow as if one did not have to serve God all the days of one's life. They therefore cried, "Away with the Jewish Sabbath," and deliberately began to perform all kinds of common labor on Sunday. The Sabbath was to be observed only spiritually, that is, one should already now, not only on Sunday but on all the days of one's life, begin to observe the eternal Sabbath in the hidden life of one's soul.

This shows convincingly that these people were not motivated by the evil desire to desecrate the Sabbath but by a spiritual impulse. The only thing they can be blamed for is that, from fear that the Romish leaven would creep in again, they lost sight too much of the practical and natural aspect of this commandment. Our Reformers therefore did not hesitate to correct this one-sidedness without shortchanging the element of truth contained in the spiritual notion. They therefore courageously opposed all superstitious elements in any ceremonial keeping of the Sabbath. And it was their spirit that still was at work in the Reformed churches in the seventeenth century, when every trace of being overscrupulous was combated as an incursion of Romish legalism. As we know, even a man such as Voetius was sometimes challenged on this point at ecclesiastical meetings.[2]

---

2. Gisbertus Voetius (1589–1676) was prominent Reformed theologian at the University of Utrecht, and so-called Voetians disputed with followers of Johannes Cocceius (1603–69), or Cocceians, concerning the proper observance of the Sabbath.

Yet it cannot be denied that people from the Lutheran and Reformed side initially went too far in combating this ceremonial aspect. Not, of course, that this superstition could ever be opposed too strongly—it must be exterminated root and branch. But they overdid it insofar as they failed to distinguish between what was Sinaitic-ceremonial and what was by virtue of creation enduring and permanent. A certain tendency can therefore be observed during those first years to explain the Lord's Day in neutral terms. Life would have been considered at its most ideal if a worship service could be held every day and thus all noticeable difference between the Sunday and the other days of the week would fall away. If this design had succeeded, there would have been no hesitation to let regular daily work continue undisturbed. But when people soon came to the realization that holding church services on weekdays benefited a few classes of society but was impossible for the masses, they realized with growing conviction that observing an intentional day of rest was simply indispensable for maintaining the religious life and thus the church itself.

When we compare what the Heidelberg Catechism says on this topic in 1563 and what Ursinus later states in his commentary,[3] we clearly notice a certain transition. In the catechism he still writes, "especially on the day of rest," that is, the Sabbath; but somewhat later, in his commentary, he already declares that "there is now just as much necessity for a certain time to be set apart in the Christian church for the preaching of God's word, and for the public administration of the sacraments, as there was formerly in the Jewish church."[4] There is thus a progression through three stages. First, the only thing derived from the commandment in a moral sense is that religion has to be practiced "all the days of one's life." Next, the rule was "that I, especially on the sabbath, that is, on the day of rest, diligently frequent the church of God."[5] And finally, practical considerations forced the concentration of worship services virtually on Sunday only and to declare the ordinance of the day of rest indispensable for the life of the church of Christ. In this context it is striking that Answer 103 in Ursinus's commentary, as

---

3. Zacharius Ursinus, *Explicationum Catecheticarum D. Zachariae Ursini* (Heidelberg: Johannis Halbey, 1607).

4. Zacharius Ursinus, *The Commentary of Dr. Zacharias Ursinus, on the Heidelberg Catechism*, trans. G. W. Willard (Cincinnati: Elm Street, 1888), 563.

5. Ursinus, *Commentary on the Heidelberg Catechism*, 557.

well as in that of Jeremias Bastingius,[6] still had the clause, "that I, even as on other days, and especially on the sabbath."[7] It is also striking that the words "even as on other days" were soon omitted. There is therefore no doubt whatever that the initial intent was to let the whole observance of a particular day be omitted. Next, the day of rest was placed side by side with the other days, albeit with a measure of preference. And finally the position was reached of demanding, also from Christians, a separate day of rest for maintaining the church service.

The Swiss and the Germans did not go beyond this. Wherever the day of rest was restored it was done exclusively as a means to maintain the church service. This explains why the answer to the question "What does God require in the fourth Commandment?" reads somewhat surprisingly: "In the first place, God wills that the ministry of the Gospel ... be maintained." The insight was not fully appreciated that the day of rest also has universal significance for humankind apart from the church service, and therefore would have to be maintained even if it were possible for the church service to flourish without a day of rest. And it has been even less adequately understood how the commandment concerning the day of rest bears a divine imprint that was impressed upon our entire life by virtue of creation.

Things remained this way until the Reformation movement shifted from Switzerland and Germany to England. The view of the Sabbath in the Dutch churches did not come from Geneva, even less from Heidelberg, but most definitely from England. Undoubtedly it filled a gap, but at the same time it contained a questionable element. The English Sabbath, as is well known, is unique. The "English Sunday" is found only in Great Britain, its colonies, and in North America. The excellent feature of the English Sunday is undoubtedly that it has a fixed form and that this consistency was energetically carried through in all relationships of private and public life. In Switzerland, Germany, and our country, keeping the day of rest was always half-hearted—at the domestic, social, and national level. Again and again the day of rest in all kinds of ways gave in to the demands of the world and the demands of public life. But this is not how it was among the nations of English heritage. *There everything had to make way for the*

---

6. Jeremias Bastingius, *In Catechesin Religionis Christianae* (Dordrecht: Canin, 1588); and Bastingius, *Verclaringe op den catechisme der Christelicker religie* (Dordrecht: Canin, 1591).

7. See Ursinus, *Explicationum Catecheticarum*, 760.

Sabbath. And what was recently witnessed in America, where the whole population was up in arms to enforce the closing of the World's Fair in Chicago on Sundays, is something that would simply be inconceivable in our country or in Germany.

In England the conviction took deep root that halfway measures in relation to the Sabbath would in fact end up destroying it and that only vigorous consistency would have the power to actually give the church her own day and give an entire nation the blessing of a day of rest. It is therefore not legislation that upholds Sabbath observance in England and America, but rather a deep-rooted popular custom. The people do not want it any other way, and they will not put up with anything else. The Sabbath has become an object of national pride in England. People there are fully aware of the fact that such strict Sabbath observance arose only among the English people and survives only there. They are very much aware what plentiful blessing England owes to this Sabbath observance, also in moral and material terms. On this basis it would be considered a surrendering of a piece of English life if in some evil hour this national peculiarity were relinquished.

It may be said without fear of contradiction that the English Sabbath is not only of religious and ecclesiastical importance, but is also of equal universal human and national significance. The English theologians, without having brought this point to full clarity, always speak from the awareness that the Sabbath certainly does not derive its significance only from the church service but is a requirement of God for human life. It is a blessing granted we humans, an obligation imposed on us by our God because we are human beings. This good element, which cannot be appreciated enough, is precisely what England added to the view of the Sabbath held by the Reformed churches. Enlightened people such as Voetius therefore did not hesitate to adopt this excellent addition. As we showed in our *Treatise on the Sabbath,* Voetius even succeeded in surmising the connection between the Sabbath rest and the new life of regeneration.

However, as grateful as we may be for this indispensable acquisition, we must not close our eyes to the questionable element that soon mingled with this English Sabbath observance and caused it to degenerate into a sinful Sabbatarianism. There clearly are traces of a superstitious admixture in this view of the Sabbath. They brought people back under the ceremonial law and ended up in salvation by works. There soon arose, in a rather broad circle, the notion that there was religious merit in strict abstinence from all work on Sunday. Whoever abstained from everything on Sunday fulfilled a duty pleasing to God just by doing nothing. Putting one's hand to anything that belonged to the earthly life would kindle God's wrath.

This attitude became especially questionable in those other countries where Sabbath observance was not universal (as it was in England) but survived only among a few pious folk. In England no one sees anything especially pious or meritorious in resting in the strictest sense on Sunday, for there are no opportunities for recreation or amusements, since the Sabbath is observed by the entire nation. There is no self-elevation or spiritual pride involved in zealously keeping the Sabbath rest. But this changes once this notion of the Sabbath is transferred to a country such as ours, where the public generally turns Sunday into a day of external pleasures. Anyone among us who observes his Sabbath with strictness is conspicuous and soon gets a reputation for being scrupulously pious.

And when under such circumstances the thought arises in you that also ceremonially you still stand under the fourth commandment, and that "doing nothing" in itself has a certain merit of godliness, then your heart is readily inclined to investigate ever more minutely what else you can avoid and abstain from on the Sabbath. Then eating a cold meal is more godly than eating a warm meal, and to go to sleep in an unmade bed is more godly than going to sleep in a bed that has first been stripped. And thus your soul imperceptibly falls under the power of superstition, even as happened to Israel in its later legalistic period, when people dared not even light a candle on the Sabbath as darkness fell, and sitting inactive in the dark was called godliness. When the disciples plucked heads of grain on the Sabbath it was considered a terrible sin. And when Jesus dared heal a sick person on the Sabbath it was accounted to the Son of Man as a desecration of the Sabbath. In this way people once again move from the essence back to the form. Something purely external is viewed as something holy. Works righteousness then poisons your heart before you realize it. And your Sabbath observance, which has become Sabbatarian, restores the soul-deadening evil from which free and forfeited grace had liberated our forefathers in their dissent from Rome.

Although we acknowledge frankly that our original Reformed Sabbath observance was deficient, and although we gratefully give credit to the English churches for supplying, under the guidance of the Holy Spirit, this undeniable deficiency, we nevertheless do not regret that it is still the one-sidedly spiritual view of the Heidelberg Catechism that continues to instruct our Reformed churches in the Netherlands. The starting point chosen by the Heidelberger, after all, was irreproachable. What is not stated in the catechism follows automatically if you but spin out the thread that it places in your fingers. And precisely by its principled rejection of all that hints at superstition it keeps you from straying onto paths where outward forms do glitter but where no spiritual intimacy can blossom.

§2

So God blessed the seventh day and made it holy, because on it
God rested from all his work that he had done in creation.
Genesis 2:3

Read and reread what the catechism says about the fourth commandment, and you will not be able to reach any other conclusion than that (apart from the name "day of rest") it contains not one letter about abstaining from work. The Heidelberg Catechism says that God commands two things in the fourth commandment: (1) attending church services, with all that it entails; and (2) beginning already in this life the eternal Sabbath by resting from my evil ways. Nothing more; nothing else. And when you note the care with which the catechism spells out all the things that are commanded and prohibited by the other commandments, then it is difficult to argue that Ursinus and Olevianus accidentally forgot to mention "that we abstain from all work."

Concerning the commandment "You shall not murder," they are so precise that they see in this commandment a prohibition against murdering one's neighbor by (1) belittling, (2) hating, (3) insulting or (4) killing, through (5) thoughts, (6) words, (7) looks or gestures, (8) much less through actual deeds, whether (9) by myself or (10) with others. They are equally precise with respect to the fifth, seventh, and eighth commandments. How in the world would they then only with regard to the fourth commandment gloss over so unthinkingly what for many, including Sabbatarians, is the main issue? After all, it was the fourth commandment, more than any other, about which there had been many disputes. Those among us who are preoccupied with the Sabbath question should ask themselves whether they have ever given sufficient thought to the statement about it in the Heidelberg Catechism, a document which our churches officially adopted as a confessional standard. Have they fully realized what is implied by this statement?

The deepest thought underlying this statement is found in the fourth commandment. We tried to translate this thought in the sketch we gave of the Ten Commandments as a whole, namely, that the fourth commandment posits the demand that our life on earth be patterned after the life of God. And we contend that a different understanding is not easily possible. The authors of the catechism state that in this commandment God bids us attend church and forsake our sins. Yet how do they derive this directly from Israel's Sabbath? The Jews had no church they could attend on the Sabbath. They did not maintain churches and schools. The synagogues that existed in Jesus' day only came into being after the exile. Except for the inhabitants of Jerusalem and its immediate vicinity, it was out of the question that the Jews would go to the temple every seventh day. Nor were the sacraments administered on the Sabbath. Circumcision took place on a day of fasting after the birth. The Passover was celebrated on the fourteenth of Nisan. And taking up offerings for the poor definitely did not fall on the Sabbath in Israel, since there were no deacons, and aid to the poor was arranged quite differently.

Thus the catechism's first enumeration of what the fourth commandment bids us do was not even applicable to Israel, and neither Olevianus nor Ursinus imagined for one moment that God at Sinai had commanded Israel to do the outward observances that they present as the content of this commandment. As concerns observing the day and resting from sin, they themselves say that this applies not only to the day of rest but to *all the days of our life*. And when they finally give a spiritual interpretation to the words "thou shalt not do any work" in the sense of "rest from my evil ways," that is, from your sins, no one will foist the absurdity on the framers of the catechism that they were of the opinion that on the Sabbath day not our daily work but only our evil ways were prohibited.

We are thus faced with two options. Either the Heidelberg theologians give an entirely false explanation of the fourth commandment, of which they knew quite well that it was not so intended on Sinai; or you must go down to the deepest life principle, from which flow the ceremonial Sabbath for Israel and the spiritual Sabbath for us. This deepest life principle is that you as a human being are created in the image of God, and for that reason the nature of the divine life must be the pattern for your human life. The fact that this is indeed the principle to which the fourth commandment must be traced back is not something we have made up or the Heidelberg Catechism has devised; rather, it is revealed by God in Holy Scripture more clearly than is the case with any other commandment. For immediately after creation we find in Genesis 2:1-2 the statement concerning the life of God that he had completed the creation of the heavens and the earth and all the host of them, and that thereafter, on the seventh day, he rested from all the work he had done. This statement about the life of God is followed in verse 3 with this commandment: "So God blessed the seventh day and made it holy, because on it God rested from all his work that he had done in creation." Here a reason is given for the institution of the Sabbath. The principle, the motivation, of this commandment is laid bare in so many words, and this principle, this motivation, is sought in this, that what God does must be the pattern of life for us humans. It is stated as clearly as possible: "So God blessed the seventh day and made it holy, because on it God rested from all his work that he had done in creation."

We will here not go into the other explanation of these words. It is discussed in our *Treatise on the Sabbath*. Let us simply note that Scripture here points to a certain rhythm in the life of God. First rest, then a work of creation of six days, and then a seventh day, which becomes the Sabbath because on this day he stops creating. And now in this fourth commandment we are commanded to be imitators of God as his beloved children and to see to it that our life reflects the life of God. In order to remove all doubt, the commandment itself once more reminds us firmly of this pattern, for after the commandment the law goes on to say: "For in six days the LORD made heaven and earth, the sea, and all that is in them, and rested the seventh day. Therefore the LORD blessed the Sabbath day and made it holy" [Exod 20:11].

It is perfectly true that in the reiteration of the law in Deuteronomy 5, Moses omitted these words and instead pointed to the fact that the Lord led Israel out of Egypt with a mighty hand (see Deut 5:15), but this does not change the matter as such. In the first place, because here too God's work is pointed to as normative for our human life. Second, because the redemption of Israel from Egypt, even as the redemption through the cross for us, is the most compelling reason to regulate our life in accordance with God's life and to be imitators of God as his beloved children. If this starting point is firm (we honestly do not see what could be brought against it), then the explanation of the fourth commandment by the Heidelberg Catechism, even though it is imperfect, comes to stand in an entirely different light. Indeed, it appears to be on the right track.

Here on earth our lives our sinful; they do not follow the pattern of God's life. Someday, when sin no longer exists, things will be altogether different. Then the life of God's elect will proceed uninterrupted according to the standard and pattern of the life of the Lord. But this cannot be the case as yet, for two reasons. First, because the consequence of sin is still at work and God's children must still work in the sweat of their face. Second, because prior to our death God's work of grace does not bring about a complete check on sin. A double spoke therefore remains stuck in the wheel of our life. Twin obstacles stand in the way, preventing us from letting our life proceed in accordance with the pattern of the life of God: the slavish toil which remains imposed on us because of sin, and the incompleteness of our redemption.

From this it follows that children of God lead a kind of double life on earth. On the one hand, they still live life as it has become because of sin—what you might call their ordinary earthly life. But on the other hand, they also lead a heavenly life, both in the hidden life of their soul and in the time they spend in prayer and worship. At no point can these two spheres of life be sharply separated. If things are well with you, it should be possible to follow the marks of your heavenly life even into your sleep and your dreams; but conversely, even when you are at prayer your earthly life will interfere. Although you cannot completely separate these two on earth, it can be done be done in a relative sense. Indeed, it must be done. You must always pray; but this does not take away that some moments during the day are more directly suitable for prayer, while other moments would be very unsuitable.

Even if you hold on to the demand that the basic attitude of your heart throughout the day should be one of prayer and thanksgiving, you well know that there are times in your life when prayer within you falls silent. Moments that drive you to prayer and that are meant for prayer are then ones you would not want to miss.

What is so clearly noticeable in the case of prayer applies to the whole contrast between the spheres of your ordinary earthly life and your spiritual heavenly life. Here too we might say, very spiritually: my heavenly life is part and parcel of my entire earthly life, and I do not need a separate sphere for that heavenly life of my soul. Many mystical fanatics say this, only to be bitterly punished by the results on account of the recklessness with which they wanted to be wiser than the Lord. The Lord "knows our frame; he remembers that we are dust" [Ps 103:14]. He knows that the effort to remain conscious of our heavenly life during our daily life far exceeds our strength.

For this reason, he has given an organization to this heavenly life on earth in the form of the church—a separate sphere where this life could express itself. Not, as the fanatic asserts, that we limit piety to the church and deactivate our spiritual life in the world. Children of God cannot do this. But they do look forward to the day of rest, and they bless the life of Christ's church, in which they repeatedly enjoy spiritual rest, receive solace, and are spiritually equipped. This enables them to reenter life in the world, following the day devoted to rest and worship, with better prospects for spiritual victories. The purpose is therefore not a spiritual life on one day in the church, and then a spiritless life for six days in the world. Rather the reverse: to enrich us with spiritual provisions and spiritual weapons on the Sabbath, in order to continue the following six days with less danger on our pilgrimage through this hazardous life.

Looked at from this perspective, the explanation the catechism gives of the fourth commandment is entirely correct. The grand idea behind this commandment is that your human life should proceed according to the pattern of the life of God. This idea cannot be realized in the normal course of life, not even for God's children. The consequences of sin in our work and toil, and in our inner lives, prevent this. The only thing possible is that the higher life constitutes its own sphere in the midst of this earthly life, and for this God gave you his church on earth. The very first condition of this commandment is therefore that in the church of God you are offered, in contrast to everyday life, a sphere that enables you to be imitators of God, as his beloved children. This carries on and carries forward the work of redemption in you. Quite correctly, therefore, the first thing that this commandment urges is that the church of God be maintained. Not the church as the body of Christ, because that exists as a matter of course. Rather, the church of Christ in its external manifestation and ministry. If there is no church in the place where you live, there is only life in society and in the home, and your environment lacks that particular sphere which is given for the higher life in the ministry of the church. Obedience to this commandment therefore demands in the first place that you maintain such a church ministry, if there is one, and that you benefit from it. And that, if such a sphere is lacking, you make every effort to establish such a church ministry in the Lord's name.

It is not enough, however, that this higher life has its own circle where you can refresh and nourish yourself spiritually. The fruit of this church ministry must be manifest in your everyday life. Therefore, the second demand is that, spiritually strengthened and equipped by the church, you will let go of your evil ways each day of your life. You will let God work in you, and thus live the eternal life already in this earthly life, albeit from a distance and to a limited extent. In summary, the explanation of the Heidelberg Catechism amounts to this: the demand of this commandment is that your life be in accordance with the pattern of the life of God. As this is not automatically the case, the church services are required to create a proper sphere for your higher life and to nourish and equip you in that sphere. The fruit of this sphere must be that more of the pattern of the life of God becomes visible in you as sin is restrained and God's work is reflected in your life.

Up to this point there is nothing with which to find fault in the catechism; its explanation proceeds from a very deep and correct notion of the fourth commandment. Only one point should have emerged more clearly. More attention should have been paid to the succession of time in a seven-day cycle. It is a trait of our human life that we are not always the same. We get tired from work, and then sleep refreshes us. We become exhausted, and then our hunger and thirst demand food and drink. This means we cannot mix work and sleep, and that there must be distinct moments in which we take nourishment. This also holds for the spiritual realm. There are also spiritual moments when we need rest to feed and strengthen ourselves again. You do not know the human heart if you think that a person can continually pause and refresh themselves while working. This demands not only that there be a separate sphere for your higher life in the church, but also that there be a fixed structure, and that in the flow of days there be a specific day on which you can more particularly receive this spiritual nourishment. The catechism has not, it must be acknowledged, paid sufficient attention to this. It does speak of "the day of rest," but it does so more as a concession to praxis than as a consequence of God's ordinance.

This is not problematic, however, for it automatically flows from the principle that the catechism identifies in this commandment. If our human life is to proceed in accordance with the pattern of God's life, and if Scripture reveals to us that God completed his work of creation in six days and then rested from his work, then we humans, created in God's image, are also designed for such a cycle of seven days, in soul as well as in body. The church has well understood this by holding fast to the cycle of seven days in all countries and in every age, and by demanding that one in every seven days be devoted entirely to the life of the church and the nourishing of the spiritual life of God's children.

§3
> *Thus says the* Lord *of hosts: If you will walk in my ways and keep my charge, then you shall rule my house and have charge of my courts, and I will give you the right of access among those who are standing here.*
> Zechariah 3:7

Coming now to the primary principle that is expressed in the fourth commandment, we stand by our conviction that the pith and marrow of this divine ordinance is to be "imitators of God as his beloved children." This is exactly what Calvin says in his commentary on Genesis 2:3. There Calvin writes that God "he dedicated every seventh day to rest, that his own example might be a perpetual rule."[8] Thus, everything that is said in connection with this commandment about resting from work, attending church, and so forth is a derived rule, a logical consequence. But the actual principle that is established and sealed by this fourth commandment is the demand that our human life must not follow whim and caprice but be guided by the divine model.

Our human life is not an original life. It is a life that is tied to the image of God. For we are not created as something original but we are created in the image of God. The first commandment demands that we will not assail God as God from our own status as *persons*, the second that we will not oppose God with the world of our *senses*, and the third that we will not violate the name of God with our *name*. The fourth commandment does not address our personhood, or our world, or our name, but our *life*. It demands that our life does not conflict with God, and that to keep this from happening we should order our life in accordance with the pattern of God's life.

Only one of the many consequences that can be derived from this principle, the most striking one, is thrust into the foreground. Many more things are involved in the sixth commandment than murder, even though only murder is mentioned as the most striking instance. Similarly, many other things are involved in the eighth commandment than merely theft, even though only theft is mentioned as the worst transgression. So it is also the case in the fourth commandment. Behind this commandment stands much more than just observing the Sabbath. It covers, in fact, our whole life. Yet only observing the Sabbath is mentioned, because this is the point that makes you most aware of the force and significance of this commandment.

---

8. *CCS* 1:106.

You fail to appreciate the import of this commandment if you think that it can only be transgressed and violated by desecrating the Sabbath.

The seventh commandment only contains a prohibition against adultery. On that basis, someone could falsify the law by claiming that fornication and all kinds of unchastity are permitted because the seventh commandment only and exclusively condemns adultery, and adultery is possible only for married persons. For the same reason, we cannot limit the fourth commandment exclusively to what it specifically names. Instead, we need to penetrate to the root and principle from which this commandment springs. That principle, as Calvin put it, is that God's own example might be a perpetual rule. We humans, in other words, are under obligation to order our lives in accordance with the pattern of God's life—to be imitators of God as his beloved children. In short, the life of God, to the extent that it has been revealed to you, constitutes a pattern for your life, a pattern you must adhere to. As God worked six days and rested on the seventh day, you too, after working six days, should rest on the seventh.

Implicit in the fourth commandment are such biblical injunctions as these: Be holy, for I am holy. Be merciful, even as your Father is merciful. Forgive each other, as the Lord has forgiven you. Be perfect, as your heavenly Father is perfect. Be imitators of God. The richest revelation at the beginning of Scripture is that we have been created in the image of God, and the richest revelation toward the end of Scripture is the mystery that we are "children of God." A single golden thread connects, therefore, our creation with our completed redemption. The all-dominant thought, accordingly, of both the beginning point in our creation and the endpoint in our redemption is that our life must correspond to the life of God—albeit with our creaturely limitations. This main thought—that our life is to correspond with the life of God—is sealed in the fourth commandment and placed before us in the example of observing the Sabbath.

While we humans are in many respects related to the plant kingdom and the animal kingdom, human life far surpasses the life of plants and animals. Yet this higher position that we occupy relative to plants and animals does not consist in possessing an independent life. To desire this is precisely the satanic thought that casts our whole life into sin. Our honor and our glory consist only in this, that God was mirrored in man and that therefore the life of man can and must mirror the life of God. This means there is no arbitrariness. Instead, your life must be subject to a rule, to fixed ordinances that God determines, and which flow directly from the life of God. As God rested on the seventh day, your life is to be rhythmically divided by the number seven. He forgives, therefore you must forgive. He is perfect, so you must be perfect. This is the warp and woof of Scripture. *Be holy, for I am holy. Be imitators of God.*

The authors of the catechism also sensed this when they derived a general ordinance from this fourth commandment, namely, "that all the days of my life I rest from my evil works, allow the Lord to work in me by His Spirit, and thus begin in this life the everlasting sabbath." Surely this shows that the commandment not only applies to observing the day of rest but encompasses the whole of life. Its aim is that our own self-will and intractability will end and that God himself will direct our life according to the pattern of his own life. This will happen in such a way that, in our existence here on earth, a life will glimmer like the life as it will be in heaven.

Granted, the catechism expresses this symbolically, in accordance with the symbolic, archetypal meaning of the Sabbath. But the conclusion of the catechism amounts to the same basic principle of the fourth commandment. It applies not only to Sunday but to every day of our life. It serves to restrict our self-will and self-conceit, allowing us to be governed according to the pattern of God's life. Its fruit is that in our earthly life bears the stamp of the life that awaits us in glory, when "we shall be like him, because we shall see him as he is" [1 John 3:2]. Any small-mindedness must therefore be banished. Children of God must henceforth not think of the fourth commandment exclusively in terms of a day of rest. For three centuries the catechism has taught our churches otherwise, instructing us that this commandment applies to the whole of our human lives. Preaching about this commandment falls short when it sticks exclusively to the Sabbath question. A higher standpoint must be taken. It must go back to the general ordinance of God for the whole of life. The Sabbath rule must be viewed in the light of this general ordinance. The blessing of this commandment, which up to now has been limited almost exclusively to the keeping of Sunday, must be extended to cover our whole human existence.

It follows that the two things the catechism mentions—in the first place the church service and in the second place letting God work in us all the days of our life—are not separate things but flow directly from each other. The connecting link is the keeping of the Sabbath. We thus get three ideas. First, we should yield to God all the days of our human existence, so that he can transform our human life according to the pattern of his divine life. Second, in keeping with the revealed rhythm of the number seven in the divine life, we should also apply this rhythm in our human life, and therefore observe a day of rest. And third, for this to be so, we are to reveal in our lives the church of Christ and fill with her content the otherwise empty day of rest. As each commandment, including the fourth, is associated with particular sins, they drive a wedge between two opposite life spheres. Without sin there would be only one current, one breath, propelling all of life in the same direction. There would be no choice and no contest. The antithesis and conflict that commenced in paradise arose simply from the *possibility* of sinning. Had that possibility not existed in paradise, just as it will be entirely absent in glory, no antithesis would ever have arisen in Adam's spirit. No struggle would have waged in his innermost soul. Even the probationary commandment would have been unthinkable.[9] But since the incursion and proliferation of sin, the antithesis has penetrated life itself and has transferred this contest to our very existence. Everywhere now two currents flow and contrary winds blow, causing turbulence in the swells of life and breakers on its shores. Two lives in one existence. On the one hand, there is human life as it tries to construct itself from earthly forces according to human insight. Over against this is that same human life but as it is influenced inwardly by God, bearing a heavenly imprint and everywhere running counter to all that is earthly and self-conceited human life.

This is not yet a contrast such as that between demonic and divine. For then the earth would have to be destroyed, no longer susceptible to conversion and hence to redemption. This is not how it is. There is always one point that these two spheres of life have in common, and that commonality lies in creation, in that which common grace preserves and upholds of creation. Hence the points of contact and hence the possibility that this heavenly new life of the eternal Sabbath can to some extent be embodied in the church. This embodiment is of course imperfect, veiled, and often distorted. Yet the life of grace and rebirth, the life out of God and according to the pattern of God's life, takes on a certain form. It is not simply a utopian dream. Nor is it merely an object of hope. It is observable here on earth. We can say of a particular person, or family, or village that you can

---

9. Kuyper is using the term "probationary commandment" to refer to the following command given by God to Adam: "You may surely eat of every tree of the garden, but of the tree of the knowledge of good and evil you shall not eat, for in the day that you eat of it you shall surely die" (Gen 2:16–17). Kuyper provides a detailed discussion of the implications of this commandment in *CG* 1.25.

observe something of the higher life in them, whereas we need to say of another person, family, or village that they still sleep under the shroud of indifference.

These two life spheres exist, therefore, side by side and penetrate each other. The extent to which you surrender your sympathy, your exertion, and your devotion to the one or the other sphere tells you whether the heavenly life prevails in you, or whether you lie submerged under the pressure of the life of the world. Children of God do not already live entirely in that higher life, with all their strength, every moment of their lives, as though they have been pulled up entirely from that lower life. That is what the monks imagined, and that is the ideal that the ascetics pursued. But the result showed the inner truth of the apostle Paul's statement, "Not that I have already obtained this or am already perfect, but I press on to make it my own" [Phil 3:12]. This is precisely the source of the danger that causes us imperceptibly to fall away again from the divine nobility given to us when we were born again, and to sink back into the world. God's commandment opposes this danger and the sinful inclination of unbelief. You shall not, and must not, sink back into the earthly sphere. You need to allow yourself to be breathed upon by that higher life. God's life has to be the pattern and ordinance of your life. That is why you are to observe the day of rest. It will ensure that again and again the power of that worldly, earthly life is broken. Making manifest the church of Christ on the day of rest will allow this higher, spiritual life, to penetrate and permeate the common life of the world. Obeying the fourth commandment *every day* of our lives consists of two things that our catechism identifies, first negatively and then positively. The negative is that you must let go of your evil ways. The positive is that you must let God work in you. And it is from the joining of these two that the heavenly life—the eternal Sabbath—is born here on earth.

The catechism's handling of the fourth commandment is therefore deeply Reformed. It demonstrates the truth and purity of our Calvinistic confession, which seeks the praxis of the Christian religion precisely in "the dying of the old man, and the making alive of the new."[10] For this letting go of our evil ways is nothing other than the dying away of our old selves; and letting God work in us is nothing other than the coming to life of our new selves. This is, on the one hand, a manifestation of the life that must be put to death; on the other, a manifestation of the life that must be

---

10. Heidelberg Catechism, LD 33, A 88.

awakened. This awakening is never the fruit of what we do, but only of our willingness to place our spirit at the disposal of God the Holy Spirit so that he can accomplish his work in us.

Letting go of our evil ways is an expression of *liberation*. It marks children of God as being slaves to sin who are, against their own desire and will, repeatedly brought to doing all kinds of unholy work in the service of Satan and the world. But to the degree that the higher life gets more control over them, they get out from under this servitude. The evil dominance is broken, and in the end they can blissfully rest from their former sin. Even the urge to do it falls away, or at least its driving force has ceased. There is now room for letting God work in their heart.

Children of God cannot do two things at one and the same time: bowing under the yoke of sin and letting the Holy Spirit work in them. If the divine work in their will is to continue, that yoke of sin must first be lifted from their shoulders. There must come a glorious moment of reprieve and liberation from the tyranny of sin that allows the Holy Spirit to break through and gain in them a firm foothold. These two aspects are thus always related. Every day of their lives, God wants to grant his children moments when the yoke of sin is lifted from their shoulders. It is in those precious moments that the Holy Spirit wants to work in God's children. When God is at work in you, you let go of your evil ways. Inversely, when you let go of your evil ways, the working of the Holy Spirit becomes manifest in you. This will become evident not just in pious feelings and religious experiences. Thanks to God's work, it will also propel us to work in God's power, resulting in a life of tenderness of conscience, gentleness, humility, and patience. Through it, something of the heavenly Father is mirrored in his child; a spark of light begins to shine whereby our heavenly Father is glorified.

This ordering of our life according to the pattern of God's life is not, therefore, a question of imitation in the literal sense of the word. For how could human beings, in their creaturely limitations, ever live up to the life of God? The very thought is offensive and absurd. But the life of God does contain a holy order, a pattern of what this life allows and what it repels, a steady course that reflects a norm. So we are bound, within our creaturely limitations, to order our life in such a way that it corresponds to the holy order, the decisive pattern, and the steady course that is found in the life of God. This can only be achieved if we let go of the reins and surrender the control and direction of our *external* life to God's providence. In the same way, we need to yield the control and direction of our *internal* life to the indwelling Holy Spirit.

§4

There remains a Sabbath rest for the people of God.
Hebrews 4:9

A separate treatment is needed of the catechism's statement that the fourth commandment charges us to commence the eternal Sabbath already here on earth. This statement appears to be derived from Hebrews 4:9, which says that "there remains a Sabbath rest for the people of God"; and Hebrews 4:11, where believers are strongly admonished "to enter into that rest." What is intended in the epistle to the Hebrews is necessary, therefore, to gain a clear insight into the eternal Sabbath.

The point of departure in Hebrews is the appeal to Psalm 95:11: "Therefore I swore in my wrath, 'They shall not enter my rest.' " Psalm 95 is a hymn that urges singing praises to Yahweh, worshipping him, and surrendering completely to him. This on the grounds that it is he who made us, so that he is our God and we are the people of his pasture, the sheep of his hand. Yet the evil of the human heart goes so far that by nature human beings hate God and are inclined to resist him. This is apparent from what happened at Massah and Meribah in the wilderness. If there was ever a time when the whole nation of Israel should have clung to the Lord after its redemption from Egypt, it should have been then. But the opposite happened. The people grumbled against Yahweh and caused him grief. This angered him to such an extent that he said, "For forty years I loathed that generation and said, 'They are a people who go astray in their heart, and they have not known my ways.' Therefore I swore in my wrath, 'They shall not enter my rest.' "[11]

From this the writer to the Hebrews infers that, given the danger of forsaking God is still great, believers of the new covenant must always watch and struggle in order not to exclude themselves, like Israel, from God's rest. But this raised the question in the New Testament church whether that rest of God was still open to enter. Israel in the wilderness was offered the rest that awaited them in Canaan. But Israel forfeited that rest and did not enter Canaan, dying instead in the wilderness. But how could there still be an entering into the rest of God, since Christians no longer wandered about in the wilderness and there could be no question of "entering Canaan"?

---

11. *Note by the author*: The word "rest" here translates the Hebrew word for "Sabbath."

To counter this objection, Hebrews makes an appeal to Psalm 95, which was sung so many centuries after the entry into Canaan under Joshua and which had been given to the psalmist by God. In that psalm, the Lord calls to his people, "Today, if you hear my voice, do not harden your hearts, as at Meribah, as on the day at Massah in the wilderness." This would not make any sense unless in David's day the entry into the rest of God was still open.

It follows that the offer of the promise to enter into God's rest was still valid after Joshua, and in the days of David, and therefore also today, according to Hebrews. Thus, all God's people throughout the ages had to be offered the promise that if they persevered in the faith they would enter into the rest of God. For the writer to the Hebrews, the rest in Canaan was offered not only to Israel; the promise still holds that there is a rest for the people of God.

How are we to understand this? What connection is there between the rest in Canaan and the rest that remains for the people of God? And how can the intended rest be called the rest of God? For the writer of Hebrews expressly states that the rest that remains for the people of God is the same rest in which God rests. It is the rest of Genesis 2:3 that is quoted in Hebrews 4:4, "God rested from all his works." The rest with which God rested following the completion of his work of creation, the rest that was promised to Israel in Canaan, and the rest that remains for the people of God—these three must in essence be one. In order to understand this, each of these three must be further elucidated.

When it says of God that after six days of creating he rested, this cannot be taken to mean doing nothing or complete idleness. Christ's words, "My Father is working until now, and I am working" [John 5:17] flatly contradicts and precludes this. The resting of God can therefore be called resting from the initial work of creation—the bringing forth and ordering, the calling into being of the creaturely sphere. The work of creation bore a unique character. It involved calling into being that which was not—bringing about the object to which God would extend his divine excellencies.

But now this object existed; heaven and earth were finished. The work God had undertaken had come to an end because the creation on which the gaze of God's omnipotence and wisdom could rest had come into being. But this rest did not involve letting go of this creation. It was, rather, a resting in this creation such that God maintained it, rejoiced in it, and brought it toward its ultimate goal.

A similar course was prefigured for the descendants of Adam, in whom God delighted [Prov 8:31]. A path was designed for them whereby through the fulfilling of God's commandments, and thus through moral-creative work, they would eventually cease from this work and receive eternal life as a reward for that work. Assume that sin had not intervened and human beings had finished their work, then after completing their moral-creative work they would have entered their rest. This rest would have been everlasting life. And the eternal rest of human beings would have coincided in perfect harmony with the eternal rest of God. This follows the pattern that, as human beings are created in God's image, their existence must reflect the course of God's life. The end of their path through life must be entering into full fellowship with their Creator.

The resting of God of which we read in Genesis 2:3 is therefore not the complete rest that will come at the end of time. It is the rest of God with regard to external creation, but God's rest from spiritual creation in the human world would only be entire when the human race had completed its course. Then, forever at one with their Creator in the kingdom of glory, human beings would radiate the full counsel of the Lord in all its splendor.

This would also have been the case had sin not intervened, since Adam did not yet possess eternal life but had received its promise. God's rest from spiritual creation would, therefore, only reach its full completion when Adam entered into that eternal life. But this is even more true now that sin has intervened and thus the whole work of grace still had to follow the work of creation. This work of grace alone would make possible the kingdom of glory, and with it the full realization of the rest of God. This brings us to the second point that requires our attention. We wanted first to elucidate God's rest, but now we come to Israel's rest in Canaan. This rest can only be symbolic. For it cannot be that Canaan would be for the Jews the actual heaven where they would live forever, so that the entrance into Canaan was equal to the entrance into eternal life. Canaan's rest was not the eternal rest itself but a representation of the eternal rest. Even as Israel in the national sense would find rest in Canaan, so also would the child of God find eternal rest in the heavenly Canaan. As the writer of Hebrews puts it, Joshua had not led them into the true rest, the essential rest; this great work would be completed only through that other Joshua, whom we worship in Jesus as our Lord and King.

We must avoid, however, understanding this symbolic meaning in a superficial sense. An example would be applying it to the Trek of the Boers from the Cape to Transvaal.[12] God selected Canaan deliberately to be the inheritance of his people. It was a garden of delight, overflowing with God's riches as no other country. In that land God had elected Zion as the place of his rest. He had designated it as the place for his sanctuary and had ordained that in that place sacrifices were to be brought and ceremonies were to be held. In all countries, and among all peoples around Canaan, an unholy power reigned. Yet in that small country of Canaan God had ordained a holy order and a ministry of reconciliation from which would go out the salvation of the world. In that Canaan lay therefore the germ of the coming spiritual salvation for the whole world and of a faith that put people at peace with God.

There is more. God's rest that is to come, into which all of God's elect shall enter, was not a purely spiritual ideal. One day it would be revealed in a rich splendor that would shine on a new earth under a new heaven. The heavenly Canaan will therefore not only consist of a blessed spiritual experience but will also possess an external, tangible splendor which for God's elect will forever be the world they behold. God's rest after the six-day creation is precisely God's resting in the creature he fashioned. The richness of external creation cannot be absent in the eternal rest of God. Canaan was therefore more than a symbol; it also bore a *typical* character because the salvation of the world would spring from it. Again, the external nature of Canaan was not be understood in an exclusively spiritual sense; it also carried a prophecy of the external glorious reality that will take effect when Christ comes on the clouds and the new earth under the new heaven will be revealed. Those who in the wilderness, and later in Israel, rejected this symbolic and typical Canaan rejected at the same time all that the symbol stood for and all that was initially given in this type. Conversely, those who embraced the symbol in faith entered into more than the visible Canaan. At the same time they embraced, along with their external riches, a spiritual, internal treasure.

The third rest to which our attention is directed is *the rest for the people of God*. This will not receive its full manifestation until the kingdom of glory commences and the archangel proclaims: "It is done" [Rev 21:6]. Only then will that which was merely symbolized in Canaan shine in full reality and

---

12. A reference to Dutch-speaking settlers (Boers) in southern Africa, who migrated eastward to Transvaal in wagon convoys (the Trek) in the 1830s to free themselves from the British colonial administration of Cape Colony.

perpetuity. And precisely for this reason there did still remain a rest for the people of God, a rest which had to come because the promise of entering it had been fulfilled symbolically but not yet in reality. For the people of God this resting is in part resting *from* something and in part resting *in* something. In the absence of sin, Adam would have entered into that rest as soon as he could rest from his meritorious works and receive the reward of eternal life. For us, who are conceived and born in sin, that rest will begin only when our striving will cease, as we have died to sin and been released from life's miseries. But that is still only a resting from sin, vain works, and misery. In and of itself this would simply issue into a quiet idleness of doing nothing. Resting from sin, vain works, and misery must, therefore, be accompanied by a resting in something positive, a resting in the rest of God. Since this rest of God, as we saw earlier, is not a doing nothing but an ever-deeper immersion in his work, so also will this rest of God not be a sitting passively. It will, instead, be an ever-greater immersion in, and therefore richer enjoyment of, all that God has accomplished. This then shall be the eternal Sabbath, when everything is finished and the eternal enjoyment will begin.

When our forebears wanted to settle for the first time in our country, they first had to reclaim our soil from swamp and seaweed, build dykes and polders to recover the land; they had to create our soil, as it were. Only when that work was finished did they enter into their national rest. But they had not reclaimed the soil in order to stand on it idly, but to live on it, to live for it, and to enjoy it. To use another image: Scripture not infrequently compares this eternal rest to a banquet. In advance of a banquet, hard work is needed to prepare everything. But once everything has been prepared, the fatigue ends, not in order to sit down at the prepared meal with one's hands in one's lap, but to sit down and enjoy what the banquet offers.

This then is the eternal Sabbath to which "he who works until now" calls his elect, and to which one day he will lead them. But this leaves a final question to be addressed: namely, How can we begin this eternal Sabbath already here on earth, and in what way is this enjoined in the fourth commandment? This requires that we pay attention to three things.

In the first place, note that our faith does not embrace the covenant of works but the covenant of grace. The center of this covenant of grace is the cross of Golgotha, and from this cross sounds the blessed shout that all is finished. To believe in Christ and his atonement is therefore to rest from all work whereby we might earn salvation and to rest in the finished work of the Lord. To believe is to rest from being reproached by our conscience, from being pursued by guilt and sin, as well as from trying to weave our garment of holiness ourselves. It has already been finished. The guilt has been atoned. The law has been satisfied. And a good conscience accrues to us as a gift from the Father of lights. All unbelief, all doubt, all lack of faith therefore means falling back into struggle, wandering again in the wilderness, being again pursued and driven. And every return to faith means to come out again from under that struggle, and from being driven, in order to enter into the rest that Christ has obtained. "Come to me, all who labor and are heavy laden, and I will give you rest" [Matt 11:28]. This is not yet a beholding, still less the full enjoyment of the eternal Sabbath. We still walk by faith. But through the marvelous energy that lies in this faith, God's children, insofar as their guilt and their conscience are concerned, enjoy the glorious privilege of beginning *in this life* the eternal Sabbath.

The second point concerns our external life, with all the sorrow and weariness of spirit that the world and its misery cause us. For you cannot escape them, and they will continue to burden you until your death. Nevertheless, if you are truly a living member of his body, the sting of that suffering has already been put to death within you by Christ. This is seen most clearly in the martyrs who were robbed, separated from their loved ones, incarcerated in filthy holes, harassed and tormented, provoked and tortured, and in the end most cruelly put to death. They nevertheless did not succumb under all this bitter suffering but sang psalms and rejoiced in God. For this reason, the Holy Spirit is called the Comforter, because it is he who transforms your experience deep within your soul, causes you to undergo the troubles of life in a different way, and makes you more than a conqueror through Christ who gives you strength.

This leads us to the third and final point, namely, the heavenly joy which the Lord gives his elect to enjoy *here on earth*. Not always, mind you. Sometimes the elect traverse very dark paths, as through the valley of the shadow of death. Also, their love is not always warm, their heart is not always sensitive, and the gate of heaven sometimes feels closed to them. But now and then a moment of heavenly refreshment comes to them. A blessedness flows through their breast which no worldly glitter can give them. Experiencing this depends on whether indwelling sin is stirring within them. They carry such sin until the day they die, but they can either allow it to stir, or they can bind it so tightly that it does not stir at all. To the degree that the sin dwelling within them is shackled, rather than given free rein, their ears open up to the heavenly music and a heavenly joy radiates in their heart.

If all this is possible, it must also be a reality. Thus God wills, in this fourth commandment, that all his elect and his gathered children on earth will, already in this life, begin that eternal Sabbath.

It is therefore a desecration of the Sabbath and a violation of this fourth commandment whenever you put your faith "out of service." Instead of resting by faith in the finished work of Christ, you sink back under your guilt through unbelief, or put your hand to vain works in an effort to earn your salvation. Thus it is a desecration of the Sabbath and a violation of the fourth commandment whenever, instead of triumphing by faith over the suffering and sorrow of this world, you succumb under your sorrow and adversity. This leaves you unable to do anything because your state of unbelief prevents Christ from giving you strength. It is also a desecration of the Sabbath and a violation of the fourth commandment, finally, whenever you allow your indwelling sin to disturb your inner peace by its stirring and goading. This closes off your heart to the heavenly joy that can descend into your soul.

Do not object that this is highly spiritual. It is simply what our catechism says, and the life of God's children must be highly spiritual. It cannot be otherwise. Because you have been created in God's image, your human life must be ordered in accordance with the pattern of God's life. This is and remains the requirement and the rule of the Sabbath: even as God rested from his work, so also shall you.

§5
*From new moon to new moon, and from Sabbath to Sabbath, all
flesh shall come to worship before me, declares the* Lord.
Isaiah 66:23

In this concluding section on the fourth commandment, we will discuss what the Catechism mentions first: maintaining the gospel ministry and education. We have already seen how this obligation is linked with the letter of the fourth commandment. The fourth commandment teaches that your life shall proceed in accordance with the pattern of God's life. As God rested after his work, there must also be rest for you after your work. This rest of God is not about doing nothing but about eternally being occupied with the glorification of his Name. The eternal Sabbath must, therefore, begin in this life. But in order for it not to vanish into thin air but to take on a tangible form for you, the church of Christ represents a sphere of life that is entirely of heavenly origin.

Those among our brothers and sisters who are inclined toward the mystical should take this instruction especially to heart. For we often encounter a measure of indifference toward the visible church in those Christians who are mystically disposed. To them it consists merely of forms and external shapes that have nothing to do with salvation. All the desire of their soul is directed toward the inner good and an intimate fellowship with the Eternal Being. It therefore does not matter to them whether the church to which they belong is profoundly corrupted. They do wish it were different, but now that this is the way it is, they will not lift a finger toward reforming their church. They are content to be left alone, "in a little nook with a little book," so that they can feast on devotional food for their soul.[13]

There is great benefit, of course, to this warmth of the mystical life. A piety that is devoid of this holy mysticism shrivels or ossifies. All religion is, after all, ultimately mystical at root. It is beyond comprehension how a strong and joyful faith can exist without a mystical union of the soul with Jesus. Given that no one comes to the Father but by him, how can you long for intimate fellowship with the eternal Being if your soul does not burn with a mystical love for Jesus? But as indisputably true as this is, it remains equally true that it is not for us to chart a course through this devout mysticism. The history of the church throughout the ages repeatedly shows how mystically disposed souls who fended for themselves fell into all kinds of heresy and even into all kinds of moral aberrations. Virtually all the circles in which this mystical self-conceit was dominant degenerated into freethinking and dissoluteness.

Strive therefore with all your heart for the deep mystical life of your soul with Christ, but remain at the same time godly. For all godliness consists in the first place in this, that you do not choose your own path in this mysticism but that you walk in the ways of the Lord. The Lord has laid out these ways for you in his Word, and the mysticism of your heart can therefore remain healthy only when you subject yourself to that Word. The first demand of that Word is not that you "taste your delights" but that

---

13. This paragraph is directed at the kind of Reformed people among whom Kuyper lived and worked as a pastor in Beesd, his first parish, from 1863 to 1867. They emphasized experiential religion over intellectual assent and formal adherence. They often preferred frequenting the conventicles rather than the official worship services.

God will be glorified through you, in the manner he has laid out for you. Even though it seems quite profound and quite spiritual to experience all manner of internal bliss, if these spiritual delights become the main thing and the glorification of God's Name does not continue to occupy the first place in your thoughts, then your piety is self-seeking. It lacks the self-denying character that does not ask, "How will things be good for me?" but quite otherwise: "Whatever I experience, let the honor go to God." Isaiah stressed the importance of remaining true to God's Word when faced with false teachers: "To the teaching and to the testimony! If they will not speak according to this word, it is because they have no dawn" [Isa 8:20]. Let this be the bridle that is applied to the mysticism of our heart. It pleased God to give his church not only a spiritual but also an external existence, and to establish in this external church his ministry to be maintained and kept pure by his children. Therefore, no mysticism, no matter how heartfelt, can release a single child of God from this obligation. Any child of God who relieves themselves of this obligation is not obedient to God.

This is not to value dry formalism over inspired warmth of feeling. A church that is arid has slipped off its spiritual foundation. Our purpose is precisely the reverse: to remind those brothers and sisters who by grace are richer in their interior life that they have an obligation. This obligation is not to turn away from the external church because of its lack of warmth, but rather to deepen and warm up the life of the church through the glow of their own hearts. The gifts of the Spirit are divided on earth. To the one the Lord gives more clarity of belief, to the other more fervor of soul. It is precisely through the joining together of both these elements that the true life of the church begins to blossom. The mystical soul cannot do without fellowship with persons who have received more doctrinal clarity, and the latter cannot do without fellowship with their mystical brothers and sisters. What God has joined together, they must not separate. Obedience is better than sacrifice, and anyone who arrogantly separates themselves from fellow believers to whom other gifts have been given deprives both themselves and those believers. They do not walk in the obedience of faith. See how beautifully our catechism joins the two when it addresses the fourth commandment. It brings together, on the one hand, the mystical element, as God works in us we begin in this life the eternal Sabbath. But also, on the other hand, and even mentioned in the first place, the demand of truth: to maintain the gospel ministry and education, to use the sacraments, and to contribute to the relief of the poor.

The fact that education is mentioned implies much more than is generally assumed. According to Ursinus's commentary, the word "education" here refers in the first place to the universities and not, as has been thought somewhat one-sidedly in recent times, to Christian day schools for children. Nevertheless, when we look at the root of the matter we find that both are implied here.

God has, in his mercy toward us, revealed his truth. But he has given this truth to the world in a written form which initially was couched in languages that are entirely foreign to us. Furthermore, he does not give us this truth in a ready form such as we need for our human consciousness. This does not mean of course that someone who learns these foreign languages, and then investigates how the church has gradually extracted the truth from this gold mine of the Word and poured it into a form that our consciousness requires, can therefore be deemed to understand God's truth. The natural person does not accept the things of the Spirit of God [1 Cor 2:14]. And a young person who desires to enter the ministry of the Word and reckons that their external studies sufficiently equip them for the ministry is utterly in error. Those who attend only the university on earth and remain strangers to the university of the Holy Spirit are in danger of giving their congregation stones for bread. But as strongly as we state this, we must equally strongly state that neither is there benefit in the opposite situation.

For there are those who imagine that inner spiritual enrichment is sufficient and that they who know the academy of the Spirit can bypass and despise the earthly academy. This is generally untrue and flatly contradicts Scripture. Note that we say generally. There are exceptions. It cannot be denied that it may please the Lord, according to the needs of the time, to bestow in a very special way on this or that person not only spiritual insight but also insight into the Word and the gift of speaking. Our Reformed churches explicitly acknowledge this in the well-known article 8, and they have never hesitated to open up the ministry of the Word to anyone who indeed appears to be "singularly gifted" for serving the church.[14] It would be possible to draw up not so short a list of people who were thus gifted over

---

14. This article (7a in modern Reformed church order) reads: "Those who have not received the prescribed theological training but give evidence that they are singularly gifted as to godliness, humility, spiritual discretion, wisdom, and the native

the centuries and who have in a rare manner edified God's church. This fact deserves mention if only because it necessarily strikes down the pride and vainglory of those who pride themselves on their study and knowledge of languages. All pride is an abomination to the Lord, and even as the person of study has been appointed by God to shame all spiritual conceit, so does the person of singular gifts exist to remind the person of study that they are nothing in and of themselves.

That said, it is certain that education at both "academies" must be the rule. Almost all people of influence whom God has given to his church over the centuries, specifically our famous Reformed theologians (in England as well as in the Netherlands) — Calvin and Bullinger, Voetius and Walaeus, Perkins and Owen, Brakel and à Marck, Comrie and Smijtegelt, and so many more — were educated both formally at the earthly academy and inwardly at the academy of the Holy Spirit. This is why the catechism puts so decidedly in the foreground that education, too, must be maintained.

The Anabaptists have always denied this, and it is precisely against this error that our Reformed churches have impressed this on its congregations. What is the issue here? Well, it could have pleased God to put his kingdom of grace entirely outside the kingdom of nature, which is precisely what the Anabaptists insist on. Then, of course, God's children would not have had to be involved with human study, with science or with scholarship, and they would have found in their Bible the truth in a clear, readily understood form, so that without further study or thought they merely had to repeat the words of Scripture. But this is not what God was pleased to do. Grace links up everywhere with nature. It is fallen Adam who is raised. It is corrupt nature that is restored and re-created. Correspondingly, the truth is deposited in Scripture as in a gold mine, but it must be extracted. Study and scholarship must serve to complete this grand work. That is why our Reformed forebears not only established schools for the training of ministers but also strongly urged the establishing of universities where all liberal arts and sciences would be taught in the fear of the Lord. The church of Christ must be able to raise her head with honor in this world, and she can do this only if Christianity confesses the truth of God in all areas of knowledge and takes part in all fields of study. For our forefathers the training of preachers was never the goal they pursued. Their schools were

---

ability to preach the Word, may, by way of exception, be admitted to the ministry of the Word."

to excel in all fields of learning, and it was in such schools that prospective ministers of the Word had to be armed to glorify God as his servants in the midst of the congregation.

Precisely from this perspective, and by dint of the same principle, we acknowledge that Christian education for children is implicit in the maintenance of schools of which the catechism speaks. For if in the church of God the truth is proclaimed, there has not only to be someone who speaks but also those who hear. This hearing cannot go well unless the hearers have been instructed since childhood in the ways of the truth. For hearing in the church is not merely listening but also comprehending, entering with one's whole consciousness into what is being said, and thus also entering spiritually into what the preacher says. This is impossible if our children are educated in a pagan context and then are transferred once a week on Sunday into an entirely different world of ideas. Such unprepared hearing means hearing sounds but not understanding anything. People then fill the pews but have no connection with what is being said. The disastrous result is that preachers, in order not to speak above the heads of their listeners, must restrict themselves to first principles. Unable to move on to higher things, they become hollow and boring. For preaching to blossom, therefore, it is necessary not only that there be schools where preachers learn to preach, but also schools where hearers learn to hear.

But there is more. In the church there must be no priestly tyranny: the freedom of the children of God must be upheld. This freedom will be lost if church members are not capable of reading Scripture in such a way that they learn to understand its meaning. They also need to be able to better themselves by reading spiritual writings. Rome shows what becomes of the church when her members do not read.

The absence of good Christian schools promotes clericalism, the evil against which the whole Reformed church in every country took a courageous and robust stand. But while the Anabaptist sought to leave the world, the Calvinist wanted to glorify God *in the world*. Thus it is also necessary for church members that, by receiving a good education in their youth, they are equipped to fulfil with excellence any kind of trade or office. For this to happen, they need to be well instructed during their youth in matters of society. This will allow them later to honor Christ in the midst of society. Every child of God that excels in their profession is an honor to Christ's church.

This goes even deeper if you pay attention to the ideas of maintenance and bringing Christian alms in the catechism's response to the fourth commandment. The church's ministry takes a lot of money to fund, especially when you add in costly missionary work. This money can be collected by begging, asking Jews, Roman Catholics, and unbelievers to deposit money for our churches in the national treasury, and allowing ourselves be paid from their money. But this goes against the honor of Christ's church. It makes the church of Christ dependent on the unbelieving power of government. It hinders the continuing purification and reformation of the church. And it fosters clericalism, because it places the ministers, being paid by the state, outside the congregation. History shows that nothing has spoiled the church so much as alien money, alms received from the state. The early Christians did not even consider this—they paid for everything themselves. Our churches under the cross in the sixteenth century did the same. And those churches that have come to spiritual flowering in our time have followed the same principle.[15]

If this is so, a great deal of money needs be collected. It has been calculated that this amounts on average to six guilders per person, to which then must be added at least another four guilders per person for schools and missions (the number of persons include, of course, the children and the poor).[16] Where can this money be found? It must of course come from the annual incomes of the members of the congregation. The money must be earned and acquired in civil society. The beautiful rule of Calvinism is this: through her preaching the church is to elevate and inspire her members, including in the fulfilling of their God-given occupations. The members of your church should, as good Calvinists, earn more than others through the faithful execution of their duties; through greater zeal; through putting more of their heart into their work. It is precisely from these extra earnings that the money should come for maintaining the ministry of your church and all that is associated with it.

Sound preaching must make us Calvinists more sober and thrifty, so that we are left with more disposable income. Such preaching should make us manage our households more economically. With greater earnings and fewer expenditures, plenty of money should become available for the

---

15. For a discussion of state funding for church ministers, see *OP*, 21.II.305.
16. *Note by the author*: A church of a thousand souls requires at least 6,000 guilders for its worship services and diaconate, and another 4,000 guilders for schools and missions.

ministry of the Lord. For this very reason, our schools must be maintained—schools that are practical and reputable, organized on Reformed principles, and capable of equipping members of the church for their conduct in society. Everything is interconnected in this way. The church itself should not establish the schools, nor run them, but she should promote their health and well-being. Conversely, the schools must be one of the means to make the ministry of the church financially viable and to keep the quality of the preaching at a high level.

In reflecting on the catechism's handling of the fourth commandment, we shall not cover the ministry of the church as such. This is discussed in the sections on the church and on the sacraments.[17] Nor shall we discuss here the Christian ministry of charity, in part because it belongs to the doctrine of the church[18] and in part because it will be discussed later, in connection with the eighth commandment.[19] Concerning charity, let us only say here that Calvinism does not reckon on the existence of pauperism in its own circles. This is because good, sound preaching, vigorous church government, and good schools must make pauperism among church members almost impossible. Within our own circles, it is primarily helpless widows and orphans who need to be cared for, as well as those who are temporarily in need through illness or accident. Our calling does involve, however, taking care also of those who are outside our circle. Jesus went through the country to take care of the blind, the deaf, the sick, and the demon-possessed, and to feed the hungry. The task of Christ's church, accordingly, is to take her place in the midst of society and act as a benefactor to those who have sunk into poverty, and as a helper to those who suffer and are in distress. Although we know how far we fall short in this, the ideal must be repeatedly stressed. Preaching, even more than diaconal services, must counter the poverty in our own circles. As already noted, the fruit of preaching must be that Calvinists become increasingly successful in their occupations, thereby acquiring the means to uphold the honor of Christ in the world through open-handed generosity.

---

17. Kuyper deals with these topics in his treatments in *E Voto* of Lord's Day 21 and Lord's Day 25 (not included in this anthology).

18. See *On the Church*, 27–28, 32–33, 146, 160, 186–87; *CG* 2.67.4–5:664–66; *PR* 2.II.21.2–4:284–86.

19. Kuyper's discussion in *E Voto* of the Catechism's treatment of the eighth commandment is included in this anthology. See "You Shall Not Steal," 33–81.

Even though preaching still lacks such effectiveness, it is making progress. The realization is gradually gaining ground that the sermon is not a training ground for amateurs, nor an endless repetition of what everybody already knows, but a power that changes the life of the congregation.

May such powerful preaching increasingly become the norm. We do not need sermons that try to be titillating or entertaining and are therefore embellished with all kinds of stories and anecdotes. We need sermons that demonstrate profound thought and reflection, a depth of mystical life, knowledge of God's Word, and familiarity with spiritual and social needs. May every Sunday in all our churches be heard the voice of God, rather than of human beings. This voice will wound like a double-edged sword. It will strike down all pride like a hammer. And it will rescue and restore, with everlasting arms of compassion, all that is sinking as a result of sin and suffering.

WORKING PEOPLE AND THE CHURCH

TEXT INTRODUCTION

One of Kuyper's first publications on the social question appeared soon after he took up a pastorate in Amsterdam as a minister in the Dutch Reformed Church. It was the introduction to a pamphlet, translated into Dutch from the German, titled *Zur Arbeiterfrage. Von einem Landpfarrer für Landpfarrer und für Alle welche es lesen wollen* [On the social question: From a country parson for country parsons and for anyone who wants to read it] (Halle: Pfeffer, 1870).

The author of this 30-page tract is anonymous. It may have been written by Wilhelm von Ketteler (1811–77), Roman Catholic bishop of Mainz and the father of modern Catholic social thought. But whoever was its "country parson" author, the text is clearly influenced by Ketteler's thought. The Dutch version was published as *De Arbeiderskwestie en de Kerk. Een woord over het sociale vraagstuk. Naar het Hoogduitsch. Ingeleid door Dr. A. Kuyper* [Working people and the church. A word about the social question. Translated from High German. Introduced by Dr. A. Kuyper] (Amsterdam: Kesteren, 1871). In the Introduction, Kuyper calls for more practical engagement by the church with burning social issues.

Rejecting the argument that the church should be narrowly focused on the salvation of individual souls, Kuyper argues that the church as a prominent social institution must be concerned about whole people in their daily existence. The church's involvement in works of mercy and private philanthropy, while praiseworthy, is insufficient, he maintained. Instead merely of fighting this or that isolated social issue, the church needed to be alert and open-handed in bringing comfort and healing to all in need.

It is clear from this pamphlet introduction that in 1871 Kuyper was very exercised about the adverse social conditions of his time. He was, however, a long way off from the standpoint he took twenty years later in his magisterial address on the "Social Question and the Christian Religion," included in this anthology. There he argued that the church as an organic body of believers in society ought to address the root cause of social misery: namely, the very structure of society.

SOURCE: The text of Kuyper's introduction to the pamphlet noted above is reprinted in W. F. de Gaay Fortman, *Architectonische critiek. Fragmenten uit de sociaal-politieke geschriften van Dr. A. Kuyper* (Amsterdam: Paris, 1956), 27–29.

WORKING PEOPLE AND THE CHURCH

Aside from questions of detail and style, I am fully sympathetic to the standpoint defended in this pamphlet. Its author is a village pastor. I emphasize this because it lends particular weight to what he writes. It also characterizes the special nature of his standpoint.

It is a symptom of spiritual poverty if the church of Christ is afraid to address the burning problems of the day. Yet to date she has not dared to do so, and this pithy tract rightly reproaches her for it.

Burning problems can never lie outside the church's scope of activity. It must be granted that in a problem of this sort all kinds of purely financial, constitutional, and political issues are involved—issues for which the church cannot provide solutions. Nevertheless, these issues are only secondary, deriving their relative importance from the bigger problem that is always central to every problem, the problem of life itself.

There is not a single problem that exercises us that does not concern human beings. In all these problems, however complex they may be, human beings always play a central role; and it is because of humans as living souls that such a question is called a *burning* problem.

Now if it is undeniable that in each of these problems *humans*—or, if you will, *humankind*—is primary, then it is also indisputable that the solution must vary depending on one's view of humans, and equally, that the real solution will not be found unless humans are taken for what they really are.

Given that the question *What are human beings?* receives two diametrically opposed answers depending on whether one reckons with revelation or disbelieves revelation, it follows that the solution to such a burning problem can be expected from only two quarters: either from revelation, or from the standpoint that opposes God's Word.

The church of Christ calls herself the mother and bearer of revelation, and her ministers act as priests and interpreters. One of two things therefore: either her ministers do not believe in revelation with their whole heart, and humans for them are not really who revelation says they are; or if humans for them are really what revelation says they are, they must feel the impulse to say to those of other minds: "Your search for a solution to the problem is in vain because you do not reckon with human beings as they really are. I know who humans really are, not by my own lights, but by the light that revelation sheds upon them. Allow me, therefore, to let this light fall upon the problem and let the success or failure of my attempt be the touchstone for the soundness of the revelation that I believe in."

No one can object to that, unless one wishes to remove the beautiful word "mercy" from the church's coat of arms.

Every burning problem, after all, and above all the social problem of the working classes, arises from dire needs, wretched conditions, and painful woes, and therefore calls for the healing balm on a hurting social wound.

How could one conceive of a church of Christ that had no heart for such suffering and that did not feel the urge to let her Savior shine in this area with the majesty of his redeeming love? Is suffering humankind not the very field assigned to her, and are not "the little people of this world" the very ones that are entrusted to her care, for the purpose of showing these the power of her consolation, the strength of her life principle, and the blessing of her whole presence?

It cannot be a good thing before God, therefore, that the church of Christ in our country has been so apathetic in dealing with this social problem.

We do not want to detract in any way from what Heldring and his followers have accomplished.[1] Yet one will readily agree that to offer help for

---

1. Rev. Ottho Heldring (1804-76) was a country pastor who pioneered programs to alleviate the social hardships of his parishioners by digging wells, reclaiming land, setting up literacy classes, and establishing homes for orphans and neglected children.

existing needs, to combat an isolated social ill, and to save individual souls is not the same as tackling, with the holy zeal of faith, the *social question itself*. Moreover, what a few have done does not exonerate *the church as a whole*.

Accordingly, it might be useful if the voice in this pamphlet gets through to the members and the ministers of our church.

In the long run the world cannot respect the church of Christ if she talks about the power of the *Word of God* but does not allow that power to work when faced with human suffering.

The work of the church, it will perhaps be objected, *concerns the soul*, and if that is not meant in a narrow spiritual sense I agree; but then allow me to ask in turn whether those who work with their hands will not with their whole soul turn their backs on the church of Jesus when warm interest in the conditions of their daily life is always absent in that church.

The social problem of the working classes is here.

The church too cannot shut her eyes to it.

Regarding this problem, may the spirit of Christ demonstrate saving power!

SUNDAY REST AND HYGIENE

TEXT INTRODUCTION

A small but significant component of Kuyper's social program was legislation that would put limits on Sunday labor. There were few limits in his
time. In the national postal service, for example, mail carriers delivered
mail not only three times a day but also seven days a week.

Industrializing countries were, however, beginning to pay attention
to this issue. Great Britain as early as 1780 saw Parliament pass *An Act
preventing certain Abuses and Profanations on the Lord's Day called Sunday*, a
law which in time led to the prohibition of work in certain sectors of the
economy. In the nineteenth century, Belgium and the United States enacted
similar laws, and one of Kuyper's first acts as prime minister in 1901 was
to commission a Free University graduate to draft a bill regarding Sunday
rest and Sunday labor.[1]

On what grounds did Kuyper deem government action in this area to
be warranted? An emphasis on public health might require setting legal
limits to Sunday labor. A plea for providing opportunities for recreation
and spending time with the family also made sense. In themselves these
might be valid arguments in favor of some form of Sunday observance.
Yet in Kuyper's eyes they were insufficient. The grounds for government

---

1. The man was Tiemen de Vries, who had earned his doctorate with the thesis *Overheid
en Zondagsviering* [Government and Sunday observance] (Leyden: Sijthoff, 1899).

regulation of Sunday rest must ultimately be found in God's commandment to keep the Sabbath.[2]

It is clear from Kuyper's party program, however, that he did not envisage the establishment of the so-called theocracy some secularists feared. Indeed, if empirical social evidence lent a weekly shared day of rest, Kuyper was prepared, as the following texts show, to invoke this evidence, rather than rely solely on the Sabbath command. His aim was clearly to persuade people, whether they shared his starting principle or not, that Sunday observance served the common good and that its neglect was both harmful and costly.

SOURCE: These two articles were appended in abridged form ("Bijlage G") to chapter 6 of the first edition of *Ons Program* (Amsterdam: J. H. Kruyt, 1879), 235–39. They first appeared in *De Standaard* of July 21 and 24, 1876. Translated by Harry Van Dyke.

---

2. See also *OP*, §§69–71.

SUNDAY REST AND HYGIENE

Hygiene is one of the latest sciences to gain a public voice.[1] No school is built, no social housing designed, without its input. It supervises children's vaccination programs and inspects home sanitation systems. It looks with disfavor on our churchyards and will soon banish burials to the moors. It has instructed the state to make certain regulations and has been given authority to enforce the same. It has done a great deal of good by replacing dampness and dirt with fresh air, cleanliness and orderliness, although as true Protestants we reserve the right to review its "scientific results" with a critical eye.

We are pleased to note, however, that the science of hygiene has come to our aid on a question that is very important to us. We mean the observance of Sunday, the desirability of keeping the Sabbath. If you advocate this in the name of God, many will not hear of it. Whatever the church recommends is viewed with suspicion, and whoever has the courage to review a social question from the point of view of the church, or vice versa, is called to order with great vehemence.[2]

---

1. By "hygiene," Kuyper refers here to what is often today called "public health."
2. This sentence reflects Kuyper's experience in Parliament to this date.

Sunday observance leaves a lot to be desired in our country. The number of industries that work on Sundays is increasing. Many people demand more opportunities for entertainment on that day. For them, Sunday is turning into a curse, not a blessing. It does not refresh but exhausts. It harms rather than heals. For thousands, it is destructive of body and soul.

What to do about it? What would you advise in order to make the day of rest once again a day of rest? If you speak on behalf of religion and the church, you will not be listened to. The blue laws of New England are the butt of many jokes. On any Sunday, the temple of nature has more worshippers than the sanctuaries of the church.

But perhaps the science of hygiene will be heeded. And it has made itself heard!

There is a Society for the Sanctification of the Sunday in Switzerland.[3] This society offered a prize for the best essay recommending Sunday observance on grounds derived from hygiene. The prize-winning essay was written by a Dr. Schauenburg, a regional health official. He is very zealous in recommending that Sunday be regarded as a day of rest, and he does so as a priest of hygiene.

Let me say up front: Schauenburg is hardly a churchgoer. He writes that "among Evangelical and Catholic clergy are many honorable men. Nevertheless, for the aims and desires of the priest and his caste, not men of vitality and energy but wretched and obedient prayer lambs, broken-down folk without strength or will, are the appropriate creatures. The cleric thinks only of himself, and the world and mankind exist for his sake."[4] And: "Over ninety percent of cultured people, educated by modern science, have become estranged from the church, so that their outward adherence to a church must be deemed a show, a hypocritical gesture condemned by their own conscience."[5]

Such a man is not likely to recommend Sunday observance out of sympathy for the church. Moreover, he favors a Prussian-style government that would make it mandatory for everyone at regular times "to wash and disinfect himself, his clothes and his bed linen." He advocates public bathhouses:

---

3. The origins of the society in Switzerland, with representation throughout the country, is found in the meeting of the Evangelical Alliance at Geneva in 1861.
4. Schauenburg, *Hygieinische Studien*, 14.
5. Schauenburg, *Hygieinische Studien*, 30.

"Anybody who appeared on the street unclean in body and dress would be taken by the police to the bathhouse."[6]

We shudder to think that a radical like that might be of influence with the health authorities in our country. But no doubt he will find favor in the eyes of our most progressive liberals.

Yet it is this unexpected witness, this materialist—for he is that, too, according to the report of the medical jury that evaluated his essay—it is this man who openly urges, in the name of hygiene, that Sunday be regarded and observed as a day of rest. Will people listen to him? But what exactly does the good doctor say?

What does Dr. Schauenburg say? He says a great many things with which we cannot concur. But we are not writing a review of his prize-winning essay. We shall merely borrow a few quotations from it that seem to us quite true and worthwhile.

For example, he points to the fact, well-known from experience, that a man, after working at his occupation for six days, must have a day off. This has many benefits. "Secure against boredom and refreshed in mind and body, a human being enters the new week with riper spirit and firmer resolve."[7] Work continues to be for him "a pleasure and a blessing." With the authority of a medical doctor Schauenburg pronounces: "A human being is satisfied neither by rest alone nor by work alone but by alternating between rest and work."[8]

He reminds us that our entire physical being is based on regularity of metabolism, which makes rest pauses imperative. "Rest" in this context is not the equivalent of sleep, though that too is indispensable, especially for the brain; but both conditions, work and rest, must serve "to renew a man's strength and enhance his joy in labor."[9]

Schoolchildren too need rest. After each six-day period a day of rest must be inserted, "lest the brain be overtaxed."[10]

Adults are to devote themselves to life's tasks with all their physical and mental capacities. Yet "before exhaustion sets in, the Sunday is there, along with Sunday rest: relaxation from work, commanded by nature and

---

6. Schauenburg, *Hygieinische Studien*, 29.
7. Schauenburg, *Hygieinische Studien*, 12.
8. Schauenburg, *Hygieinische Studien*, 14.
9. Schauenburg, *Hygieinische Studien*, 15.
10. Schauenburg, *Hygieinische Studien*, 18.

law, relaxation which allows human beings to reflect on their work and evaluate it."[11]

Families enjoy Sunday in a variety of ways. "Members are at peace, meals are more relaxed, baths have been taken, clothes are washed, experiences are shared, and plans are discussed. Life takes on a different hue. There is a chicken in the pot, and beer or wine are on the table. The atmosphere is festive."[12]

For the masses, too, the common rest day is a blessing. "The common celebration of a break from work heightens the feeling of togetherness."[13]

All this raises the moral level of a nation and improves its well-being. "For nothing disrupts the functioning of skin and muscles, of the organs of respiration, circulation and digestion, and so on, more than the monotony of life and labor."[14]

Factory work on Sundays, writes Dr. Schauenburg, is ruinous.

> Factory owners who ignore this law of health science are cruel tyrants. Work on the railway may not be too strenuous, but those who do the mind-numbing work in telegraph and postal offices need even more rest than the Sunday normally provides. ... Hectic Sundays—all that traveling to exhibitions, meetings, professional conferences—that is not what the Sabbath was meant for. Such activities do not bring relaxation but double, if not triple, exertion.[15]

Finally, Sunday promotes health through cleanliness. "How often are water and soap not more effective than medicines!"[16]

It is useful, it seems to us, to be reminded of these old truths. Our various levels of government can learn from them. Would they not do well if they demonstrated that they wanted to have Sunday observed as a day of rest?

Sunday shifts by civil servants should be cut back or cut out. With the exception of unavoidable tasks, everybody, from the letter carrier to the highest official, should be able to rest on Sunday. Train schedules should be reduced on Sundays, and railway workers should have a free Sunday

---

11. Schauenburg, *Hygieinische Studien*, 19.
12. Schauenburg, *Hygieinische Studien*, 20–21.
13. Schauenburg, *Hygieinische Studien*, 22.
14. Schauenburg, *Hygieinische Studien*, 23.
15. Schauenburg, *Hygieinische Studien*, 24–26.
16. Schauenburg, *Hygieinische Studien*, 56.

at least every three weeks. Inns should be open for only a few hours on Sundays and should close a couple of hours earlier than usual. That would reduce all that traveling back and forth on Sundays and restore the day, economically speaking, to what it ought to be: a family day. Thousands would do well by it. England and America suffer no harm by honoring the Lord's Day. For that matter, one can tell from our Jewish neighbors how *not working* on the Sabbath is no deterrent to getting ahead in the world and being productive members of society.

Do not call us religious fanatics. Just reflect seriously for once how much evil is inflicted on society by the present-day nonobservance of Sunday with its hustle and bustle and dust and din. A huge amount of money, labor, and energy is now being wasted. Our national government, our city councils, all our men of influence—all people of good will—should set an example by respecting the day of rest and ought to enable those who so wish, to observe it. And just as God's commandment is supported by the science of hygiene, so the interest of the state is promoted by the influence of the church.

Do not call us purists. We just love our people. A people that dispenses with its Sunday will perish. So stop obstructing the church. And if you will not listen to the church, at least listen to the science of hygiene.

MANUAL LABOR

TEXT INTRODUCTION

The course of industrialization in the Netherlands, which had finally picked up in the 1870s, was jolted by local difficulties and slowed by a general and severe depression in the 1880s. Workers in the cities faced prolonged unemployment without insurance, daily provisions, or sure prospect of improvement. Meanwhile, the ongoing crisis in Dutch agriculture, now bereft of urban outlets for its surplus labor, was intensifying and causing increasing alarm. Although the labor violence that exploded in more industrialized Belgium and northern France at the time never erupted in the Netherlands, no one was sure of that in advance. The worst years of the depression (1882–86) thus mixed real suffering with acute anxiety.[1]

Local authorities and labor associations were overwhelmed by the situation, and the conservative-dominated cabinet in The Hague did little until, at the prompting of progressives in the States-General, it appointed committees to investigate farm and factory conditions. These *Enquêtes* (Inquests) were comparable to congressional hearings in the United States and to parliamentary inquiries in countries with the Westminster system, compiling sworn testimony in a formal report, along with recommendations for legislation. That legislation was forthcoming in 1889, courtesy of the Antirevolutionary-Catholic coalition ministry headed by Aeneas Mackay (1838–1909).

---

1. E. H. Kossman, *The Low Countries, 1780–1940* (Oxford: Clarendon, 1978), 314–19.

The entire process received ample, and often acute, commentary across the spectrum of Dutch opinion. Kuyper entered in with the following series of articles in *De Standaard* during February 1889. In them he speaks not only to immediate concerns, though he does that with a fine eye for detail, but to the structural problems, ideological premises, and broader consequences of industrialization as a whole. This was applied political philosophy conveyed at a rapid pace—the seven articles appeared every other day! In conveying it, Kuyper intended that his lay audience would thereby receive a quick overview of the main issues, as well as some calming hope, and a license for appropriate rage.

Some classic Kuyperian motifs run through this piece: sphere sovereignty, the horrors of 1789–93, the celebration of a free society, the derogation of liberals and conservatives as outmoded variations on the same premise. Kuyper's class consciousness is more pronounced than usual, however, and poses a challenge to his usual theme of law and social order. His solution is to unleash full class combat, albeit within tight rules and a legally constituted matrix of formal institutions. Thus Kuyper comes to some of his most innovative suggestions for solving the "social question": enhance the rights of labor with a modern version of the old guild system, install labor councils to match business cartels, settle their disputes through binding arbitration, balance and so stabilize the entire system through parliamentary representation by social function as well as by geographical district. These proposals were never enacted. But they show a philosopher with an eye for the concrete; a steadfast leader ever willing to experiment; and a devotee of both order and freedom facing up to new social circumstances.

SOURCE: These articles originally appeared in *De Standaard*, February 8–22, 1889, and were reissued as a brochure with the title *Handenarbeid* (Amsterdam: J. A. Wormser, 1889). The text is reproduced here in full except for a few minor deletions of repetitive summaries or commentary on local events. A translation by Reinder Bruinsma, with an introduction (adapted for this present volume) and annotations by James D. Bratt, first appeared in *Abraham Kuyper: A Centennial Reader* (Grand Rapids: Eerdmans, 1998), 231–54. Adapted and edited by Harry Van Dyke.

MANUAL LABOR

I. THE FOUNDATIONS OF THE BUILDING

A nation lives by labor, but labor takes many forms. There is physical and intellectual labor, precision work and unskilled work, labor that demands mental concentration, and labor that requires almost exclusively an exertion of the muscles. If there is going to be a "code of labor," therefore, it will be more correct to speak of a code of *manual* labor, as this is the type of labor that is facing more and more difficulties.

The question of manual labor is of great importance for society because the class of citizens occupied in it is so large; in our country the majority have it as their sole means of existence. Thus, the condition in which manual labor finds itself inevitably exerts an influence on the entire social and domestic condition of the greater part of our nation. Naturally, every Netherlander is eager to know whether this majority is doing well, has a reasonable existence, and is prospering morally, or whether it is depressed by worries, tending toward discontent, and declining in morals.

In the long run, manual labor is of the greatest importance for the very security of our society. However phlegmatic our nature may be, however calm the Dutch pace of life, history clearly teaches that a confrontation cannot be avoided if the majority of the population lives for many years with anxiety and resentment and so grows weaker in its moral fiber. The social question so far has not taken that threatening form in our country only because the spirit of discontent and moral decline has remained confined to a small portion of those who work with their hands. Agricultural workers in particular have not been affected until now, although it must be feared that before too long the slump in the prices of land and agricultural products will give free play to evil spirits in this domain too. You can already see something of this in the north.

Apart from the question whether the social order is sufficiently armed to deal with a violent eruption, it is beneath the honor of the government and the dignity of our people to ignore such a serious matter until the situation runs out of hand. Apart from its urgency and threat, our government and our people ought to open their eyes to this unsatisfactory situation and ask themselves seriously whether the legislator is entitled and equipped to help alleviate this pressing need. This is demanded of wise government; it is demanded by justice, which elevates a nation; it is demanded also by the tender compassion that may be expected of a baptized nation.

But even if the legislator believed itself entitled to take any measure and agree to any demand, it is far from certain that it would be able to arrest the diminishing regard for manual labor. The very fact that we participate in a global market and that therefore conditions in other countries influence our situation makes this improbable. Besides, preventing *all* misery and alleviating *all* poverty is a problem that will always escape solution. Finally, the course of world history shows that great nations, after a period of glory, tend to enter a period of spiritual exhaustion and, once sunken in this spiritual miasma, become inferior to other nations in every form of life.

Therefore, it is high time that moral forces be considerably strengthened among the common people. "Being content with little" will help to cultivate patience in times of sorrow and hardship, while looking toward a higher ideal will draw the tranquil eye away from the world and its desires. At stake is the happiness of the people. If these moral forces enable you to teach the larger part of our nation to be content with little and in that condition also to catch the luster of a higher ideal, you have achieved more than if you artificially raise wages 10 or 15 percent. For if people lack moral fiber, a prevailing discontent will result only in a new demand that wages be raised another 10 percent.

Yet, for the present we will set these moral forces aside. We will stay silent as well about the contribution that the marvelous power of love can make to improve the circumstances of many through graciousness, compassion, and liberality. Here we are concerned only with the legislator, and so we face the question: What can lawmakers do to eradicate from our society this imbalance which unmistakably burdens a considerable part of the population and robs it of its happiness? We must courageously and openly acknowledge that the social democrats are right when they maintain that the situation calls not only for the *physician* but most certainly for the *architect* as well.

Let us clarify what we mean.

At first, the well-heeled class regarded the social question as a schoolmaster does a couple of rascals in his class. Liberals and conservatives alike demanded to know what the meaning was of all that noise and fuss. Their sacred doctrine was nonnegotiable: the *laissez faire, laissez passer* philosophy was the bedrock of wisdom. A national system such as ours, born from these sagacious depths, *had* to be an El Dorado for all. Granted, there was inequality, but this was simply the struggle between the stronger and the weaker in which the weaker was just "predestined" to succumb. Complaints or resistance were uncalled for. All this grumbling had to stop, the sooner the better. But if it did continue and if the people sooner or later raised their fists, what of it? One simply reinforced the police and made sure to have enough loyal troops. That would be the end of it.

Less than 20 years ago this fairly described the general feeling among our ruling elite. But since then, mainly due to the nobler policies of other nations, the crass arrogance and complacency expressed in this chilling egoism began to soften a little. No, the complaints were not so totally unfounded. There were indeed abuses. From a variety of causes, the much-lauded system of liberal wisdom had not been able to realize its ideal in every aspect. The social *organism* was still perfectly in order, but here and there some less desirable phenomena had found their way into its constitution. And thus, it was gradually admitted, the *physician* has to be called in, and the pharmacist has work to do.

To be sure, not all liberals want to go to the same length. Listening to the diagnoses of Quack and Levy, we notice that Levy laughs it off by recommending cough syrup, while Quack—a man of serious study, with a kind heart and a tender mind—would not object to the cost of some iron pills and, if need be, some minor surgery.[1] Even so, this usually separates

---

1. Isaac A. Levy (1836-1920) was a lawyer from Amsterdam and a member of Parliament. Hendrick P. G. Quack (1834-1917) was a professor of economics at Utrecht and Amsterdam. Both men belonged to the more progressive liberals who favored addressing the social problem by broadening the franchise.

the liberals from the social democrats on the issue. The liberals are looking only for a medical solution, whereas the social democrats want to tackle the social problem from an architectural angle. They argue that society cannot be salvaged by eliminating a few abuses, since the evil does not reside in these but in the *entire structure* of our social system.

For the time being we will leave aside the question whether their arguments are correct and in particular whether their new design is practicable. But on this we agree with them: when a house creaks and warps, the notion of making some superficial repairs and applying a coat of paint without first examining the supporting walls, joists, and foundations is not serious. It's not even serious from the point of view of our liberals, who live by *reason* and know nothing of divine ordinances. After all, their standpoint implies that those foundations, walls, and joists have been constructed by human consent and accordingly can always be changed if human wisdom so indicates. Here indeed the liberals and social democrats meet. Both do the building themselves. Neither the liberals nor the social democrats in their politics know anything of a God who built everything. In this respect Jonkheer Six[2] yields nothing to Domela Nieuwenhuis.[3]

The real issue between them comes down to the following. The liberals were the first to come on the scene; they built the house according to their design and now demand that the social democrats, who came afterwards, accept the dwelling, though they are willing to throw in some repairs. For their part the social democrats say: *Your whole house is useless. Let's together demolish it and then build, at our shared expense, a new house according to our design. You'll be amazed how much better we both like it.*

Liberals cannot object to this on principle, but we antirevolutionaries can. Our response is that one must distinguish. The design of the house we now inhabit shows a part that has been ordained by God and must be preserved in any reconstruction. But, to be frank, the same design has not a little that we do not find particularly attractive since it is a product of the liberals, and this part can be reconstructed in a different way *without contravening* divine ordinances. Critique of this part of the house must remain free, and the suggestions of other architects should be heard. The

---

2. Willem Six, Esq. (1829–1908), member of the Dutch ruling elite, was a model of classical liberalism and a conservative devotee of the national church.
3. Ferdinand Domela Nieuwenhuis (1846–1919), a former Lutheran pastor, was a member of Parliament and a radical socialist who later embraced anarchism.

existing situation should not be regarded as perfect so long as it has not passed the test of criticism with honor.

II. ECONOMIC AND POLITICAL INFLUENCES

We have now clearly indicated in what respect the social democrats deserve a hearing and in what respect they do not. They are right when they refuse to be fobbed off by the liberal landlord with some repairs and some paint and insist instead on a thorough inspection of the foundations, walls, and joints. But they are wrong insofar as they assume that not God the Lord but social democracy is to ordain the design of society's house. That said, liberals have no defense over against social democrats, since both refuse to reckon with God's ordinances, making the difference between them merely a personal one: namely, whether it is the liberal or the social democrat who knows more about building. In this competition the liberal has the advantage since he has already erected the house, while the social democrat only has one on paper. But the competition can only increase, because the social democrat wants to build on the site where the house of the liberal stands.

While these two architects fight it out, we need to pay attention to two equally important matters. First, it is important that the class of people who live by manual labor be able to buy good quality and quantity with the money they earn. Wages will always remain relative. In more than one area a farm laborer who earns five guilders is in fact much richer that a laborer in Amsterdam who gets eight or even ten. The government has all sorts of ways to influence the price of consumer goods. Enclosing a city within narrow walls will make the houses expensive. Building good roads will let people live farther away. Border tariffs have an influence on the price of goods. Excise tax on salt, soap, and sugar is paid by all. Land tax, license fees, and the poll tax are figured into the price of houses and goods. In brief, our entire fiscal system is like the web of a spider, where each vibration is transmitted along all threads from the center to the outer edges.

As for agriculture, we recently pointed to our unsuitable inheritance laws whereby the continuity of large farms, which need a lot of manual labor, is continually in jeopardy. Endless partitioning in turn has led to a higher density of population. A greater number of people engage in bidding wars for the small pieces of land they want to rent. It has happened that landowners who at one time received only twelve hundred guilders in rent from a farm got more than two thousand after the land had been partitioned. That means an extra eight hundred guilders which has to be paid by the lower class.

Then too we see how the law guaranteeing freedom of movement can burden each laborer at any moment with 10 or 12 competitors. "Where there is carrion the eagles will gather." And those eagles arrive just as often from other provinces as from across the border. Large public works projects also figure in, for when the government creates extra work of 10 years' duration or longer, it attracts a large group of manual laborers who, on that basis, get married, live, and make plans. Then when the work is suddenly finished this immense crew of laborers is left empty-handed.[4]

We could add much more, but this will suffice to illustrate how the fiscal policy and administration of a country affect the situation of the manual laborer in all sorts of ways. Accordingly, not only the structure of society but also the manner in which the national household is run is a powerful factor that either benefits the laboring class or oppresses it. Even if you assume that any kind of household will cost money and that it is fair

---

4. Under the title "Unemployment" Kuyper's paper, *De Standaard*, carried the following asterism on November 11, 1885, as the Dutch economic depression worsened: "In years past, England etc. ... suffered the fever of unemployment, too, even worse than we do today. That's when Potgieter [E. J., 1808–75] translated Hood's 'Lay of the Labourer' for us. And although that translation was a dismal failure, nevertheless by the 'Lay of the Laborer' and 'Song of the Shirt' Potgieter helped us feel what England's workingman was struggling with then and what is still happening in our own cities today.

"Back then the unemployed in England suffered in large numbers, suffered hopelessly, suffered horrible deprivation. Only the 'poor rates' offered relief.

"We cannot let our fellow man die of hunger. To say: 'Go and be warm' is not Christian. But also, given the scope of the problem, help does not come via vague promises. Even less should it be perceived as extorted by threats; it is unacceptable that our laboring population sink ever lower morally to the dismal level of demanding money by intimidation.

"We are not just facing a need but a situation that needs to be regulated, a set of circumstances that requires provision.

"If back in 1874, when the Antirevolutionary caucus in the [Second] Chamber urged regulation, and if this demand had been met by the adoption of a Labor Code, our misery today would not be half of what it is. We would have our guilds, and through the guilds a set quota of laborers for every trade, and through that a drop in the marriage and population figures so that the entire imbalance between work and workers would be eliminated.

"So in our opinion there should be no further delay. A Labor Code must be passed now. For the time being, consider England's 'poor rates' the only remedy. A few thousand guilders won't suffice. A few tons should do!"

for all classes to share in this expense, it is obvious that the share a particular class can bear depends on the relative prosperity this class enjoys. Understandably, then, the people who live by manual labor demand a better deal since their situation has been declining.

It does not follow, of course, that every change these folk desire is possible, or even prove profitable for them. But that does not remove the urgent necessity for a thorough investigation of this aspect of the social question—not only because the people want it, but because God requires the government to be *fair* in its dealings.

This automatically brings up the third key element in this question: *politics.* In the past, when government was elevated more highly above the different social classes, politics did not get involved in the class struggle. Precisely because of her lofty position, government was conscious of its calling to stand in the breach for the weaker classes and to defend them against the stronger. When the psalmist extols the King of kings with such words as "O LORD, who is like you, delivering the weak from him who is too strong for him" [Ps 35:10], he is highlighting the most beautiful pearl in the crown of our rulers: to defend the weak and needy, lest they be oppressed by the big and powerful.

But sure enough, the liberals put an end to this noble conception of government too. Liberalism robbed the king of his majesty and gave him some tinsel by way of compensation. A king made of marzipan. The power to rule was no longer with the king but with the majority in the Second Chamber, which explains why liberalism had no scruples whatsoever in its attempts to acquire that majority. Seeing that the Second Chamber does not in fact represent all classes but only one, namely the *bourgeoisie*, the metamorphosis that occurred came down to this: the king remained king in name but the actual power of government was transferred to the well-heeled, the propertied class. At the time it consisted of about 100,000 people, representing a household population of about 400,000—approximately one-tenth of the country's population.

This has triggered repugnance and disturbed our civil peace. For if it could not be denied that whoever has the power of government can, both by the rearrangement of the foundations of society and by the mode of management, exert a predominant influence on the fate and the condition of the various classes in their conflict of interests; and if de facto this governing power was now placed in the hands of one of these classes—then the dreadful suspicion *had* to arise that this ruling class would abuse its power to strengthen its own position and weaken that of the others. And so was born the demand for *universal suffrage*—on the liberal standpoint a most reasonable demand, if only on the cogent grounds that any other system is purely arbitrary. For on this standpoint, to require that voters have a certain level of prosperity would be an aggravated form of tyranny. But the issue concerns precisely those who lack that prosperity. Their fate is mainly in the hands of those who control the government. This control lies with the majority of the voters, and the vote is given only to the well-to-do, that is, only to those who in this social lawsuit represent the party versus the less privileged.

We do not say that the social democrats are one whit better in their intentions. On the contrary, they intend the very same thing as the liberals but with virtually the reverse outcome. Their system, too, puts the power of government in the hands of the two chambers. These chambers are elected by all the people. Among these people the less privileged are in the majority. Therefore, all power should be in the hands of the less privileged. Then the voters who live by their manual labor will use the power of the law to change the foundations of society, the political system, and above all the tax rates, so that the liberal bourgeoisie will be in just as unpleasant a position under the democrats as the democratic majority currently is under the press of the liberals.

Whatever means we might advocate for solving the problem, this much is beyond doubt: it would be childish prattle, or worse, to see the social question as simply a matter of a few repairs and a coat of paint. The social question in actual fact touches (1) the very foundations of society, (2) the entire mode of governance, and, not least, (3) the principle of authority, *the* political issue par excellence.

III. THE GOVERNMENT'S JURISDICTION

The jurisdiction of the government has hardly come into play with the three cardinal issues discussed so far. For, returning to our point of departure, this competence is not in dispute so far as the *political* question is concerned. Once the government assumes the right and the duty to seek the will of the nation in its governance, to rule only in close consultation with the provinces and other councils on the basis of a mutually agreed-upon Constitution and with recognition of the historical rights and liberties of the people, then it is only natural that the suffrage can be extended to all adult citizens if need be. For now, we shall not discuss whether this would be desirable, but there is no doubt about the government's right to do so.

The same is true of the fiscal laws. If it were convincingly shown that the present system of taxation imposes an unfair burden and if the government felt it prudent to shift this burden in various ways, all would agree that it would have the legal competence to do so.

Finally, as to the *foundations of our social system*, the government, ruling as it does by the grace of God, would be totally outside its jurisdiction to loosen or move one of the divinely ordained foundations. But where these foundations were laid not by divine command but merely by the magistrates' design, the current magistrate could no doubt change what its predecessors effected, so long as it did not violate historic or individual rights. For instance, should the government feel that collective ownership of land would make the Netherlands a happier nation, then there could be no doubt that the government might proceed toward this preference so long as it took adequate measures to reach this goal without violating anyone's acquired rights.

Thus, the road is open in a threefold respect. *Politically*, the government may not let the Second Chamber become the sole governing body; *fiscally*, it may not introduce communism; with respect to the *principles* on which communal life rests, it may not violate God's ordinances or historical rights. But avoiding this threefold snag, should the government deem it desirable to introduce universal suffrage, shift the tax burden, and improve the foundations of society, it would *not* be legally incompetent to do so.

The matter would take on a totally different color, however, if we were to ask more precisely whether the government has the jurisdiction to exercise *direct* influence on manual labor as such. The social conditions of the common people who live by manual labor are only *indirectly* determined by the political, fiscal, and social structure of the community. They depend *directly* on whether manual labor as such is flourishing or languishing. If there is ample demand and generous reward for that labor, and if it can take place under circumstances that elevate the manual laborer, this class of common folk will prosper. But if it is hard to get work, if the pay is meager and must be done under demeaning conditions, this class as a whole will languish.

The question is whether the government may directly interfere in this area. Does it not overstep its bounds when it creates work or prevents competition, raises wages or shortens the workweek, and in general supports manual labor by making it available only under such conditions that ensure that the manual laborer is also respected as a *human being*?

We believe it beyond doubt that the government does *not* have this right, at least not in the absolute sense. State and society are not identical. The government is not the only sovereign in the country. Sovereignty exists in distinct spheres, and in each of these smaller circles this sovereignty is bound to primordial arrangements or ordinances that have been created not by the government but by the Creator of heaven and earth. Only in one instance can these sovereign entities tolerate, or even demand, government intervention: when two or more of these spheres collide at their common borders and a great imbalance between their respective powers makes it likely that the more powerful entity would expand excessively and the other would be disproportionately pushed back. To take an example, the point of contact between the sphere of capital and the sphere of manual labor *formally* is always a contract—either explicitly entered into or tacitly assumed. Because the authorities are involved in court cases about contracts, this is the formal point that lies within the reach of the government.

This poses the question: Should the state allow any kind of contract, or do the authorities have the right to stipulate that *every* contract dealing with such matters must presuppose or include certain conditions? Then the next question: Is a government authorized to punish noncompliance when such contractual conditions which it deems essential are not met? This was the reason, in our critique of the factory labor bill proposed by Mr. Ruys,[5] why we wondered whether the legislation would not have approached the question more correctly if it had taken up the matter under contract law. As this proposal attempts to intervene *directly* in a domain that is sovereign in its own sphere and governed by its own laws, we deem this bill a first step on a road that will leave every sphere of society at the mercy of the magistrate. Our warning, *Principiis obsta!* [resist beginnings!], was therefore not superfluous.

Let's take it from still another vantage point. It is our deepest conviction that the government has no jurisdiction to stipulate how labor matters must be regulated, not even in the form of a contract. The States-General do not remove this objection. For although the States-General represent the people

---

5. G. L. M. H. Ruys van Beerenbrouck (1842–1926) was the minister of justice in the Mackay ministry, the coalition cabinet of the Right which Kuyper in general supported from the sidelines via the pages of *De Standaard*.

as a single entity, they do not adequately represent the *subentities*, such as capital and labor, which may collide with one another. For that reason we have always insisted that labor be organized on a basis regulated in law. *Capital* is of course already strongly represented in the provincial states and other councils; it is firmly entrenched in the highest circles of the government and possesses its own organizational network in the chambers of commerce. *Labor* stands on the opposite side, unarmed and defenseless. Private labor associations do not constitute a counterbalance, since they must camp in the open field *outside* the framework of the law. The least that should be done, we think, is to immediately create chambers of labor which the government shall be obliged to consult. But this is not enough. "Chambers of labor" will remain an odd element so long as they are not rooted in the organization of labor as such. Capital has only *one* form, but labor has *many*. Therefore, if labor is to be organized it must have a structure that accommodates *each of its forms*. We do not care whether one wants to use the old label of *guilds* for this type of organization. Nobody wants to restore the guilds in their ancient form. But we do demand that the Revolution acknowledge—and we would prefer a confession of sin before the end of 1889—that it made an enormous mistake when it demolished the traditional organization of labor without replacing it with something new. Society is not served by a tabula rasa as we have had now for almost a century.

IV. THE OLD GUILDS

The deterioration of society that resulted from the destruction of the organization of labor has once again focused our attention on the ancient system of guilds. We should take care that this never lead to a movement which intends to restore the ancient guilds in their historic form. It was an unforgivable mistake for the Revolution simply to abandon the existing organization of labor without putting a better one in its place. But it was a laudable act and not an error that in the second half of the past century more than one country in Europe abolished the antiquated guild system as it existed at that time.

The blame lay with the Revolution. Not as if France struck the first blow and other nations simply followed. In Germany the law of September 4, 1731, had already laid the ax at the root of the tree,[6] and Emperor Joseph II through his edicts of 1771 and 1772 hacked away mightily at the trunk.[7] What the Revolution accomplished was this. First, long before the storming of the Bastille, the Revolution disseminated among the nations the false promise of untold earthly happiness, also for the working class, through unbridled freedom. Second, clothed with authority for the first time in France, the Revolution suddenly in 1791 (after a futile attempt by Turgot in 1776) brushed aside every organization in the sphere of labor with a single stroke of the pen.

The misguided *idea* that boundless liberty would solve everything and the rude *example* of turning everything overnight into a tabula rasa eventually inspired most governments to go in a similar direction. And even though in Germany free enterprise in the form of freedom to practice any trade was not fully recognized until June 21, 1869, and even though Germany and Austria (witness the law of March 15, 1883) still honored some remnants of the ancient guild system, we should recognize that the *guild system* has in fact been replaced by absolute "liberty" and that the languishing remains of the old corporations seem to continue only as obsolete curiosities without exerting any real influence on the course of affairs.

The ancient *guilds* were doomed to fail because they were taken over from *Roman* into *Germanic* law and thus could not but come into conflict with the character of the new European way of life. A better way would have been to follow Solon's approach in Athens instead of trying to imitate ancient Rome. Solon allowed private initiative to come into its own. He did not allow the government to get involved in business but merely stipulated that manual laborers constitute their own class of citizens, that nobody be allowed to have two trades at the same time, that foreigners from the outside be allowed to offer competition only if the local craftsmen agreed. Furthermore, he gave industry the right to be sovereign in its own sphere and to make its own rules, the only restriction being that it was not to decide anything contrary to the law of the land.

This was possible in Athens since there a tradesman was regarded as an honorable citizen. In Rome this was not the case. Most manual laborers in Rome were slaves; for free men to join them was considered a humiliation.

---

6. Prussian king Frederick William I (1688–1740) suppressed the craft guilds as part of his campaign to improve the army.

7. Emperor Joseph II (1741–90), inspired by Enlightenment ideals, abolished serfdom and eliminated guild restrictions.

Their corporations were looked down upon with contempt. They were strictly regulated and forbidden to raise fees and prices even in times of economic hardship or steep inflation. They were liable for losses due to shipwrecks, and during the empire they were subjected to extortion. Such were the guilds which, transferred on that basis to the towns that Rome built along the Rhine, the Danube, and the Meuse rivers, contained the seeds of political strife. There were the townsmen, and there were the members of the guilds. Inevitably, the ambition arose among of the guilds to resist the burgher patricians, to demand equality with the other townspeople, and finally to try to acquire power over their fellow-townsmen. Well organized, heavily armed, confident of a numerical majority, these guilds not seldom declared war, losing sight of their craft's well-being in their hunt for political power... .

Yet it cannot be denied that, even in this extremely defective form, the guild system served society well, particularly in regions such as Flanders and Holland, where it did not rest on such a strong division between two classes of citizens. Thanks to the guild system in the sixteenth and seventeenth century, our craftsmen were not only outwardly prosperous but so skillful in their trades that the most exquisite products were made in the Netherlands. The craftsman was a kind of artist in his workshop, and the rest of Europe learned real craftsmanship from us.

Today, however, the struggle is no longer between the craftsmen and the townsmen who purchase their products. A conflict has broken out in the world of manual labor between "masters" and "journeymen." That overriding fact makes it wholly unsuitable to resurrect the guilds in their old form as a solution to the social question. Any new rules should pay attention to two things. First, care should be given to what the crafts themselves require, taking into consideration what the purchasing public demands, so that neither will the crafts be destroyed by unrestricted freedom nor the public be exploited by the industrialists through overly stringent regulations. But also, second—and this is the main issue—no new forms of organization will be able to solve the social problem unless the reciprocal relationship between the factory owners and employers, on the one hand, and those who actually perform the work, on the other, is arranged in such a way that the workers regain a sense of security in life.

Today this sense of security is totally lacking, for four reasons. (1) Employers now have, in steam and machinery, a power at their disposal which for a good part makes them nondependent on manual labor.

(2) The amassing of large capital makes it possible for industrial enterprises to expand on such a scale that small concerns barely manage to survive. (3) Unrestricted freedom of movement for workers, even from other countries, allows unsustainable competition with the local craftsmen. (4) All workmen, whether young or old, are now casual laborers without a long-term contract; so long as payment of their wages is up to date, they can be dismissed tomorrow.

These are the precious fruits of unbridled liberty, this is the grievous result of the dogma of *laissez faire, laissez passer* that our liberals proclaim as the highest wisdom. Today this confronts us with the bitter misery that divides the lower and higher classes of society in hatred, resentment, and passionate anger. For it could not but make the manual laborer among us, as in imperial Rome, a kind of being to whom no human existence need be guaranteed, a sort of *appendix* to the machine. And once again this numerous class reacts by fighting without restraint to defend its right of existence. It does so, first, by creating its own organization and meeting coercion with coercion in *the strike.* Second, through anger, as in Belgium and northern France, where workmen are turning against the machines that compete with them and setting factories on fire. Also, by demanding that society be organized in such a way that it will be saved from the tyranny of capital. And finally, if all else fails, this class reacts by entertaining the notion of overturning, top to bottom, the entire social order which it perceives as being the cause of its misery.

Our authorities thus have a choice. Which do you want? Either put an end to the tension that undeniably exists between the employers of the industrial enterprises and the manual laborers—not by putting them off with empty promises but by truly eliminating the abuses and creating a climate for properly organized modes of cooperation. Or, if you don't want this, accept that things stay on a war footing and that you will inevitably have to contend with a war that the workers have already started against the machine, against capital, and against the social order.

This being the situation, the antirevolutionary believes that the false liberal principle of *laissez-faire* which has given rise to all these problems must be abandoned, the sooner the better. It must not come to a war between citizens. The government has the duty to ensure that organization take the place of disorganization and that both parties have the opportunity to furnish the building blocks for this organization freely and independently.

V. CHAMBERS OF LABOR

The chambers (or councils) of labor that have been proposed from more than one quarter can never give us the positive elements of the ancient guilds. Furthermore, their efficiency is unthinkable without the prior organization of labor.[8] ... We do not oppose the idea of a chamber of labor but, on the contrary, will support any initiative to have them established, even today, in whatever imperfect form, so long as it is clearly understood that this would only represent the *first brick* for the house and that *the entire house* would still have to follow.

In this respect what was done in the Middle Ages shows us how to proceed. When people around the eleventh century first attempted to organize the guilds, the authorities saw the need to be involved in establishing some rules for the system. But far from pretending that this had settled the matter, they understood their regulations to be nothing but the *scaffolding* for the guilds, which now would build the actual *house* themselves. Not the government but the guilds themselves developed their own organization and regulations, autonomously and fully "sovereign in their own sphere." As the building of the house progressed the authorities removed its scaffolding bit by bit. Contact with the authorities in the fourteenth and the fifteenth century did not primarily concern the guilds' organization but the *political* privileges they demanded, particularly those touching their share in local government.

This is the route to take today as well. We believe the government would make a definite mistake if it were to initiate too many rules. Even today it can do no more than erect the *scaffolding*. And it would then in all likelihood be preferable, at least for the time being, to have the "chambers of labor" represent *labor* only. Let all laborers who can prove that they have regularly earned wages in the same locality for at least a year elect such a chamber in each town or in each group of villages with a combined population of some twenty thousand inhabitants. The role of such a chamber would for now be limited to giving advice. But if it had the freedom to establish suborganizations in various crafts and groups to gather data on which to base their advice, we would see emerging a grassroots organization with an official character that would help us proceed step by step. Having been initiated by the stakeholders themselves, it would guarantee that it would not be too far removed from reality.

---

8. At this point, Kuyper briefly describes the problems he sees in various proposals.

Our existing chambers of commerce could also gradually be altered and expanded in such a way that they would develop into representative bodies with suborganizations for the various branches of employment. Then we would be on the right track toward two advisory bodies, each from its own vantage point and aware of its own interests, offering advice to the government about the organization of and issues relating to labor. Naturally this presupposes that the government would also be informed of the advice coming from the individual crafts and that the government share the views of the chambers of labor with the chambers of commerce, and vice versa, in order to hear comments from both sides.

This approach would be much, much more profitable than the best *inquest*, which by its very nature is incidental and bears no lasting fruit, gathers its data atomistically, and does not lead to organization, does not allow its advice to spring from life but itself goes out in search of it. It would also create the opportunity to establish *councils of arbitration* composed of appointees from both the chambers of commerce and the chambers of labor. If suborganizations for separate branches are established, their boards could, depending on the nature of the conflict, nominate members for these councils of arbitration.

If more *general* issues were at stake and the government wanted a more general kind of advice, what objection could there be to having each chamber of commerce elect a delegate to a *general chamber of commerce* and, likewise, to have a *general chamber of labor* consisting of one delegate from each local chamber? These bodies could be established within a year and then develop themselves further, on condition that the details of its organization be left to the chambers of commerce and labor themselves. The government would do no more than lay the first brick and determine the general design. This would have the advantage of satisfying the generally felt need for an organization within a legal framework and furnishing the government with much better advice than would be possible through an inquest. Furthermore, whatever is brewing in different parts of the country would be vented, the councils of arbitration would have a solid basis, and a foundation would have been laid for further construction.

Another condition would be—and this we stress—that the government not establish such an organization in an effort merely to reconcile employers and employees. Two other objectives should be pursued as well, and this leads us back to the guilds. In the first place—to mention this only in passing—we should also pay attention to the undeniable and inevitable clash between *those who purchase* and *those who produce* the goods, particularly with reference to foreign imports. Secondly, more care ought to be given to the development of *national craftsmanship*. Precisely this common interest joins the employer and employee together. Do our institutions fully understand our times? Can we revive the spirit that would *improve* them relative to those in other countries? Can this be accompanied by further educating our working class in *head, heart, and hand*, so that in knowledge, loyalty, and skill they might successfully compete with other countries? Then we would reach the point where currently clashing interests would melt together again. Then a better day would dawn for employer and laborer alike. Our national ethos would be strengthened, our national identity enhanced, and the wellspring of national prosperity would flow more freely.

Alas, the liberal school fetish has caused incalculable damage to our country's manual labor force. Our young tradesmen could recite the names of the rivers of Asia, but they had not learned how to work skillfully with their hands.[9]

VI. CHURCH, SCHOOL, AND POLICE

The liberal approach to the social question bore its bitterest fruit in the foolish arrangements it made for *church, school,* and *police* in its interaction with society. The liberals wrought such immense damage here that it is highly questionable whether the results of their recklessness can still be undone.

Those with sound political insight have long acknowledged that the best way for the state to care for the church is to leave her alone as much as possible. What is delicate and tender in nature wants to be spared and respected, as it tends to lose something of its splendor when handled by secular agents. It would have been much better if our politicians in 1813[10] had moved in a direction that would have led to a gradual disappearance of all official ties between state and church over a period of, say, twenty years. It would also have been much better if by means of some careful transitional measures and compensation for historic rights the financial tie between state and church had been cut. It would have made the churches

---

9. A dig at the public school, with its overemphasis on intellectual learning based on a rationalist pedagogy. See the following chapter for further critique of the education installed by the liberals.
10. Reference to the reorganization of the national church at the end of the French occupation.

get used to living from freewill offerings. America demonstrates how this is the safest route from a political and financial but also a religious and moral standpoint. To this noble policy America owes its political stability and the vitality of its religious life, which no other country can match, while at the same time there is no other country where the ministers of religion are so well respected and paid.

But our liberals felt they were too clever to take such a solid policy as their rule. Not that they fought against it in theory. Far from it. They inscribed "Separation of Church and State" on their program in extrabold gilded Gothic. Only, their thinking was: "We may yet be able to make use of the church in our attempts to liberalize the simple people a little more!" They first tried to do that in Belgium, in the *Collegium Philosophicum*,[11] until this backfired in 1830.[12] When their attack on the Catholic Church had failed and Belgium had been separated from us, the liberals tried to make up for their failure by creeping into the Dutch Reformed Church. This is what they proposed: (1) all clergy were to be educated at state universities; (2) the professors would mainly be recruited among liberals; (3) synodical administration was to be completely in liberal hands; and (4) the regulations of the church were to be gradually transformed into a set of rules governing an ethical-religious association without a common confession. And so they set to work. The whole country was flooded with liberal clergy. Everywhere the old religion was to be eradicated. The light of the gospel was to be hidden under a bushel, while *their* light was to be kindled throughout the church.

The failure of this policy is already apparent. Liberalism is discovering too late, to its regret and shame, that its only achievement is to have alienated two-fifths of our people from *any* religion whatsoever and to have driven the remaining three-fifths back toward orthodoxy. Meanwhile it has been too little noted how, in its presumptuous partisanship, liberalism's failed experiment unwittingly severed all kinds of *moral* bonds in large sections of our population, infused their blood with the passion of discontent, and cruelly robbed them of the only comfort that many hard-pressed folk still have in their misery.

---

11. This institution was founded in Louvain by the central government of the United Kingdom of the Netherlands for the purpose of ensuring a more "enlightened" training of Catholic priests.
12. An informal alliance between liberals and Catholics led to the revolt of 1830 that ultimately led to the creation of an independent Belgium.

Everyone is entitled to his own opinion about the moral value of religion, but even the most ardent liberal will agree that when we compare two working-class families who live in equal circumstances except that in the one family religion radiates its kindly light while the other is inhabited by grumbling and resentment, we find the first family to be happier. That so many thousands of families have been robbed of *this* happiness—for this the liberals are to blame. Therefore we cannot accede to the pressure exerted on us from so many sides that we not deal with church matters in our political journal. The social question alone forbids it, and therefore we continue to demand the emancipation of the churches.

To a certain extent the same can be said about *education*. The liberals were also unwilling to respect the independence of the public school. On the contrary, it was to be a tool and its staff a recruiting cadre for elections. This had multiple effects. In the orthodox villages it neutralized the influence of the pastor. For the middle and higher classes of society it offered a cheap school and an effective method to train almost all their sons and daughters as free thinkers. It would alienate the lower classes from any kind of religion and—when the suffrage was extended—would incline them favorably toward the liberals. On top of all that, it provided thousands of teachers and supervisors with a chance to be awarded a lucrative post.

But in this case, too, evil carried its own punishment. Action provokes reaction. The template of a common school perverted the quality of education. The people regressed rather than progressed. The moral influence of the school broke down. The end result was that academic leadership ebbed away, leaving us with none but inferior imitators. The younger generation, coldly calculating and benumbed by the strong dose, lost all passion for ideals. Last but not least, the balance between the *intellectual* and *moral* aspects of life was destroyed among the lower class, while our laborers, clever in bookish knowledge, rapidly lost many of the practical skills needed in the trades and in business.

This process served the liberal masters well for a time but at the expense of the poor, whom the heavy emphasis on intellectual knowledge has left ill-prepared for the struggle of life. For we should never forget that the labor question is an *international* issue. You cannot isolate your country. If politicians elsewhere deal more prudently with their schools, your people fall behind their neighbors—which means, when expressed in numbers, that working people here run short of money while laborers elsewhere enjoy ample incomes.

It was a senseless partisanship in the domain of *church and school*, which resulted moreover in such an obsession with "church and school" that little attention was paid to the political and economic interests of the people. And so our colonial management deteriorated, Achin[13] turned into a disaster, market after market closed, Hamburg and Antwerp overtook us in giant leaps, foreign products pushed our own products off the shelves, and left our poor laboring class the victim of this fanaticism.

Finally, we add a word about the *police*, for the social question is such a central matter that every part of the political machinery is linked to it. A good police force, guardian of the peace, must be respected by 99 percent of the population and feared by no more than the 1 percent who are difficult and obstinate. All classes and segments of society should know that they can count on the police. Its appearance on the scene should induce order and calm among the people and disturb only rascals and troublemakers, whether old or young. "A terror for the wicked and a shield for all others."

But our police today is anything like this. One could almost say that in an evil hour it has turned into a sort of Praetorian gang with a military organization that creates unrest in the minds of the citizens, stimulating—even provoking—them to rebellion. In particular, the class from which most of our workers come appear to the police as an inferior lot who need to be kept under the masters' thumb. Whence, of course, the sad fact that the majority of this class often allies itself with the rascals and troublemakers against the police.[14]

This has a very destructive effect. People begin to see the government as an exacting, annoying, more or less hostile power. They have to yield to superior force but would oh so gladly break this shackle. Resistance breeds a feeling of satisfaction and honor to one's class. Punishment creates martyrs. And so the foolish way in which the police are allowed to act threatens rather than protects law and order and keeps rebellious sentiments alive.

To sum up, liberalism's dallying with the church has weakened the morale of the lower classes, its exploitation of the school has saddled the

---

13. The subjugation of this region in northern Sumatra, which harbored raiders on shipping in the Strait of Malacca, had met limited success by this time of writing and was not achieved until 1903.

14. A notorious instance of police provocation occurred during the "eel riot" in the summer of 1886, when police tried to stop the cruel but popular working-class pastime of eel stripping in the canals of Amsterdam. The clash resulted in 26 civilian deaths, 100 wounded, and several hundred arrested and jailed.

workingman with intellectual knowledge in lieu of practical skills, and its obsession with law and order has turned the police into an armed force which has only raised the spirit of resistance instead of lowering it.

VII. INQUEST OR ORGANIZATION?

The concepts of *inquest* and *organization* are at odds with each other. *Inquest* is based on the idea (1) that the working class remains in tutelage under the guardianship of the high and mighty, (2) that the high and mighty now have begun to realize they may not have been the kind of guardians they should have been, (3) that they are holding an inquest to find out whether this suspicion is true, and (4) that once the inquest has taken place, they will take measures as good guardians are supposed to do.

Organization, which we support, proceeds from totally different assumptions. It assumes that the realm of labor is a world of its own and best suited to be the judge of its own interests. It assumes that when these interests impinge on those of other groups, it is in the best interest of the laborers that they fight this fight themselves. It assumes that the government should come to their aid only when, through no fault of their own, the balance between the social powers has been disturbed. Hence there is no question of guardianship, only of a helping hand for the working class to get to its feet and stand on its own legs. In order to realize this in accordance with the nature of life and not contrary to it, there must be organization on both sides. The government should get its information from permanent organizations rather than a one-time inquest.

Still, we do not condemn the present Inquest and will not resist any measure which the minister of justice might take to bring it to completion. "Anything that brings to light is light." But we do hope that, once the inquest has been concluded, the minister will not be tempted to save the situation on his own by imposing measures from the top down. Any inquest must have but one purpose: to achieve an efficient organization, the sooner the better. And not until advice from this organization has reached the cabinet, shall the minister have the competency to do on behalf of the state whatever then proves to be necessary.

Thus, we have no weighty objection against the emergency act that has already been proposed. Luther once said that children should be given "apples and pears,"[15] and if the minister feels that public opinion demands this hors d'oeuvre to whet the appetite for the main course, we have no problem with that. But those who believe that this type of legislation will silence the storm are quite mistaken. That would be like the concessions of the Girondins, which merely betray weakness and increase discontent.[16]

No, organization is the important thing. Not a pseudo-organization as proposed by Mr. Kerdijk,[17] who wants chambers of industry alongside the chambers of commerce with the kindhearted admission of a couple of workers. In the present struggle commerce and industry represent a common, not an opposite, interest.[18] No, we must depend on independent organization of both capital and labor. Only when our legal system has instituted such will order come out of chaos and each interest have its natural advocate.

We should not be led astray by the German example. The German people are accustomed to being under the guardianship of the authorities and to accept any mitigation of their fate as a gift from the government. But that is not in the nature of the Dutch. We are keen on personal initiative.

---

15. In a letter to his son Reformer Martin Luther (1483-1546) speaks of a "a pretty, beautiful, [and] cheerful garden where there are many children wearing little golden coats. [They] pick up fine apples, pears, cherries, [and] yellow and blue plums under the trees; they sing, jump, and are merry. They also have nice ponies with golden reins and silver saddles. I asked the owner of the garden whose children they were. He replied: 'These are the children who like to pray, study, and be good.' Then I said: 'Dear sir, I also have a son, whose name is Hänschen Luther. Might he not also [be permitted] to enter the garden, so that he too could eat such fine apples and pears, and ride on these pretty ponies, and play with these children?' Then the man answered: 'If he too likes to pray, study and be good, he too may enter the garden'" (LW 49:323-24).

16. The Girondins were the rivals of the more radical Jacobins in the Legislative Assembly of revolutionary France, 1793-94. When their policies fell into disfavor with the Parisian crowds, they responded with small compromises and symbolic gestures only. They were executed or exiled during the Reign of Terror.

17. The Progressive Liberal member of Parliament, Arnold Kerdijk (1846-1905), was a champion of the public school and advocated tax reform and consumer cooperatives as solutions to the social question.

18. *Note by the author:* The Royal Decree of November 9, 1851, defines the existing "chambers of commerce *and factories*" as bodies to which not only businessmen but also industrialists can be nominated, both with full voting rights. If the members disagree on, for example, import duties, suborganizations within a chamber, one for commerce and one for industry, could independently inform the government of their specific point of view.

Our strength lies in the spontaneous resilience of the citizens. The air we have to breathe is called civic freedom. So there is nothing against letting the Inquest be pursued a little further and shed some more light on working conditions, and there is nothing against having some emergency legislation stop one or two abusive practices. But you will not arrive at a lasting solution.

Besides, creating such organization can be done very quickly since the government need only call a bare framework into existence, invested with the authority to further organize itself and to submit any pertinent proposals if such assistance from the government were desired. ...[19]

Only when such organization exists will no single group among the workers any longer dominate the conversation but the entire working class will find peace and quietly help to build a better house. All the issues that will eventually have to be part of a labor code—such as the relationships between apprentices, journeymen, supervisors, and employers; letters of recommendation in hiring practices; wage scales; working hours; safety provisions; sickness and old-age insurance; the care of widows and orphans; strikes; and so on[20]—will be solved in the wrong way if they are imposed on the working class from on high. They will be of benefit only if they are the fruit of cooperation between the employers on the one side and the workers on the other.

This also bypasses the legal problem of whether it is within the government's competence to intervene in these matters. In this scenario the state regulates only what belongs indisputably to its task: namely, to enable these social interests to organize themselves within a legal framework and on this basis to make their wishes known. It will subsequently give legal sanction to additional regulations that both parties may desire.

We intentionally refrain from discussing more specific problems. Whether it will someday be necessary to change our laws apropos of marriage, property, and inheritance; whether some changes in our fiscal system are in order; whether, owing to the social question, church and school will have to function in a more substantial and practical way; whether, in light of the social question, the state will need to extend the right to vote to all heads of households; and whether the government, in providing for

---

19. At this point Kuyper recalls the scheme of labor, commerce, and arbitration councils sketched above and provides further details on how they would operate.
20. See *OP*, §297.

the organization of labor, will to some extent have to follow the German example—we have our opinions on all these matters but feel we ought not to give any final answers so long as organization has not come into being.

The very understandable unrest and ferment among our laboring class, which currently voices its opposition against the state through the creation of all sorts of alliances and associations, should first be guided into legal channels. Only then can we make progress.

We would like to see this organization formed as soon as possible for another reason as well. The controversy that has erupted once again over the provincial states reminds us how foolish it is to have the upper chamber of the States-General elected by them. This is to mix political and provincial interests to the detriment of both. For this reason, already in 1878, we suggested transforming the first chamber into a chamber of interests and to have its members elected not by the provincial states but by the various social bodies, so that the universities, the large cities, commerce, industry, agriculture, and labor—and why not also church, school, and philanthropy?—would be represented in this chamber.[21]

We shall come a step closer to this ideal as soon as the chambers of commerce, industry, and agriculture on the one hand, and the chambers of labor on the other, have a solid organization, each anchored in its own soil.

---

21. For Kuyper's idea about "organic" representation in the upper house of Parliament, see *OP*, §§135–38.

THE SOCIAL
QUESTION AND
THE CHRISTIAN
RELIGION

TEXT INTRODUCTION

Kuyper delivered this address at the opening of the Christian Social Congress, which met in Amsterdam on November 9–12, 1891. The congress came about as part of a broader international Christian response to changing social conditions in light of political and economic revolutions of the eighteenth and nineteenth centuries. The Christian Workingmen's Federation (Patrimonium) cosponsored the congress, and the other sponsor was the Antirevolutionary Party, which Patrimonium had accused of favoring the middle and upper classes and never nominating one of their own in a winnable district. The congress was organized in part to head off the formation of a separate Christian labor party. This new translation has been carefully compared at every point with the first English translation by Dirk Jellema, published as *Christianity and the Class Struggle* (Grand Rapids: Piet Hein, 1950), and the second edited by James W. Skillen, published as *The Problem of Poverty* (Grand Rapids: Baker, 1991; repr., Sioux Center, IA: Dordt College Press, 2011). The four divisions and the subheadings that were added to the Skillen edition have been adopted. All references, unless indicated otherwise by brackets or identified as editor's notes, are Kuyper's; unlike the earliest editions of this piece in English, the notes are unabridged in this version. Kuyper's references have been conformed to modern style conventions where possible.

SOURCE: Abraham Kuyper, *Het Sociale Vraagstuk en de Christelijke Religie: Rede bij de opening van het Sociaal Congres op 9 November 1891 gehouden*

(Amsterdam: J. A. Wormser, 1891). Translated by Harry Van Dyke. Annotations by Jordan J. Ballor and Harry Van Dyke. First published in Jordan J. Ballor, ed., *Makers of Modern Christian Thought: Leo XIII & Abraham Kuyper on the Social Question* (Grand Rapids: Acton Institute, 2016).

THE SOCIAL QUESTION AND THE CHRISTIAN RELIGION

I. FACING THE REALITY OF POVERTY

I think I will act in accordance with your wishes if right at the outset, in this opening address, I define the purpose of our first congress as modestly as possible. Not for a moment should the idea take hold that we mean to emulate one of those impressive assemblies where specialists from every country in Europe come together to display their wealth of knowledge and show off their brilliant talents. One unfortunate result of the state's monopoly on higher education in our country is that we have not as yet produced any specialists;[1] none of us at this congress stands out as an authority on

---

1. To be sure, one may counter that the more socialist school in economic theory did receive university appointments, in our country as well as abroad. However, it should be noted (1) that when there was talk some years back of appointing a more radical economist to a chair in political economy, the appointment was thwarted and ultimately stopped by [the ministry in] The Hague; (2) that in other countries appointments went almost exclusively to *state* socialists; and (3) that the ministry, if need be, is not afraid (as became apparent recently at the State University of Groningen) to appoint a more radical economist, but only because a fundamental

economics, for example. And unless my senses deceive me, you have not come here to cross swords with the opposition in a public tournament, but rather to talk among ourselves as brothers united in the name of Jesus for the purpose of having a serious discussion of this question: What should we be doing as confessors of Christ about the social needs of our time? In other countries, too, people who profess Jesus have increasingly realized that action is needed. Think of the action of the Christian Social Workers' Party [Christlichsoziale Arbeiterspartei] in the circle around Count Waldersee in Berlin, or the Christian socialists, inspired by Maurice and Kingsley, who have joined forces in London under Rev. Headlam,[2] or the Christian Society of Social Economics [Société chrétienne pour économie sociale] of Switzerland, organized two years ago in Geneva.[3] And speaking

---

unity was assured between the professor and his more orthodox colleagues: both refuse to reckon with special revelation. However, as soon as it is a question of filling a chair in a law faculty with someone who is not only a Christian and a jurist but who wants to be a *Christian jurist*, they will have none of him, either for constitutional law or political economy. Thorbecke, who was very radical for his time, was appointed; Groen van Prinsterer was not.

2. *Ed. note*: Alfred von Waldersee (1832–1904) was a field marshal under Kaiser Wilhelm II. Prominent Christian socialists included court preacher Adolf Stöcker (1835–1909) and Rev. Rudolf Todt (1839–87), who helped found the Central Union for Social Reform and the Christian Social Workers' Party. F. D. Maurice (1805–72) and Charles Kingsley (1819–75) were Anglican clergymen and founders of "Christian socialism" in Britain. Stewart Headlam (1847–1924) was an Anglican priest whose activism was explicitly inspired by Maurice and Kingsley.

3. This association was founded in Geneva in the spring of 1888, on the initiative of Mr. Frédéric Necker. I call attention to the following articles in its bylaws:

    ART. 1

    The goal of the Christian Society of Social Economics is to gain insight into prevailing social conditions in Switzerland that are contrary to the laws of justice, charity, and solidarity which according to the very order of God must govern relations among men, and to bring about their reform by the use of means that are in harmony with these laws.

    ART. 2

    Placing itself outside all political, ecclesiastical, or theological interests, it appeals to all those who acknowledge Jesus Christ as their Master and who believe that applying the principles taught in his gospel is the solution to all the questions affecting the happiness of every individual in particular and the progress of humanity in general.

    ART. 3

    It accepts as members all persons who, adhering to these views and principles, wish to cooperate in whatever way toward their realization.

of Christianity in the broadest sense, think of what has been done toward a solution of the social question from the side of Catholics[4] by such capable

---

Art. 4

It proposes to attain its goal by stimulating, through conferences or otherwise, the study of all relevant topics, by issuing publications from time to time, by taking up contact with associations that pursue a similar goal, and finally by affirming through all possible means the duty incumbent upon Christians to work toward the moral and material well-being of the masses.

Art. 5

The foregoing provisions may not be changed by the General Assembly unless the proposed changes have been approved by three quarters of the members of the Association.

In the opening address by Mr. Necker on Feb. 18, 1889, the goal of the Society is explained further in these words: "It is therefore not enough to help the unfortunate privately, or even to combat this or that cause of the suffering. We must find out whether we cannot take collective measures more generally and get at the misery in all its sources at once. We must acquire special knowledge, for these complicated problems are not solved with instinct or enthusiasm. That is what our discussion must be about. At the same time, all members [of the steering committee] agree that, in order to acknowledge that Christ has come to bring to mankind salvation and healing of all their ills, the true remedy can only be found in the application of his teachings."

Thus our conclusion is that it was not only useful but necessary to establish an association that can guide Christians in gaining better than usual insight into the current conditions of the social order that cannot fail to make enemies of order and especially enemies of the gospel, and to seek a solution to problems which interest all men to such a high degree.

See *Bulletin No. 1* (Geneva, 1889), 9–10. Last year the Society published *Quatre écoles d'économie sociale, conférences données à l'Aula de l'université de Genève* [Four socio-economic schools: Lectures delivered in the auditorium of the University of Geneva] (Paris: Fischbacher, 1890), a publication we recommend highly. The Roman Catholic position of Frédéric Le Play is explained by Claudio Jannet, socialistic collectivism by G. Stiegler, state socialism by Charles Gide, and the liberal or classical school by Frédéric Passy [*Ed. note*: This latter work appears in English translation as Frédéric Passy, "The School of Liberty (1890)," *Journal of Markets & Morality* 20, no. 2 (Fall 2017): 413–69]. A similar Christian association exists in France under the name *Association protestante française pour l'Etude pratique des questions sociales* [Protestant Association for Practical Study of Social Questions]. Its *Bulletin* is included in the *Revue de Théologie pratique et d'études sociales*.

4. We must admit, to our shame, that the Roman Catholics are far ahead of us in their study of the social question—very far in fact. Although the school of Le Play—who in his well-known works *La Réforme sociale en France*, 2 vols. (Paris: E. Dentu, 1866); *L'Organisation du travail* (Tours: A. Mame, 1870); and *L'Organisation de la famille* (Paris: Téqui, 1871), more or less went his own way—is not identical with the Catholic school, still we do not ignore that men like Ketteler, Christoph Moufang, Claudio Jannet,

intellectuals as Le Play and Von Ketteler; by a whole series of significant congresses in Germany, France, and Belgium; and most recently by Leo XIII in his encyclical.[5]

Albert de Mun, Charles-Emile Freppel, Charles Périn, and others have not only engaged in serious study of the social question but have also laid out the direction we should follow. *La question agraire* (Paris: Retaux-Bray, 1887), by Rudolf Meyer and G. Ardent; *Le Patron: sa fonction, ses devoirs, ses responsbilités*, and *De la richesse dans les sociétés chrétiennes* (Paris: Victor Lecoffre, 1861), by Périn; and to a certain extent also [a work by novelist] Arvède Barine, *L'Oeuvre de Jésus-ouvrier* (Paris: Fischbacher, 1879), provide many surprising insights into the practical ideas of these authors. But Catholic activity is even more impressive when we look at their frequent conferences, their periodical literature, and the associations they have founded. In particular the Unions de Patrons en faveur des Ouvriers [Employers' unions for the benefit of workers] in Belgium, about which Rev. Pierson will give more details at our congress, is an excellent undertaking that deserves to be emulated. The clear pronouncements of Cardinal Newman are familiar enough, and although German and French Catholics are somewhat divided—the former lean more toward relying on the state, the latter more toward the church alone—the encyclical of Leo XIII will probably soon bring them together. Thus Catholic activities should spur us on to show greater energy (although Catholics *here at home* are still mostly inactive)—all the more so since we Protestants can learn more from the Roman Catholics than from the Knights of Labor in America, who did start out under Stephens in 1869 by requiring an oath on the Bible but abandoned it already in 1878 at the order's assembly in Philadelphia. At the assembly in Richmond in 1886 the entire order went over to socialism lock, stock, and barrel. The Christlichsoziale Arbeiterspartei, too, gave us less by comparison, both because it leans too much in the direction of state socialism and because it fails to penetrate to the fundamental principles involved. Precisely the latter is being done by the encyclical, and what is more, it deals solely with those principles that all Christians hold in common and that we too share with our Roman Catholic fellow countrymen.

For the Knights of Labor, see the informative work by Arthur Hadley, *Socialism in the United States* [*Ed. note*: Although Arthur T. Hadley commented widely on economic matters, including the Knights of Labor, efforts to locate a work by this title have been unsuccessful. Kuyper may have intended to refer here to the work of another prominent economist of that era, Richard T. Ely, such as *Recent American Socialism* (Baltimore: Johns Hopkins University Press, 1885), and "Socialism in America," *North American Review* 142, no. 355 (June 1886): 519–25], and Amédée Villard, *Le Socialisme moderne; son dernier état* (Paris: Guillaumin, 1889), 190. A good survey of the Catholic movement is Landelin Winterer, *Le socialisme international; Coup d'oeil sur le mouvement socialiste de 1885 à 1890* (Paris: Lecoffre; Mühlhausen: Gangloff, 1890).

5. *Ed. note*: Frédéric Le Play (1802–82), French engineer turned sociologist who launched the systematic study of the family in industrial society; Wilhelm von Ketteler (1811–77), bishop of Mainz, pioneer of Christian social thought in Germany; Leo XIII, encyclical letter *Rerum Novarum* (May 15, 1891).

We Have Been Too Slow to Act

Our own entry, therefore, does not come too early but too late. We lag behind others when we could have been in the vanguard. After all, before a single voice had been raised by Christians outside our borders, Willem Bilderdijk, Isaäc da Costa, and Willem Groen van Prinsterer had already called our attention to the social problem.[6] As early as 1825 Bilderdijk addressed the lower classes in this vein: "You sigh and languish in poverty and decay, While luxury feasts on the fruit of your hands."

And in the face of this problem he parodied the false theory of philanthropy when he introduced a classical liberal as saying: "The land is weighted down with paupers: To a work camp with them! Good riddance. They're only rascals on relief that we pity, but even the deserving poor cost far too much. The poor are hungry, sure; but do they have a job? What use are they when jobs for them are lacking?" By contrast, Bilderdijk put his finger on the sore spot by calling Christians to repentance in the opening lines of his volume of biting verse: "Whenever a people is fated to perish in sin, in the church the disease of the soul will begin."[7] Some fifteen years later, da Costa lashed out with equal relentlessness at the plutocracy—the "rule of money," as he called it. He pictured the social problem—then imminent, today all too real—in the following contrast:

> Here, disproportionate luxury, outwardly healthy, glowing
> with youth, but inwardly scorched, destroying the sap of life,
> as like a cancer, undoing the balance between the classes. ...
> There, muttering at toil that gives no bread; free men weighed
> down by yokes, at sites where walls blaze night and day with

---

6. *Ed. note*: Willem Bilderdijk (1756–1831) and Isaäc da Costa (1798–1860) were Dutch poets associated with the Réveil ("revival"), an evangelical reform movement in the Netherlands with similarities and connections to evangelical revivals elsewhere in Europe, including England and Switzerland. Guillaume (Willem) Groen van Prinsterer (1801–76) was the leading member of the "confessional" party in the Dutch Reformed Church and founding father of the antirevolutionary movement in Dutch politics.

7. W. Bilderdijk, *Nieuwe Oprakeling* (Dordrecht: J. de Vos, 1827), 43, 46, 47. R. A. Kollewijn, *Bilderdijk, zijn leven en werken* (Amsterdam: Van Holkema and Warendorf, 1891), 2:136, also points to this trait in Bilderdijk's reflections. To some extent one may even look upon Bilderdijk as a forerunner of state socialism insofar as he demanded that the state provide every twenty-year-old young man the chance to be in a position to marry. See his *Briefwisseling met Tydeman* (Sneek: Van Druten & Bleeker, 1866–67), 2:67ff.

heat, and cityscapes grow black from everlasting smoke, and
souls are choked by fumes.[8]

When da Costa penned this prophecy he was not parroting socialism but
speaking a quarter-century before Karl Marx founded his International in
London in 1864. And in 1853 Groen van Prinsterer frightened the members
of Parliament with his brusque declaration: "As for the ideas of socialism,
one should be mindful of the wretched condition of the lower classes, and
especially of the harm that the higher classes, through their moral corruption and false science, have brought about among the common people."
Groen declared that in socialism "truth is mingled with error, which gives
it power," and he recognized that "we must strive to improve material conditions too, the unjustness of which redoubles the influence of the socialist
error."[9] He called upon his fellow Christians to extinguish the fire when he
wrote that "socialism finds its source in the French Revolution and," like
the Revolution, "can only be vanquished by Christianity."[10] Thus we have

---

8. *Da Costa's kompleete dichtwerken* (Haarlem: A. C. Kruseman, 1861–63), 2:397; see also,
    besides his *Bezwaren tegen den geest der eeuw* [Grievances against the spirit of the age]
    (Leiden: L. Herdingh, 1823), his magnificent song "De Vrijheid" [Freedom], p. 364;
    and no less his depiction of socialist misery in London, woven into his "Wachter, wat
    is er van de nacht?" [Watchman, what of the night?], 3:87; as well as his occasional
    poem "1648–1848," 3:113ff., esp. 119.
9. *Ed. note*: G. Groen van Prinsterer, *Adviezen in de Tweede Kamer der Staten-Generaal*
    (Utrecht: Kemink en Zoon, 1856–57), 2:556–73, here 571; speech of December 19, 1853.
10. G. Groen van Prinsterer, *Nederlandsche Gedachten*, 2nd series (Amsterdam: H. Höveker,
    1869–76), 4:64. In a speech in the lower house of Parliament on June 18, 1850, Groen
    warned: "It is the misfortune of our age that democracy is put on a pedestal. It will
    do us no good to give power to the middle classes. They too are a new aristocracy and
    a new privileged class, and it will only mean a transition." G. Groen van Prinsterer,
    Adviezen in de Tweede Kamer der Staten-Generaal, zitting van 1849–1850 (Amsterdam:
    Johannes Müller, 1851), 2:125. That for the rest Groen expected improvement only
    from a better organization of society is clear from the following:
    "Our worst ailment is pauperism. Poverty, unemployment; ruptured relations
    between the higher and lower classes; no bond save work and pay; proletari-
    ans and capitalists. Where this will take us is uncertain; but there is no doubt
    where it came from. From *liberty and equality* as understood by the Revolution.
    Just one detail. When that slogan was first raised, guilds and corporations
    too had to go. The desire was for free competition; no restraints on skills
    and industry; no hateful monopolies exercised by individuals or associa-
    tions; the development of private initiative and commerce would guarantee
    a better future. Well, the future that was envisioned has arrived. Can it be
    called better? *On this point I am of one voice with the leading spokesmen of the*

been declared to be in default. And that not only by our God-given leaders, but just as strongly by the socialists. They have never stopped appealing to Christ for their utopias. They constantly hold before us solemn Bible texts. In fact, they feel the connection between the social needs and the Christian religion so strongly that they have not hesitated to present Christ himself as the great prophet of socialism and to exclaim: "There can be no talk of the failure of the Christian work of emancipation: a mere two thousand years lie between the beginning and the conclusion of the work initiated by Christ."[11]

Accordingly, a liberal of the old school, Alfred Naquet, is worried that socialism might pave the way for new triumphs for Christianity, and he reproaches socialists precisely for furthering the cause of religion despite their hatred of it. "You are doing the work of religion," he exclaims, "when you put in the foreground exactly those problems whose solution closely involves Christianity."[12] This is an unintentional yet telling tribute to the influence that Christianity can exercise in helping solve the social

---

present-day revolution. It is this liberty, this unrestricted competition, this removal, as much as possible, of the natural relationship between employer and employee, which tears the social bonds, ends in the dominance of the rich and the rule of the banking houses, robs artisans of regular sustenance, splits society up into two hostile camps, gives rise to a countless host of paupers, prepares for the attack by the have-nots on the well-to-do and would in many people's eyes render such a deed excusable, if not legitimate. It has brought Europe to a state so dreary and somber as to cause many to call out in terror: Is there no way to revive, in some altered form, the associations that were so recklessly crushed under the revolutionary ruins?"
See G. Groen van Prinsterer, *Vrijheid, Gelijkheid, Broederschap; toelichting op de spreuk der Revolutie* (The Hague: L. van Nifterik, 1848), 83–84.

11. See *Freiland und die Freilandbewegung* (Dresden: E. Pierson, 1891), 57. The quotation occurs in Theodor Hertzka, *Freiland: ein soziales Zukunftsbild* (Dresden: E. Pierson, 1890), 275. This constant appeal by socialists to Christ should be neither underestimated nor overrated. Two motives are at work here. First, it is a tool of propaganda, since they know how easy it is to gain a hearing the moment one appeals to Scripture. But it is also a misguided belief. Some socialists are indeed struck by the glaring contrast between the way Christ viewed the social need and the long-standing attitude toward this need adopted by many Christians. In both cases there is an implicit acknowledgment of the authority that Scripture still exercises, and that is a joyful sign. A utopia similar to *Freiland* has been written, besides Bellamy in his *Looking Backward 2000–1887* (Boston: Ticknor, 1888), by American Ismar Thiusen (pseud.) in his *Looking Forward; or The Diothas* (London: G. P. Putnam's Sons, 1890).

12. A. Naquet, *Socialisme collectiviste et socialisme libéral* (Paris: E. Dentu, 1890), vi.

question—an influence that comes out even more beautifully in these rich words of Fichte:

> Christianity conceals within its womb a much greater treasure for the renewal of life than one suspects. Thus far it has applied its strength only to *individuals* and only indirectly to the state. But anyone, believer or unbeliever, who has been in a position to notice Christianity's hidden driving force must grant that it could apply marvelous organizational strength also *to society*. Once this strength breaks to the surface, the Religion of the Cross will shine before the whole world in all the profoundness of its ideas and all the wealth of blessing it brings.[13]

But enough citations, friends—more than enough—to convince you that one simply cannot deny the intimate connection between the social question and the Christian religion. We feel ashamed that this conviction has not been stronger among us, or at any rate has not roused us to action much earlier. We are humbly penitent in the face of such crying need. Why has it taken so long for us to move into action in the name of Jesus?

Do you protest that this obvious truth need not be argued in a gathering such as this? I take your protest to be prompted by a spirit of self-reproach, not pride. In the face of the enormous needs of our time, needs which at every point are connected to the very core of error and sin, how could we possibly fail to look to *Christus Consolator*, who never ceases to call out with divine compassion also to our deeply troubled times: "Come unto me, richest century that ever was, yet so deadly weary and heavy, and I will give you rest."

THE CONNECTION BETWEEN CHRISTIANITY AND THE PROBLEM OF POVERTY

Let me not spend another word on the reality of this connection. The very presupposition of this congress is that we acknowledge it. But what you do expect of me—and, with your indulgence, what I shall endeavor to offer—is to lay bare the threads by which these two phenomena (on the one hand the Christian religion and on the other the social question) are intimately

---

13. These beautiful words are quoted in the foreword to *Quatre écoles d'économie sociale*, vi.

connected. To be convinced that this connection is real is not enough: it must also become concrete, so that it can raise our consciousness.[14]

As my point of departure I shall take a contrast that is plain for all to see. I mean the contrast between nature as it exists independent of our will, and our human art that acts on nature.[15] The entire social question, we should realize, arises from the connection between human life and the material world that surrounds us. Now in human life, as well as in the material world, there is on the one hand a power beyond our reach that we commonly call *nature*, and on the other there is a power originating in the human will that we may refer to simply as *art*. Our human nature is placed in the nature that surrounds us, not in order to leave nature as it is, but to work on nature instinctively and irrepressibly, by means of art, to improve and perfect it. An example is the stud farm for creating thoroughbreds. Another is the skill of the florist who does not just gather bouquets of wild flowers but multiplies and refines varieties by mingling seeds. Men heat water to make steam and cut stone to produce diamonds. They harness rushing streams that split the mountains by guiding them into safer channels, to use the water for shipping and irrigation. In short, human art acts on every area of nature not to destroy it—much less to erect a mechanical structure along-side it—but rather to unlock nature's hidden strength, or else to tame its wild force. God's ordinances require this. While still in paradise, man was

---

14. A mistake that is often made is that people associate the Christian religion solely with the world of feeling. To be sure, even in this respect its significance for the social question is great, insofar as a great deal depends on the state of feeling in rich and poor, in government officials and citizens, and even in the public interpreters and commentators. He who can contribute even a little to improve these feelings does an excellent work. But the Christian religion is mutilated when its action is confined to the world of emotions. It professes not just Christ but the Triune God—Father, Son, and Holy Spirit—for which reason its first article of faith is "I believe in God the Father Almighty, Maker of heaven and earth." This implies that the Christian religion must also have a position on our relation to nature, government, and our fellow man, including human nature and its attributes—thus a position on the very phenomena that govern the social problem.

15. I concede that the word "art" is commonly used only for those arts that call for aesthetic appreciation. Yet the word itself does not limit it to that, and usage, even today, allows a broader denotation. At bottom, "art" simply denotes a power given to man to wrestle free from the overpowering force of nature. Nowadays, free creative art is called "art" in a more restricted sense only because man's triumph over nature comes out best when he manages to portray the idea of nature more beautifully than nature itself.

given the mandate "to preserve and cultivate" the material world.[16] It was created for man to improve and perfect it. "All creatures," our confession states so beautifully, were made "for the service of mankind, to the end that man may serve his God."[17]

It follows that this applies equally to human life, both in its personal and social aspects. We neglect our duty if we allow our inner nature to run its course unrestrained and fail to come to its aid to ennoble it through the holy art of "watching, praying, and struggling."[18] Shame on fathers and mothers who let their children grow up naturally without acting upon nature through nurture and education. And it is nothing but primitive barbarism to abandon society to the course of nature without human intervention. The art of politics, too, taken in the higher sense of statecraft, intervenes so that society may develop into a community; and so that social life, both by itself and in its relation to the material world, may be ennobled.[19]

If in the course of history man had not made mistakes or fallen into error, and no crime or egoism had disrupted this natural development, human society would have run its course in peace and advanced undisturbed toward an ever-greater state of happiness. Alas, humankind did not live in such a desirable state. To be sure, among virtually all peoples human

---

16. See Gen 2:15, where it says literally: "The LORD God took the man and put him in the garden of Eden to work it and keep it." The notion of "keeping" can only mean that man was charged with barring all influence of Satan. After all, there was no other enemy, and Satan could enter Eden only through man's heart. And as for the word "work" (*'abad*), this cannot refer to plowing and digging, which is contrary to the whole character of paradise, but must be taken in the sense of that higher cultivation that human art works upon nature.

17. Belgic Confession, Art. 12.

18. *Ed. note*: A formula associated with the Réveil.

19. Human societies too are partly a work of nature, partly a product of human art. For things to go well, human art in the political and social domains should not violate nature or cripple its power, but guide and develop it. Further, it may not regulate this guidance of nature and of the nations in an arbitrary fashion, but must do so according to the ordinances of God that are given both in his Word and in the idea of man. The mistake of the French Revolution was that in its arrogance it rejected historical statecraft; in part it wanted to regress to undeveloped nature, and in part wished to remake the existing state of affairs according to its own insights. Similarly, the theory of nationalities embraced by Napoleon III was a one-sided emphasis on national character at the price of human art in this area. That said, both were understandable reactions to the sinful approach of our former diplomats, politicians, and jurists, who considered nations an abstraction, a kind of *corpus vile* [worthless body] that could be experimented with at one's pleasure.

instinct has prompted men to acknowledge certain indispensable standards for any human society, and from ancient times men of genius and courage have made many felicitous contributions in this area. But as soon as the need arose for a more elaborate ordering of the complex phenomenon we call human society, action after action was misdirected, both by those who set the tone in society and by those who held the reins of power.

HUMAN ERROR AND SIN

In both instances the series of misdirected actions was invariably caused either by error or by sin. The cause was error whenever people were ignorant of the essence of human nature and its social attributes, and unaware of the laws governing society and the production, distribution, and use of material goods. But the cause was also—and just as much—sin. Owing to men's greed or hunger for power, sin disrupted or thwarted a healthy growth of society, sometimes by violence, and then again by false practices and unjust laws. Occasionally it caused a very unhealthy development to fester for centuries. As time went on, error and sin joined forces to enthrone false principles that violated human nature and to erect out of these false principles whole systems that gave injustice a semblance of justice and stamped as normal what was actually in conflict with the demands of life.[20]

---

20. The two forces of error and sin must always be sharply distinguished if one wishes to understand the development of society. A third force is also operative, that of necessity independent of human involvement; this power can be left out of consideration here, although it is a fact that this necessity too, which is mostly the consequence of wars, insurrections, and disasters, is just as much related to sin. But in this connection we must note two other forces that give direction to society, namely the power of custom and the power of the law. The power of custom is the collective expression of a nation's predispositions and arises imperceptibly; but customs are also given a certain direction in every domain by the great and mighty of this world, and no less by the intellectuals and philosophers who by influencing the nation's ideas gradually alter the nation's predispositions as well. But besides these two influences the condition of society depends on a country's laws, especially in those states and those times in which the law is less governed by the national spirit than the national spirit by the law. Exactly for this reason every mistake committed in this area must always be accounted for in terms of sin. Sin, on the one hand by the darkening of our mind (in error) and on the other by the weakening of our will (in direct sin), turns the impact of our human art upon society into a curse instead of a blessing. This might not be noticed right away, and popular leaders and statesmen only seldom realize sufficiently their awesome responsibility in this regard. Nevertheless, in this way too God visits a righteous judgment on the peoples—peoples that are themselves the reason why human art in the social domain in part falls short and in part corrupts

This reckless play with human society was carried on among all peoples in every age. It was carried on in private life by intellectuals and property owners, and before long, under their inspiration and just as recklessly, by governments. For while it is perfectly true that the social question in the narrower sense is discussed only very intermittently, with the result that many people are under the delusion that government intervention in social problems is a novelty of our own time, yet actually there has never been any country in the world where the government did not in various ways control both the course of social life and its relationship to material wealth. Governments have done so by means of all kinds of rules in civil law; they have done so through commercial codes, indirectly also through constitutional law and criminal law. In regard to material wealth, governments have intervened by means of inheritance law, the system of taxation, import and export duties, regulations governing real estate, agriculture, colonial administration, coinage, and so much more. It has never been possible in any developed country to speak of a free, entirely instinctual development of society; human art has everywhere taken in hand the development of natural forces and relationships. But while we must gratefully acknowledge that this intervention by human art has in general brought us from a barbaric situation to a well-ordered society—indeed, while we must concede that the continuous unfolding of society reinforces our belief in an overriding rule of Providence—yet we cannot for a moment doubt that this government intervention, which often proceeded from untrue principles, in every age has made conditions unsound when they could have been sound. It has in many ways poisoned our relationships and brought about untold misery, even as the end of government should be the happiness and dignity of its people.[21]

---

so much, and why art then ends up seeking to restore its strength in the frenzy of revolution. See Louis-Mathurin Moreau-Christophe, *Du problème de la misère et de sa solution, chez les peuples anciens et modernes*, 3 vols. (Paris: Guillaumin, 1851).

21. Only from this point of view does one understand the French Revolution at one and the same time as horribly necessary and deeply sinful. State policies had gradually led the nations down impassable paths and had done such violence to human nature that a reaction became inexorable. Things had to bend or break. The statecraft of the time should have repented of its unnatural ways and of its own accord infused fresh air into the oppressive atmosphere. Failing that, the political fabric could only be torn to shreds. Nature always reacts when art tries to force it. To that extent a violent explosion was bound to come, and the French Revolution was indeed a righteous judgment of God on those who had misused the power and fortune entrusted

The inequality among men, which cannot be undone, gave the stronger an ascendancy over the weaker, as though we were not a human society but a herd of animals where the rule holds that the stronger animals devour the weaker ones. The stronger almost always managed to bend every custom and government ordinance in such a way that they stood to gain and the weaker lost out. They did not sink their teeth into each other's flesh, like cannibals, but the powerful ground down the weak with a weapon against which there was no defense. And where governments as servants of God still protected the weak, the more powerful class of society soon learned how to exert such a preponderant influence on politics that governmental authority, which should have protected the weak, became a weapon against them.[22] This was not because the stronger man was more evil in his heart than the weaker man, since no sooner did a member of the lower class rise to the top than he in turn took part just as harshly—if not more harshly—in the wicked oppression of members of his former class. No, the cause of the evil lay in this: that man was cut off from his eternal destiny and not honored as created in the image of God. Nor did men reckon with the majesty of the Lord, who alone by his grace is mighty to bridle a generation sunk in sin.

This unjust situation arose already in ancient times, of which the Preacher complains so movingly: "Again I saw all the oppressions that are done under the sun. And behold, the tears of the oppressed, and they had no one to comfort them! On the side of their oppressors there was power,

---

to them. Yet this in no way diminishes the deeply sinful character of the French Revolution insofar as it separated, contrary to God's ordinances, nature from history and replaced the will of the Creator of nations with the will of the individual. This stamped it as a movement opposed in principle to God and his Christ, and for that very reason, after a short breathing spell, it brought a corruption deadlier than the corruption it revolted against in 1789.

22. The Crown, it is said, must stand above the parties and act against the superior power of the majority in the interest of the minority whenever needed. That is correct, yet it is only a derived thesis. At the basis of it lies the more general thesis that government is the minister of God and thus must defend the oppressed in God's name, since God takes pity on the oppressed. This is how it must be in the courts when justice is dispensed. This is how it must be with the police when violence erupts. And similarly in the life of society, government through its laws and regulations must take care to preserve the balance and protect the weaker members. To view civil government as the organ and instrument of the majority of the moment is therefore a deeply sinful conception of the task of the magistracy. Then government lines up with those who are already the stronger, in order to oppress the weaker even more; this leads to reaction and anarchy, and ultimately fosters nihilism.

and there was no one to comfort them" (Eccl 4:1).[23] Think of situations like the one where Naboth was murdered so that Jezebel could add his field to the royal park of Ahab [see 1 Kgs 21:1–16]. Or if you will, situations that were forever stigmatized by our Lord in the parable of the rich man and poor Lazarus [see Luke 16:19–31], and situations against which James flung his apostolic anathema when he wrote: "Come now, you rich, weep and howl for the miseries that are coming upon you. ... Behold, the wages of the laborers who mowed your fields, which you kept back by fraud, are crying out against you, and the cries of the harvesters have reached the ears of the Lord of hosts" (Jas 5:1, 4).[24]

II. JESUS AND THE SOCIAL QUESTION

Now is it conceivable, friends, that the Christian religion, when it came into the world, did not take a stand against so criminal a state of affairs? I am sure you are aware how at the time these social conditions, worse even than those that today keep Europe and America in a state of tension, foretold the imminent fall of the Roman Empire. A truly Asiatic despotism in almost every colony of Rome maintained a system of exploitation and extortion against which great orators such as Cicero more than once raised their voice in vain. In those days, as in our day, the balance between classes was gone: brazen luxury next to crying need; immense accumulations of capital alongside pauperism, kept out of sight in the slums of Rome. Inevitably, government corruption came next. Sensuality rather than modesty set the tone in public opinion. The masses, carried away by poverty and passion, stood poised to revolt, murder, and plunder.

---

23. Many Bible readers, and also many preachers, make the mistake of reading or discussing moving words such as these without applying them directly to the reality of their own environment.

24. If words as strong as these were not found in the Bible and someone were to venture today to write them down of his own accord, he would be branded a crypto-socialist. For those who want to pin their hope on money and the power of money, Scripture is a hopeless book. The Holy Spirit who speaks in Scripture happens to consider an abundance of gold and silver more dangerous than desirable, and he deems an inheritance of millions not comparable by far to the inheritance that awaits us with the saints. This is what God attests in his Word, so I may not represent it any other way. And let no one reproach me for it, but let him realize that his criticism would attack Scripture itself.

JESUS: MORE THAN A SOCIAL REFORMER

As austere Rome, like sunny Greece, began to sink away into the morass of human misery,[25] a light arose in Bethlehem and a death cry was heard from Golgotha, awakening a new hope for the nations. This was not a new hope in the sense in which men today want to lower the Christ of God to the status of a social reformer. His honorary title, far higher and far richer, was *Savior of the world*. But still, the godliness he wrought among men holds a promise "for the present life and also for the life to come" (1 Tim 4:8)—though Jesus always emphasized that man's eternal welfare comes first, lest soul and body are destroyed in hell [see Matt 10:28]. The worm that never dies, the wailing and the gnashing of teeth in a fire that is never quenched—these were the horrors that gave Jesus no rest as he looked upon the poor human race. The joy to which he called people had to be the eternal joy of his kingdom. The heartlessness of the socialist was never found in the Savior. The socialist, for the sake of improving the lot of humanity in this short span of temporal existence, furiously and recklessly cuts off all prospects of a glory that will endure for all eternity.[26] Neither Jesus nor his apostles ever

---

25. One cannot pay enough attention to the parallel between the social conditions that preceded the fall of the Roman Empire and the social evils in the midst of which we ourselves are living today. Naturally, the forms were different then; but the imbalance was the same; and if the popular press had existed at that time and newspapers had been handed down to us, journalists would almost be able to copy whole articles from them. The moral props of that society were moldy and rotten, as they are today. Roman civilization, excelling in cultural refinements, finally collapsed. Similarly, our Western civilization will eventually succumb, unless the Christian religion, which is still a vital force, intervenes to save it. But in and of itself the danger is no less now than it was then.

    And if someone says that it was the barbarian invasions that delivered the death-blow to the Roman Empire, then we ask whether the growing power of Russia, and partly of the Chinese that hide behind Russia, has nothing to say to us today. See Moreau-Christophe, *Du problème de la misère*.

26. This heartlessness can only be accounted for by the fact that the scholars and the educated began by first undermining the belief in a life after this life, and then eradicated it. Doubt is no first step to faith, and to speak of a "hope of immortality" is tantamount to destroying belief in an eternal existence, at least with the masses. I therefore stand by my use of the term "heartless." Socialists may not personally believe in an eternal life, but neither can they prove the contrary. Is it then not heartless—equate eternal life, for the sake of concreteness, with a thousand years—to entice someone to pursue happiness for say, seventy years, and then have him pay for this with a wretched existence of upwards of nine centuries? And what are a thousand years when measured against eternity?

preached revolution. We are to be subject to every power set over us, and poor Lazarus will be avenged,[27] not while surviving on the crumbs that fall from the rich man's table, but once the rich man suffers eternal torment and poor Lazarus is comforted [see Luke 16:9–31].

If you then ask what Jesus did to bring deliverance from the social needs of his time, here is the answer. He knew that those defiant abuses had sprung from the malignant roots of error and sin, so he confronted the error with truth and broke the power of sin by shedding his blood for that sin and pouring out his Holy Spirit into the hearts of his own. Rich and poor had lost touch as a result of losing their common focus on God, so he called both back to their Father who is in heaven.[28] He realized that the idolatry of money kills nobility in the human heart, so he held up the "service of Mamon"[29] before his followers as an object of profound contempt. He understood the curse that lies in capital, especially for men of great wealth, so

---

27. I do not shrink from using the word "avenged." Scripture forbids us to abandon this idea. "You will only observe with your eyes and see the *punishment* of the wicked," says Ps 91:8 [NIV]. This idea is not at all out of step with what Jesus teaches us in the Gospel: in his parable about Lazarus he lets him *see* the anxious suffering of the rich man, and he even has the rich man appeal to Lazarus' pity to deliver him from his pain.

28. That this really is implied in the name of Father is evident from Mal 2:10, where the prophet asks in the name of the Lord: "Have we not all one Father? Has not one God created us? Why then are we faithless to one another, profaning the covenant of our fathers?" The Lord's Prayer, too, clearly expresses the same thought. In that prayer the poor prays for the rich, that God may give him his bread for that day, and the rich prays the same for the poor. Nowhere does this prayer talk of *me* or *I*, but always of *we* and *us*: "Our Father in heaven, forgive *us* our debts. Give *us* this day *our* daily bread" [Matt 6:9, 12, 11].

29. "Mamon" (not "mammon") is a word in Aramaic that means "capital." It is personified by Jesus in Matt 6:24, to place it directly opposite Jehovah. Mamon is often spoken of in the same breath with the golden calf, but wrongly so. The worship of the golden calf in the desert did not stem from greed; the Israelites had all sacrificed their gold to make that golden calf; besides, what they worshipped in this calf was not gold but Jehovah, under the symbol of a power of nature. No, the scriptural term that serves as the stigma of the worship of capital is the worship of Mamon. The sinful nature of this worship consists in this, that the rich possess wealth not as belonging to the Lord but as though it belonged to them—which then exacts its price in that they fancy they are master of their money whereas money becomes their master. See Otto Wittelshöfer, *Untersuchungen über das Kapital, seine Natur und Function* (Tübingen: Laupp, 1890), who may not be writing from our perspective yet who clearly shows the power inherent in capital. See also Johann Karl Rodbertus, *Das Kapital. Vierter sozialer Brief an Von Kirchmann*, ed. Theophil Kozak (Berlin:

he called out to them to stop accumulating capital and laying up treasures on earth where moth and rust corrupt and thieves break in and steal (see Matt 6:19, 20). Jesus turned away the rich young ruler who could not decide to sell *all* that he had and give to the poor (see Matt 19:16–22). The heart of Jesus did not nurse hatred against the rich but a deep compassion for their pitiable state. Serving Mamon is hard, and it is easier for a camel to pass through the eye of a needle than for a rich man to enter into the kingdom of heaven (see Matt 19:24).[30] Jesus got angry only when the possession of money led to usury and harshness. In one of his parables, the man who refused to forgive his debtor is given over to tormentors and branded as a wicked servant who knows no pity.

By Personal Example

Nor did Jesus limit his work to moral motivation. He practiced what he preached. Where poor and rich were at odds he never chose the side of the wealthier but always joined the poorer. He was born in a stable, and while foxes had holes and birds of the air had nests the Son of Man had nowhere to lay his head (see Matt 8:20).[31] His apostles were not allowed to raise funds; they were to go out without purse or provision. True, one of them carried a purse, but that was Judas, that terrible man who was seduced by love of money and sold his soul to the Devil.[32] The powerful trait of compassion is

---

Putttkammer & Mühlbrecht, 1884), and Franz Stöpel, *Das Geld in der gegenwärtige Wirtschaft* (Minden: Bruns, 1885).

30. Too little notice is taken of this trenchant statement of Jesus, and too few sermons deal with this text. This saying does not rebuke the rich but shows compassion and pity for them. The struggle to repent is so much more difficult for them than for the poor. In light of one's eternal well-being it is an advantage to be poor. Well-considered, a rich man who becomes a true child of God is a double manifestation of God's liberating grace. There is just one thing the Lord does not tolerate: when a rich man dares to oppress a poor man! Then the Lord's wrath is kindled, as is so clearly shown in the parable of the unforgiving servant (see Matt 18:23–35).

31. Jesus had no possessions and no earnings. He lived on gifts of love. I prefer to emphasize this rather than the fact that Jesus had been a workingman. In this I follow Scripture, which tells us nowhere that as a youth Jesus did carpentry work. Not that I would deny this; I even consider it probable; but it is not part of the Gospels' message. However, the Gospels do oblige us to point out that Jesus belonged to the have-nots and lived off gifts of money and goods.

32. Judas carried the money bag (John 12:6; 13:29). To be the treasurer is always dangerous. Dealing with money makes a man materialistic. Money as such has a bad influence on a man's heart. That is why it is so unhealthy for a nation when banking

inscribed on every page of the Gospel whenever Jesus came into contact with the suffering and the oppressed. He did not reject the people "who do not have the law" [Rom 2:14], but drew them to himself. He would not quench the smoking flax [see Isa 42:3]. He healed the sick. He did not shy away from touching the leper. And when the crowd grew hungry, even though they did not yet hunger after the bread of life, he supplied more than enough loaves of bread and more than plenty of fine fish (see Matt 14:14–21).[33]

In this way Jesus coupled theory with practice. His theory was in tune with the prayer of the writer of Proverbs: "Give me neither poverty nor riches; feed me with the food that is needful for me" (Prov 30:8). It is a prayer from which the apostle draws this lesson for the lover of money:

> For we brought nothing into the world, and we cannot take anything out of the world. But if we have food and clothing, with these we will be content. But those who desire to be rich fall into temptation, into a snare, into many senseless and harmful desires that plunge people into ruin and destruction. For the love of money is a root of all kinds of evils. It is through this craving that some have wandered away from the faith and pierced themselves with many pangs. But as for you, O man of God, flee these things. (1 Tim 6:7–11)[34]

---

and the stock exchange become dominant. And that is also why it is precisely the man of high finance for whom the chance to learn to bow humbly before his God is so remote. Bilderdijk realized this when he wrote Da Costa: "It requires no explanation that merchants and professional gamblers have no Christian faith." See Kollewijn, *Bilderdijk, zijn leven en werken*, 2:137.

33. When reading stories such as these we tend to put the emphasis too exclusively on the miracle. Yet the Gospel writer introduces the story by saying: "When he went ashore he saw a great crowd, and he had compassion on them." Jesus helped out with bread and supplemented it with fish; his distribution to the poor was not scanty but generous. Those who have to do the hardest work should be fed the heartiest food.

34. The word that our authorized version [the *Statenvertaling* of 1637] uses for the root of all evil is *geldgierigheid* [miserliness]; but that is not how to read it today. To be a miser today is to commit the sin of stinginess. A miser hoards his money and does not want to spend any of it. But in the seventeenth century *geldgierigheid* meant exactly what it says in the original Greek: *philargyria*, that is, hungering, lusting, after money. Today we call this *geldzucht* [avarice]. There are today, alas, money-grubbers among those who call themselves Christians who live a lavish lifestyle and then think: "I am certainly not tightfisted, so this root of all evil does not apply to me."

But Jesus' "theory" also implied, inversely, that the poor man ought not to grumble, nor let himself be goaded into bitterness and so vent his worries in anxious questions such as, "What shall I eat, or what shall I drink, or with what shall I clothe myself?" "For the Gentiles seek after all these things, and your heavenly Father knows that you need them all." And then follows what is exactly the reverse of what the socialist teaches: "But seek first the kingdom of God and his righteousness, and all these things will be added to you" (Matt 6:25–33).

ORGANIZING THE CHURCH

Such is the "theory." It cuts both ways: it cuts the root of sin in the human heart of both rich and poor.[35] But then the theory is also followed up with the heart-conquering practice of devotion, of self-sacrifice—and yet more: of a divine compassion that first pours all the balm at its disposal into the wounds of suffering mankind, and then finishes, for rich and poor alike, by going as a lamb to the slaughter and as a sheep that is mute before her shearers (see Isa 53:7).

Those acts alone, my friends, that message, such a death, would certainly have been enough in and of themselves to exercise an influence for good on social relations. Overthrowing the idol of Mamon and refocusing life's purpose from earth to heaven must by themselves have brought about a complete revolution in people's outlook on life.

But Jesus did not stop there. He also organized. He sent out a church among the nations, an organization that was bound to impact society in three ways. First, through the ministry of the Word, to the extent that the Word constantly combats the lust for money, comforts the poor and the oppressed, and points to a glory without end in exchange for the sufferings of the present time [see Rom 8:18]. Second, through an organized ministry of benevolence that in the name of the Lord, who is the single owner of all goods, demands the community of goods in the sense that it will not be

---

35. Jesus flattered no one, neither rich nor poor, but put both in their place. That is why Jesus has such high standing. Prominent men in our society generally look down upon the poor and flatter the rich, or else they scoff at the rich while flattering the poor. This is contrary to the Christian religion. Both must be convicted of their sin. Still, it is true that when Scripture corrects the poor it does so much more tenderly and gently; and, by contrast, when it rebukes the rich it uses much harsher language. However, our poor too will gradually lose the faith if they pin their hopes on all kinds of help from the state instead of relying solely on their Father who is in heaven.

tolerated in the circle of believers that a man or a woman should go hungry or lack clothing. And third, through instituting the equality of brothers so as to offset differences in rank and station. He abolished all artificial divisions between men by joining rich and poor in one holy food at the Lord's Supper, as a symbol of the unity that binds them together not only as "children of men" but also, more importantly, as those who are bowed down under the same guilt and have been saved by one and the same sacrifice in Christ.[36]

It is a fact, therefore, that as a direct result of the coming of Christ and the spread of his church among the nations, society became markedly different from what it had been during the pagan era. Roman society of that time was a striking example of what Jesus once called "whitewashed tombs, which outwardly appear beautiful, but within are full of dead people's bones" [Matt 23:27].[37] The whited sepulcher of Rome crumbled into ruins. And short of claiming that the new social order which in due time arose on those ruins corresponded in any way to the ideal that Jesus cherished, yet we may gratefully acknowledge that it gave birth to more tolerable social conditions. No longer did earthly welfare weigh heaviest in public estimation; eternal well-being also carried weight. Slavery was severed at its root and subjected to a moral criticism that ultimately spelled its demise as an institution. The poor and the orphans began to be cared for. The prohibition of usury helped to discourage the accumulation of too much capital. The higher and lower classes approached each other more freely on a more equal footing. And although the contrast between surplus and scarcity was not

---

36. Far too little attention has been paid thus far to the fact that Jesus not only preached but also organized. His circle of 3 disciples, then 12, and then 70, already spoke of an organization; but not until the installation of apostles and deacons and the commission to proclaim the Word and administer the sacraments was that gigantic organization called into existence that has gradually spread to all nations throughout the centuries. And now it is worth noting how this organization was instituted not only for securing the eternal welfare of its followers but most definitely also for removing social ills. This organization produced these twin fruits precisely on account of its divine simplicity. This fact alone tells us that the church abandons her principle when she concerns herself only with heaven and fails to relieve earthly need, and that our diaconates will have to function very differently if they would truly honor Christ.

37. On this, see Charles Letourneau, *L'evolution de la propriété* (Paris: Vigot Frères, 1889), 332ff., and Louis Morosti, *Les problèmes du paupérisme; la vérité sur la propriété et le travail*, 2nd ed. (Paris: A. Ghio, 1887).

eradicated, no longer did excessive luxury clash blatantly with grinding poverty. Society was not yet where it should be, but it was set on a better course. And if the church had not strayed from her simplicity and heavenly ideal, the influence of the Christian religion on political institutions and societal relationships would eventually have become dominant.[38]

For that to happen, however, the pace of evangelizing Europe was too rapid and the diversity of peoples to be assimilated too massive. The conversion of Constantine was a signal for the church to wed herself to worldly power, thereby cutting the nerve of her strength. Hence the gradual infiltration of the church by the world. In the place of disciples who went forth without purse or provision came richly endowed prelates seated in magnificent palaces; and the fisherman from Galilee was succeeded at the head of the Church of Rome by popes surrounded by princely pageantry. A Julius II or a Leo X seemed more intent on paganizing Christendom than on Christianizing the world.[39] The salt had lost its savor and social corruption regained its former strength, a corruption that was checked but not conquered in the countries of the Reformation and that continued to fester in those parts of Europe that remained Roman Catholic. Here, royal absolutism and aristocratic pride in the end evoked the unbearable social

---

38. On this, see the work of Wilhelm Endemann, *Die national-ökonomischen Grundsätze der canonistische Lehre* (Jena: Friedrich Mauke, 1863), vol. 1, in B. Hildebrand, ed., *Jahrbücher für Nationalökonomie und Statistik*. Indeed, the rise of a "system of economic theories and economic policies, developed with phenomenal consistency," was due to "the basic principles of the Christian religion." See Wilhelm Roscher, *Geschichte der National-Oekonomik in Deutschland* (Munich: R. Oldenbourg, 1874), 1:11.

39. In this connection we should certainly not forget that the voluntary poverty of the monastics was an attempt to carry on the original tradition, and to that extent the vow of poverty was a well-intentioned protest against growing worldliness in the church. But, aside from the question whether such vows are lawful, it is a matter of historical record that the monasteries of that age turned the vow of poverty more and more into a fiction. And even if they had remained more faithful to their ideal, the monastics could never have made amends for the immeasurable damage that the church herself inflicted on social relationships by her pursuit of worldly splendor. As long as she was persecuted the church flourished and ennobled social relations. When she came into a position of honor under Constantine it was at the price of her moral influence. As a result she had no choice but to throw her weight on that side of the balance of power that was exactly opposite to where Jesus had put it.

tension that at last erupted in a revolution on French—that is, Roman Catholic—soil.[40]

III. THE SOCIALIST CHALLENGE

The French Revolution, a revolution that every consistent thinker who professes Christ simply must oppose, did its evil work not so much in that it ousted the Bourbons from the throne, nor in that it made the middle class more powerful than clergy and nobility, but in that it completely overturned people's worldview and outlook on life.

While the Christian religion teaches that the union of authority and freedom is guaranteed by the fundamental principle that all men are subject to God, the French Revolution cast out the majesty of the Lord in order to set up an artificial authority based on individual free will, an authority that resembled the kind of scaffolding nailed together of loose planks and beams, which at the first storm wind will creak and collapse. While the Christian religion teaches man to appreciate life on earth as part of an eternal existence, the French Revolution denied and fought everything that falls outside the horizon of our earthly life. While the Christian religion speaks of a paradise lost, a state of purity from which we fell, and for that reason calls us to humble repentance, the French Revolution saw in the state of nature the standard for what is normal for humans, incited us to pride, and replaced repentance with a liberalizing of man's mind and spirit. Still more, while the Christian religion, as the fruit of divine compassion, introduced the world to a love that wells up from God, the French Revolution opposed

---

40. On the considerable influence that the Protestant Reformation had on the improvement of social conditions, read Roscher, *Geschichte der National-Oekonomik in Deutschland*, 1:82–120. It is worthy of note that Roscher dates the weakening of this influence from the rise of territorialism, a system of political economy that had its roots in the Lutheran Reformation, not the Calvinian. He does not hesitate, therefore, in acknowledging that our country in particular gave the first impulse toward more correct economic insights. "It is beyond dispute that economic primacy in Europe passed from Upper and Central Italy to Holland" (223). Compare Étienne Laspeyres, *Geschichte der Niederländischen National-Oeconomie* (Leipzig: S. Hirzel, 1863).

What I say about Catholic countries in no way speaks of antipapism, but facts are facts, and as long as Catholics persist in painting Calvinism as the root of the Revolution we are obliged to point to the notorious fact that the great Revolution broke out in a Catholic country, that still today southern Europe and South America are entirely Roman Catholic and at the same time the most revolutionary, and that the throne is nowhere safer than in Protestant countries.

this with the egoism of a passionate struggle for possessions. And, to get to the real point that lies at the heart of the social question: while the Christian religion seeks the dignity of the human person in the relationships of an organically integrated society, the French Revolution disrupted that organic tissue, severed those social bonds, and finally, with its atomistic tinkering, left us with nothing but the solitary, self-seeking individual that asserts its independence.[41]

With that, the die was cast. Inevitably, given this wrenching apart of everything that gives human life its dignified coherence, this change gave birth to both deep-seated social distress and a widespread social-democratic movement, as well as an extremely complex social problem that is now facing every nation. I do not deny that other factors contributed to the deterioration of social relationships, such as the application of steam power to machinery, along with faster communication between countries and rapid population growth.[42] But I do stand by my assertion that neither the social question, which now holds two continents in feverish tension, nor the social-democratic movement, which today threatens the public order in

---

41. This is the pivot on which the whole social question turns. The French Revolution, and in the same way, present-day liberalism, is antisocial; and the social distress that today disturbs Europe is the evil fruit of the individualism that was enthroned with the French Revolution. In France especially this has never been understood by most Christians, including Protestants. As is well known, the school of Vinet chose individualism, of all things, as its basic premise. Guizot alone saw deeper and there-fore better—at least in his second period. This explains why most French Christians, led by De Pressensé, became fellow travelers with the revolutionaries and why their example was followed in other countries as well, our country not excluded. [Ed. note: François Guizot (1787-1874) was a right-wing liberal in the French government, but after the 1848 revolution he renounced his liberal past. Edmond de Pressensé (1824-91) was a student of theologian Alexandre Vinet (1797-1847) and served as a pastor of the Evangelical Church in Paris. He was appointed senator for life after holding a seat in the French National Assembly, where he was a staunch advocate of the separation of church and state.]

42. It is just as one-sided to try to explain the social ills almost exclusively in terms of steam power and machine production as it is to shut one's eyes to these factors. Usually, however, the effect of the machine is overemphasized. If morality and per-sonal faith had not been so defiantly undermined by the French Revolution, the class struggle would never have assumed such formidable proportions. Machines and steam simply present us with an inner contradiction: steam power improved the lot of the worker and relieved drudgery, but the endless division of labor dulls the mind, lowers the value of manual labor, and when one machine can do the work of a hundred it puts ninety-nine men out on the street.

Europe and America, could ever have assumed such ominous proportions if the principles of the French Revolution had not brought about so radical a change in the consciousness of nations, classes, and individuals.[43]

SOCIAL DISTRESS

In the first place, then, the French Revolution was bound to bring about profound social distress. This followed from its very nature: first, it made the possession of money the highest good, and then it set every man against his fellow man in the pursuit of money. It was not that the revolution's program mentioned money, or that her more inspired spokesmen did not coax more idealistic tones from their harps. But the theory, the system, could only end in kneeling before Mamon, simply because it cut off the prospect of eternal life and directed men to seek happiness on earth, hence in earthly things. This created a base atmosphere in which everything was valued in terms of money and anything was sacrificed for money. Add to that the demolition of all social organization, followed by the proclamation of the mercantile gospel of *laissez faire, laissez passer*, and you will understand how the "struggle for life" was ushered in by a struggle for money. The law of the animal world, dog eat dog, became the basic rule for all social interaction. Love of money, chasing after money, so the apostle had taught us, was the root of all evil. Accordingly, no sooner had this evil demon been set loose at the beginning of the nineteenth century than no plan seemed too subtle, no trick too sly, no deception too shameful to those people who—through superiority of knowledge, position, and capital—took money, always more money, from the socially weaker members of society.

This would have happened even if the opportunities at the start of the struggle had been equal for both parties. But it turned out to be much worse when the opportunities were so manifestly unequal. On the side of the bourgeoisie there was experience and insight, ability and solidarity, ready money and ready influence. On the other side were the peasantry and the working class, destitute of knowledge and deprived of resources, and compelled every morning by the need to feed mouths to accede to any

---

43. This change is most apparent nowadays in the entirely different outlook on life found in the great cities and the rural areas. It explains why the lower rural classes, even though their condition is often more wretched than that of the lower urban classes, actually live happier lives and complain far less than their counterparts in the city. One can also discern this in Patrimonium [*Ed. note*: A Reformed workers' association founded in 1876]. How vastly different its tone from that heard in socialistic groups!

conditions, no matter how unjust.[44] A person did not need to be a prophet to predict the outcome of this struggle. It simply could not end in any other way than in sucking all surplus value toward the capitalists, big or small, to leave the broad lower strata of society with only so much as appeared strictly necessary for keeping them alive as instruments for feeding capital (since in this system labor counted for nothing more).

And so a social situation hitherto found only among the Jews—"at one extreme of the social divide the millionaires, at the other end the toilers and drudges, poor as dirt"—gradually became the social situation of all Europe, but now without the palliative of family ties and compassion for poverty-stricken coreligionists that has always had an ameliorating effect among our Jewish fellow citizens.[45] And so the current situation in Europe consists of a well-fed bourgeoisie ruling over an impoverished working class that exists for the purpose of steadily increasing the capital of the ruling class, and is doomed to allow those who are no longer of any use to capital to sink into the morass of the proletariat.

And this social distress is made still worse by the bourgeois practice of instilling false needs in the poor by making a display of its wealth, and of undermining the contentment that can leave men happy with little by

---

44. This fact simply cannot be denied. Inevitably, capital absorbs more and more capital until it meets a resistance it cannot break. That resistance, in the present context, is the fact that workers cannot possibly make ends meet at present wage levels. Whatever else one may say, Lassalle is perfectly correct in saying that this iron law of wages is the curse of our society. And yet this law is the natural consequence of *laissez faire, laissez passer*—or if you will, of unrestricted competition. Capital absorbs more capital in this way not because of any evil purpose, but simply because it does not meet with any other power of resistance short of "to be or not to be" of the workers—of the instruments that feed capital. See Ernest Gilon, *Maatschappelijke nooden*, trans. G. Keller Jr. (Amsterdam: H. Gerlings, 1889). The complete system of *laissez faire, laissez passer* is given in Adam Smith's *The Wealth of Nations*, 3 vols. (London: Cadell and Davies, 1812 [1776]). This work is edited and annotated, among others, by J. F. Baart, *Adam Smith en zijn onderzoek naar den rijkdom der volken* (Leiden: Van Der Hoek, 1858). In the meantime, John Stuart Mill in his *Principles of Political Economy*, 2 vols. (London: John W. Parker, 1848), has put a lot of water in this economic wine. See also Thedor Hertzka, *Die Gesetzen der sozialen Entwicklung* (Leipzig: Duncker & Humblot, 1886).

45. I am prepared to acknowledge the sincere efforts liberalism has made to advance the lower class. But what did it offer them? Reading, writing, and arithmetic! And what did it take away from them? Faith, the courage to live, and moral energy. What did it withhold from them? Trade schools and a share in capital.

igniting in them—all the stronger in the measure that there is less for the poor to enjoy—a feverish passion for pleasure.[46]

SOCIAL DEMOCRACY

With the same iron necessity the system gave birth, in the second place, to a social-democratic movement, with its open proclamation of a coming revolution. The French Revolution had written on her blood-red banner not only "liberty" but also "equality and fraternity," and the French peasants and the French workers were certainly not the last ones who, singing the Marseillaise, had rushed to the battlefield in the wars of the French Republic to lay hold of these precious ideals. But alas, the equality they dreamed of turned out to be an increasingly offensive inequality, and for the promised fraternity they got a reprise of the fable of the wolf and the lamb.

Was it not natural, then, that the suffering class of society began to ask: "With what right are these drastic conditions imposed on us? They told us we were as good as anybody else and that the numerical minority had to submit to the majority. Well, aren't we the majority, the largest segment of the population by far, the overwhelming masses? And is it not a violation of the basic premise of the Revolution, and a mockery of the sacred rallying cry for which so much blood has flowed in Paris, that a new aristocracy—this time an aristocracy of much lower caliber, an aristocracy of money—stands poised to lay down the law to us, to put its foot on our neck, and so reinstate the evil once overthrown with such incredible exertions by the Voltaires and Rousseaus and the heroes of the Bastille? Give us—yes, us too—the voice in affairs that is owed us according to the system of the Revolution itself. Then we shall outvote you and install a totally different social order that will once for all deliver the deathblow to privilege and finally, finally, give us what your fine theory promised us but that you never gave us."

In all seriousness, friends, I cannot see how anyone who is not an opponent but a supporter of the French Revolution can have objections, based on sound logical grounds, to this demand from social democrats. From their

---

46. In this respect, the displays in our shop windows do more evil than people realize. In many ways they stimulate covetousness and create needs that, if not eventually satisfied, leave behind a feeling of bitter discontent. Similarly, the excessive luxury of our school buildings has done harm to a class of pupils who at home can never live in such a grand style. Happiness is not an absolute but a relative concept. He who awakens needs that he is in no position to satisfy shoulders a big responsibility and commits an act of callous cruelty.

standpoint at least I must give them my unconditional support. Once the false theory is granted, social democracy, and it alone, is consistent.[47] And as for the common reproach that it is wrong at least in this, that it openly preaches revolution and declares that if need be it will not shrink from using violence, of this too I do not see how one can condemn it in the name of the French Revolution. Or did the dignified gentlemen of the party of the Girondins[48] *not* preach revolution? Did men really sentence Louis XVI to death on the ground that the social order may *not* be breached?[49] Did the spiritual forebears of our liberals and conservatives really shrink from using violence during the September Massacres?[50] But surely to raise these questions is to lapse into absurdity when the dull thud of the guillotine still echoes tragically and troublingly in our ears and when only recently the centennial of the storming of the Bastille[51] was celebrated by all Europe's liberals as the commemoration of a most praiseworthy act of heroism. How can one who has himself not hesitated to wade through streams of blood to achieve his goal, turn other people over to public contempt when they in turn, if caught in a tight corner, would reintroduce the guillotine?

Of course I shudder as I utter these words, and everything with which the Christian religion inspires us recoils with horror from statements such as these. But when comparing the social democrat to the liberal, I cannot fault him. It is using a double standard, it is hypocrisy or self-deception, for those who were born of the Revolution—indeed, born of regicide—to count it as a mortal sin in their own spiritual children when they in turn so much as dare to speak of "drastic measures."[52]

---

47. It is not enough to say that the social-democratic movement issues from the liberal theory. It must also be stressed that the liberal calls for a totally arbitrary halt on a trajectory that according to his theory has to be followed. Thus the liberal has spiritual kinship with the social democrat, but unlike him he is in the wrong, because he is arbitrary, self-serving, and inconsistent.

48. *Ed. note*: The Girondins were early participants in the Revolution who preached moderation yet voted in favor of deposing the king.

49. *Ed. note*: The main charge for which King Louis XVI was condemned to death was that he had "conspired against liberty."

50. *Ed. note*: In the September Massacres during the Revolution, crowds in Paris dragged imprisoned "traitors to the sovereign people" from their cells and murdered them.

51. *Ed. note*: Early event in the Revolution, when a prison fortress was captured by a Paris mob that set the prisoners free and lynched the garrison.

52. It is indeed passing strange how many of the ordinary citizens in our country at one and the same time condemn the advocacy of force on the part of the social democrats and yet praise the French Revolution to the skies. Surely it won't do to say that

THE SOCIAL QUESTION

But now I come to a more attractive subject. The French Revolution had a third consequence, this time in the reaction to it. After bringing about the social distress and giving rise to the movement of social democracy, the revolution also called attention to the social question. Not that the social question is raised for the first time today—rather, it was debated in ancient times, along both the Euphrates and the Tiber, in both Sparta and Athens. It resurfaced when the feudal system made inroads, and again centuries later when it had worn out. And, to add a fact from our own history, it was resolved twice on Java, once when the cultivation system was introduced, and again when it was abolished.[53] In any case, to speak of a social question today means in the most general sense to raise grave doubts about the soundness of the social structure in which we live. The result has been a public debate about firmer foundations on which a more effective social edifice can be erected, this time more livable.[54]

In and of itself, therefore, to raise the question in no way implies that the answer must be found in a socialistic sense. The solution adopted may be quite different. Just one thing is required if the "social question" is to be real for you: namely, that you realize that the current condition of society cannot be continued, and that this condition cannot be explained from

---

the September Massacres were merely *excesses*. After all, without *revolution* there would have been no Revolution in 1789. Every liberal, even if one does not hold the excesses against him personally, nevertheless bears responsibility for the revolutionary use of force. What it comes down to is that force is considered legitimate when used to the advantage of the liberals but is abhorred the moment it tends to undermine their power. Hence in 1845, also in our country—in [the liberal daily] the *Arnhemsche Courant* at that—there were allusions to regicide, and today the appearance in Parliament of a social democrat offends "respectable" liberals. See Eugen Jäger, *Die Französische Revolution und die Soziale Bewegung* (Berlin: Puttkammer, 1890).

53. *Ed. note*: Kuyper discusses the rise and demise of the colonial government's system of compulsory cultivation in his work *OP*, §§251–56.

54. These essential characteristics of the social question must be carefully kept in mind. That is not to say that the social structure has to be taken down wholesale and replaced with a brand-new one. History always asserts its rights, and there can never be a question of total demolition. Even when men fancy they are busy doing so, they aren't really; history's influence is too powerful. But neither can you say that the job is done after you have applied a few dabs of paint and replaced a roof tile here and there. No, you must definitely cordon off the house and put up scaffolding. The structure won't do any longer. The repair that is required is far too comprehensive for that. See Anon., *Personal and Social Evolution with the Key of the Science of History* (London: Fisher Unwin, 1890); Hertzka, *Die Gesetzen der sozialen Entwicklung*.

incidental causes but from a fault line in the very foundation of our social order. If you fail to realize this and think the evil can be exorcized by fostering greater piety, kindlier treatment, and ampler charity, you may think that we face a religious question, or a philanthropic question, but not a *social* question.[55] The social question is not a reality for you until you level an architectonic critique at human society as such and accordingly deem a different arrangement of the social order desirable, and also possible. With regard to the impossibility of continuing the current condition of society, born as it is of the individualism of the French Revolution, I think there can be little difference of opinion among Christians. If a human heart still beats in your breast and the ideal of our holy gospel has ever inspired you, then every higher aspiration you may have must cry out against the current state of society. If this situation continues, life will become less and less a heaven and more and more something of a hell on earth. Our society is drifting away from Christ; it lies prostrate before Mamon. The very foundations of the earth, as the psalmist would lament (see Pss 11:3 and 82:5), are tottering under the steady goad of the most brazen egoism. All the joists and anchors of the social edifice are shifting, disorganization is breeding demoralization, and the drunken revelry of some people in the face of the mounting need of others reminds you more of a decomposing corpse than of the fresh bloom and robust energy of flourishing health.[56]

No, things need not stay this way. We can do better than this. And conditions can unquestionably be made better in the way of—I do not shrink from the word—*socialism*. Only, do not take the word in the sense of social democracy but in the sense, in itself so beautiful, that our country is not (to speak with da Costa) "a heap of souls on a hunk of soil" but a *community* willed by God, a living human *organism*. It is not a mechanism assembled of component parts, nor a mosaic that forms a "fragmented surface," as

---

55. I am not saying that the religious and philanthropic aspects of the problem are unimportant, but merely that one who looks no further and extends his antennae no further than this has not yet come in touch with the social question.

56. Applying blush to your skin does not make it less dull but only worsens your unhealthy complexion. So it is with our society. It lives with more cultural refinements; it clothes itself more stylishly (though not more beautifully); it pretends to be glowing with youth. But he who is no stranger to the dressing rooms of high society, and sometimes sees the matron in her negligee, knows all too well how faded and jaded she actually looks.

Beets[57] calls it, but a body with members, standing under the law of life that we are all members of one another, so that the eye cannot do without the foot or the foot without the eye [see 1 Cor 12:21]. It is this human, this scientific, this Christian truth that the French Revolution ignored, denied, insulted. And it is at bottom the individualism born of this denial that all of today's society is moving away from.[58]

SOCIALISM IS NO TEMPORARY FAD

You are mistaken, therefore, if you believe that present-day socialism owes its rise to the confused utopias of fanatics or that it stems from the brains of starving hotheads. Marlo, who in three thick volumes first discussed the "organization of labor,"[59] was a very learned university professor. Rodbertus, who championed the cause of the working classes even prior to Karl Marx, had been a minister of the king of Prussia in 1848.[60] Marx himself, the founder of the First International, belonged to the upper class and married

---

57. *Ed. note*: Nicolaas Beets (1814–1903) was a theologian of the ethical-irenical school and author of a collection of poems, *Brokkelvloer van rijmspreuken* (The Hague: M. M. Couvée, 1891).

58. The beautiful word "social" should not be left to the private preserve of social democrats. Christianity is preeminently social. The beautiful picture that the apostle Paul paints for us of the social nature of the church in 1 Cor 12:12–27 and no less in Eph 4:16 is *mutatis mutandis* equally applicable to human society. In fact, we believe that, rightly viewed, the original organism of humanity, now purified, has been resurrected in the church of Christ. See F. D. Maurice, *Social Morality: Twenty-One Lectures Delivered in the University of Cambridge* (London: Macmillan, 1890).

59. Karl Marlo, *Untersuchungen über die Organisation der Arbeit, oder System der Weltöconomie*, 3 vols. (Kassel: Wilhelm Appel, 1853). [*Ed. note*: Karl Marlo, pseudonym for Karl Georg Winkelblech (1810–65), taught chemistry in Kassel, Germany, and spent the last twenty years of his life writing in favor of common ownership of the means of production.]

60. Rodbertus was for a short period minister of worship in the Auerswald–Hansemann cabinet; see Georg Adler, *Rodbertus, der Begründer des wissenschaftlichen Sozialismus* (Leipzig: Duncker & Humblot, 1884). His first work was *Zur Erkenntnis unsrer staatswirthschaftlichen Zustände* (Neubrandenburg: Barnewitz, 1842). His most extensive publication is *Zur Erklärung und Abhülfe der heutigen Creditnoth des Grundbesitzes*, 2 vols. (Jena: Mauke, 1876). [*Ed. note*: Johann Karl Rodbertus (1805–75) was a gentleman-economist from Pomerania, a province of Prussia along the Baltic Sea. He was a pre-Marxian socialist who wrote widely on land rents, overproduction, economic crises, the labor theory of value, and similar topics.]

into a ruling family.[61] Lassalle moved in the circles of high society.[62] Henry George was an American from a respectable family.[63] And Schaeffle, in 1871, who went so far as to advocate the collective ownership of land, capital, and the means of production, was a minister of the emperor of Austria.[64] Thus it was almost impossible at times not to burst out laughing when until recently socialism would be talked about, also in our own circles, as something peculiar to the riffraff. One almost wonders whether people read at all, or stay in touch with the times. Did Quack speak to deaf ears when in eloquent prose he introduced the whole family of socialists to our educated

---

61. Like Marlo and Rodbertus, Marx was a man of outstanding erudition and scientific talent. His critique of the Hegelian philosophy of law was masterful, and his work *Das Kapital. Kritik der politischen Oeconomie* (Hamburg: Meissner, 1871) was first of all a scholarly study. For those who find this work too demanding, Gabriel Deville wrote *Le Capital de Karl Marx, résumé et accompagné d'un aperçu sur le socialisme scientifique* (Paris: H. Oriol, 1883). [*Ed. note*: Karl Marx (1818–83) was the chief theoretician of the communist movement and in 1864 helped organize the First International Workingmen's Association.]

62. Lassalle indeed circulated among the higher classes. In 1864 he was killed in a duel with a Moravian prince who was his rival in seeking the hand of the daughter of an ambassador. His forte was oratorical talent more than scholarship, yet he more than anyone caused the socialist ideas to become widespread in Belgium. [*Ed. note*: Ferdinand Lassalle (1825–64), after studying philosophy in Breslau and Berlin, became a lawyer and a social activist who founded the first political party for German working men advocating universal male suffrage.]

63. Henry George, the apostle of land nationalization, is best known for his book *Progress and Poverty*, which he wrote in 1877–79 especially in connection with the situation of the Jews. The dedication in this fascinating book is touching: "To those who seeing the vice and the misery, feel the possibility of a higher social state, and would strive for its attainment." More than 300,000 copies have already been sold. In the edition of Kegan Paul of London, this work of 400 pages fine print costs only ƒ0.60. [*Ed. note*: Henry George (1839–97) was a newspaper editor and political economist who played a major role in the rising labor movement in America. His widely popular book *Progress and Poverty* taught that the chief cause of poverty was "unearned wealth" from land rents, and that the solution lay in taxing the value of land.]

64. Dr. Albert Eberhard Friedrich Schaeffle was minister of trade in the Hohenwart cabinet. His main work is *Das gesellschaftliche System der menschlichen Wirthschaft*, which in a short time went through three editions. It was published in two volumes by Laupp in Tübingen. [*Ed. note*: Albert Schaeffle (1831–1903) was a professor of political economy in Tübingen and later in Vienna. In his translated work *The Quintessence of Socialism* (London: Swan Sonnenschein, 1889) he argued for collective ownership and a planned economy.]

public?[65] Indeed, have people never even heard of Plato, the greatest of the Greek philosophers, who drafted and recommended a scheme for a full-scale socialistic arrangement of the state?[66] Such extreme ignorance about the aims of the socialist movement may have been excusable twenty years ago, but today it would lead only to policies that are hopelessly out of date.

In the meantime, the socialist movement has already given birth to four different schools. It has spontaneously and simultaneously given a rude awakening to the "satisfied bourgeoisie" in every country of Europe. It has found its advocates in a whole string of universities and is making the printing presses groan under a constant stream of scholarly studies. It has gradually gained so much in depth and scope and significance that Chancellor Bismarck follows its lead and Pope Leo has circulated an encyclical about it. The German emperor even inaugurated his reign by convening a congress in Prussia's capital for preparing an international solution to the social question.[67]

---

65. H. P. G. Quack, *De Socialisten: personen en stelsels*, 3 vols. (Amsterdam: P. N. Van Kampen & Zoon, 1875-92). [*Ed. note*: Hendrick Peter Godfried Quack (1834-1917), a liberal who was sympathetic to the plight of the working classes began as a professor of political economy at the University of Utrecht, a post he exchanged after ten years for a senior position at the Bank of the Netherlands, eventually becoming its director.]

66. For those who do not understand any Greek, three of his dialogues, *The Statesman*, *The Republic*, and *The Laws*, are accessible in excellent translations by [Friedrich] Schleiermacher. A brief but reliable overview of Plato's political system is found in Zeller, *Die Philosophie der Griechen* (Leipzig: Fues, 1875), 2:756ff. As is well known, Plato carried his socialist and even communist ideas to such lengths that he even abolished the family and wished to declare child-rearing a task of the state.

67. This was a happy move by the Kaiser, even though the result fell far below expectations. Actually he committed plagiarism, because the proposal he took up had already been discussed by Switzerland.

Regardless, little progress will be made this way. The social question can indeed only be solved internationally; but before the several nation-states realize this and venture to act with the energy required, more particularism will have to be overcome than can perhaps be realized short of a general combustion throughout Europe. Instead we are moving in a direction where each nation again thinks only of itself with regard to social problems, and with regard to economic competition each nation is beginning to live at war with all the others, at most seeking security in narrow trade blocs. No one has (unintentionally) brought out this international element more clearly than J. H. von Thünen in his *Der isolirte Staat in Beziehung auf Landwirthschaft und Nationalöconomie*, 3 vols. (Rostock: G. B. Leopold, 1842).

Truly, it will not do to bury our heads in the sand. There is no strength in scoffing at the slogan "Justice for All," in declaring Domela Nieuwenhuis[68] a social outcast, in letting the ignorant masses jeer, "All the socialists in a herring barrel." Socialism is in the air. The social wind, which can at any moment turn into a storm, is swelling the sails of the ship of state. And it may safely be said that the social question has become *the* question, the burning life-question at the close of this century. Indeed, in the whole of this century, so fraught with problems, no problem has emerged that reaches so deeply into the life of the nations and agitates public opinion so vehemently.[69]

The common characteristic of all the forms and stages in which this impressive movement has thus far appeared, is a rising sense of community—of the rights of community and the organic nature of society—in opposition to the one-dimensional individualism with which the French Revolution has impregnated our society, along with its corresponding economic school of *laissez faire, laissez passer*. This zeal for the social principle is so strong that it has led to a battle over property rights and a war on capitalism, given that the individual finds his strongest bulwark precisely in his property. Absolute property rights have allowed immense fortunes

---

68. *Ed. note*: Ferdinand Domela Nieuwenhuis (1846–1919) was a Lutheran pastor who turned socialist and later anarchist. He supported the Dutch labor movement but ultimately chose for a revolutionary solution to the social question.

69. Nothing is more foolish than to view socialism as a passing storm and a cloud that will evaporate. It is certainly true that the socialists are internally divided and still lack leaders unselfish and high-minded enough to call into being a global action. Their congresses are mostly scenes of tumult, and their publications abound in barbed civilities. But it is a mistake to view the social question as a temporary inconvenience. On the contrary, the very fact that the socialists, despite their many differences, have made gigantic steps forward shows the dynamic force that social democracy propagates. Don't forget that the International was founded only in 1864, that shortly thereafter it fell apart, that the new association still has a very deficient structure, and yet that the social movement after only a quarter-century has thrown all Europe into turmoil. Particularly since the 1889 congresses in Paris its activity has made disturbing advances. Villard, *Le Socialisme moderne*, like the above-mentioned writing of Abbé Winterer, *Le socialisme international*, paints a convincing picture both of the enormous dimensions of this movement and of the significance of the centennial celebration of the French Revolution for its revisionism. See also August Sartorius von Waltershausen, *Der Moderne Sozialismus in den Vereinigten Staaten von Amerika* (Berlin: H. Bahr, 1900) [ET: *The Workers' Movement in The United States, 1879–1885*, ed. David Montgomery and Marcel van der Linden, trans. Harry Drost (New York: Cambridge University Press, 1998)].

to be amassed, which now form an insurmountable obstacle preventing society from doing justice to its sociological nature.[70]

The Unity and Diversity of Socialism

Thus the socialist movement in all its branches stands united in opposing individualism. But no sooner is the question raised about what should be demolished and what should be erected in its place, than *tot capita tot sensus*—there are as many opinions as there are heads. After all, people who do not believe in God, to whose eternal ordinances we are to submit, and who do not attach much importance in the life of nations to historical development that never permits its intrinsic law of life to be violated with impunity—such people look upon the entire structure of contemporary society as nothing but a product of human convention. Hence they consider themselves perfectly justified in razing it to the ground. Nor do they shrink from the gigantic task of building anew on the vacant plot.

Of those who think along these lines, the most radical is the nihilist. He realizes that everything hangs together in life and he therefore believes society cannot be saved so long as every last remnant of our deadlocked civilization still stands. Hence he wants to start by destroying everything, literally everything. His ideal is to return to the time immediately after the flood. He does not halt until he has reached *nihil*—nothing.[71]

---

70. Of course we are not denying that greed and envy play a big role in the social question. As persons, the members of the class that now complains are no better than the men of the class that has "arrived." People who were poor and became rich usually turn away from socialism; and on the other hand there are no more dangerous socialists than people who have lost their fortune. But evil passion does not call into existence a lasting world movement. The power of socialism does not stem from its covetous desire, but rather from the moral demand of societal life. This demand speaks to men's conscience; here throbs its lifeblood; on this demand religion places its seal. The attack on private property only entered the picture long after this inescapable righteous demand. See Gaëtan Combes de Lestrade, *Eléments de sociologie* (Paris: F. Alcan, 1889); Friedrich Elbogen, *Die Erlösung: sociale studien* (Zurich: Schröter & Meyer, 1889); and Charles Secrétan, *Etudes sociales* (Paris: F. Alcan, 1889).

71. To understand a nihilist, read the portrait of one painted in *Germinal* by Zola, who now has also become a Christian socialist. Actually, the *perhovtri* in Russia go even further by forbidding all marriage in order to make our hopelessly corrupted human race die out; see *Allgemeine Evangelisch-Lutherische Kirchenzeitung*, no. 40, Oct. 2, 1891. A historical survey of nihilism is found in Nicolai Karlowitsch, *Die Entwicklung des Nihilismus*, 3rd ed. (Berlin: Behr, 1880). It did not arise until 1875

A degree less radical is the anarchist. He laughs at this idea that the very houses and tools are infected and instead locates the virus only in government and in every force and function that emanates from government. For the anarchist, the demolition will have gone far enough once government is abolished. No more state; only a society. Then the golden age will arrive in due course.[72]

Still less radical are the social democrats. They would keep both state and society, but a state that is merely the organ and house manager of society. The state should be so arranged that the *many* households are dissolved into the *single* household of the state and that in this one household all citizens share equally. True, there are nuances among them: relentless fanatics who preach rioting and looting, alongside men such as Liebknecht[73] who hope to triumph through parliamentary action; a Schaeffle who advocates common ownership of land, capital, and the means of production, next to the ordinary collectivist who would have the state own only the land and the means. But at the end of the day their paths all converge in one and the same ideal: a state that absorbs all individuals into itself and looks after all individuals equally.[74]

---

and first drew attention as a result of the assassination attempt on General Trepow. Today its strength is broken, but the idea of nihilism is not gone. That idea will return as soon as social democracy pursues its aim with any consistency and wakes up to the influence of the historical past on current conditions. See also Alphons Thun, *Die Geschichte der revolutionären Bewegungen in Russland* (Leipzig: Duncker & Humblot, 1883).

72. The anarchists owe their significance to the Russian writer Bakunin, and as for their organization and the development of their ideas even more to General Kropotkin and Johann Most. Their central committee is stationed in London and its publication was *Die Freiheit*. They were most active in France, Switzerland, Belgium, and North America, where the famous Chicago trial [following the Haymarket affair of 1886] broke their back. Their slogan was "Propaganda of the deed." And at a congress held in London in July, 1881, the rule was adopted that "to achieve the goal we pursue, that is, the annihilation of sovereigns, ministers, clergy, nobility, big capitalists, and other exploiters, all means are legitimate."

The Paris Commune of 1871 differed from anarchism in that it wanted to destroy central governments but keep the *commune*, that is, the organization of the local community.

73. *Ed. note*: Wilhelm Liebknecht (1826–1900) was the cofounder of the Socialist Labor Party of Germany, which abandoned revolutionary activity in favor of forming the opposition in Parliament and meanwhile educating the working class.

74. The French *possibilists* in particular, as well as the German social democrats under Liebknecht, work for reform through parliamentary action. They hope to strengthen

At a fair distance from these social democrats you find the state social-ists. They reverse the above position, albeit with a variation, by placing the authority of the state high above society, but then also charging state authority with the task of guiding the movement of society in a top-down manner.[75] This school has found its enthusiastic spokesmen in Rudolf Meyer, Adolf Wagner, and partly in Emile de Laveleye, along with many others; and it has finally found its ideal statesman in Bismarck.[76]

As for the historical school, its strength lies less in a practical program than in scholarly research. It hopes to be able to dispel the illusion that current conditions and legal relationships are of a timeless nature. It thus

---

their position through a moderate stance. Although they do not reject the idea of revolution, they consider it wrong to push this to the foreground, and they expect more from the one bird already firmly in their hand than the two in the bush. Quite distinct from these more practical social democrats, however, are the theoretical social democrats such as Schaeffle. They do nothing else than design a plan for erect-ing a new society, and they abstain strictly from anything that smells of agitation and violence. The label "collectivist" hails from these theoreticians and really belongs only to them. See M. Schönberg, *Die Ziele und Bestrebungen der Sozialdemokratie*, 10th ed. (Leipzig: Levien, 1890).

75. *Ed. note:* State socialism was the name given to Bismarck's legislative program of the 1880s to help the German working classes and draw them away from other forms of socialism. The program included health insurance, accident and disability insurance, and old-age pensions. Because prominent academics wrote in support of it, it was nicknamed *Katheder-sozialismus.* Their ideal resembles what today we call the welfare state.

76. This school emerged from conservative quarters in Germany, so is native to that country. In his book *Le socialisme d'Etat* (Paris: Calmann Lévy, 1890) Léon Say gives a neat description of this state socialism—to warn the French against it! It is the antipode to social democracy in that it is imposed from the top down. Nevertheless, from its standpoint it has been a strong advocate for the common people, and Rudolf Meyer contributed not a little to the rise of the socialist movement through his book *Der Emancipationskampf des vierten Standes in Deutschland*, 2 vols. (Berlin: Aug. Schindler, 1874–75). State socialism has also given rise to the Christian school of Todt and Stöcker. Emile de Laveleye is not exactly what one might call a state socialist, but his position in fact follows the same line. Adolph Wagner called his school the *sozialrechtliche* [the social justice school]. He agrees with Schmoller more than other authors. His chief work is his textbook for political economy [*Lehr- und Handbuch der politischen Oekonomie*], of which three volumes have come out thus far: vol. 1, *Grundlegung*, 2nd ed. (Leipzig: C. F. Winter, 1879); vol. 5, *Finanzwissenschaft*, 3rd ed. (Leipzig: C. F. Winter, 1884); and vol. 6, *Fortsetzung* (Leipzig: C. F. Winter, 1880). He supports Stöcker.

prepares public opinion for change, and it investigates what would make for orderly change.[77]

Add to this list the less doctrinaire liberals. One can detect among them a growing inclination, on the one hand, to become more conservative—that is, to make the necessary concessions for preserving the status quo—and, on the other hand, to become more radical by enlarging the political influence of the lower class in order to improve its lot and to curtail the self-destructive privileges of the propertied class.[78]

To complete this brief summary, finally, I add the cynical pessimists. These men acknowledge that something is smoldering in the house of our modern civilization. They will even concede that there is a fire and that if the fire is not checked the flame of an all-destructive revolution will soon break out. Yet they declare at the same time that extinguishing the fire will simply prove impossible. Thus they prophesy with stoic calm that our modern civilization, like the ancient Near Eastern and Greco-Roman civilizations, is destined to sink into Nirvana.[79]

---

77. The historical school is a broader name for the so-called *Katheder-sozialisten*, a term of contempt that Oppenheim gave them. Gustav von Schmoller, Erwin Nasse, Lujo Brentano, and M. Schönberg were the founders of this group, which bears close affinity with state socialism. Their system is especially directed against the Manchester school, and to the extent that it aims more at historical studies it is creating a following and finding support also outside Germany's borders, that is, in Letourneau, *L'Evolution de la propriété*; Alfred Fouillée, *Propriété sociale et la démocratie* (Paris: Hachette, 1884); and others.

78. The radicals on the one hand come close to state socialism, on the other to *Katheder* socialism, at times so close that the boundary line is erased. Their group, also in our country, is not yet organized as a school—hence their differences about state involvement or private initiative are not visible all that much. That the liberals are also moving over to the left is less the result of conviction than of the desire to stay on top by means of timely concessions. Still, the socialistic trend of our age is too powerful also for them to be ashamed of the name "socialist." Even Naquet exclaims: "I for my part am profoundly socialist"; see his *Socialisme collectiviste et socialisme libéral*, 202. And Frédéric Passy, in his lecture of April 9, 1890, about the "Ecole de la liberté," is no more inclined to waive the honor of the label "socialist."

79. The same pantheism that wipes out all differences in the moral domain and dares to place Nero next to Jesus as an equally intriguing contemporary also leads in the sociological domain to the most shallow and cynical fatalism. The situation is wretched, concludes the pessimist, but there is no way to improve it. We slide down the incline until we sink into the abyss. All this is our destiny. And then perhaps, on the ruins of our civilization a wholly new building program can commence. *Perhaps?* But these pessimists know nothing of the enduring dynamism that lies hidden in the

IV. A CHRISTIAN APPROACH TO THE PROBLEM OF POVERTY

If I am not mistaken, friends, with this hasty sketch I have achieved my goal of highlighting the threads by which the Christian religion must be woven together with the problem of poverty. What remains for me to do in this final part of my address, therefore, is to take up these threads one by one and show you what direction they ought to give to our study of the problem and to our response to it.

But first I must clear up one final question which, if left unanswered, would probably nullify the force of my argument. The question is this: How can I call social democracy a fruit of the French Revolution and at the same time contend that it is opposed to the basic principle of the French Revolution?

This apparent contradiction stems from the fact that the individualistic character of the French Revolution is only a derived principle. It is not its root principle from which it drew its dynamic. That root principle is its defiant cry *Ni Dieu, ni maître!* [No God, no master!] Or, if you will: humanity's emancipation from God and from the order instituted by him. This principle gives rise to two lines, not just one. The first line is the one that leads you to dismantle the existing order and leave nothing standing except the individual with his own free will and his supposed supremacy. But alongside this line runs another, at the end of which you are tempted not only to push God and his order aside, but also to go on and, deifying yourself, sit in the seat of God (as the prophet said [see Ezek 28:2]), and from your own head you create a new order of things. That's what social democracy is doing. Yet even as it is busy doing so, it gives up very little of the individualistic starting point. Underneath the social structure that it seeks to erect—allow me to use an image from the building trade in Amsterdam—it still drives the piles of popular sovereignty, and hence of individual wills, through the medium of universal suffrage.[80]

---

heart of the Christian nations and that can therefore rise above that which spelled ruin for Babylon, Athens, and Rome.

80. It is the age-old problem of the one and the many that recurs here. The starting point of both social democrats and liberals is individualistic, the individual person, and hence Pelagian free will. That the dynamic of the French Revolution is also operating in the social democrats is clear from their continually recurring demand that adult male individuals should rule the affairs of state and society by majority vote. They do not even *understand* our demand that the starting point should be the family.

RESPONSE TO SOCIALISM

But this only in passing. The question that now demands our full attention is this: What attitude should Christians adopt in the face of the socialist movement?

And then it is beyond question that we too should be moved to profound compassion by the disorder of our society and the great distress that has resulted from it. We may not, like the priest and the Levite, pass by the exhausted traveler who lies bleeding from his wounds, but like the good Samaritan we ought to be moved by a holy compassion for him. Yes indeed, people are suffering; there are crying needs.[81] Those needs may not yet be so great in the circles of our regular tradespeople, but they certainly exist among the proletariat behind them, and no less in certain rural areas. Think of Friesland.[82] And then I join Bilderdijk and say: God has not willed that a person should toil away and still not have enough to feed himself and his family, let alone that someone with able hands and a will to work might, just because there is no work, die of starvation or be condemned to begging.[83]

---

81. *Ed. note*: In a prayer at the congress, Kuyper had prayed: "They cannot wait, not a day, not an hour."
82. *Ed. note*: In this northern province, desperate farmhands walked off the job. They staged mass demonstrations and compiled blacklists of farmers who hired those willing to work. Events such as these formed part of the background of the Social Congress; see Harry Van Dyke, "How Abraham Kuyper Became a Christian Democrat," *Calvin Theological Journal* 33, no. 2 (November 1998): 420–35.
83. Bilderdijk, letter clxi in *Briefwisseling met Tydeman* (Sneek: Van Druten & Bleeker, 1866–67), 2:76–83, expressed himself in very strong terms:
    "There is nothing for it but to restore civil society to its original purpose. If there is land, let men cultivate it. If there is shipping or fishing, let men expand it. If these three are not enough, organize factories and see to it that everyone can find work for his hands and arms and so provide bread for himself with a wife and children. Oblige all to work and install free and compulsory industry, free and compulsory agriculture. Attach honor to free and shame to compulsory labor. Let no one who steps forward be without honest labor, and have no tolerance for begging. Land, shipping, fishery, and industry—these will support the working classes. No more is needed. Whoever aims to profit from this arrangement is driven by a wrong spirit. If money is lacking at the start, it will be a duty to raise the funds, just as it is for national defense; *frustra armis tuemur, quos fame necamus* ['It is vain to protect with weapons those whom we kill through starvation']. *Prospicere subditis* ['Looking after subjects'] includes, besides protection against foreign and domestic violence, also the *subsidia vitae* ['life's necessities'] and the *promotio subolis perpetua, quâ non tantum conservetur sed et augeatur res*

To be sure, if we have "food and clothing" the apostle would have us be content with these (see 1 Tim 6:8 or Prov 27:26).[84] But there is no excuse for a situation in which our heavenly Father with divine generosity causes an abundance of food to come forth from the ground and that through our fault this bounty is distributed so unequally that while one person has more than enough to eat the other goes to bed with an empty stomach—if he even has a bed. And if there are people who want to defend such abuses by invoking—God forgive them—the words of Jesus, "For the poor you always have with you" [John 12:8], then out of respect for God's holy Word I must register a protest against such a misuse of Scripture. I must ask those who so judge first to study the same Scripture, so that they can see

---

publica ['constant promotion of offspring which not only preserves but also increases the state'].

"There you have in broad outline what every country should make the primary duty. What matters is not to deliberate how to get rid of the poor or prevent their increase, but to make them well-off through work and have them increase in chastity and godliness. He who does not know this does not know how to govern; he who does not want this is an enemy of mankind (whether he means well, according to his lights, or not).

"It is true that this becomes more difficult to the extent that perverse commerce has made money more common and so made life's necessities more expensive, which at the slightest recession increases poverty and spreads want, creating incalculable misery. But where there is a will there is a solution. For it is not the quantity of money but its circulation that creates wealth and produces enough surplus."

And in a more general sense he writes:

"Only, all is tainted because money has been made the end-all and be-all instead of a mere means of exchange. As long as this persists the misery will continue and become rampant. This is the great plague that has gone out over Europe, and only those who have the seal of God on their forehead and rest in His providence are immune to it and refuse to work or beg for money but despise it. These few do suffer; yet God will feed them.

"He is no less harsh against high finance and the service of Mamon: 'All the nations of Europe serve this Mammon, and their only recovery lies in overthrowing the false system. The case is irrefutable. *No bread* for those who are willing to work clashes with the basic law of all work: "In the sweat of thy face shalt thou eat bread." ' "

84. This follows from the creation and the curse. God himself created us with such a nature that we are subject to metabolism: our bodies need food, which is then consumed so that we must eat again. Likewise, the curse, on account of sin, has made it necessary both to clothe our bodies out of shame and to shield them against the cold.

how conditions for the poor in Israel were almost luxurious compared to the wretchedness in which our proletariat are sunk.[85]

If you then ask me whether charitable giving should increase even more, then I answer without a moment's hesitation, *most certainly!* But I hasten to add that a charity that knows only how to give money and not how to give one's self is not yet Christian love. You will not be blameless unless you also give of your time, energy, sympathy, and resourcefulness to help end such abuses once and for all. You will remain blameworthy until you leave nothing unused that lies hidden in the storehouse of your Christian religion for combating the cancer that is destroying the vitality of our society in such alarming ways. The material need is appalling, and the oppression is great. And you fail to honor God's Word if you should ever forget that Christ himself, just as his apostles after him and the prophets before him, invariably took the side of the suffering and the oppressed against the rich and the mighty of this world.

But even greater, and more appalling, is the spiritual need of our generation. When in the midst of our social misery I observe the demoralization that follows on the heels of material need, and hear a raucous voice that, instead of calling on the Father in heaven for deliverance, curses God, mocks his Word, insults the cross of Golgotha, and silences whatever voice still testifies in his conscience—all in order to set aflame, as in a rage, everything untamed and brutish in the human heart—then, my friends, I stare

---

85. The words in John 12:8, "For the poor you always have with you," do not establish a *rule* but state a *fact*; they do not say that it ought to be so, but at most that it will always prove to be so. Second, it will not do to conclude from a concrete saying about that period that Jesus was at the same time prophesying about *later centuries*. And in the third place, this totally overlooks the reproach hidden in these words. The Greek here does not have *meth' hymōn* but *meth' heautōn*, that is, you will always have the poor in the social circle you are forming. This was said to Judas and his ilk—people who carry the money bag and handle it the way Judas did.

I hope this comment clarifies my saying "God forgive them." As for the very tolerable condition of the poor in Israel, see the fine rectorial address by my worthy colleague D. P. D. Fabius, *Mozaïsch en Romeinsch recht* (Amsterdam: J. A. Wormser, 1890), 69ff. On the same page a footnote also explains the statement in Deut 15:11, "For there will never cease to be poor in the land." [*Ed. note*: Paul Fabius taught law at the Free University of Amsterdam. He was an exacting and meticulous scholar, and his political sympathies were decidedly conservative; during the preparation for the congress he had angrily accused Kuyper of doing no more than taking his cue from the socialists.]

into an abyss of spiritual misery that moves me to pity almost more than the most grinding poverty.

This spiritual misery, too, cries out in reproach of us as Christians. Were not almost all those who now rage once baptized? And following their baptism, what has been spent on those thousands to make them understand something—at least something— of the true love of God that there is in Christ Jesus, instead of the caricature of the Christian religion against which they now utter their curses? And when the poison of the French Revolution crept undetected into the veins of the social body, what have we Christians done in our country to stop the poisoning of the lifeblood of society? Indeed, when at last the evil erupted and the social disease assumed epidemic proportions, what has been our contribution toward offering medicine and balm for its cure? Only now are we making our first feeble attempt by means of a social congress to face up to society's deadly struggle. By this time, our Christian intellectuals should already have been laboring for twenty or thirty years with something of the earnestness and scholarly approach of a Marlo or a Schaeffle to plumb the depths of this desperate situation.[86]

Spiritual and Social Problems

There is so much damage to make up for! Just consider the issues involved. Of primary importance is the majesty of our God. Although I shall presently discuss some concrete measures, we must first take up those general

---

86. This point cannot be emphasized enough. We too, for our part, ought to be engaged in study and action. We will not make any progress in tackling the social question with sentimental talk or shallow generalities. That was the mistake of the earlier communists and utopian dreamers such as Fourier and Proudhon. Socialism is a power to be reckoned with precisely because of its studies and serious research. To be convinced of this, go through the historical surveys of Quack, Winterer, Villard, and others; or, better yet, the systematic studies of Deville, Block, and Blondel. Of Gabriel Deville I recommend his work *Le Capital de Karl Marx*. Even more extensive is Maurice Block, *Les progrès de la science économique depuis Adam Smith*, 2 vols. (Paris: Guillaumin, 1890); it comes in two volumes and is rich in citations. And a work without a historical survey but providing a summary of the history in the course of expounding its own system is *La question sociale et sa solution scientifique* (Paris: Guillaumin, 1887), by Jules Edouard Blondel. It is therefore most desirable that the law faculty of the Free University furnish us with advice on this score.

To see the difference between the old and the new research method, compare Wilhelm Roscher's *Geschichte der National-Oeconomik in Deutschland* with Johann Joseph Rossbach's *Geschichte der Gesellschaft*, 8 vols. (Wurzburg: Stuber, 1868–75).

ideas that give shape and color to our entire outlook on life. We are neither plant nor animal; being human is our badge of honor; and because we are human we live first of all as conscious beings, and our sense of happiness or unhappiness in many ways is governed by our notions, ideas, and general concepts. Therefore the first article of any social program that is to bring healing must remain: "I believe in God the Father Almighty, Maker of heaven and earth." This article is today being erased. Men will no longer hear of God in politics. Not because they do not find the poetry of religion charming, but because to say "I believe in God" is to acknowledge that there is a divine order for nature and a divine ordinance for our conscience—a higher will, to which we creatures have to submit.

Today, everything has to be a free product of human creativity. The social edifice has to be erected according to man's whim and caprice. That is why God has to go, so that men, no longer restrained by natural bonds, can invert every moral precept into its opposite and subvert every pillar of human society. Does that not point us in the direction we ought to go precisely when dealing with the social question? As Christians we are to emphasize as strongly as possible the majesty of God's authority and the absolute validity of his ordinances. For all our condemnation of the rotting structure of our society, we are never to help erect any structure other than one that rests on the foundation laid by God.[87]

Just as surely, in the second place, we Christians are to take sides in the controversy between state and society. If you, like the social democrats, allow the state to be absorbed by society, you deny the political authority that God has established to uphold his supremacy and his justice. Conversely, if you, in line with the state socialists, allow society to be absorbed by the state, you offer incense to the deification of the state. You will be putting the state in the place of God and destroying a divinely ordered, free society for the sake of the apotheosis of the state. Against both positions we Christians must uphold the view that state and society each has its own sphere, or, if

---

87. This point is paramount in the whole social question. If I do not reckon with God I am entirely free in reconstructing society and can make it as I please. Man then becomes the maker of society in the strictest sense of the word, and he will violate natural laws wherever they stand in the way or push aside the moral law whenever it forms an obstacle. However, if the starting point is belief in God, who created both our human nature and the nature around us and gave laws for both, then all human social action is bound to the ordinances of God in nature and in the moral law as taught by Scripture.

you will, each has its own sovereignty, and that the social question cannot be properly resolved unless we respect this duality and thus honor political authority while also clearing the way for initiatives from society.[88] If, in the third place, the question is raised whether our human society is an aggregate of individuals or an organic body, then all those who are Christians must place themselves on the side of the social movement and against liberalism, simply because God's Word teaches us that we are made of one blood and joined in one covenant [see Acts 17:26–31]. And we must do this no less because both the solidarity of our guilt and the mystery of the atonement on Golgotha are absolutely incompatible with all such individualism and point instead to the cohesive whole that is human society.[89]

If then the pantheist, and inspired by him the pessimist, call out to us that the process of history, however fatal and miserable, cannot be disturbed—that an iron fate governs the course of human life and that we must first wade through this river of woe in order to arrive perhaps in later years at happier circumstances—then it is our duty as Christians, with God's Word in hand, to resist this false theory of blind fate as well as the false system of culpable passivity. On the basis of our confession of God's providence we are to separate, also in society, what is good from what is evil.

---

88. Denying this duality leads either to state absolutism and state deification, or to anarchy. No third possibility exists. You cannot have a constitutional state unless the duality of government and people is recognized and the relation between the two is regulated in law. The capital error of our constitution, which gives half of legislative power to Parliament, is on that account so very questionable. All monism on this point leads to pantheism. The theism of the Christian religion demands the duality and therefore the contrast between the people as subject to God and the government as servant of God—the institution to which God has entrusted the care of the people.

89. On the atomistic standpoint the entire gospel would collapse. For then there would be no incarnation of the Word, no Head of the church, no original sin, and therefore no atonement through the blood of the cross. It would be a fatal uprooting of all Christian certainty, beginning with a denial of original sin and solidarity in guilt, followed by a denial of the glorious doctrine of the covenants. This is the very reason why Christians must firmly defend the organic and therefore the social character of human life. This comes to expression in a most moving way in the commandment to love one another. See Adolf Jäger, *Die soziale Frage im Licht der Offenbarung*, 2 vols. (Neu-Ruppin: Rud. Betrenz., 1891); Hans Lassen Martensen, *Socialismus und Christenthum*, trans. from the Danish (Gotha: Rudolf Besser, 1875); Rienzi (pseud. of Henri Hubert van Kol), *Christendom en socialisme* (The Hague: Rh. W. Raadgeep, 1882); and, though presented somewhat oddly, Paul von Lilienfeld, *Gedanken über die Socialwissenschaft der Zukunft* (Hamburg: E. Behre, 1873–79), 2:403ff.

With a sword at our side and a trowel in our hand, we must simultaneously contend against what has been found untenable and reinforce what has proved beneficial.

Or if, in the fifth place, the hot-headed zealot, in direct opposition to this passive pessimism, tries to set fire to the house and through wild revolution hopes to clear the ground for erecting the new building, then it is just as much our duty as Christians, with the apostolic Word on our lips, to warn against all violation of authority, to oppose boldly every act of violence or lawlessness, and to insist loudly that the line of historical development must never be carried forward except through gradual transition and along lawful avenues.[90]

In the sixth place, if the social question places the issue of property on the agenda, and the one claims that property rights are absolute while another wants all private property to be converted to communal property, then the person who lives by God's Word must oppose this with the only true theory that God gave us in his ordinances. In God's name he has to bear witness that there can be no question of absolute ownership except in the case of God himself, and that all our possessions are only held on loan from him. We manage our possessions only as a form of stewardship. This means on the one hand that none but God the Lord can release us from our responsibility for managing those possessions; but on the other hand that we can never have any other property right than in association with the organic coherence of mankind, hence also with the organic coherence of mankind's goods. Thus what the social democrats call "community of goods"

---

90. Revolution and history stand only partially opposed to each other. After all, next to the regular process of history there is just as much the disruption of this process through violence. The only defense against revolution as a principle and as a fact is the apostolic word: "Submit yourselves to the higher powers" [see Rom 13:1; 1 Pet 2:13] understood according to the Calvinist interpretation that this passivity finds its limit only in the command to obey God's Word. To be sure, according to the *secret* counsel of God, mutiny and insurrection have their place in history as divine judgments; but God's *revealed* will does not sanction disobedience except for God's sake, and even then never otherwise than as passive resistance. Our forefathers therefore always insisted that the Dutch Revolt against Spain was not a revolt of the people but a legitimate defense of defenseless people by the *magistratus inferiores* [the lower magistrates]. See Voetius, *Catechisatie over den Heidelbergschen Catechismus*, ed. Poudroyen (Dordt, 1662), 636ff., where this question is clearly explained in the spirit of our forefathers in short questions and answers.

existed neither in ancient Israel nor in the first Christian community.[91] On the contrary, an absolute community of this kind is everywhere precluded in Scripture. However, Scripture does preclude just as surely any presumption of a property right on the strength of which you could dispose of your property absolutely, as though you were a god over it, without taking the needs of others into consideration.[92]

Furthermore, if both collectivists and also advocates of the nationalization of land have made a separate issue of the question of the land, then it is appropriate for us as Christians neither to arrogantly ridicule such a notion, nor to shrug our shoulders at such a thorny issue, as though God's Word gives us no guidance here. Our conscience alone won't let us. We hear how in Scotland three-fourths of all the land is in the hands of 14 persons, and how not so long ago one of those 14 who had purchased a new

---

91. This is clear from Acts 5:4, where Peter says: "While it remained unsold, did it not remain your own? And after it was sold, was it not at your disposal?" This shows, first, that Ananias owned still more land; second, that to sell it was not mandatory; third, that giving or not giving the money after selling it remained his free choice. Neither Calvin nor any Reformed exegete understood what we read in Acts 3:44–45 as describing a "community of goods." The only thing that can be inferred from these verses is (1) that the wealthier brothers sold a considerable portion of their property in order to distribute a portion of the proceeds to the poorer brothers, and (2) that the deacons' chest in the days of the apostles was still so full that no one suffered want.

92. It is imperative that Christians come to realize that the absolute definition of property right, which the French Revolution and its associated economic theory have pushed to extremes, is not necessarily the correct one at all. That realization is best acquired by tracing historically how property has been defined in constantly changing ways throughout the ages and among all peoples. To that end we recommend the work by Letourneau, *L'Evolution de la propriété*, a thorough study that offers an ethnological and chronological survey of the way property has been regulated among different peoples and in different centuries. Once you are convinced through this historical survey that our concept of property is hardly the only one, nor the most attractive one, take this concept, which stems from Roman law, and place it next to the concept of property in Scripture—that God alone is owner because he alone is Creator, and that we are stewards of his goods—and instantly you have a concept of property to work with that is nonsocialistic and yet sociological.

The words from the parable, "Am I not allowed to do what I choose with what belongs to me?" (Matt 20:15), do not in any way indicate a Christian theory of property right. They simply occur as a detail in a parable, taken from life as it was then. Merely think of the parable of the unjust steward [Luke 16:1–12]. Moreover, this concerns only the right *to give away* what one owns. See P. Poulin, *Religion et socialisme* (Paris: Lacroix, Verboeckhoven, 1867), 210ff.

tract, inhabited by 48 families, simply evicted the almost 300 persons living there in order to extend his game preserve. If we hear this, surely an inner voice tells us that a "right" like this to dispose of land from which bread for the consumer must grow just cannot be right, as a matter of principle; and treating ownership of land the same as ownership of goods must run counter to God's ordinances. Israel's laws laid down quite distinct rules for land ownership. The fertile field is given by God to all the people, so that all the tribes of Israel might dwell on it and live off it. Any regulation of land ownership that does not reckon with this explicit ordinance ruins land and people.[93]

Oh, it is so profoundly untrue that the Word of God only calls us to save our souls. No, God's Word poses firm ordinances and draws unmistakable lines also for our life as a nation and for our common social life; and we Christians are unfaithful to God's Word if we disregard this fact and

---

93. In my address at the congress I could not say more [about land nationalization, an idea floated by the leadership of Patrimonium in Friesland]. That would have preempted discussion. Hence I confined myself to the general comment that use of the soil cannot fall under the common law of property. This is evident from the distinctive nature of the soil, which is not the product of man's work and is merely worked upon by man. It is also evident from the special legislation about the land that God gave Israel—by which I do not suggest that we should at once adopt laws that were laid down for Israel, but only that God has lifted this characteristic feature beyond the reach of our criticism. After all, even more strictly than in the case of goods, God himself is Owner of the soil (see Fabius, *Mozaïsch en Romeinsch recht*, 25). To be sure, it does not follow from this that our salvation lies in land nationalization, nor that Mr. Van Houten's idea must become law. But whoever haughtily mocks all such proposals and ideas and brands them as "socialist" is guilty of superficiality and skepticism. Agrarian legislation will always be difficult. Just think of Ireland. Yet that is where the Salisbury Ministry has not honored the sacrosanct nature of land ownership. Compare Henry George's work of 1879, *Progress and Poverty*, cited above. In addition, see J. Stoffel, *De oplossing der sociale kwestie door opheffing van het privaat grondbezit* (Deventer: A. W. Hovenaar Rutering, 1889); Dr. Homo, *De nationalisatie van den bodem* (Haarlem: Met & Meylink, 1883); H. George, *Sociale vraagstukken*, trans. J. Stoffel (Deventer: W. Hulscher, 1884); A. von Miaskowski, *Das Problem der Grundbesitzvertheilung in Entwicklung* (Leipzig: Duncker & Humblot, 1890); and H. von Wendel, *Die landwirthschaftliche Ankaufs- und Verkaufs-Genossenschaften* (Berlin: Parey, 1886). And for a new essay aimed at solving the social question, see O. Effertz, *Arbeit und Boden: Grundlinien einer Ponophysiocratie* (Berlin: Puttkammer & Mühlbrecht, 1889), ix, who adopts the idea of Petby that "Arbeit ist der Vater, die Erde die Mutter der Güter, das Gut ist also als Kind des Vaters Arbeit und der Mutter Erde an zu sehen." ["Labor is the father and soil the mother of goods, hence goods are to be viewed as the children of father Labor and mother Earth."]

conveniently allow our theory and our practice to be determined by the opinion of the day or by prevailing laws.[94]

The Power and Clarity of God's Word

At almost every point in regard to the social question, God's Word provides the most specific directives. Think of the family, whose immediate destruction is being advocated; of marriage, which some men would transpose into free love; of family ties between the generations, which some propose to dissolve by repealing laws of succession; and no less of births, which they wish to regulate by law. Did not Bilderdijk—to start with the last issue— even before he knew of Malthus, denounce, on the basis of God's Word, all such agitation as an *impium facinus*, a godless deed, contrary to God's positive ordinances; a *homicidium posteritatis*, a murder of unborn offspring?[95]

For precisely the same reason we may never, so long as God's Word has authority among us, be opposed to colonization. God's earth, once cultivated, can produce food aplenty for more than double the millions who inhabit it today. And what else is it but human folly to crowd together in a few spots on the globe so that people have to hide in cellars and slums, while whole regions elsewhere, a hundred times the size of our entire country, await the plough and the sickle, or where thousands of herds of the most magnificent cattle roam without an owner. "Be fruitful," says the divine commandment; but also: "fill the earth" (Gen 1:28); and not: "crowd together on a little plot within your narrow borders."[96] For indeed, marriage, which

---

94. Scripture gives us not only ideas but also specific ordinances. Christians who say that they bow to God's Word yet in their social and political exertions march with the men of the French Revolution live a double life: they are of two minds and show that they do not understand Scripture and the power of the Word.

95. See his *Briefwisseling met Tydeman*, 2:77.

96. Emigration and colonization cannot be recommended enough, since even though Malthus's law that population grows at a geometric rate while the food supply only at an arithmetic rate has in the meantime proven false—see his *Essay on the Principle of Population*, 7th ed. (London: Reeves and Turner, 1872); and Charles Knowlton, *An Essay on the Population Question* (Rotterdam: Van der Hoeven & Buys, 1878); and the opposite view in Henry George, *Poverty and Progress*—that still does not erase the fact, now that hygiene has considerably lengthened life expectancy, that the population is increasing far too rapidly for the land now under cultivation; its limitation can only be found in a lower birth rate or in mass starvation. That the solution is not the adoption of a two-child system is demonstrated in France; see Franz Mehring, *Social Reform und Ueberbevölkerung*, quoted in Otto Zacharias, *Die Bevölkerungs-Frage in ihrer Beziehung zu den sociale Nothständen der Gegenwart*, 4th ed. (Jena: Mauke,

suffers harm as a result of such crammed geography, must be held in high honor by Christians, and God punishes us with all the calumny of the sin of sensuality and the curse of prostitution when we resist his ordinance in this matter.[97]

Thus the same Word of God prefigures and prescribes the family household as that wondrous creation from which the rich fabric of man's organic life is to develop. Here too you need not hesitate; you know what you have to do. We do not have to organize society; we have only to develop the germ of organization that God himself implanted in our human nature. Away, therefore, with false individualism, and anathema on every effort to break up the family! In the civil society on Dutch soil, at any rate, where for three centuries family life has flourished as a source of resilience, the dismantling of this primary foundation of our society must never be allowed—at least not with our consent.[98] The issue is no different when it comes to labor. Specifically with regard to physical work, which speaks most loudly in

---

1883), 36, who is likewise opposed to the two-child system and all physical means [of contraception], yet holds a brief for "moral restraint."

This painful, thorny question cannot be settled with a simple appeal to the words "Be fruitful" unless one also adds "and fill the earth." Colonization must therefore be made more prominent. Of the 1,434 million people who inhabit the earth today, 1,000 million live on one seventh of its surface. That leaves six-sevenths for only 434 million people, that is, 3 or 4 souls per square kilometer. Even after subtracting glaciers, deserts, and steppes there remain 56 million square kilometers, that is, a region as large as all Asia, which could provide abundant food for hundreds of millions of people. See Wilhelm Votsch, *Die Vertheilung der Menschen über die Erde* (Berlin: Habel, 1884), 44.

97. The means suggested by the advocates of the two-child system have promoted prostitution to an unbelievable degree, and it is an outrage that in our enlightened age these means of sin are openly recommended in the major newspapers of the leading centers of culture. But even apart from this issue, the social question is to a high degree a moral question. The service of Mamon turns into the service of Ashtoreth. A woman's honor is for sale for money, and poverty then encourages putting oneself up for sale. See Louis Martineau, *La prostitution clandestine* (Paris: Delahaye, 1885); Louis Reuss, *La prostitution au point de vue de l'hygiène* (Paris: J.-B. Baillière, 1889); Emile Richard, *La prostitution à Paris* (Paris: J.-B. Baillière, 1890); plus the many publications elicited in our country by the strong initiatives of H. Pierson. [*Ed. note*: Rev. Hendrik Pierson (1834–1923) was the director of an asylum for ex-prostitutes, a home for unwed mothers, and an orphanage. He played a leading role in the European movement to abolish the legalization of prostitution.]

98. For this reason, and this reason alone, we must oppose tuition-free schools, school meals, school showers, and so on. It is one thing to wonder whether parents who have no money should not be given money to help them take care of their children.

the social question, what stands out is the divine ordinance: "By the sweat of your face you shall eat bread" (Gen 3:19).[99] But standing next to it is also this word: "The laborer deserves his wages" (Luke 10:7). And you shall not defraud him of his wage (see Jas 5:4), much less withhold it from him (see Deut 25:4). The Lord says expressly through Moses: "You shall not oppress a hired worker who is poor and needy" (Deut 24:14); his wages may not even be kept with you overnight (see Lev 19:13). You shall honor the workingman as a human being, of one blood with you; to degrade him to a mere tool is to treat your own flesh as a stranger (see Mal 2:10). The worker, too, must be able to live as a person created in the image of God. He must be able to fulfill his calling as husband and father. He too has a soul to care for, and therefore he must be able to serve his God just as well as you. That is why he has a right to a Sabbath—a right that is especially important for one whose work tends to pull him down to a material level. The worker, too, was created by God as a frail creature, as one whose strength breaks under sickness and accident and also diminishes with age. And even then, when he can no longer toil in the sweat of his brow, he should be able to eat bread from the labor of the days of his manly strength.

So speaks God in his Word, and your workman reads that too. He must read it, and he should read it. And when he reads it, does not God's Word itself give him the right—no, not to grumble, even less to revolt, but at least to *complain*? May he not lodge a complaint against a social order that deprives him so painfully of that which an ordinance of divine mercy had intended for him? And although this suffering is felt by few of us personally, should it not weigh upon us for our brothers' sake? With God's Word in hand, may we hold back from leveling a withering critique on so diseased a society? Indeed, quite apart from the question of public relief, may we be at ease so long as that society is not reformed in accordance with God's Word? To treat the workingman simply as a "factor of production" is to violate his human dignity. Worse, it is a sin that goes squarely against the sixth commandment, "You shall not kill"—which also covers killing the workingman socioeconomically.[100]

But the state should never take child-rearing away from the parents. That weakens our national strength.

99. Bathing in sweat, but then also eating bread.

100. Work too is a divine ordinance, one that is governed in the first place by the question how we are to view the worker. And then the answer is clear: we are to view the worker as a human being, created in the image of God, sin-ridden, destined

A brief word, finally, about public relief. God the Lord unmistakably laid down the basic rule also for the calling of government. Government exists to administer God's justice on earth and to uphold that justice. Thus its duty is not to take over the tasks of family and society; the state should withdraw its hands from them. But as soon as collisions arise from contacts between the different spheres of life so that one sphere encroaches upon or violates the divinely ordained domain of another, then a government has the God-given duty to uphold rights against arbitrary acts and to push back the stronger party in the name of God's rights to both spheres. What a government may not do under any circumstances is to grant legal protection to one sphere and withhold it from another. A commercial code—I stand by what I said in Parliament back in 1876[101]—also calls for a labor code.

---

for an eternal existence, and here on earth called to take his stand in society as a husband and a father, to share with us the ups and downs of sickness and health, youth, maturity, and old age. Cardinal Newman and Pope Leo XIII rightly agree with this, and Mr. Van Houten's critique may show that these facts by themselves cannot solve the question, yet in no way does he prove that ours is not the right starting point. We may not be at peace with the social order until it offers to all men an existence worthy of human beings. Until such time it will remain a target of our critique. Only, do not expect a solution from monetary help from the state. That will always be humiliating for a person's sense of self-worth as well as debilitating for our national strength. The help the state must offer is better legislation. Even the various brands of socialism only half recognize this; see F. J. Haun, *Das Recht auf Arbeit* (Berlin: Puttkammer & Mühlbrecht, 1889); Edmond Guillard, *Protection et organisation du travail* (Paris: Guillaumin, 1887); James E. Thorold Rogers, *Work and Wages* (London: Swan Sonnenschein, 1890), 154ff.; David Ricardo, *Rente, salaires et profits* (Paris: Guillaumin, 1888); N. G. Pierson, *Grondbeginselen der staathuishoudkunde*, 3rd ed. (Haarlem: Bohn, 1891), 109; Conrad Bornhak, *Die deutsche Sozialgesetzgebung* (Freiburg: Mohr, 1890), 9; and Falckenberg in his fine dissertation of 1891 [*Ed. Note*: This is perhaps a reference to Paul Falkenberg, "Der Eigentumserwerb von dem veräußernden Nichteigentümer nach Handelsrecht" (diss., University of Leipzig, 1891)]. See also the introduction in L. Smith, *Les coalitions et les grèves* (Paris: Guillaumin, 1885), and the important discussion about "weekly rest from the social point of view" at the international congress held in Paris under the chairmanship of Léon Say; see *Congrès international du repos hebdomadaire* (Paris: Guillaumin and Fischbacher, 1890).

In the labor question, too, the atomistic approach corrupts everything: work by the hour and by the man-hour, when in fact two organic ties govern work: first, that of the work to be rendered (think of field work as compared to work in a large factory); and second, that of the life cycle of the workingman (youth, manly strength, old age, illness, and health).

101. See my *Eenige Kameradviezen uit de jaren 1874 en 1875* [Selected speeches in Parliament from the years 1874 and 1875] (Amsterdam: J. A. Wormser, 1890), 191-97. [*Ed. note:*

Governments should give workers their rights. Labor, too, should have the opportunity to organize itself and stand up for its rights. And as for the other type of state aid, which consists of distributing money, not justice, under whatever form and pretext: that sort of aid, to be sure, was not precluded from Israel's laws either, yet there it was kept to a minimum. Therefore I say, unless you wish to weaken the working classes and break their natural resilience, always limit any material assistance by the state to the smallest dimensions. An enduring solution for nation and country, hence also for our working classes, is found only in powerful private initiative.[102]

So then, no more arguments are needed, friends, to show that the outlook on human life afforded by the Christian religion provides—for virtually all aspects of the social question—a fixed starting point from which to attempt a concrete solution to each problem. We do not stumble around in the dark. The principles against which we are under obligation to test present-day conditions and current legal relations are clearly expressed in the Word of God. We fall short in our sacred calling as Christian citizens if we shirk the solemn task of reconstructing whatever appears in conflict with God's will and ordinances.

A Balanced Perspective

And yet, I may not end with this. For even if we pursued the path of justice to the end and succeeded in having measures passed that improved the legal situation, we would still never attain the goal God has in view. Legislation by itself will not cure our sick society unless at the same time drops of the medicine enter the hearts of rich and poor. Sin is such a terrible power that it makes a mockery of your dikes and dams. Regardless of your legal system, time and again sin will inundate the terrain of human life with the waters of desire and self-interest.

The actual date of the cited speech was November 28, 1874.]

102. Our ARP, too, must take care not to be carried along by state socialism. Even though we stand directly opposed to the individualism of the Liberal Party, we nevertheless subscribe wholeheartedly to the warning given by Goshen, which Léon Say, *Le socialisme d'Etat*, 214, translates thus: "If we have learned anything from history, we could say that the self-confidence of the individual and the respect of the state for natural liberty are necessary conditions for statehood, the prosperity of society, and the greatness of a people." The whole antirevolutionary program is set up along these lines. It would indeed be safest to concentrate all our strength on the organization of labor and labor contracts.

So I come back to the point I started from a moment ago: because we are conscious beings, almost everything depends on the standard of value that our consciousness brings to bear on life. If this present life is all there is, then I can understand why people want to enjoy it before they die and why they are haunted by the mystery of suffering. And therefore it is your standing duty, you who profess our Lord Jesus Christ, to place life eternal in the foreground for both rich and poor, and to do so earnestly, so that it grabs hold of people, and emphatically, so that it pierces their soul. Only those who reckon with a life everlasting know the true value of this earthly life. If outward possessions, material goods, and sensual pleasures are all that is intended for man, then I can understand the materialist and do not see what right I have to reprove the glutton and the hedonist. Therefore it is your duty, children of the kingdom, to seize every occasion and use every means to impress upon rich and poor that the peace of God is a much greater treasure and that the spiritual well-being of man is of much greater worth.

In the face of poverty, too, it is an open question just how you arrive at contentment and happiness. That depends by no means solely on the sum of your possessions. It depends first of all on the needs that are aroused within you, and on the kind of needs you want to have met. The socialist may sneer that this dismisses the poor with "pie in the sky," but the facts say otherwise.

If you are familiar with our Christian families, including families with the lowest incomes, then you know how much the fear of God can do for those who have only a sober portion of worldly goods. You will have observed how that little portion is elsewhere squandered in alcohol addiction and sin but is twice blessed in the case of the Christian workingman; you can testify how even in a poor household human dignity comes into its own in husband, wife, and children; and you will have thanked God for the generous share of happiness and bliss that they enjoy despite their limited resources.

No, the core of our working people do not ask, and they do not beg. On the contrary, they sometimes give generously to those who have less than they do.[103] I feel strongly that anyone who sets himself up as a prophet

---

103. Nothing enriches our Christian working classes so much as strict abstinence from strong drink. With the money thus saved thanks to self-control, they enjoy better food, and God places a double blessing on their meager portion. That blessing results especially from the fact that they do not allow their desires to be stimulated by false stimulants. After all, where such stimulants are at work one is never satisfied and

among our people and causes these fundamental elements of their consciousness to waver is guilty of cruel and pitiless conduct. Equally cruel for
the same reason is the modern theology that is preached from the pulpits,
sowing the seeds of doubt in people's hearts about our eternal destiny. No
less cruel was our public school, which dragged the children down from this
lofty standpoint. What the Christian school has done through this alone for
the suffering of our people, when it restored to thousands upon thousands
of families this only reliable standard of value for our life, our goods, and
our joys, cannot be estimated highly enough.

But this means, friends, that among those of us who are better off, the
whole of our life should be preaching the same holy principles. You who
were given more may not willfully fly in the face of those principles by
going back to your immoderate attachment to earthly possessions—giving
the impression that for you the enjoyment of luxury means more to you
than anything else, or even worse, that you share only grudgingly what
you have received from the Lord as your Owner. Then the less fortunate
do not believe what you preach. And they would be right; for all our sense
of truth revolts against a theory about happiness in the hereafter that only
serves the purpose of keeping poor Lazarus at arm's length here on earth.

There cannot be two different faiths—one for you and another for the
poor. The really decisive question in all this is simply whether you recognize in the less fortunate, indeed in the poorest of the poor, not just a *persona
miserabilis*, a wretched creature, but someone of your own flesh and blood
and, for Christ's sake, your *brother*. It is exactly this noble sentiment, sad
to say, that has been weakened and blunted so brazenly by the materialism
of our age. Yes, you know them too, those wealthy owners who are alarmed
by the socialist threat and now, from fear of this threat, reach for all kinds
of social improvements that none of them ever thought of before. But at
least among us who profess the Lord, let a more perfect love—I plead with
you—cast out all such fear. There is no room in our ranks for those who
wish to march with us in order to safeguard their money box. This is holy
ground, and he who would tread on it must first rid the soles of his feet
of his egoism. The only voice permitted here is the stirring and eloquent
appeal of the good Samaritan whispering in our ears. People are suffering

---

therefore never happy. This can be seen in high-income families that still complain
loudly and never know the peace of having their needs satisfied. Desire always asks
for more, and to stimulate desire is to arouse dissatisfaction and so spoil happiness.

all around you, and these people are your brothers, your natural kin, your own flesh and blood. You might have been in their place and they in your more pleasant position.

The gospel speaks to you of a Savior of humankind who, though he was rich, still for your sakes became poor, that he might make you rich [see 2 Cor 8:9]. The gospel makes you kneel in adoration before a Child born unto us, but born in a stable, wrapped in swaddling clothes and laid in a manger. It points you to the Son of God, yet one who became the Son of Man and crossed the land from affluent Judea to poor, despised Galilee to turn to those who were in need or pressed down by sorrow. Indeed, it tells you about this one and only Savior who before he departed from this earth stooped before his disciples in the garb of a slave, washed their feet one by one, and then got back on his feet and said: "I have given you an example, that you also should do just as I have done to you" (John 13:15).[104]

TIME FOR ACTION

The beauty of a love that comes from God and wells up within you does not display its glory when you allow poor Lazarus to quiet his hunger with the crumbs that fall from your richly laden table [see Luke 16:20-21]. All such charity rather insults a manly heart that beats no less in the poor man's breast. Rather, this love shines forth when, just as rich and poor sit down together at the table of the Lord's Supper, so you feel for the poor man as for a member of the body and you feel for your hired servants and maids as for children of men, human beings like yourself. A well-meant handshake is sometimes sweeter for a poor man than a generous gift of alms. A kind word, spoken without condescension, is the sweetest balm for those grieving with loss. Divine compassion, sympathy, suffering *with* us and *for* us—that was the mystery of Golgotha. So you too, in solidarity with your suffering brothers, must share in their pain. Only then will the sacred music of solace begin to resonate in your words, and then, driven by sympathy and compassion, you will spontaneously make your actions fit your words.

---

104. How offensive, when churches distinguish between gentlemen and burghers, and burghers and the poor, preferably with a separate "chapel" for the poorest members. It becomes even more offensive when during the Lord's Supper the gentlemen do not want to sit next to the workmen, and when in regions where ear irons are still worn, the ladies with the golden irons go first, to be followed by the women with the silver ones. Such practices are pagan. Christ wants us have affection for each other as *brothers and sisters*.

Indeed, *actions*, acts of love, are also crucial. Obviously, the poor man cannot wait until the restoration of our social structure has been completed. Almost certainly he will not live long enough to see that happy day. Nevertheless, he still has to live; he must feed his hungry mouth and the mouths of his hungry family. Robust aid is therefore called for. And however much I am inclined to commend you for your sacrificial giving—and this is true, by the grace of God, of many of you—yet the holy art of "giving for Jesus' sake" [see 2 Cor 4:11] should become much more developed among us Christians. All poverty relief by the state, never forget, always leaves a blot on the honor of your Savior.[105] Show compassion, therefore, to the depressed and the oppressed. Nothing is more suited than this compassion to make you "imitators of God, as beloved children" [Eph 5:1]. The sacred motive of mercy contains the secret of the heavenly power that you as Christians can exercise. For that wondrous motive makes the miser generous and opens the lips of those who are dour by nature. And when you are then moved to empower the poor through counsel, leadership, and initiative to row against the current of suffering in society, then you will not be at a loss for helpers, but then all real (not just nominal) Christians will vie for the great honor of assisting in this ministry of mercy to your suffering brothers in Jesus' name.

Men and brothers, may this high and holy motive govern our meeting together at this congress. Let none of us boast of the good work that we are about to undertake, but let there be instead a quiet self-reproach that we are meeting only now. And may the happy fact that the men of Patrimonium[106] are meeting and consulting with fellow Christians from the upper class be for us a token of peace, and may it be an inviting prophesy that mutual trust will soon be fully restored among us.[107]

---

105. It is perfectly true that if no help is forthcoming from elsewhere, the state must help. We are not allowed to let anyone die of hunger so long as bread still lies molding in so many breadboxes. Also, when the state helps it must do so quickly and adequately. (An indictment of our poor law!) But for that very reason it deserves emphasis that public relief is and remains, not our badge of honor, but a stinging indictment of the church and the rich—the consequence of a liberalism that undermined the strength of the church and made the rich egotistical.

106. *Ed. note*: Reference to the delegates from the Christian Workingmen's Federation that cosponsored the congress. The other sponsor was the ARP, which Patrimonium had accused of favoring the middle and upper classes and never nominating one of their own in a winnable district. The congress was organized in part to head off the formation of a Christian labor party.

107. I speak of "restoring" trust because at the most recent annual meeting of Patrimonium it became apparent that this had been undermined. There was a

And if you ask me, finally, whether I dare to place any hope in this congress—the hope that we shall at least come a little closer to solving this burning question of the day—then do not forget that the social problem is a global problem, a problem of an eminently international character, one which on that account can never be definitively settled within the narrow boundaries of our small country. What the future will reveal also with respect to this question depends on a host of factors that are not within our power. It could be that our long-provoked God, in his righteous judgment, will allow some very troubling days to come upon us, if not immediately, then in the not-too-distant future. These are the secret things that also at this congress we leave to the Lord our God (see Deut 29:29).[108] But while we await whatever may come, we do have his revealed commandment: to do, also at this congress, whatever our hands find to do, and to do it with all our might [see Eccl 9:10]. May God the Lord grant his blessing to that end.

And furthermore, what is beyond dispute for all of us is this: if our violently disturbed society is yet to be rescued, then our fast-dying century will have to recognize Christ as its Savior. I therefore close with a prayer that I know lives in everybody's heart. It is this: should this rescue be delayed and the stream of iniquity rise still higher, may it never be said of us Christians that because our faith, whether it be among the higher or the lower classes, was so lukewarm, we kept our society from being rescued and we forfeited the blessing of the God of our fathers.[109]

I thank you.

---

reason for this. Workingmen cannot devote time to studies, and the men among us whose duty it is to make the social question a topic of concentrated study from a Christian perspective have thus far woefully fallen short in fulfilling this duty. The lower class feels this, and that feeling breeds mistrust.

108. He who does not believe in the power of the Christian religion to lift society out of a condition not unlike bankruptcy can only conclude with P. Jacoby, *Etude sur la sélection* (Paris: Baillière, 1881), 535, that the civilized nations of today are destined to sink into barbarism and to be succeeded by younger nations that are still in an underdeveloped state. See Letourneau, *L'Evolution de la propriété*, 495. See also especially the excellent work by James Fitzjames Stephens, *Liberty, Equality, Fraternity* (London: Smith, Elder, 1873).

109. I have deliberately included in these notes references to some interesting titles in order to be of service perhaps to those among us who are still complete strangers to this field.

DRAFT PENSION SCHEME FOR WAGE EARNERS

TEXT INTRODUCTION

During his second term as a member of Parliament, Kuyper wrote a series of articles in which he proposed a design for a comprehensive, mandatory pension plan for the working classes. The plan would provide pensions for the elderly, widows, and orphans, as well as insurance against sickness, disability, and unemployment. The series of eighteen articles appeared in *De Standaard*, April–May 1895. At the request of the Christian workers association Patrimonium, it was then published in a separate booklet of 102 pages.

Source: Abraham Kuyper, *Proeve van pensioenregeling voor werklieden en huns gelijken* (Amsterdam: Wormser, 1895). Translated, abridged, and annotated by Harry Van Dyke.

DRAFT PENSION SCHEME FOR WAGE EARNERS

There is a movement afoot to provide old age-pensions for the working classes. It is generally agreed that a wage earner should be eligible for a pension at the age of 65. However, the age of 60 might be better, for workers are then past their strength. But a plan starting at 65 may have a better chance of being accepted. To lower it to age 60 would then be the next step.

Our working classes live on subsistence wages and therefore cannot save for old age. Yet their low wages benefit all of society through lower prices for goods. If prices could be artificially raised to finance a savings plan, wage earners could be assured an annuity in old age. But we all know that the agricultural and industrial products cannot be raised in that way; foreign competition alone makes this unfeasible. Even if its prices were raised, society as a whole would not be willing to pay for such a savings plan. Saving has to start with the stakeholders themselves, at a young age.

We have always maintained that working people who have spent their working days in honest labor have a moral right to a pension when their strength begins to fail. Not as a right which they own, or have earned, or can sue for; but a right grounded in ordinances imposed by God on humankind. As our laws are made by human beings, they can never perfectly capture divine justice. They are partial, incomplete, and sometimes feeble. At times they are very deficient expressions of the justice demanded by God.

Today, by the law of the land, elderly working people are for a good part poor and helpless. But by the standard of justice this ought not to be so.

In times past, a slave was paid for at the time of purchase or else was born on the plantation and reared at the owner's expense. In either case a slave owner had to *pay up front* before he could benefit from a slave's work. That was phase one. During phase two the slave performed work and was housed and fed. Then came phase three, when the slave got old and could no longer work, yet was still housed and fed at his owner's expense. These are the natural phases of a human life as ordained by God. Thus the owner was obliged to spend money on the elderly slave by divine ordinance. Divine justice assured that the slave had a right to an "old-age pension."

Now then, do our wage earners, who are free people, deserve less than the slave? Our answer is: neither less, nor more, but the same.

The case of the slave is obvious. The case of working people is more complicated because they have free will.

The abolition of slavery, later also of serfdom, brought working people a wonderful privilege: personal freedom. No longer in bondage to others, they could now make their own decisions and take responsibility for themselves and their families.

Freedom is often mistaken for being able to do what you want. But true freedom is to shake off unnatural bonds and to put on natural bonds. To be free means to be unhindered in your natural development and to live in the relationships that belong to your nature according to the created order.

Working people, both before and after their death, are obligated to care for their loved ones and to care for themselves in old age, when they are no longer able to work. To make this possible, two conditions have to be met: they have to negotiate an agreement with their employers about a living wage; and they have to band together with their fellows to limit competition in the labor market. Alas, neither condition can be met. A false individualism has made them impossible. The law of supply and demand rules supreme. In the old days, guilds at least provided some bond. But since the French Revolution, society is trapped in the antisocial system of limitless competition.

This being the case, can the working classes better themselves *without outside help*? Merchants and manufacturers can, because they are few in number and can band together. Not the millions who work from Monday to Saturday; they lack the time and the means to form a united front. The rise of trade unionism was a hopeful development, but today it is lapsing into socialism. Why? Because not *all* workers join unions. If they did, the problem would be solved at one stroke.

Clearly, only the government can help. But how? By temporarily enrolling the working classes in a real organization of lawful interests. Failing that, the labor movement will take on a political character and in the end will destine the government itself for abolition.

After surveying various proposals to alleviate the problem of poverty in old age (as by Napoleon and William Booth), Kuyper turns his attention to the proposal of his friend Mr. William Hovy for businesses in the Netherlands.

The Association of Dutch Employers, known as Boaz, emerged in the wake of the Social Congress of 1891. Its chief mandate is to awaken the conscience of employers regarding their employees. Its vision is that at least *Christian* employers, propelled powerfully by the Word of God, conduct themselves toward their employees in such a way that they can stand before judgment of God.

Quite naturally, therefore, Boaz has raised the issue of pensions. It has asked its members what, in the light of God's law, can be demanded of employers that is to the benefit of their workers. Boaz had the good sense to invite Willem Hovy to introduce this subject.[1] He has been convinced of the necessity of pensions for years. At the brewery of which he is the senior director, he introduced a pension scheme that works well. He has insisted that this is about neither doling out alms nor philanthropy. It is, instead, about ensuring that honest workers in their old age can enjoy the fruit of their working years. For this reason it is essential, according to Hovy, that the government intervenes. Private ventures, tried in a variety of ways, have fallen short.

As a business leader with outstanding commercial expertise, Mr. Hovy did not hesitate to state the following in his report:[2]

---

1. Willem Hovy (1840-1915) was a business leader in the brewing industry. His friendship with Kuyper is noted in this anthology's editor's introduction by Peter S. Heslam.
2. See the lecture by Willem Hovy, "Pensionnering voor loontrekkenden," published in the monthly periodical *Boaz* (March 1894).

If only the universal introduction of old-age pensions could be achieved on a voluntary basis! That would be far preferable to having it imposed by law. Thus far, however, every attempt at voluntary adoption has failed terribly. I need only remind you of the attempt made in 1881 by the Workingmen's League Patrimonium, for which a great deal of preparatory work was done. I remind you of the call sent out in 1882 by a committee recruited by the Association for the Promotion of Factory and Handicraft Industry. That committee of more than a hundred members included many prominent citizens, *inter alia* five cabinet ministers; five provincial governors; members of the First and Second Chamber of Parliament; the mayors of cities, including Amsterdam, Rotterdam, Utrecht, and Leeuwarden; several university professors; and other authorities. This call urged all stakeholders to attend a meeting in which important information would be shared about establishing a General Dutch Pension Fund for Workers. It included these words:

> We ask you urgently to show your interest by attending this meeting. This will assist in the setting up a fund which, strongly supported and well managed, will ensure the future happiness of the Dutch worker. No finer opportunity has been available for a long time to demonstrate that the Dutch people as a whole has a heart for working people and acknowledge their service. Should, with your cooperation, the fund become a reality, something will have been accomplished that will be of benefit for the whole of the Netherlands.[3]

Finally, I remind you of the serious and well-intentioned attempts made only a few years ago in this city, in particular at the initiative of the mayor at that time, Mr. Van Tienhoven. The result of this was the founding of the so-called Employers Union. Its aim was that every workman would have a pension book and that one-third of the premiums would be paid by the workman and for two-thirds by the employer. The idea was that when a

---

3. See E. Bergsma, *Het pensioneeren van werklieden* (Rotterdam: H. A. Kramers & Zoon, 1882), 20–24.

worker moved from one employer to another, the latter would be obliged to carry on what already existed, with the result that at the end of their working lives, workers would be assured of a pension to which their various employers would have contributed.

These endeavors have led to very little. This is despite the hard work, and attention to detail, that went into setting them up. We think back with gratitude, for example, for all the work done by our esteemed and beloved Bart Poesiat for the pension and relief fund for workingmen and their widows. We are also grateful for the zeal with which Jacob van Oversteeg sought to make this program popular. However, the voluntary system has foundered. Hence the choice remains between regulation by law, or no regulation. I do not hesitate a moment to prefer the former.

Mr. Hovy therefore is the unconditional ally of those who, with us, want to see pensions made mandatory through government legislation.

> To arrive at an acceptable situation, pensions must be regulated. The employer should follow the example of the ant, which makes provision in advance, lest when the need arises the burden is too heavy. Christian employers should do this of their own accord, but all employers need to do it. Therefore I believe that somewhat greater pressure is necessary to overcome human selfishness.

> That pressure has to come from the power that is intended by God to protect the weak, namely from government. I am afraid of all government meddling in spheres outside its own. But I do believe that government has an important task to fulfill when it comes to raising the moral consciousness of the nation, counteracting the arbitrariness of those who have the power, and protecting the weak over against the strong. Government has already accepted this role in the laws regulating the labor of women and children. But to prevent unfair impoverishment, the government has just grounds to demand that, besides wages, something extra is paid to provide for living costs during old age.

Mr. Hovy also agrees with us that providing pensions is not enough. Sickness and disability must also be provided for. Provision should also be extended to the widows and orphans workers leave behind.

To achieve this goal, Mr. Hovy proposes that the working man himself makes provision for his wife and children should he come to die, and that the provision of his pension, if God spares his life, should be solely the obligation of the employer.

There is something beautiful in this idea of dividing provision. Employees take care of their loved ones, while their employers take care of them—on the express condition that the pension is not regarded as poor relief but as a portion of the earned but *as yet unpaid* wages. An employee can, therefore, demand a pension of their employer, just as they can demand payment of their weekly wages. Moreover, Mr. Hovy is so generous that he regards the three guilders that has been accepted everywhere else as too little; he would like to provide a pension that would ensure double that amount for elderly workers.

To show how this could be done, he offers three examples:

1. From the age of 24 and up, an employer pays 30 cents weekly for his worker's pension. At age 65 that will yield a pension of 6 guilders a week, climbing to 12 guilders a week when the worker turns 70 (because contributions have been made for such a long time and the worker cannot be expected to live many more years). If contributions are not begun until age 34, the 30 cents per week entitles the worker to a pension of only 3.33 guilders at age 65 and 6.66 guilders at age 70. If started at age 40, those figures are 2.15 and 4.30 guilders a week; and so forth.

2. Twenty guilders annually are paid for the workers. At the age of 65 that will give them a pension for their own weekly contributions, starting at age 24, of 50 cents; at age 26, of 48 cents; at age 27, of 46 cents; and so on. All one needs to do in this case is perform the addition to arrive at the amount of weekly benefits—amounts that increase considerably again if contributions are made till the age of 70 without drawing a pension.

3. Employers may wish to contribute an amount for their workers only at certain times, when the firm has prospered and can therefore afford it; one year they contribute 100 guilders per workers. If started at age 24, this sum will ensure workers receive a weekly benefit at age 65 of 2.50 guilders. If it

is possible to keep this up for three years in a row and contribute 100 guilders each time, workers will be assured at age 65 of a weekly pension of 2.50 plus 2.40 plus 2.30, or 7.20 guilders. All that for an outlay of 300 guilders! Of course the contributions can be made at irregular times and some years can be skipped over when the financial resources do not permit; the pensions will adjust according to the means.

The amounts mentioned here take into account that when the insured person dies before age 65, the premiums that have been paid are not returned. It can also be stipulated that the premiums will be paid back to the blood relatives, but then the contribution amounts will increase.

I trust these modest proposals will illustrate and clarify the situation. As it has been said, "It matters not which method is selected—circumstances will have to decide that—so long as the goal is pursued."

Unquestionably, this report brings honor to the annals of Boaz. It deals with a topic that is entirely in line with that organization. Its handling of the subject is prompted by Christian conscience. And it indicates a way forward that holds out the promise of complete and ample provision.

We join others therefore in thanking Mr. Hovy for what he as the mouthpiece for Boaz has offered. At this stage in the discussion, we refrain from offering any criticism, except on one point.

However noble it is for the members of Boaz to want to shoulder the entire burden of providing for pensions, it seems to us that this will not work as a general policy. If it were introduced by law, our exports would lose out to foreign competition. If all our workers were placed at industrial firms of the size of Mr. Hovy's brewery, then pensions could indeed be arranged in this way. But that is not the case. The pension scheme we need encompasses all workers, men and women, and not just industrial workers but ordinary laborers, including those who earn a living with pen or needle that is too modest for them to put some of their earnings aside for their old age. In the case of small firms employing no more than one or two people, the idea of self-insurance does not work, and the balance shifts in favor of the competition.

At a hundred or more employees, the mortality rate does not differ all that much. Ten or twelve factories with approximately the same number of workers would, on average, be taking care of an equal number of pensioners. But if the number of your employees is three, two, or one, then this rule does not apply. With firms of this size, an employer may have to pay an additional pension to those paid by a competitor who had an employee who died early and is therefore free of that obligation.

This inequality would be prevented if all employers retired their workers by taking out an annuity for them at age 65 and onward; but many firms cannot afford to outlay such a large sum up front.

Any move from one employer to another would also be problematic. After all, under the proposed scheme practically no employer would hire someone over 50 years old because they would risk being stuck paying that person's pension. Moreover, the right remains to lay off workers at the end of their contracts. The temptation would be strong to dismiss the more elderly workers.

However excellent the proposal may be for large industrial firms, it does not solve things for the work force as a whole. Should this scheme be made mandatory, all employers, large or small, would have to make an annual payment into a government fund for every worker they employed that year. Amounting to a wage raise, this would make it more difficult for them to compete against foreign imports. They would no longer need to fear domestic competition because all employers would be equal. But their foreign competitors, who pay much lower wages, can produce more cheaply and will rob them of customers in the global market.

Again, it does credit to Boaz as an employers' association, and to Mr. Hovy as a Christian employer, that they are willing to take on the burden of paying for pensions. Nevertheless, Mr. Hovy will concede that other factors are at play here that will make it unavoidable that certain adjustments are made to his ideas.

We leave it at these cursory comments for now. A newspaper article, to remain readable, cannot discuss such schemes in greater detail. As serious proposals, their main points are clear enough. Following this brief introduction, readers can judge for themselves which avenues offer the best prospects for arriving at the intended destination. We also assume that, insofar as pension schemes are being introduced in Germany and elsewhere, our readers will be acquainted with the relevant legislation.

After concluding this survey, Kuyper examines his option of government involvement in providing security for workers in their twilight years.

Is it acceptable to antirevolutionaries to have government involved in an insurance scheme for wage earners? Well, I proposed this very thing in Parliament twenty years ago, and I repeated it in my commentary on the manifesto of the Antirevolutionary Party, *Our Program*.[4] But was I right?

Let me begin by stating that such involvement does not belong to the permanent attributes of government—in contrast to its task to administer justice, always and everywhere. That is government's unique calling, its normal task. An abnormal task may present itself only when others fail to perform their duty or when special circumstances make intervention mandatory. For example, child-rearing does not belong to the task of government, but child protection from serious parental neglect or abuse does. Then government has to get involved, though only to withdraw again once parents are fit to take back what is their natural task. Similarly, care for the poor does not belong to the task of government, but when pauperism spreads and philanthropy falls short and starvation is imminent, government *inaction* would be criminal. Misguided laws and ordinances can also create unhealthy situations in society, the kind that private initiative cannot hope to rectify; then again government has the duty to make up for the mistakes it made earlier.

If asked whether government involvement in the social question in general, or specifically with old-age security for the working classes, belongs to the *normal* task of government, we would say no.

In a normal situation, society has all the means at its disposal to ensure the smooth running of employment, including wage labor. And if private initiative is able to take care of any problems that arise, government should stay out. Its unique mandate does not cover this.

But if social conditions have become so desperate that private initiative is powerless to do anything about it, government must intervene.

Such intervention should not permanently displace private initiative, but instead should assist private initiative, strengthen it, and so conduct affairs that before long government can withdraw again.

---

4. Abraham Kuyper, *Ons Program* (Amsterdam: Kruyt, 1879). See also the English translation of the second, abridged edition of *Ons Program*, *OP* 20.III.§§292–98:344–50.

We therefore believe that government must get involved in the problem of poverty in old age. It has been delinquent for far too long in tackling the issue.

The stipulation that government involvement should be only temporary should not be taken in an absolute sense. If a just situation cannot be restored through temporary measures, fixed legislation—statute law with coercive power and backed by sanctions—may be called for.

Just as society's activity in trade and commerce eventually required government regulation, so wage labor has come to need enduring legislation to guide and protect it. And this level of involvement by government will not be temporary but permanent. Just as commerce received its commercial code, so the activity of the working classes has matured to the level where it needs a properly legislated code of laws, a labor code.

For this reason, we have distinguished sharply between two entirely different questions: Should government regulate a pension scheme? And: Should government support pensions financially?

Regulation will be necessary. The days when we could rely on natural bonds will never return. And to expect voluntary participation in an insurance scheme *by all* workers is naïve; it does not reckon with sloth and sin; and it would install a system that showed the same deficiency a hundred years from now. Only mandatory participation can ensure enduring success for an old-age pension scheme.

Financial support of such a scheme by government is another matter. We think that would be wrong.

From the start the intention should not be for government to follow its own ideas and impose them on labor. Instead, it ought to offer support in such a way that private initiative is not paralyzed but reinforced. The scheme should eventually be able to throw away the crutch and walk on its own two feet.

That is why we have argued for installing chambers of labor for advising the government before anything is done. And that is also why we have endeavored to help settle the franchise question, so that the working classes themselves can be part of the consultation about this issue.[5] Unless reason

---

5. For Kuyper's passionate involvement in the debates at this time about extending the franchise, see Harry Van Dyke, "Abraham Kuyper and the Continuing Social Question," *Journal of Markets & Morality* 14, no. 2 (Fall 2011): 641–46, and James D. Bratt, *Abraham Kuyper: Modern Calvinist, Christian Democrat* (Grand Rapids: Eerdmans,

forsakes us, we cannot imagine that the sitting Parliament can achieve anything successful in this delicate matter before the lower classes are given the vote. The legislation to deal with this issue must not be concocted by some clever jurists but, guided by true principles, *should arise from life itself*. To be solid, it should not be designed *theoretically* but must link up with private initiative in continuity with history.

For the above reasons, we refuse to endorse government intervention in regard to the social question, whether it be by appealing to the *common good* or by invoking the rights of the *community*.

We reject as revolutionary the political theory that sees the state as "the community"; and an appeal to the elastic and chameleonic concept of "the common good" would in this case take us further than we are allowed to go.

In our eyes there are three lawful grounds for our proposal: (1) government is obligated to act temporarily on behalf of its subjects when they are unable to fulfill their normal duties themselves; (2) government ought to ensure the public regulation of rights whenever they are imperiled in the private sector; (3) government has the bounden duty temporarily to support the weak when they are threatened to succumb to pressure.

Three areas illustrate these duties of government: education, marriage, and poor relief.

Education is a task of the home. But when parents fail to realize this task, government has to assume it, at first in its entirety, later partially.

Marriage does not stem from the state; if anything, the state stems from marriage. Marriage originates outside the state; its essence is complete in and of itself; it is of a private nature and practices its sovereignty according to a higher norm. With a view to persons and goods, however, governments everywhere have realized their duty to include and guarantee marriage rights in their legal systems.

Similarly, poor relief. It is the task of the church and the household. To slide it onto the government is to slide down the slippery slope toward communism. But when abusive conditions have caused pauperism to exceed the capacity of private charity, the government takes action to protect the weak.

We shall not deal here with all the social problems that beg regulatory measures. We want to focus on the pension question as the most urgent

---

2013), 228–33, as well as "Christ and the Needy" and "The Reefs of Democracy," in *On Charity and Justice*.

problem at the present time. The level of wages today are simply too low for wage earners to be able to afford insurance. Hence they need help.

After completing the 18 articles, Kuyper added another one in which he summarized his draft of a pension plan in 24 theses.

1. Government involvement in pensions must honor three principles. First, when citizens turn out to be unable to do what they should normally do for themselves, government should temporarily do it for them. Second, government is duty-bound to protect rights if injustice results when they are left in the care of the voluntary sector. Third, government is called to temporarily support every integral part of national life that would otherwise collapse.

2. Every insurance plan to be considered must exclude the notion of charity. Alms are for not for those who can work and who do work, but for those who are poor, either through their own fault or through no fault of their own.

3. Any sound pension plan should proceed from a universal insurance scheme against every burden incurred by the working classes through sickness, accident, unemployment, old age, or death.

Even though for the time being only old-age pensions can be introduced, the whole package of insurance schemes must be taken into consideration for any regulation regarding such pensions to be effective.

4. Whatever the pension plan, the government's intention must be to make the legal framework enduring, yet also to withdraw government assistance and involvement as soon as feasible.

5. No regulation may be introduced except after consulting the parties involved, which in this case is workers and owners.

6. The insurance should extend to men and women who work for wages that do not exceed, say, six hundred guilders annually.

7. The scheme should not be uniform throughout the country or for all categories but should relate proportionately to varying wages, living standards, and living conditions.

8. The government ought to make participation in the insurance plan mandatory for apprentices, tradespeople, artisans, clerks, and so on that are in service. Their registration in the scheme would impose obligations and guarantee certain associated rights.

9. The plan should cover six eventualities: sickness, disability, unemployment, widows, orphans, and old age.

10. The registration of a trades people should oblige them between the ages of 20 and 22 to deposit into the scheme 1 guilder per week. This sum of 150 guilders per year shall be supplemented with 100 guilders from the government. In addition, for 40 weeks of the year, registrants are to pay 25 cents per week; for the sum thus invested they are entitled to a pension of 3 guilders per week, starting at age 65. If the tradesperson dies and leaves behind a spouse and children, the spouse is to be entitled to a week's pension for 1 year and each of the children a week's pension till the age of 14.

10b. Sickness and disability insurance should be the responsibility of employers, as part of the risk of employing persons.

11. Insurance against unemployment (other than seasonal) should be charged to the registrants collectively, up to a maximum of 25 cents per week, spread over 40 weeks per year. Any deficit or surplus would be settled annually with the government.

12. Under normal circumstances, these arrangements would cost the government approximately 40,000 x 100 guilders a year, plus a surcharge to the unemployment fund—thus a sum of between 4 to 5 million per year, offset by a reduction in poor relief.

13. Widow and orphan allowances would cost registrants 150 guilders, payable in a lump sum, followed by 10 guilders per year, plus approximately 10 guilders per year for the unemployment fund. Twenty guilders a year is not even 40 cents a week, which comes down to 6⅔ cents per day, or less than 1 cent per hour.

14. Employers would need to insure their workers against sickness and disability, which would amount to just 20 guilders and thus equal a raise in wages of 1 cent per hour.

15. Such an arrangement would discourage unmarried workers in their early years from squandering their money and entering marriage at too young an age.

16. The administration of the funds should include employers and employees, with the aim of making it independent as soon as possible, under government supervision.

17. Existing insurance companies could be used for sickness and disability insurance, provided such companies are accredited and inspected by the government.

18. Since such a plan, if introduced in 1900, would not reach its full effect until 1942, the intervening years would need some form of bridge financing.

19. For the intervening years, extending the *right* to a pension, or to widow and orphan allowances, would have to be abandoned for those who have today already reached the age of 55, as otherwise financial resources would be exceeded.

20. Those between ages 23 and 25 would be obliged, by way of exception, to pay the registration fee, whereby they would acquire the full rights of registered workers.

21. Those between ages 25 and 33 should have the option of acquiring the full rights of registered workers through voluntary payment of higher annual premiums. This option could be made mandatory.

22. Those between ages 39 and 55 should have the option of insuring themselves exclusively for a pension through paying higher annual premiums, any shortfall during these sixteen years being topped up by the government.

For the first year the government would face an expenditure of 6 million guilders, the following year of just under 5 million guilders, soon decreasing to less than 3 million, ending in 16 years.

Since not all will avail themselves of this option, the payable amounts will not be nearly so large.

23. Employers should be obliged for the sake of those who choose the options described in articles 21 and 22 to pay a diminishing premium, calculated over all their employees, until such time as the normal regulation becomes fully operative.

24. A plan like the above would wrest workers from pauperism in the future and offer at least some assistance during the intervening years.

Kuyper appended two more articles "to forestall any misunderstanding."
They dealt with poor relief customarily delivered by the church.

We oppose on principle the growing pressure to assign care of the poor to the state and to submerge it entirely in *public relief*. If today we ask the state to make sacrifices for the poor we do so only as an exception, as a temporary measure to remedy a situation that has arisen in part because of misgovernment. At the same time we do so in order to escape, the sooner the better, too big a role for government in caring for the poor.

Antirevolutionaries are firmly of the opinion that this demand is in line with their principles. As early as 1854 Groen van Prinsterer wrote, "Our goal must not be the regulation of public charity but its eradication," though he added that "we do not want public relief to stop immediately, to declare on the spot that patients are healed and demand of them that they act as restored. ... What we want is not that the subsidies are immediately cancelled, but that the current situation be subordinated *to a different system*."[6]

Calvinism took a permanent stance on this question when it reinstated the diaconate in its original form. A diaconate is unknown to the Lutheran church; the episcopal Church of England did not restore it; and although it cannot be said that the medieval church, under Rome's hierarchy, neglected care for the poor, yet it had developed into something quite different from the ecclesiastical office of poor relief. The Calvinist churches restored the diaconate as a ministry of mercy. Wherever they could develop unhindered, such a ministry appeared, and consistories soon incorporated deacons.

To be sure, we have often drawn attention to the fact that in the eighteenth century this ministry was allowed to slide. Deacons collected and distributed perfunctorily. And Reformed theology failed to work out the fundamental idea behind the diaconate and adapt it to changing conditions.

But this neglect does not undo the fact that the Calvinist approach to poor relief should take its starting point in the diaconate. That said, two comments are in order.

First, the diaconate was never meant to confine its aid to churchgoers, but was concerned about the poor in general. Just as God makes his sun to rise on the evil and the good, and sends rain on the just and the unjust, so the material aid administered by deacons was to benefit all who were needy. Particularly the stranger and the sojourner were to enjoy the benefit of hospitality.

Secondly, this ministry was intended exclusively for the needy. It was not meant to care for the aged, the widows and orphans among our working classes. In fact, the lowliest day laborers were asked to contribute to the deacon fund, thus reinforcing his sense that if receiving charity can be harmful, giving to charity elevates and ennobles.

---

6. See G. Groen van Prinsterer, speech in the second chamber, May 12, 1854, in *Handelingen van de Staten-Generaal, 1853-1854* (Den Haag: Algemeene Lands-Drukkerij, 1854), 809.

As often as the collection plate goes around in a church consisting of members of all classes, and everyone without exception puts something into it, a moral act of great significance is taking place. The widow's mite, which Jesus praised, has been highly esteemed for 18 centuries [see Mark 12:41–44; Luke 21:1–4].

However, the whole system presupposed a normal situation, one in which a willing worker could earn a living wage and only the needy had to rely on charity. But no sooner does an abnormal situation arise—one in which even the willing become needy and have to rely on alms—than the effectiveness of this system falls short. Then a broad class of people join the ranks of the needy, without work and without rights, victims of an industrial crisis. They are forced to buy on credit, become impoverished, grow bitter, and in the end deliver themselves over to pauperism or communism.

In that situation, the need is so great that the diaconate is powerless to relieve it. Only help from elsewhere can provide what is needed. This reflects negatively on the diaconate and charitable donations begin to decline. The idea takes hold that aid that can make a real difference must come from elsewhere. Church collections for the poor used to bring in astonishing sums; today they amount to little to be proud of.

It gets worse. The diaconate is the expression of the morally elevating thought that help and care for the needy do not come from human beings but from God. What the rich and the well-to-do possess is not theirs but belongs to God; they are the stewards of it, and God commands them in his Word to set aside some of it for the poor, without revealing their name. In this way the money for the poor remains strictly God's money, and God has appointed deacons to distribute his money to the poor in his name.

That is showing love in the most delicate and least self-serving manner. Recipients are not humiliated and do not become beholden to anyone. They receive their alms from the same God from whom the rich man receives his wealth.

But if the situation turns dire, the diaconate becomes inadequate, and hence discredited. Then *voluntary philanthropy* enters the scene to try and improve on the diaconate. This time, however, God is left out of the picture. Human beings are giving of their *own money*. They are pleased with their own generosity and pride themselves in it. Without meaning to, they humiliate the poor and make the poor beholden to them.

As a result it soon becomes apparent that private philanthropy, too, falls short. Then state assistance rushes in, with a double advantage: when the funds dry up it can coerce contributions through taxation; and its regulations and inspectors can create some order in the chaos of pauperism.

The end result is that the church is up against the state. The state is the rich and powerful body, the church the poor and powerless institution.

At first sight, admittedly, aid to the poor is more effective and people shout for joy—unless they recall deeper-lying principles. When they do that, they will say that love is higher than coercion, that moral gain is only real when giver and receiver together bow before God, and that the end result will show one of two things: either coercion will make way again for love, for God's sake and to the church's credit; or else coercion will gain the upper hand, but only to have the state absorbed into society and at last to see society and government sink away into communism.

Thus, although we fully concede that in the current social upheaval the diaconate cannot possibly hope to succeed in alleviating the flood of misery that is inundating the nation, yet we must insist that unless aid to the needy comes from God, through the church, it will demoralize people and corrode the very fabric of society.

Our three basic tenets still stand: (1) alms are to be given only to the needy; (2) alms are to be offered to God, thus in secret; (3) alms, which belong to God, are to be distributed by his servants.

But our ideal does not fit reality. So what are we to do?

First, we must take care to preach the Word. All our earthly goods belong to God, and we are only stewards of them. What is left over after providing for our household is intended by God to serve other people's needs rather than being spent on luxuries and excesses, or to be donated with our name attached, so that we can parade our generosity and thus humiliate the poor. To give in secret ought to become the norm, and deacons should again be respected as distributors of what belongs to God.

Secondly, the diaconate should become an object of study. What has become routine, ill-understood, and therefore corrupted must be lifted up again and shown to be a holy work of love.

For these two measures to be adopted, and for our ideal to regain acceptance, will take time. Meanwhile, another problem has arisen that requires an answer, not from the church but from the state.

Poverty is rife. This impoverishment did not occur because God laid more suffering on humankind. Epidemics have actually decreased, wars have become less destructive, and the soil produces crops more abundant than ever before. But impoverishment has arrived on a large scale because the condition of the lower classes has been disorganized. Their weak and outdated organization has been removed, and they have been left to struggle along in a false, chaotic position in an entirely new situation.

Poverty arose as a result of an entirely new production method that was introduced without legal protection for the many millions whose lives were impacted by it. Other factors included duty-free trade, and new monetary regulations. Workers used to be masters of their work; today the work is master over them. They have become incidental to their work, and work is centered on capital. If the lower classes remain without rights and without defenses in our society, either they will seek their rights through violence, or the poison of pauperism will penetrate ever deeper into our social fabric.

We are not implying that violent action would be justified. But history shows that leaving a powerful class of people in intolerable conditions always ends in violence. For this reason it is incumbent upon government to do three things:

1. Revise the laws and regulations that gradually worsen the situation, so that they stop doing further damage.

2. Provide temporarily for those needs where it has been demonstrated that they cannot be remedied from elsewhere.

3. Create a situation in which only the destitute and those who have hit bottom through their own fault will have to rely on philanthropy.

These three measures are interconnected. If only the second were done, it might perpetuate the existing situation. In providing aid, the government should not disqualify a needy person who is supported, in however small an amount, by a diaconate. And if public relief is legislated, as in England, such that it is made a duty of government and a right of the poor, one lands on a slippery slope where no halt is possible.

That is why we have strenuously advocated that working people organize themselves, something that was expressed in the demand for a labor code. This is because the idea of a labor code promises a future in which, once all kinds of organizational regulations are adopted, all this will ultimately find its permanent codification.

That is why we have continued to argue for chambers of labor; for employment contracts and contracts for farm tenants, with binding stipulations; for registration of apprentices, tradespeople, and artisans; and lately for an insurance plan for the working classes, in order to provide for old age, disability, and unemployment and with a view to widows and orphans who are left behind without help.

The liberals, who wanted to make such provisions available as a favor, and therefore as charity, evidently did not grasp that this was a bad idea that would completely overturn the insurance scheme we proposed. We antirevolutionaries must insist that the atmosphere of charity must be removed for all who can work and have worked and who are willing to work. For only then can genuine works of charity be revived so that all those for whom they are meant will be truly helped in their need and will then be morally lifted up.

Provided this receives firm commitment, we have no objection whatever to public relief, since the time will arrive when it will automatically cease.

After all, if our system is adopted, the working classes within 40 years will be fully protected against the impoverishing effect of old age, illness, accident, unemployment, and death. This major decrease in the numbers of poor people will cause pauperism to lose its force. And it will allow the diaconate once again to raise its head with honor and to provide aid to those who by divine institution may lay claim it.

PROTECTIONISM AND MATERIALISM

TEXT INTRODUCTION

During fall 1898, Kuyper left the Netherlands for a tour of the United States of America lasting almost five months. During this time, he received an honorary doctorate in law from Princeton University, delivered the famous Stone Lectures on Calvinism at Princeton Theological Seminary, visited areas with significant Dutch-American populations (including Michigan, Iowa, Illinois, Ohio, and New York), and visited the US president at the White House.

On returning home, he wrote up his impressions of America in a booklet of some 200 pages titled *Varia Americana*. As the title suggests, it touched on a variety of aspects of American life that he had found remarkable. A seasoned traveler and keen observer, he included aspects he had long admired, albeit from a distance. Kuyper expressed both concern for the materialism he encountered and appreciation of the prosperity and cultural flowering of the nation's Gilded Age, predicting the nation's rise to become a world leader. He drew lessons from this in support of the moderate protectionism his party advocated for the Netherlands.

SOURCE: Two extracts from A. Kuyper, *Varia Americana* (Amsterdam/ Pretoria: Höveker & Wormser, n.d. [1899]), 28–33, 49–54. Translated and abridged by Harry Van Dyke.

PROTECTIONISM AND MATERIALISM

EXTRACTS FROM *VARIA AMERICANA*

America has a system of nearly exclusive protection. It does not only levy retaliatory tariffs to "get even" with foreign countries that close their borders to American products, or to give support to a languishing or newly started industry. On the contrary, it has incredibly high tariffs in a truly protectionist sense, making imports of foreign manufactured goods virtually impossible. In New York, for example, an ordinary pair of French kid gloves costs 7.50 guilders, while an American pair of almost equal quality costs 2.50 guilders.

I am not recommending similar import duties for our country. During the last election, the Antirevolutionary Party supported import duties only when tariffs elsewhere cut us off from the chance of fair competition. One must never forget that the United States is a "world unto itself"; with a population of 70 million, it has a huge market for its domestic industry, and it is rich in natural resources such as metals, lumber, and coal. And because it stretches over temperate and warmer climate zones, it grows tobacco, cotton, wine, and every kind of fruit. It is a country that literally lacks nothing, a situation that cannot be compared to ours.

Meanwhile, our free-trade fanatics tend to condemn any tariff whatsoever against products from abroad that compete with our own. They allow duties only on what we can grow or manufacture ourselves. But in America neither of the two major parties will ever adopt free trade. In a sharp exchange with a newspaper in the West, it was emphasized to me that Democrats, no less than Republicans, favored high tariffs; they differed only in the motivation. Democrats want the revenue that tariffs generate, but they do not wish to cut off all foreign competition.

History helps us understand this difference. The Republican Party is the heir of the old Whigs transplanted from England to America and bringing with them the principles of our viceroy, King William III. This also explains why almost all Dutch Americans have joined the Republicans, not the Democrats. Democrats are eulogists of the principles of the French Revolution. Their spiritual father is Jefferson, who in 1793 defended those principles against Washington and Hamilton. Our immigrants would have none of this, and only Pella, which is not of Calvinist origin, supported the Democrats. Moreover, socialists always side with Democrats when push comes to shove.

From our point of view, the Republican platform adopted in Chicago in 1896 contains not only positive points but also negative ones. On the whole, however, Republicans are definitely antirevolutionary, while Democrats see Jefferson as the founder of their party, as their program of 1896 expressly stated. Embracing individualism, the Democrats care so little about social problems that they look favorably on free trade and approve of tariffs as long as they create revenue.

In the Netherlands, two main arguments are pitted against every proposal to raise or expand import duties. The American experience gives the boot to both arguments.

The first argument is that raising tariffs impoverishes the lower class in favor of the well-to-do. Wages in America are, however, higher than everywhere else. Moreover, the majority of workers vote, in every election, for the party that supports protection. Ample statistics show that even when tariffs are raised, so do wages. The manufacturing sector has flourished and boosted the general standard of living. Even now, companies attract temporary workers from abroad in order to help meet their orders.

According to the second argument, higher tariffs lower imports and therefore also lower exports. In reality, the very opposite is the case. America's balance of trade shows a growing surplus every quarter, enabling it to buy back European stocks in its railways and to make its interest payments in manufactured goods.

Give it another few years and America will redeem all its debts in Europe, develop into a major investor in Europe's industry, and at last vie with Britain in controlling much real estate on the Continent.

Thus, what we have seen in the case of Germany has been confirmed in America: despite the pessimistic prophecies of the free-traders, higher tariffs raise a people's standard of living and improve a nation's balance of trade.

... Life in America exists under the shadow of the almighty dollar. Money flows in colossal amounts, and no expenditure seems too great. Male typographers earn 18 dollars and females 15 dollars a week, while press and steam engineers earn as much as 20 dollars a week (or 50 guilders and 37.50 guilders respectively). A husband and wife without children, if they are skilled, can make 80 guilders a week between the two of them. Of course, unskilled laborers earn wages even lower than 15 guilders. But money flows almost everywhere throughout this country, in generous amounts.

Unquestionably, this has led to the worst kind of service to mammon. A person can become a capitalist or a millionaire faster than in any other country in the world. This fact ignites the passion for making money. It affects young and old. The humblest shopkeepers and the lowest office clerks lie in wait for a chance to amass a pile of money. This fosters a speculative craze unheard of in Europe. While people engage in physical sports, financial sport is uppermost, including reckless gambling.

Asking *how* people make money is secondary; the main thing is *that* they get their hands on it. Hence that sudden rising and falling on the social ladder of people who at first had nothing, then rapidly became millionaires, then were reduced to poverty again, and then, thanks to some daring moves, become even richer than before. *Parvenues* are unknown, except among wealthy black Americans and sometimes among immigrants who have become wealthy. But for ordinary white Americans, becoming rich is not unusual.

What does arise when the dollar reigns is a *money aristocracy*. The respect shown the lucky man who struck it rich through speculation borders on hero worship. Only among the descendants of old Dutch and English colonists can one really talk of a generational aristocracy. In all other cases, the level of one's money determines one's social status. While the unions want the level to come down, the trusts want it to go up. And since there is more than bread for all classes, no one even thinks of introducing social legislation. Dr. Caroll D. Wright, the commissioner of labor, frankly admitted that only if the need became dire might the public be persuaded to share with the lower class what is now given graciously, through private initiative.[1]

Fighting for the dollar appears so pleasurable to Americans that, instead of voluntarily allaying the social struggle through timely legislation, they prefer to battle it out directly. Both sides are organizing themselves in the expectation that "strikes" or "boycotts" will decide the issue. Fighting has become the passion. A truce would disappoint them. Spectators spend thousands on boxing matches, and thousands more on betting for either fighter. The same passion is poisoning American society. No bullfights are held, as in Spain, but people are fighting, dollar against dollar, on the social battlefield.

While this passion makes people keen, quick-witted, and shrewd, it also threatens society with crass materialism. In some circles it feeds excessive opulence. It sorely tests the idea of honesty, and among those whose greed is not tempered by a moral counterweight, it encourages crime on a large scale.

Only its robust religious life has spared America from succumbing under this money fever. This comes to symbolical expression in the "clerical tickets" issued by the "railroad kings," allowing clergy to travel for half-price on all nonluxury trains. This religious spirit reinforces moral sense, curbs the evil of alcohol, and counteracts greed by fostering a level of generosity in charitable giving that is unknown elsewhere. The wonderful practice of tithing that Christianity has encouraged has accustomed rich Americans to take delight in giving. Not infrequently, they endow churches, seminaries, and mission stations with millions of dollars of gifts, and extend such generosity to the arts and sciences. Without such princely liberality, America would have suffered much deeper moral decline under the dollar's hegemony.

Those who today are working to undermine the spirit of religion among its people, to weaken the authority of Scripture, and to replace religiously

---

1. Caroll D. Wright (1840–1909) was a statistician who served as the first US commissioner of labor.

motivated giving with mere philanthropy do not know with what social peril they are threatening the American union. There is a growing sense that a revision of the Constitution would not be too high a price to pay if it could block unbelievers from cutting, at irreparable harm to America's future, its religious elevation, which is still the mainstay of America's national strength.

HUMAN TRAFFICKING

TEXT INTRODUCTION

As prime minister of the Netherlands from 1901–5, Kuyper served as minister of interior affairs. That role involved him in a wide range of matters, including requests from private organizations for government subsidies. If the cause was worthy, as in the following case of antitrafficking, he was keen to respond positively. He preferred, however, to use the instrument of matching grants to guard against easy handouts, as is illustrated in this brief extract from parliamentary proceedings.

Source: Abraham Kuyper, *Parlementaire Redevoeringen* [Parliamentary speeches] (Amsterdam: Van Holkema & Warendorf, 1909–12), 2:614–15. See the Dutch Hansard, *Handelingen van de Tweede Kamer*, session of December 12, 1903, pp. 862–63. Available at www.statengeneraaldigitaal.nl. Extract from a budget debate in the lower house of Parliament. Translated by Harry Van Dyke.

HUMAN TRAFFICKING

Mr. Speaker, I thank the honorable member, Mr. Helsdingen,[1] for his plea, though he could have seen from the documents that urgent requests and fervid pleas are not necessary in order to hold a brief for the interests of this association.[2] The association has approached me and has been able to see for itself that there is nothing I would rather do than come to its aid. In my view, the association can be assisted in two ways. The first is by giving it a gratuity. This would not, however, solve the issue since it is much more important for the association that the government promotes the same goal as pursued by the association. I am convinced about what causes the great

---

1. Willem Helsdingen (1850–1921) was a founder of the Social Democratic Workers' Party (*Sociaal-Democratische Arbeiderspartij*, or SDAP), a Dutch socialist political party. There are slight discrepancies between the official record of the parliamentary proceedings (published as *Handelingen van de Tweede Kamer*) and Kuyper's published *Parlementaire Redevoeringen*. For example, the *Handelingen* credits the question Kuyper is addressing to J. Th. de Visser (1857–1932) a member of the Christian Historical federation. De Visser referred to an international protocol agreed on in Paris in July 1902 to combat "white slavery" by keeping strict surveillance at ports and railway stations of those escorting women and girls to places of employment. For the official version of the extract translated here, see the *Handelingen*, session December 12, 1903, pp. 862–63, available at www.statengeneraaldigitaal.nl.
2. The association to which Kuyper refers is the Association for the Care of the Interests of Young Girls (*Vereeniging ter behartiging van de belangen van jonge meisjes*). Kuyper makes reference to a line in his budget ("the documents") reserved for expenditures to combat the abuse in question.

evil that young women from the countryside are lured to the big cities where often they become morally compromised. It lies in the fact that they are lured by false advertisements and hiring agencies that are without a conscience and are then placed in dubious positions of service.

I have therefore begun consultations with my colleague of the Department of Justice to see whether this evil can be checked. I also intend to give the association strong support, provided I can determine whether it is possible to record which young women from the villages go to the big cities and on which days. This information cannot be gathered from their change-of-address certificate[3] because they leave the village without applying for one; they first go to see if they can get a position, and then they apply for a moving certificate in writing.

It therefore occurred to me as desirable to get the mayors of the villages and the mayors of the cities to take action so that the departure of those young women could be noted immediately. That would be the best way, with the help of the association, to keep an eye on the young women and take care that they not fall into the wrong hands. I believe I am doing what I can. The mayors have declared to me that they will give their support.

The honorable member will perhaps ask: If this is all true and the association so strongly supports the cause,[4] why not give it a grant right away? To that I would like to say that, considering the great interest that is at stake here, I share his view that this matter concerns the moral character of our nation. However, the contributions from private donors seemed to me very low.

The policy customarily adopted by the department in a case like this is as follows. When private initiatives with limited support request aid, they must first increase their support base. Whenever the government has been willing to give aid to an association, provided private support of it increases, this support does indeed increase. When an association later returns with the same request, its record of contributions typically shows a marked increase.

Thus, instead of obstructing an association we are helping it, because the initial refusal to provide it with a grant is precisely the means to give

---

3. The public registry (or registry of civil status) of a municipality would issue such certificates to residents moving elsewhere.

4. *Handelingen*: "and the association gives you such strong support"—which should perhaps read: "and you give the association such strong support."

it a boost. If an association with a small membership had immediately received a grant, the amount would have been relatively small, whereas if the following year it turns out that contributions have increased, the government grant can be proportionally higher. I am therefore happy to assure the honorable member that it will not be my fault if I do not succeed in including a good subsidy for this association in next year's budget.

SOCIAL ORGANIZATIONS UNDER OUR OWN BANNER

TEXT INTRODUCTION

In autumn 1907 Kuyper wrote a series of articles in which he discussed the question whether Christian employees and employers should form confessionally based, or faith-based, organizations. The first three articles addressed the need for faith-based trade unions in the light of the growing influence of radicalism in the Dutch labor movement. The fourth article dealt with employers associations, and the fifth described group representation.

Source: Abraham Kuyper, *Sociale organisatie onder eigen banier* (The Hague: Bootsma, 1908), a collection of five articles reprinted from the November 13, 15, 18, 20, and December 13, 1907, issues of *De Standaard*. Translated by Harry Van Dyke.

SOCIAL ORGANIZATIONS UNDER OUR OWN BANNER

A news item from Rotterdam about the founding of a Protestant Union of Postal and Telegraph Workers, with the motto "Door plicht tot recht,"[1] shows that the movement to establish "trade unions under our own banner" continues apace and is gaining ground, including among the lower ranks of civil servants.

The strenuous objections repeatedly leveled at separate labor organizations apparently no longer have a hold on the stakeholders, a fact in which we greatly rejoice.

In itself, and apart from the realities of life, there would undoubtedly be greater strength in having a single union that embraced all members of an industry, service, or occupation. As in other areas, unity would bring greater power. And if that power is put to use in accordance with sound

---

1. This translates as "through duty to right" (acquiring rights by virtue of performing duties).

principles and a measure of self-restraint, the goal that organized labor strives after would be attained sooner and better.

However, that avenue cannot and must not be followed, and to the degree that it has been followed, those steps should be retraced, the sooner the better. In a *federation*, to be sure, cooperation with other trade unions is permissible; but a *fusion* would mean the death of the vital principle that has given birth to our separate Christian action.

It is simply not true that a labor organization is concerned only with the material interests of bread and butter and can therefore unite all workers in the struggle for better living conditions, regardless of people's spiritual background and convictions. The extremists in the radical camp themselves emphasize that the spiritual element cannot be divorced from the material element. And they preach the doctrine that all spiritual developments arise from the economic factor. Indeed, the link between soul and body, between a person's spiritual and material existence, hence also between spiritual and material starting points, is undeniable.

The talk is always, even in educational circles, of *resources* rather than *persons*. Even government documents speak of "human resources." Such is the distortion of language with which materialism regales us.

In antiquity, not even slaves were mere machines. Human life itself forbids this. Wherever humanity acts, unique persons are active, with their own consciousness, their own inclinations, their own wills and responsibilities. To a certain extent it can even be said of a thoroughbred horse or a purebred dog that these noble animals are more than machines. And however far anarchism may have strayed from the only sound paths along which a nation can progress to greater happiness, it has always opposed socialism by championing the freedom of the individual against the tyranny of the community.

Granted, many people lower themselves beneath their true destiny to the level of machines, stifling their conscience and silencing their will. But even with them, this lowering is only *relative*. Even in the case of small children or their caregivers, we are always dealing with human beings; and what makes a human being *human* is directly opposite to the essence of a machine.

In every company, craft, trade service, occupation, or profession, moral ordinances play a crucial role. It is not true—it is a popular lie—to say that the position of wage earners is governed solely by economic laws. When push comes to shove, one worker condemns as reprehensible what another deems legitimate and commendable. Higher principles constantly affect people's conscience and cause them to part ways.

In the Middle Ages, the connection between work and higher principles was expressed by linking guilds to the church. This link, though quite natural, was too direct. It did connect work to principles, but not everyone realized the specific nature of this connection.

The necessary clarification did not come until rival worldviews manifested themselves in society. This antithesis repeatedly confronted working people with the choice between what was morally acceptable and what, according to moral criteria, would be irresponsible. Not until syndicalism gained a firm footing and allowed itself to be led by radicals *in a clear violation of conscience* did people begin to realize that even in the organization of labor, the spiritual element must be given a voice.[2] And whenever people talked about taking action, the choice they faced went beyond legal and illegal. In fact, it soon became apparent that the radical labor movement embraced a distinct outlook on life and was increasingly dominated by a definite worldview that was making that movement subservient to a spirit in the political and social arena that was diametrically opposed to the Christian worldview. This worldview did not limit itself to the economic sphere. But it made that sphere serviceable to propaganda for a spiritual vision that sought to call into being a totally different order of society. It wished to turn religion and education upside down, as well as politics and ethics, so that a wholly different worldview would triumph.

***

Thus, not just Christians subscribe to the view that the material position of wage earners can never be divorced from their moral convictions and spiritual life. The radicals in the labor movement protest equally against the impossible split between spiritual and material factors; they constantly use the syndicalist movement to advance their goal of a political and spiritual revolution. They put a material goal in the foreground, but to achieve that goal they avail themselves not only of material means but even more

---

2. Syndicalism was a movement around 1900 that proposed replacing a free-market economy with a socialist system in which businesses were owned and operated by the workers. The movement called for work stoppages, general strikes, and anarchist agitation.

of spiritual means. Anarchists end up condoning any means whatsoever, even the "propaganda of the deed," that is, of murder. They uproot all moral stability and proclaim that justice and morality change with popular opinion, so that people reorder their moral concepts and call good today what yesterday they condemned as immoral.

Radicalism realizes increasingly that moral standards cannot be eradicated as long as religion binds people's conscience to God's will. Hence it does not cease trying to tear apart that bond. Thus it stands diametrically opposed to the religious and moral convictions of every Christian nation. It spreads itself worldwide, with a view to breaking this spiritual resistance in the nations. It disrupts the peace of civil society by calling for an unrelenting class struggle. At the end it awaits the rise of the morning star that will announce the great day of the revolution which, after army and police have been weakened by antimilitarist forces, will deliver state and society into the hands of a mob hungry for loot and leaders hungry for power.

How could Christians possibly join organizations led by such people? If they witnessed to their beliefs in membership meetings, would they reap anything other than scorn? And would they not be jointly responsible for the decisions taken in the meeting? Would their beliefs not be weakened by the toxic atmosphere in which godless principles were constantly presented with great aplomb as if they were established facts?

Many Christians who came to this realization after a bitter experience decided to withdraw from trade unionism. Because the radicals had misused their organization they condemned all organization as such. They could not conceive of an organization based on their own Christian worldview, so they stood aside and left the labor movement in the hands of the radicals.

This only served to promote the very evil they condemned! The radicals now were master of the field. Their program, their conduct, their press gave the watchword. Most union bosses were carried away by the radical press. And in the end the radicals could boast that they alone represented working people and that their spokesmen alone championed the rights of labor, both inside and outside Parliament.

This is the situation in more than one country. Just look at Italy and Spain, England and America. Only sporadically does one hear of Christian social action in those countries, and it is of little or no influence.

We cannot be thankful enough that our country has seen Christian social action. It predates the radical movement, is still expanding, and in 1903 proved capable of defying the radicals.[3] But it must go forward and rally more and more Christian workers under its banner. Every new trade union that honors the kingship of Christ is to be warmly welcomed.

***

There are three reasons for advocating separate Christian trade unions: (1) to dispose of the false impression that the radicals represent the whole of the working class, (2) to keep Christians out of bad and dangerous company, (3) to unite all Christians in the land and empower them to improve their industry and defend their common interests.

Nothing would be more mistaken than to conclude that Christian trade unions only exist to stave off the influence of socialism. They exist chiefly to look after their own interests, not to serve outside interests. They are there to benefit their members; promote their specific trade, improve the quality of their work, guard against laws and regulations that might be disadvantageous to their trade, study improvements to their trade in other countries, attract younger workers to become members, and oppose social evils, especially the abuse of alcohol among their members. They are also to attract workers concentrated in the urban centers but no less those workers in the trade who live in smaller towns or who are scattered across the countryside. These organizations are to see to it that, on the one hand, they foster a Christian spirit of self-reliance, and on the other, that they establish a relationship with employers in keeping with Christian standards.

When Boaz was founded, Christian business leaders were strongly encouraged to ask whether their treatment of their workers was the way God would want. The same applies, of course, for members of workers' unions. They too have a responsibility toward their boss. This relationship must not be arbitrary but based on God's ordinances. In other circles, inflammatory speech suggests that workers can conduct themselves toward their employers in any way they please and relate to them only on a footing of armed peace. Our banner, in contrast, requires that both employer and employee place themselves before God and ask: Lord, what would you have us do? This should be the attitude of those who work for employers who hold up our banner, just as much as of those who are hired by employers

---

3. Kuyper is here referring to the railway strike of 1903, which occurred during his term of office as prime minister.

who have no regard for higher ordinances. In labor unions our people need to be a witness for Christ. And the general public needs to acknowledge that our workers are aware of their position, are united in standing up for their interests, and so enter the fray for higher moral principles that they contribute to civic spirit and orderliness in society. That means, then, that not one trade or craft and not one service should be left behind. Every business sector, including the service sector, should be covered under our banner—not just in general, but also locally, both in private enterprise and the civil service, and in all their branches.

Once strong in separate organizations, we can join forces with other organizations whenever common interests are at stake, at least for defined goals—never for action that would tarnish our banner. If for the sake of cooperation we were to surrender our independence and abandon our principles, we would render ourselves powerless, become the tool of others, and undermine the vitality of our people. To prevent this, a national federation of all Christian organizations is highly desirable. There have been repeated calls for a second Social Congress, but for this to be worthwhile the impetus for such a congress must come from the trade unions, and that will not happen if each of them stays on its own without seeking nationwide ties.[4] A national organization could send representatives to a labor council, and such a council could organize an annual or biennial congress for discussing shared interests. It could also take in hand the kind of social teaching and action that Roman Catholics have been so successful at.[5]

Four things, therefore, need to be taken care of: (1) Every tradesman should join an existing union. (2) Every trade that is still without a union should organize one. (3) All local unions of the same trade or service should combine into a national organization. (4) These national organizations

---

4. A second congress did not convene until 1919. The first Christian Social Congress was held in 1891, sponsored jointly by two organizations in the founding of which Kuyper had played a leading role: the ARP and the Christian Workingmen's League Patrimonium.

5. Kuyper often expressed admiration for Catholic social teaching and action and encouraged collaboration between Protestant and Catholic movements. The Protestant ARP and the Catholic People's Party (KVP) enjoyed close relations at the political level and shared power in coalition cabinets. In 1980, the ARP and the KVP merged with the Christian Historical Union (CHU) to form the Christian Democratic Appeal (CDA), which has also enjoyed many electoral successes.

could then come together and create a central organ for looking after the common interests of all unions.[6]

All this will take much effort, time, struggle. It is a huge project that awaits completion. But the lofty goal that we pursue is worthy of such dedication. It is intolerable that the organizations under the banner of Christ are weaker than the organizations which, consciously or unconsciously, undermine the Christian vitality of our nation.

EMPLOYER ORGANIZATIONS

Moving from working people to employers, it is important to differentiate between large and small firms. Tradesmen and retailers belong to a different social class than the capitalists who run large factories or companies with the help of appointed directors. It is true that department stores, with their powerful capital, are penetrating the retail market, and capitalized land ownership is penetrating agriculture, but it can still be said that the common divisions largely hold. Among employers there is a middle class and there is big industry, and these two groups are increasingly at odds with each other.

The conflict that arises now and then between employers and employees is of a different kind in the case of these two groups. Employers with a staff of no more than a dozen persons in their store or trade look altogether differently at their people than directors of large enterprises who every week pay the wages of hundreds of workers. In retail stores and in the trades, moreover, employers know their staff by name and therefore have an entirely different relationship with them. Happily, an amicable relationship often develops between these employers and their employees, especially in those firms where the owners and their children work alongside wage earners. In rural settings, it is not uncommon for farmers to eat at the same table as their hired hands.

The sharp conflict between employer and employee is therefore not found among this middle class. Instead, it mainly arose in big industry, mining, manufacturing, construction, and transportation.

But even though the conflict broke out in big industry, it has had an impact on the middle class. Radicalism in all its branches has altered the

---

6. Nine national Christian trade unions founded such a central organ the following year, on May 13, 1909, under the name Christelijk Nationaal Vakverbond (Christian National Labor Federation).

spirit of the working classes, and the armed truce between employers and workers in big business has gradually penetrated small-scale enterprises. As a result, the former amicable relationship has been damaged, even in small firms of only five or six employees. In some cases, it has been replaced by indifference, discontent, and antagonism.

The middle class, accordingly, finds itself caught in a twofold struggle for survival. On the one hand, private employers that ply a trade or run stores must compete with the superior power of big capital that tries to poach their customers; and on the other hand, they must wage a struggle with their workers who continually push for higher wages, shorter hours, and better working conditions, thereby only aggravating the struggle with big capital.

The position of the "middle class" (taken here and in what follows as the class of store owners) has imperceptibly come under threat to such an extent that this class has finally realized the need to defend itself and to make itself strong by organizing itself.[7] Belgium and Germany have led the way in this, and Tutein Nolthenius deserves honor for having promoted this movement in our country.[8]

Initially this movement tried to gain strength by means of an unnatural resistance to any obstacle in its way, in particular by protesting against cooperatives. Fortunately, that is now behind us, and in general people have begun to realize that the battle cannot be won by going against the stream of life, but that the middle class, like every class, has to gain strength by improving itself. It needs to do so by making itself indispensable to its customers and clients, and organizing its members more effectively.

Regarding the organization of store owners, the question has been raised whether store owners who are Christians should get involved in the movement as it now operates, or whether they should organize themselves under their own banner.

Anarchists, social democrats, and radicals are inciting a spirit of revolution and unbelief among the workers. If this spirit was to be promulgated within the store owners' movement, then it would be the duty of Christians

---

7. Kuyper's use of the term "middle class" in this section has similarities to the German term *Mittelstand*, which is often used to refer to the owners of small- and medium-sized companies (SMEs), which together form the backbone of the German economy.

8. Pieter Marius Tutein Nolthenius (1814–96) was a Dutch member of Parliament who advocated economic measures to alleviate poverty.

to form a separate organization of their own. No Christian employers should allow themselves to be taken up in any organization that poisons minds and supports revolutionary aims.

So far, however, this has not been the case. The middle-class movement, like the Farmers Federation, is entirely business-like and is more inclined to protest against rather than to promote all revolutionary impulses.[9] In the absence of the forces that drive working people to form separate organizations, there is currently no reason why Christians among the middle class should separate themselves. This is all the more advisable since the number of prospective members among the middle class is so much smaller than among the working classes.

Christians who are small employers and store owners ought to defend common interests that are of a purely business-like nature. Such matters are best defended together. Should the situation change, it will be necessary to switch to other measures. For now, however, there are insufficient grounds for separation, provided every Christian employer, when genuine Christian principles are at stake, has the courage and the energy to stick up for them.

But although there are as yet no grounds why the Christian employer and the Christian retailer should not participate in the organization of the middle class, this does not absolve them from the responsibility to become more conscious, within a separate organization like the one we have in Boaz, of the special obligations that rest on members of the middle class and the agricultural class who confess Christ.[10]

In the movement represented by Boaz, questions come up for discussion about what is and is not permitted, about honest dealings, and especially about our duty toward workers. Such issues, when addressed from a Christian standpoint, often require a distinct solution. Individual Christians cannot come up with viable solutions, nor can they do so by joining a group of people who do not share their principles.

---

9. The term "business-like" in this sentence translates the Dutch term *zakelijk*. Kuyper uses it in this section to denote pragmatic, matter-of-fact affairs that are nonideological.

10. Boaz is the name of an association of Christian employers noted in the editor's introduction to this volume by Peter S. Heslam. The association was established in 1892 largely through the efforts of Kuyper's friend and colleague Willem Hovy (1840–1915), a successful beer brewer. It was reorganized as the Association of Christian Employers and Wholesalers in 1918, and as the Federation of Protestant Christian Employers in 1937.

Against this background, the keenly felt need arose that led to the founding of Boaz. Christian employers and retailers are still advised to join Boaz, and to find in Boaz what the general middle-class organizations cannot give them.

In the agricultural sector, it is altogether possible for farmers so to organize themselves that Christian principles form the basis of action—either separately or in conjunction with the Farmers Federation. Most farmers, after all, still adhere to a Christian perspective. This cannot be said, however, of most participants in the middle-class movement. That is why, for the time being, its activity needs to be restricted to practical matters.

All this leads to the conclusion that Christian employers and retailers would do well to join the organization of the middle class, provided that they also develop Boaz as an organization under its own banner that stands ready to serve the middle-class movement with excellence, as a supplement and corrective.

GROUP REPRESENTATION

Group representation is quite different from the role of trade unions and does not make them superfluous. Its basic idea was first applied during the term of office of the previous cabinet to the national printers, and then more elaborately among the personnel of the national railway.

The printing office employed many people who lived in such poor housing that the director had to deal with a constant barrage of complaints. In response to this situation, an employees' standing committee was installed. It could let the wishes and concerns of workers be known to the director, who in turn could inform workers of any changes deemed desirable. In this way, a representative body arose to maintain good relations between employer and employees and to serve the interests of both. The arrangement enjoyed the enthusiastic approval of the newly appointed director, and thanks to his cordial cooperation the experiment has been very successful.

Group representation was introduced at the national railway in response to that well-known anarchistic adventure: the strikes of 1903. On the one hand the government saw itself compelled, in the national interest, to curtail employees' powers; on the other hand it felt obliged to install a form of group representation in order to safeguard their rights. [11]

---

11. The government Kuyper refers to was led by the cabinet in which Kuyper served as prime minister.

One should not think, however, that this was a new invention. Less complex versions were already functioning in more than one large factory, here at home as well as in other countries. In a large plant with hundreds of workers the need arises automatically to have a mouthpiece for conferring with the employer. Thus, group representation is a natural phenomenon.

In smaller workplaces, employers can be in direct contact with each of their employees. Only when their numbers grow is it necessary to choose about ten names to maintain this contact on behalf of the entire workforce.

Government employees also have desires and concerns they wish to bring to the attention of their superiors. To facilitate this, various departments and offices of the civil service have developed the appropriate legal organs.

The purpose of group representation is, therefore, to make manager-worker relations friendlier, to encourage mutual consultation by removing hindrances, and to consider the practical impact of proposed changes. The advantages are that the organization's management deals with its own employees, that politics can stay out of it, and that conflicts can be avoided. Thus it will be a good thing if all companies and all services adopt this form of representation, once their workforce exceeds a certain size. It works best when the groups are formed at the local level, as this helps facilitate the parties' consultation.

None of this means that trade unions are redundant. Unions represent the unity that is lost in group formation. Their aim is to improve their trade and profession and to strengthen solidarity among their members. From this higher standpoint they can have a wholesome influence on group representation. Labor organizations can leave contact with employers to the groups and deal only indirectly with employers. That takes away the revolutionary character that so easily insinuates itself into labor unions, a trait that has serious consequences not only for industry but also for the civil service.

It remains to be seen whether group representation can be made mandatory for the service industry in the private sector, but it already can be for the public services, where its introduction is highly desirable. If left undone, the trade unions will increasingly attempt to dictate to the government what it wants, losing its integrity as a result. Clashes will be unavoidable. And civil servants will gradually lose the sense of the distinct nature of the public sector.

FEEDING THE NATION'S WORKERS

TEXT INTRODUCTION

During election campaigns, Kuyper often devoted short articles in his daily newspaper, *De Standaard*, to defending his party's stance on key election issues. To draw attention to the importance of these articles, they were marked with three asterisks in the form of an asterism. Offprints of these asterisked articles would be printed in large numbers and widely distributed. On the eve of the Dutch general elections of June 12, 1907, seven such articles were published together in a brochure. The fifth was titled "Feeding the Nation's Workers" (*Den Nationalen Arbeid Voeden*), which had originally appeared in *De Standaard* of June 7, 1909. In it, Kuyper explained why the Antirevolutionary Party had always been in favor of some level of import duties. It was in part, he explained, to increase revenue for financing social programs, but also to stimulate domestic industry, thereby helping to increase better-paying jobs for ordinary working people. He marshals several arguments, backed by statistics, in favor of some form of protectionism.

The influence of Kuyper's perspective was reflected in the policies of the government that was formed in the wake of that summer's elections. That government, a coalition of Protestant and Catholic parties under the premiership of the antirevolutionary Theo Heemskerk (1854–1932), enjoyed a clear majority in the lower house and remained in office until 1913.

SOURCE: Abraham Kuyper, "Den nationalen arbeid voeden" [Feeding the nation's workers], offprint in *Voor den Slag* (Utrecht: Ruys, 1909), 12–14. Translated by Harry Van Dyke.

FEEDING THE NATION'S WORKERS

As early as 1878 our paper *De Standaard* urged raising the tariff for import duties, and the Antirevolutionary Party has spoken with growing conviction, especially since 1897, in favor of increasing the revenue generated by those duties.

Other parties adopted the same line. Even the liberal cabinet minister Sprenger van Eyck introduced a measure which caused the amount to rise from 6 to 12 million.[1] In the elections of 1901 the vote for raising the tariffs was almost unanimous. The new cabinet included it in its program of action, and Minister Harte tabled a carefully drafted bill to that effect.[2]

With our defeat in 1905 this bill perished as well. The new liberal cabinet once more championed free trade. The difference is again an issue in the coming elections of 1909. The Left says: "Open your front door, so everyone can walk right in." The Right says: "Put a lock on the door of your home,

---

1. J. P. Sprenger van Eyck (1842–1907) was minister of finance in the liberal cabinet of 1894–97.
2. Jan Harte van Tecklenburg (1853–1937) was minister of finance in the Kuyper cabinet of 1901–5.

and admit only those who will comply with what you, the home owner, demands."[3]

The question of free trade is far too complicated for most voters to understand, but there is one thing which the simplest voter can grasp and which alone is enough to condemn our country for sticking with free trade.

Voters, take note.

Europe has 19 states, and 17 of them have put free trade behind them. Only two still adhere officially to free trade, namely, Britain and the Netherlands. But even in these countries, opinions are almost equally divided. In Britain the party that wants to break with free trade is gaining ground daily, and in our country absolute free trade was defeated already in 1901. Add to this that more than one British colony has abandoned it. And what is more, all American and Asian countries continue to resist it.

Thus it can be said that virtually *the whole world* realizes that free trade is unprofitable, except for half the British and not quite half the Dutch. Moreover, Britain chose for free trade only after she had first become master of the world market *by means of protectionism*, and she chose for it in such a way that her import duties were still higher and her excise taxes still lower than ours.

Britain has a population eight times ours and in 1908 collected the equivalent of 415 million guilders in duties, which for our country would be proportionally equal to upwards of 50 million; yet we collected only 15 million. In addition, Britain levied 432 million in excise taxes, which for us would amount to 54 million, whereas we collected over 57 million.

So what do you think of free trade now? Evidently leading statesmen around the world tell you: *free trade really doesn't work.* Only a Dutch elite is telling you: *free trade, or we are lost!* On top of that, half the Dutch and half the British oppose it, and Britain applies the system quite differently than we do. Do you really believe that our small elite know better than the whole world? And would you still want to go along with a system that has been abandoned or is tottering everywhere else? Common sense tells you otherwise.

---

3. For almost a century of Dutch politics, the parties of "the Left" consisted of the full gamut of conservatives, liberals, socialists, and anarchists who avowed to do politics in a pragmatic, religiously neutral or secular mode, while "the Right" included both conservatives and progressives who sought to have their policies guided by Christian principles. Kuyper numbered himself among the progressive wing of Christian political action.

You will be told: be careful what you choose. If you raise the tariffs, your commerce and shipping will tumble. But what is that prophecy worth if you know that in Germany, which levies very high duties, foreign trade in 1890 approached 54 million tons and rose to 104 million tons by 1905? What a tumble!

And as for the shipping trade, note that Germany's merchant marine had just under 962 tons in 1871 but registered 2.4 times as many tons in 1906.

Those who defend free trade on the basis of "fair exchange" will always collide with these two arguments: (1) that this Dutch wisdom is contradicted by the rest of the world, and (2) that a country with high import duties, such as Germany, doubled its trade in 15 years and more than doubled its maritime shipping after adopting protective measures.

Meanwhile, raising our revenue from tariffs in order to pay for social legislation is by no means the only reason why the politicians of the Right oppose free trade. They have always emphasized, rather, that their goal is no less than to have our manufacturing sector flourish and so allow the nation's labor force to spread its wings more widely. In other words: to increase our prosperity and improve working conditions for our wage earners.

Just look at beer, confections, and cigars. Beer is taxed at 23 percent, confections at 20 percent, and cigars at 10 percent. A high rate therefore. But it so happens that no branches of industry are doing better than breweries and confectionaries and cigar factories. By contrast, for the making of virtually all other consumables we are letting all the wages be earned by laborers in foreign countries while our labor force can only watch as their manufactures enter our country as finished products. This explains why our well-to-do are at a loss what to do with their money, why investing in securities is the rule among us, and why financial investing has given rise to the evil of speculating on the stock market, which sets us back millions each time a crisis hits.

Granted, with higher tariffs some articles will cost more, but how does it hurt you if you have to pay 25 guilders more per year and your wages go up by 50 in the same year? I'd say you're still 25 ahead! Just look across the border. Tens of thousands of Dutch laborers travel to Germany because they know they can earn higher wages there. And they even send money to their families back home to boot.

The argument that higher tariffs will lower exports is likewise contradicted by the facts. The level of German exports did not go down but went up: it stood at 31 million tons in 1897, but by 1905, thus only eight years later, it had risen to 44.5 million tons.

To top it off, we do not nearly have the level of protection guaranteed in Germany and the United States. Our sole aim is to match tariff for tariff. If a foreign country charges our exports, say, 10 guilders, then we want the foreigner to have to put down 10 guilders for importing his goods into our country. It is simply intolerable that manufactured goods can all freely enter our country and that the labor costs paid by us are paid out to the foreign worker while the Dutch laborer runs short of wages.

We are not bent on ruining Rotterdam or Amsterdam, but Hamburg and New York clearly demonstrate that a vigorous port can actually gain from higher tariffs, gain significantly in fact. The only thing to avoid is that the rest of the country will be sacrificed to an imaginary fear in our commercial ports.

So do not lightly skip over this plank in our election platform. Raising the tariff is the obvious means available to us to stimulate our business and industry, to benefit our national labor force, to finance sound social legislation, and (also of moral importance) to bridle the mammon of speculation which has ruined so many families and has often resulted in suicide.

THE SOCIAL QUESTION (1909)

TEXT INTRODUCTION

After the fall of Kuyper's cabinet, following the bitterly fought general election of 1905, Kuyper took a break from politics. He embarked on a nine-month journey through the countries bordering the Mediterranean Sea. He expected, however, a return to power for the coalition of confessional parties, preferably under his leadership. This expectation was not unwarranted, since the coalition had lost power on the basis of district seats but had won the popular vote.

Kuyper never returned, however, to the cabinet table. Nevertheless, he did return to the Second Chamber after winning a by-election in the fall of 1908 and played a key role in securing victory for the coalition in the general election of 1909. He did so in part through his prolific journalism, which included a series of editorials in his daily *De Standaard*. In the issue of June 5, 1909, he published an asterisked piece titled "The Social Question" (*Het sociale vraagstuk*). It countered the most recent promise the Liberal cabinet had made to introduce state pensions. In forthright language, Kuyper explained why the antirevolutionaries opposed government pensions in favor of an old-age insurance scheme. Such a scheme, Kuyper argued, would uphold the dignity of the wage earners, since pensions in old age are in reality rightfully earned, yet deferred, wages.

SOURCE: Abraham Kuyper, "Het sociale vraagstuk" [The social question], in *Voor den Slag* (Utrecht: Ruys, 1909), 5–7. The 17-page publication titled *Voor den Slag* [Before the battle] was an election brochure published on the eve of the general elections for the lower house of Parliament, June 12, 1909. It reprinted seven articles that had appeared the week before in *De Standaard*. Translated by Harry Van Dyke.

THE SOCIAL QUESTION (1909)

As you look over our Antirevolutionary election program you will be struck immediately by the heading printed in gold lettering: The Social Question.

The first to raise this comprehensive subject in parliament was our party, way back in 1875.[1] The first labor law was put on the books by the Mackay cabinet.[2] And the first to submit a definitive solution to this question was the Kuyper cabinet, which tabled a complete set of three bills: (1) a new labor law, (2) a health insurance scheme, and (3) a disability and old-age insurance plan, not to mention an extension of the Occupation Injuries Act. From the outset we called for a labor code, after the example of the commercial code, and before long we listed the headings for such a code.[3] If we are once more victorious at the polls it will again be an Antirevolutionary who

---

1. Kuyper was first elected to parliament in 1874, and his early activity focused on the question of education funding, which was set within the larger context of the government budget and social policy. Kuyper's parliamentary speeches in December focused on the national budget. See *AKBE* 1875.08, p. 91.

2. The first Christian coalition government of 1888–91 was formed by the Aeneas Mackay (1838–1909) of the ARP. The labor law referred to is the Arbeidswet of 1889, which put an end to farm and factory labor by children under the age of 12, to be enforced by government inspection of the workplace.

3. See *OP* 20.III.§§292–98:344–50.

will bring the solution to the social question one step closer. The Liberal parties may for their part take pride in their Occupation Injuries Act, but certainly not as a model specimen of legislation.[4]

But be on the alert! The Liberals are now popping up with a slogan that could spoil everything again for working people. They are calling for *state pensions!* If that slogan were ever to triumph, it would completely sidetrack the social question and deeply disappoint the working classes.

To be sure, it sounds wonderful and looks quite good. Workers will have nothing to pay, and when they reach the age of 70, a free pension will fall into their lap. What a generous offer!

But suppose for a moment that the Liberals win the elections and form the government, then a child can figure out that nothing will come of their fine promises except bitter disappointment.

Even a pitifully small pension would require them to have 12 million guilders ready at hand every year. Well, on paper that is easily fixed, but even if the lower house approves it, the upper house is certain to vote it down, and the whole thing will be shelved, leaving the working people empty-handed. Then the issue will have to be revisited from the beginning four years from now.

So tell one and all, and open the eyes of working people before it is too late. All that talk about state pensions can only end up crushing their hopes.

Even if we imagine the impossible—that the upper house goes along with the mad scheme—what would working people actually get?

Their plight is that many of them can no longer work at their trade by the time they are 50 or 60. By that time they are either disabled or worn out. And they will all be left uncared for, while only the 70-year-olds will be helped—and even then with a weekly supplement that is altogether inadequate for the more skilled laborer. The 1905 proposal guaranteed an annuity far in excess of 300 guilders; the Liberal proposal less than half that![5]

---

4. The act became law under the Liberal government of 1897–1901. It was a modest first step in social legislation, and last-minute concessions to employers on the part of the government created a great deal of uncertainty when it was implemented.

5. This is a reference to one of Kuyper's legislative bills that died on the Order Paper when he lost the elections of 1905. His bill proposed an old-age insurance scheme to which both employers and employees would contribute through premiums. For the plan as presented as a member of Parliament in 1895, see "Draft Pension Scheme for Wage Earners," in this volume.

We know that they promise you that the rest will be taken care of later. But then the government will have to spend not 12 but 80 million guilders a year on it. To dangle before our eyes the prospect that such a vast sum will somehow be found is to mock and trivialize the plight of working people.

Should the government ever adopt the fatal scheme of state pensions, then it is safe to predict that it will end in a fiasco and that four years from now we will be no further along than today. Worse, from year to year we will take a step backwards because the conservatives are lying in wait to torpedo the grand plan of old age insurance.

Besides, do working people desire *pensions*? Are they not too proud for that? Are we allowed to tempt them to rely on *public relief* and afterward live out their days on the public purse? Do their pride, their sense of dignity, not object to spending their old age among the ranks of those living off public handouts?

What most concerns working people is *insecurity*. What will become of them and their families if they fall ill and lose their income? What will happen to their loved ones if they contract a chronic ailment and hunger knocks at the door? What will they live on, once they turn too old to ply their trade and earn their bread? The well-to-do have no idea what such anxieties mean: their income continues when they are ill, and they are insured when their ability to work comes to an end. But working people are constantly pursued by those anxious questions. Fear of the future haunts them.

If you can persuade employer and employee to set aside a small portion of their weekly wages and so spread the risk over large numbers, a load is lifted from their heart. Then they have peace of mind about the future. And above all, they then need not thank anybody for it because they have earned it all themselves and paid for it from their own well-earned wages.

That is what working people long for: to be insured against any eventualities in the future and to know that they owe this peace of mind solely to their own effort and sacrifice. This preserves the dignity of the working people. This alone allows them to enjoy what we who are better off have enjoyed for centuries: security about their living conditions without offending their sense of honor.

If you vote for the Right, and the Right forms the next government, such security will be a reality within the next four years, and there will be support when needed for the disabled elderly, for men and women, for widows and orphans, and that support will have been furnished by working people themselves.

This is the choice you face at the ballot box: with state pensions, in four years' time, *nothing*; with mandatory insurance, in four years' time, *every need provided for*.

And who of you, who kneel in adoration before Christus Consolator, can hesitate when facing that choice, even if you do not personally benefit from an insurance scheme? For what is *consolation* other than that those who are not themselves acquainted with poverty show *compassion* to the needy and the oppressed?

Is it not a core Christian principle that we should carry one another's burden, and is insurance not a God-given means to bring this rich idea into practice?

And who would deny that it is a Christian premise that working people should receive a level of wages for their labor to enable them to live off it, not only when they are well and working but also when they are weak and worn.

To be sure, the poor we have with us always, and love makes it a point of honor to come to their aid. But who would dare consign the working classes as a whole to the ranks of the poor? True, if our working classes were without sin it would not be necessary to make the insurance *mandatory*, for then everybody would insure themselves voluntarily, and that should be our long-range goal. But so long as the sins of thoughtlessness, carelessness, and laziness are still so prevalent that mandatory participation must be used to combat this sin. It is a respectable obligation that the government asks of its citizens. Just open God's Word to see how in Israel the disposal of property was curtailed in favor of the needy, and you will realize that the government falls short in its proper task if it hesitates to intervene in this case.

And therefore, voters of Antirevolutionary stock, drive the champions of state pensions into a corner. Nothing of what they promise can ever be realized in our country. The only solution lies in mandatory insurance. Everything that is proffered as pensions from the public treasury is nothing but public relief, and that goes directly against your Antirevolutionary principles.

INDUSTRIAL
ORGANIZATION

TEXT INTRODUCTION

A significant event during the Kuyper Ministry (1901–5) was the great railroad strike of 1903. It started on Wednesday, January 28, when unionized dock workers in Amsterdam refused to handle the cargo of companies employing nonunionized workers. Next, the union of railway and tram (streetcar) personnel, nursing their own long-standing grievances about poor working conditions and long working hours, called a sympathy strike. The action caused serious disruption of all transportation by land and water throughout the country. By Saturday evening, January 31, management acceded to all demands. The labor movement (with the exception of the Christian labor organizations) rejoiced in their swift victory and began to contemplate further action. The following Tuesday, Kuyper responded with the editorial in *De Standaard* that is provided below in an abridged translation.

The labor unrest of 1903 entered a fresh stage when the Kuyper government tabled a bill to "safeguard the public interest" by outlawing strikes in the transportation sector. Labor leaders now called for a nationwide general strike to protest this "strangulation law." Although the general strike petered out within a few days, and the government had installed a committee of inquiry into workers' grievances, Kuyper's reputation as a friend of the working classes suffered a severe blow.

In 1910, Kuyper, now no longer a cabinet minister but still a member of parliament, resumed his discussion in *De Standaard* of the need for reform of labor relations encompassing owners/managers and workers. He did so in four editorials from April 23-30, 1910, which also appear below in abridged translation. All five editorials shed light on Kuyper's contribution to an "architectonic critique" of modern society. In the decades of debates and associated legislation that followed them, his ideas contributed to a growing tradition of consensus politics. This became known by the end of the century as the "polder model" of national socioeconomic policy: the tripartite cooperation between employers, labor unions, and government to agree annually on wage moderation, job protection, and fiscal restraint.

SOURCE: *De Standaard*, February 4, 1903, and April 23, 26, 28, 30, 1910. Reprinted in W. F. de Gaay Fortman, *Architectonische critiek; fragmenten uit de sociaal-politieke geschriften van Dr. A. Kuyper* (Amsterdam: H. J. Paris, 1956), 142-60. Translated, edited, and abridged by Harry Van Dyke.

INDUSTRIAL ORGANIZATION

If anything became clear last Saturday, it was that a good organization can wield enormous power. Suddenly, on the order of labor union leaders, virtually all employees, without hesitation, went on strike at virtually all railway stations and depots throughout the land. Why? Because the unions wanted it.

Do all those thousands of workers understand exactly what the issue is? Hardly. We asked some of them why they were on strike, and they answered: "Well, you see, sir, we got word from headquarters that we had to go on strike." When asked why headquarters wanted this they replied: "Because of the scabs." When asked when they might go back to work, the reply was: "When headquarters says so."

No doubt some strikers would have given better answers, but most of them are satisfied as long as they can be sure that the action is "against the capitalists." They are the workers who have been made "conscious" of their struggle. But whether conscious or unconscious, they all show that they know one thing for sure: they bow unconditionally to the organization. If the union leadership gives an order, they fall in line, regardless of personal freedom. As the leadership understand the true interests of its members, following it without question will bring them a step closer to utopia.

Purely from the point of view of organization, all this commands admiration. It does social democracy—which the unions brought into being—proud. And they are not holding back in expressing their admiration for this result.

Nevertheless, there is a very questionable side to this whole phenomenon. And even social democrats would rail against such well-drilled, tightly organized masses if an organization of equal strength were arrayed against them.

Meanwhile, such a counterorganization does not exist. There is no body opposite the powerful one-sided organization that the social democrats have created. They have organized the *workers,* but what we have needed for a very long time is an organization of *industrial work.*

That whole area has been disorganized. Guilds were abolished, but no substitutes were put in their place. Everybody did what was good in their own eyes and used this power vacuum to rake in whatever they could. Over the years, bitter complaints from the working classes were more than justified, given the high price they were paying. It was to be expected that these people, educated in state schools and estranged from the Bible, seeking only bread and butter, would eventually rise up when leaders stepped forward. Social democrat leaders gained their confidence and promised them what they wanted, once they gained power.

To gain power, organization was needed. We have seen how union leaders in the past controlled the diamond workers of Amsterdam and today control the railroad workers throughout the country. This grave situation would not have arisen if there had been a proper organization of industry.

But that is not what successive governments wanted. When Dr. Kuyper 25 years ago advocated the desirability of creating a code of labor, he was roundly laughed at.[1] Even the progressive members of Parliament thought it was impracticable.

Now that the tables have turned, it is generally agreed that it is high time that labor and industry were regulated by law. No one can deny that this would have been far easier a quarter-century ago. The social unrest of so many years has come home to roost. Management has not helped itself. The workers have helped themselves. What has transpired cannot be undone.

---

1. Even during his time as prime minister, Kuyper continued to write editorials in his daily *De Standaard,* although he would refer to himself in the third person.

Many voices for social healing will now clamor for attention; ideas for remedies and reforms will abound. Meanwhile, the workers will perfect their organization. After what happened last Saturday, they will hold on to their viewpoint with even greater determination, and they will be averse to changing their tactics. Whoever wants to come with recommendations now in 1903 will have to have a cool head, a sharp eye, and a warm heart for the needs of the working classes and for the field of labor and industry in its entire scope.

***

Long before this year of 1910, we urged the legal organization of industry in its dual composition of employers and employees. To a certain extent, these two parties have conflicting interests. Lower wages for the employees result in higher profits for the employer. Higher wages will enable employees to improve their standard of living. Workers are bound to think: the owners of our company are making big profits; why can some of that not be paid out to those who work for them?

That is how things work, but only up to a point. If wages are too high and company owners can make as much or more through investments, they can choose to live off their interest and close their firms, putting their employees out of work. Conversely, if wages are too low, their workers will be poorly fed and housed and will perform less well on the job, depressing productivity and thus eating into profits. Owners and workers do, therefore, have some common interests. Good economics dictates that both the conflicting and the common interests be so arranged that owners and workers both gain the maximum benefit from their relationship.

At this point in time, no such arrangement exists. As a result, labor and management are on a war footing. Workers form unions and demand higher wages and shorter workdays. Owners are often forced to give in, but in response to the labor movement they have begun to form employer organizations. The resulting standoff causes constant unease.

In Germany, weavers, miners, and recently also construction workers have formed nationwide organizations. In response, the employers have formed their own nationwide organizations in each of these sectors. When a partial strike broke out recently in the construction industry, employers joined together to order a general lockout throughout the country, except for Hamburg and Berlin. Production will halt, probably for many weeks, and both parties will suffer.

There is also a third party, the nonunionized workers. They cannot work because of the lockouts, and if they try they will be hounded as strikebreakers. Police protection will be necessary. In Amsterdam, employers on the way to the office were molested by striking workers and had to be escorted by the police. Personal security will remain at risk, and the conflict of interests will only intensify as long as no laws are passed to regulate it.

***

As early as the 1880s in our country, it was felt that *something* had to be done to reconcile conflicting interests. However, the seriousness of the situation was not fully appreciated. Especially feared at that time was freedom for management and labor to meet separately and to discuss among themselves which policies and guidelines to recommend before submitting them to joint consultation. When socialism began to organize the workers separately, on their own, it was believed that our sober nation would not see the excesses witnessed elsewhere. That was still the belief at our Social Congress in 1891. As a remedy, it recommended chambers of labor, with equal representation of labor and management and with the mandate to advise the government and to mediate and arbitrate conflicts.

However, the law that established them was implemented in the weakest form. Comparatively few chambers were installed, and little interest was shown in the election of members for these bodies. To be sure, the information and advice they offered was often valuable. Yet they lacked the power to make their words stick.

***

Social action was not led by chambers of labor but by individual trade unions. There was no regulatory cohesion. The interest groups engaged in debilitating guerilla warfare, rather than consulting to solve their issues together. Imposed top-down by the government were a factory act, the labor contract, and liability and compensation acts. But barely were they implemented when their inherent defects became apparent: the laws ignored the diversity of industry, they laid down often ill-fitting restrictions, and they only served to aggravate labor-management disputes.

The problem is illustrated today by the debates about state pensions. In the absence of private schemes, the government will soon be making up any shortfall in old-age provisions from the public treasury. This extreme state intervention in turn encourages the advocates of total state abstention. But the latter are floundering, caught in an individualistic mindset and lacking the fortitude to let the organic nature of industry come into its own. They regard corporations as strictly private affairs. Only due to the present-day abuse of power by the trusts are they beginning to acknowledge the public-legal character of industry.

All our coal, for example, used to come from German firms, but now our coal mines in Limburg threaten to diminish the demand for German coal.[2] The German coal syndicate has reacted by no longer supplying coal to Dutch firms that also wish to use local coal. Thus it tries to lord it over an important sector of the economy in a foreign country! In America as well, Roosevelt and Taft have had to take on trusts and syndicates that threaten to take control of entire branches of commerce and industry.[3] These sectors are indispensable for a free people and a free economy. This fact encourages socialists to argue for state intervention through public ownership of these sectors.

All this lends support to the conviction that every firm of any size does indeed have a public-legal side to it and that a more desirable situation shall only be achieved when government comes to the aid of private enterprise by providing it with *a legal framework that enables industry to regulate itself* and by means of regulatory power to compel the unwilling to cooperate, and in this way to honor once again the organic nature of commerce and industry. For precisely for this purpose, the company must become to a many-sided organization that is legally ratified; government regulation and private enterprise need to work together in the right proportion.

***

---

2. The Netherlands, with its relative lack of natural resources, was able to open its first large-scale, publicly owned coal mine in the southern province of Limburg in 1899.
3. Kuyper is referring to Republican politicians Theodore Roosevelt (1858–1919) and William Taft (1857–1930), who served as the 26th and 27th presidents of the United States, respectively.

The first requirement for a well-designed industrial organization is that all groups of firms are legally obliged to create their own organization that encompasses the entire country or a specific part of the country. The distinction between organized and nonorganized companies must end.

It may previously have been deemed impossible to organize, say, the construction industry, for the whole country. Results have shown, however, that even in a country ten times larger than ours, Germany, this is quite feasible. Even in the United States, many such organizations exist.[4]

Such an organization inevitably needs to encompass employers, on the one hand, and employees, on the other. Participation in a firm's elections for these bodies must be made mandatory for both parties, for only then is there assurance that the entire firm is represented. Care must also be taken, by means of proportional representation, that a simple majority does not outvote and drown out minorities.

Under this arrangement, every firm (or every combination of firms) acts through two bodies, one involving the employers and one involving the employees, each representing all points of view. Each body meets separately to deliberate and decide, and to appoint, say, six members to the higher, mixed organization. This mixed organization has its chairman appointed by the government and is given independent regulatory powers. Ongoing consultation between the groups is thus encouraged, while the final decision rests with the mixed body, although any final decision should need more than a bare majority.

This higher body can then determine whatever needs regulation, such as the apprenticeship system; technical training; working hours (differentiated by age, region, and type of industry); wage levels (according to skill, trade and age); unemployment provisions; and insurance plans against illness, disability, and old age; all differentiated by branch. Employers and employees can work together to increase production and markets, and in general, each within their sphere of influence, promote the flourishing of their companies. They can draw up rules governing contracts, factory regulations, days off, Sunday rest, and so much more—all in the context of their companies and therefore directly relevant and practicable.

---

4. Examples of such professional and industry associations, which are either explicitly or implicitly granted licensing monopolies by state power, include the American Bar Association and the American Medical Association.

Still more is needed. Industrial organization, to be effective, needs the legal competence and executive power to enforce its regulations. While government coerces compliance in a formal sense, industry creates the substance of the regulations that will hold for the entire sector.

No doubt it will take some doing before employers and employees are ready for this form of cooperation. After so many years of hostility, the two parties will have to grow in mutual trust. But experience has shown that where anarchy is replaced by sound organization, former passions are extinguished and old distrusts melt away. To be sure, large companies have increased the distance between employer and employee, but again, experience has shown that both parties are best off when the company flourishes.

Finally, a neglected question is how best to improve what is produced in order to be a match for foreign competition. Currently, both parties concentrate almost exclusively on scoring off each other; their eyes are fixed on private and immediate gains. The promotion of our national, communal interest will not improve until labor and management are organized in such a way that industry itself regulates the common interests of all who work in the economic sector.

THE SACRED
ORDER

TEXT INTRODUCTION

Kuyper's project was, in large part, to discern and advocate the ways in which "the sacred order of the world" related to the various spheres of human life. Even as an elder statesman, aged 75, he pursued this project with energy and conviction. The following piece provides an example, as Kuyper weighs the merits of free trade and protectionism. Participating in the election campaign of 1913, he uses intellectual and empirical arguments to propose that protective tariffs are legitimate in a world in which nations are not equally endowed in terms of economic assets and conditions. Such tariffs help build a country's prosperity and honor the providential order of separate national communities. For situations in which the playing field between national is level, free trade may provide the best prospects for mutual prosperity. But free trade as a universal absolute requiring world-wide adoption needs to be opposed as an idolatrous dogma that flies in the face of empirical evidence and the sacred order of things. In ignoring its practical limitations, its ideological advocates support a kind of cosmopolitanism that downplays national characteristics and reflects the folly of the Tower of Babel. Kuyper's words reflect the age of Western imperialism in which he uttered them and provide a sounding board for subsequent debates about the promise and pitfalls of the global economy.

SOURCE: Abraham Kuyper, *Heilige Orde* (Kampen: Kok, 1913). Text of an address given at a preelection meeting of the *Bond van Antirevolutionaire Kiesvereenigingen* [Federation of

Antirevolutionary Electoral Associations] of Amsterdam, May 30, 1913, extract from pp. 12–18. Abridged, translated, and annotated by Harry Van Dyke.

THE SACRED ORDER

Gentlemen! It did not take much for your board to persuade me to come over and address you at this time. Forty years ago, I initiated the revival of our antirevolutionary movement. I also played the role of midwife when your federation was born. In the 27 years that I worked in Amsterdam, first as a pastor, then as a journalist, and finally as a professor, I became more than half an Amsterdammer. This I remained when I left, and this I still am. So I feel very much at home among you.

On this occasion I would like to call your attention to the theme of "the sacred order of the world," as the poet Bilderdijk called it.[1] There is a sacred order of God in the life of the nation, a sacred order in the life of the state, and no less a sacred order in the education of our children. Allow me therefore to examine how that order relates to the three great questions of tariffs, suffrage, and education. All three questions face a confusion of human inventions that run counter to the sacred order. We must resist these with

---

1. Willem Bilderdijk (1756–1831), the Dutch poet to which Kuyper refers, wrote about the sacred order (*heilige orde*) in words Kuyper cites on the title page of the published version of his speech: "Heilige Orde dezer wereld, Die den scepter van gezag, Over nachtbeurt voert en dag, En een kroon spant, rijk ompareld." From Willem Bilderdijk, *Vermaking* (Rotterdam: A. F. H. Smit, 1828), 1. With these words, Bilderdijk echoes Jer 33:25, which speaks of the God having established "my covenant with day and night and the fixed order of heaven and earth."

holy energy in the coming election campaign if we are to remain true to our principle.[2]

The campaign will be tough this time. In 1909 you managed to capture three of the city's nine districts. Brothers, I say to you: carry on! I am confident you will keep your three seats and perhaps even add a fourth. But each of you must not fail to work hard in the campaign, for even small margins can defeat us. The Liberals' gerrymandering of districts has meant that in 1905 we gained the majority of the popular vote yet won fewer seats than the opposition. So we cannot flag in our efforts to return to office the present cabinet made up representatives from parties on the political right.

[After reviewing the record of the sitting cabinet, Kuyper turns to the topic of tariffs.][3]

If the present cabinet is returned, a key issue will be to see its proposal to raise import duties approved and passed into law. You may say: we are Amsterdammers, and as Amsterdam lives from trade, higher tariffs will kill our commerce.

Indeed, that is what free-traders would have you believe, but surely you don't buy that? It is the sacred cow of the Left, but when the Left was in office they did not abolish tariffs—in fact, they raised them slightly. In theory the Liberals condemn tariffs; in practice they maintain them. Except for Britain, no nation in the world practices free trade. Germany's tariffs are three times higher than ours. In 1890 it imported 31 million tons and exported 22 million; today these figures have tripled to 75 and 66 respectively. You may say that this must refer to Germany's trade by land, but tariffs must have destroyed its merchant marine. This is incorrect. In 1871 Germany had 147 steamships, in 1899 it had 1,223, and today that number exceeds 2,000.[4] Britain has a dominant position in world trade, but this predates her embrace of free trade; earlier, her high tariffs boosted her manufacturing industry, and she also dealt a deathblow to India's industry by transferring the profitable business to Manchester and Birmingham.

For too long our country has failed to protect its industry. Belgium's smokestacks far outnumber ours. Germany used to send its agricultural

---

2. The election campaign culminated in the Dutch general election of June 17 and 25, 1913.

3. The cabinet consisted of four Antirevolutionaries, three Catholics, and two independents. The prime minister was Antirevolutionary Theo Heemskerk (1852–1932).

4. *Note by the author:* The clearest survey of maritime shipping appears in J. G. Bartholomew, *Atlas of the World's Commerce* (London: G. Newnes, 1907), table 24.

workers to our farms to help in the harvest, but since it adopted protective tariffs it is our workers who migrate east in droves in order to share in Germany's prosperity. We are told that, because Wilson has replaced Taft, Washington will soon lower its tariffs.[5] America's tariffs will still, however, be much higher than what our government is proposing.

I realize that some of our industrialists have profited from our lower standard of living. But higher tariffs would merely sacrifice the personal interests of some individuals to the greater good of the whole. Industry in general will gain from higher tariffs. Judging by the experience of our nearest neighbors, moreover, higher tariffs will raise the standard of living of the nation as a whole.

The mere rumor of the plan to raise our tariffs has already caused our neighbors to begin to arm themselves against them. Yet our liberals oppose this plan. Free trade is their dogma, and they are fanatical about it. Belied by the facts, these zealots go against nature and replace objective observations with their subjective arguments, in defiance of the sacred order of things.

If all nations were equal in natural resources, favorable geographic conditions, and work habits, and if they could compete on fair and even terms with all other nations, then indeed all tolls at the border would be contrary to the nature of things. But that is not how things are. That is not the sacred order of this world that a higher Providence offers human beings. Humankind is divided over peoples and nations. Divine government has provided some with great riches, others with less, and still others with a meager share. This inequality determines the life of nations, and given their unequal opportunities nations cannot dispense with tariffs to protect themselves.

Some people may respond by saying: we don't give a fig about those natural boundaries; we sail the world's oceans that wash the shores of every country, so why worry about international competition? But then I reply: just as the tower of Babel tried to stop any dispersal of humanity, so free trade would have the *national* element replaced by the *universally human*. Merchants, in love with trade and commerce, easily lose sight of their homeland and turn cosmopolitan. Soon they feel like a world citizen.

Let me not be misunderstood. I am not suggesting that there can't be situations that call for free trade. Protective tariffs (other than for exotic

---

5. Kuyper is referring to the William Taft (1857-1930) and Woodrow Wilson (1856-1924), the 27th and 28th presidents of the United States, respectively.

products) would of course be contraband for a country rich in natural resources, endowed with fertile soil, enjoying easy access to foreign countries in all directions and populated by a technically capable people. What is praised, and preached to us, is free trade as the *only* system, free trade as *dogma*, free trade as a requirement for *all* nations and peoples, free trade as the greatest discovery to be salvaged from the maelstrom of human existence. I say with Friedrich List that it would end in killing national life and breaking the sacred order.[6] The faithful follower of Adam Smith, Thomas Cooper declares, in contrast, that we must reckon only with human beings and humanity and that a nation is nothing but a *nonentity* that has no actual existence except "in the heads of politicians."[7] This stands in direct opposition to the sacred order. The divine order in nature presents us with a humanity divided over unequal nations. Even at the consummation of the ages, Holy Scripture lets us hear praises for the Lamb that are not sung by one undivided humankind but by distinctive nations, tribes, and peoples. In contrast to it stands the human dogma of free trade, aimed at nullifying the sacred order and once again erecting a tower of Babel—which God judged and then destroyed. In exceptional circumstances, free trade can be very valuable, but as a dogma it is an unsparing tool that levels all difference and cuts the bonds that hold a nation together.

---

6. *Note by the author:* Friedrich List, *Gesammelte Schriften* (Stuttgart: Cotta, 1850–51), 3:132. [*Ed. note:* Friedrich List (1789–1846), a forefather of the historical school of economics, held that free trade would result in the subjection of the less advanced nations to the predominant manufacturing, commercial, and military powers of the world. The only condition allowing for free trade as a beneficial policy, according to List, would be near equality among the nations in industry, civilization, political development, and military power.]

7. Thomas Cooper (1759–1839), onetime president of South Carolina College, was an Anglo-American scholar known for his strong defense of free speech and free trade. See Friedrich List, *The National System of Political Economy*, trans. Sampson S. Lloyd (London: Longmans, Green, 1885), 122. See also Thomas Cooper, *Lectures on the Elements of Political Economy* (Columbia: Telescope, 1826), 19: "Hence the moral entity—the grammatical being called a *nation*, has been cloathed in attributes that have no real existence except in the imagination of those who metamorphose a word into a thing; and convert a mere grammatical contrivance, into an existing and intelligent being."

THE SOCIAL QUESTION (1917)

TEXT INTRODUCTION

Kuyper was 78 years old when he sat down to rewrite his political testament, published as *Anti-Revolutionary Staatkunde* in 1916–17. It had been almost 40 years since he wrote his first version, published as *Ons Program* in 1879. Now, as then, he needed around 1,300 pages to expound his political manifesto. As he explained in the preface to volume 1 of *Anti-Revolutionary Staatkunde*, what he offered was not a work on *political theory*. That subject was far too broad and would require more time that he still had at his disposal. What he was providing, instead, was his view of what made for practical politics in the antirevolutionary tradition. All the same, that first volume was subtitled "The Principles" and dealt extensively with concepts such as government, sovereignty, justice, state and church, and the function of political parties. By contrast, the second volume, the shorter of the two, tackled more practical topics such as budgets and the role of the auditor general, provincial and municipal jurisdictions, public decency and public health, foreign affairs, colonial policy, and, once more, "the social question."

Kuyper was able to work on *Anti-Revolutionary Staatkunde* at a steady pace, especially since hearing loss kept him from attending too many sessions of the First Chamber (of which he was still a member). Increasingly, he wrote, this impediment "confined him to the study." His publisher later reported that Dr. Kuyper had submitted regular installments, finishing the last one in December 1916, exactly as had been agreed on a year and a half earlier.

In the preface, Kuyper confessed that his earlier political commentary (*Ons Program*) was the work of an autodidact. At university he had studied neither law nor politics; he was first of all a theologian and second a church historian. But, he explained, growing contact and communion with old-style Calvinists, which he considered the country's silent majority, had led him to broaden his horizons. It persuaded him that a treasury of Calvinist political thought lay dormant and needed to be heard. He had tried to do this, he explained, first in *Ons Program* and later in *De Gemeene Gratie* (see *Common Grace*). Long aware that the work of 1879 was both deficient and insufficient, he was glad now to have the time to improve and update it.

So much had changed over the four decades between *Ons Program* and *Anti-Revolutionary Staatkunde*, not least regarding the social question. The class war appeared to be intensifying. The popularity of socialism was growing. As prime minister, Kuyper had had to deal with a potentially crippling railroad strike in 1903. Labor relations were under severe strain, requiring of employees and employers greater cooperation and consultation, rather than strikes and lockouts. What aspects of Kuyper's "architectonic critique" of society could be developed to defuse such social tensions? This was the burden of the section of *Anti-Revolutionary Staatkunde* from which the following abridged extracts are drawn. Clearly, for Kuyper, it was high time for a review of the practical measures implemented, and an outline of what still needed to be achieved.

SOURCE: Abraham Kuyper, *Antirevolutionaire staatkunde met nadere toelichting op ons program* (Kampen: Kok, 1916–17), 2:492–534 (abridged abstracts from ch. 18). Translated and annotated by Harry Van Dyke.

THE SOCIAL QUESTION (1917)

THEN AND NOW   §1

Almost half a century ago, in 1878, I drafted a basic rule for solving the social question. It stated that the Antirevolutionary Party "acknowledges the necessity to contribute better than at present, also by means of legislation, toward making relations between the various social classes answer as much as possible to the demands of God's Word."[1] This formulation echoed my speech in the Second Chamber on November 28, 1874, and was reiterated in my speech in the chamber of November 22 and 23, 1910.[2]

The state of the social question in our country has changed considerably since 1874. The solution proposed at that time by the liberal member of Parliament Mr. van Houten could not satisfy me.[3] It is noteworthy that the Communist International, which began its activities in our country in

---

1. See *OP*, 331. The quoted "rule" is article 19 from the party program adopted in 1878.
2. See Abraham Kuyper, *Eenige Kameradviezen uit de jaren 1874 en 1875* (Amsterdam: Wormser, 1890), 191–97; and *Verslag der Handelingen van de Tweede Kamer der Staten-Generaal gedurende het zittings-jaar 1910-1911* (The Hague: Algemene Landsdrukkerij, 1911), 455–57.
3. Samuel van Houten (1837-1930) was a progressive member of Parliament and propagator, among other things, of birth control.

1873, invited me, who was then still a pastor, to a public debate with one of its spokesmen. I declined because I could immediately see that we differed radically in basic starting point, even though we agreed that labor needed protection *in law*.

§2   ANXIOUS FEELINGS

These first attempts at addressing the social question in our country instilled much anxiety. Countermeasures were contemplated. Rumors circulated that noisy demonstrations and street riots, prepared in secret, would soon break out. I still remember hearing a group of young working women in Amsterdam yelling: "We have loved long enough! Now we want to hate!" This was answered from across the canal by the then popular ditty: "All the socialists in a herring barrel!" A systematic approach was lacking. The individualistic approach of John Stuart Mill meant well but destroyed all social cohesion. As Rawson Birks pointedly observed: " 'The greatest happiness of the greatest number' has been its professed aim, and 'the greatest discontent of the greatest number' would almost seem, from the present signs of the times, to have been the result actually achieved."[4]

We were fortunate enough in the Netherlands to see the establishment of a Christian counteraction in the form of the Christian labor organization Patrimonium. This action helped fence in our Christian working classes, as it were, and kept them from being infected by the spirit of revolution. In more revolutionary circles, however, the spirit of the Paris Commune lived on. The barricades threatened to go up in all Western countries, and some capitalists thought they might have to save themselves by quitting the Continent. Not even the army was immune to this spirit.

§3   TOWARD COLLABORATION

By 1880 this movement for turning society upside down was brought to a halt. Saner minds prevailed, and even Marxists decided that consultation and constructive action was the means to arm the masses—not with pistols and daggers but with knowledge and perseverance. Both Liberal and Christian statesmen openly acknowledged the need for improving the lot of the working classes. Around 1880 we entered a phase in which a more serious and systematic approach to the social question was embarked

---

4. Thomas Rawson Birks, *First Principles of Moral Science: A Course of Lectures Delivered in the University of Cambridge* (London: Macmillan, 1873), 11.

upon; society would not yet be turned upside down but merely for window dressing.

HOLY SCRIPTURE §4

Initially, Christians felt they could not join the nascent labor movement. They certainly believed that mutual aid and charity were needed, but they were slow to realize that at stake were fundamental *rights* and that the social question was an issue concerning *justice*. Did Scripture, they asked, not condone even slavery as a normal phenomenon? Not even the apostle Paul dared question the right of a slave owner (though he softened it by speaking of brotherly love). And in ancient Israel, was the owning of slaves not legitimate (though they might go free after seven years)?

Granted, in the sin-ridden evolution of the human race, slavery was an inevitable phase which no doubt had benefits. The short epistle of James does not even mention slavery, but what we do read there is very instructive: "Behold, the wages of the laborers who mowed your fields, which you kept back by fraud, are crying out against you, and the cries of the harvesters have reached the ears of the Lord of hosts" (Jas 5:4).

Two facts must be recognized. First, the relation between servant and master varies from age to age and culture to culture, and no uniform response will do; what once was condoned is now an abomination. And second, each phase has its own evils, today including evils that can be exorcized only through godliness and love of neighbor. The present state of social relations has juridical, economic, religious, and ethical dimensions. We must work to change a variety of social relations and strive for a more just economic order. Society needs constantly to undergo the operation of moral and religious forces.

OVERCOMING CLASS DIFFERENCE §5

The entire social question hangs on the relationship between master and servant. When egoism rules, masters demand the maximum and servants offer the minimum. Throughout the centuries, men have looked for a system that would once for all end this opposition. The latest and largest attempt at this is socialism, but even the early Christians tended toward a form of common ownership. "They had all things in common" (see Acts 2:44), not because of an apostolic injunction but voluntarily, in a paradise mood: no more "mine and thine," no more competition, one holy household under God. The same arrangement has been tried throughout history, but just as in Jerusalem it has always ended in bitter disappointment. When the apostle Paul later had to go around collecting funds for the impoverished church of Jerusalem, a judgment was pronounced on the mistake of the early church.

Communism may look attractive, but since everyone carries sin in their heart, experiments with communal ownership always increase misery. If the International ever succeeds in setting up a state based on communal ownership, it can expect the same sorry outcome.

§6 ## MARXISM WATERED DOWN

The "whole Marx" has long been abandoned, but socialism still stands for a comprehensive endeavor to abolish once for all the opposition between the haves and the have-nots, between employer and wage earner, between rich and poor, and to hand over all material aspects of life to a central power that will administer the whole and distribute all goods. Society will have no struggles, no privileges, no inequalities. Thus, once again a harking back to paradise, or a premature anticipation of the new earth. Not that socialists think in those terms. They are simply convinced that the time is now ripe for realizing the classless society.

§7 ## PUBLIC SERVICES

Has private ownership indeed had its day? In his book *Progress and Poverty*,[5] Henry George blamed all social woes on the unequal distribution of the land. Governments were to nationalize, or if need be confiscate, all land and put it at the disposal of all citizens.

Though its application was impracticable, George's proposal contained an element of truth. Similar to his solution, big cities have felt compelled to bring the provision of gas, water, burial grounds, and public transport under their control, and since the outbreak of the dreadful war in 1914, national and local governments have been obliged to regulate the food supply, its sale, and its price levels.

Sometimes communal ownership can therefore be necessary for a time. Some governments, to increase revenue, have even given themselves a monopoly—France in tobacco and salt, our East Indies in opium.

---

5. Henry George, *Progress and Poverty: An Inquiry into the Cause of Industrial Depressions and of Increase of Want with Increase of Wealth* (New York: Doubleday, 1880).

NO SUPPORT IN SCRIPTURE §8

Thus, while certain conditions have given socialism reasons for its utopias, it cannot appeal to Scripture. Biblical history covers many ages, each with its own demands. Only three facts remain valid throughout: (1) what obtained in paradise and will again obtain in the consummation is not susceptible of implementation in the current sin-disrupted state of the world; (2) every historical period brings with it its own demands; and (3) under these varying periods of culture one demand stands and never changes: *love your neighbor as yourself.*

The middle term in the revolutionary slogan "Liberty, Equality, Fraternity" is incapable of realization. Nothing is so unequal as the human world, and the stamp of uniformity imprinted on our modern culture chokes life and is a veritable curse.[6]

GUILDS HAVE OUTLIVED THEMSELVES §9

The labor movement of our time is a response to a radical change in social conditions. The old craft and commercial guilds operated on a comparatively small scale and embraced both employers and workers who were on intimate terms with each other. The workers were treated well and did not have to work at night or on Sundays. In the textile trade, cottage industry ensured that fathers were not separated from their families. Social contentment supported the peace of society. Unfortunately, guilds did not keep up with changing times.

NEW DEMANDS §10

The changing times brought the steam engine, which revolutionized the world of labor. We saw this when steam cranes came to unload ships and three men did the work that used to take twelve. The technical revolution brought manufactured goods within reach of more people. Growth in demand caused an expansion of the labor force, loosening the intimate bond between employers and their workers, especially when factories and plants grew to enormous size. Increasing alienation from employers fostered cooperation among the workers in the defense of their rights and interests. Labor solidarity first included all those in the same workplace, next it was extended to an entire branch of industry, and then it reached beyond the borders to include fellow workers internationally.

---

6. See Kuyper's speech of 1869, "Uniformity: The Curse of Modern Life," in *AKCR*, 19–44.

§11

EMPLOYERS HESITATE

At first, employers disputed the right of labor to act this way. This led to bitter conflicts and only gradually—thanks in part to the leadership of the Roman Catholic clergy—did the mentality change. In Belgium, Catholic employers even went so far as to organize annual retreats in order to ask themselves before the face of God whether they were doing right by their employees. When I helped organize Boaz,[7] I hoped to attach something similar to the new organization, but our Calvinist circles proved not yet ready for such a practice of examining one's conscience. Nevertheless, our eyes have been opened to the demands of a new era, witness books like those by Slotemaker de Bruïne[8] and Smeenk.[9] In the modern firm the old intimacy between employer and employee has made way, by law, for a formal regulation of the rights of each. Each party has its own organization and strives to reconcile interests. On the line of Stuart Mill ran only one locomotive, that of employer individualism; today, by contrast, the workman's locomotive has obtained in public opinion equal rights to the track.

§12

ORGANIZATION IS A MUST

In England, and partly also in America, the clash of interests had not taken on this form, and a more pragmatic organization of labor was achieved. Yet the factual conflict could no longer be ignored, and the fundamental antithesis found on the continent of Europe blew over to Britain, where even the International gained a foothold. We may deplore this, but it should not discourage us. The issue at stake, fraught with many seemingly insoluble difficulties, simply demands resolution, and only organized action on both sides can hope to achieve this. International commerce prohibits purely

---

7. Boaz was a Christian employers association, founded on January 18, 1892, for the purpose of fostering "awareness of employers' obligations to their subordinates" and of improving "not only their businesses but also the religious, moral and social condition of their subordinates." In 1897 it adopted a program of action in support of Sunday observance, grain tariffs, a national mortgage bank, small-claims courts, and improved housing and pensions for the working classes. In 1918 Boaz was split into three organizations: for farmers, retailers, and other entrepreneurs, based on the sovereignty of God, civil obedience, and love of neighbor.

8. J. R. Slotemaker de Bruïne, *Christelijk-sociale Studiën* [Christian social studies], 3 vols. (Utrecht: Ruys, 1908).

9. C. Smeenk, *Voor het sociale leven. Handboek ten dienste van de christelijke vakorganisatie en de algem. arbeidersbeweging* [For social life: Manual for Christian trade unions and the labor movement in general] (Rotterdam: Libertas, 1914).

national solutions, and countries blessed with rich natural resources will be able to guarantee their working classes a higher standard of living than poorer countries. All these factors need to be taken into account.

DIFFICULTIES §13

One difficulty is that not all members belonging to one of the interested parties will join their organization. Employers may insist on their freedom *not* to join and to hire only workers who likewise shun organizations. Similarly, an employee may be content to work for a "decent boss" and decline to join "those rabble-rousers."

Indeed, some labor unions are run by agitators instead of leaders. Socialists especially can storm and rage against all employers or workers that they happen to dislike. We all know how they will sometimes harass people during a strike and even picket private homes. It is also true that serious workers cannot always attend union meetings where you sometimes have to listen to language no one should be forced to hear. And when you protest you are laughed at, if not jeered.

Equally repugnant are decisions arrived at in these meetings which your conscience can only condemn and which you simply may not support.

England and America tend to have more sober unions, but here on the Continent socialist fanaticism prevails—the very cause of its failure to achieve its goals.

ORGANIZING APART §14

To organize was imperative, but our people could not join the organizations that had arisen. This led, here and elsewhere, to efforts to start *separate* organizations based on a Christian foundation. Catholic employers and Catholic employees took the lead in this, with the assistance of their church. Generally, however, they would not accept Protestants as members. In our textile region of Twente, a cooperative venture of Catholics and Protestants was in full swing when the Catholic clergy disapproved and opposed it.[10] Although the two groups still work together on a small scale, it became clear that collaboration in social and economic affairs was out of the question. Accordingly, the Catholic side pressed for their own purely Catholic organizations. We on our side did the same, and the Antirevolutionary Party

---

10. This ecumenical initiative during the 1890s was led by Father Alphonse Ariëns (1860–1928).

tried to stimulate it from the beginning. Patrimonium took the lead, soon followed by a variety of more specialized unions and associations.

§15 ## PECULIAR DIFFICULTIES

Among our people, however, no local church or national synod provided the necessary guidance. It was always a question of individuals who joined. So what was there to prevent others from *not* joining? This detracted from the general nature of the organization. A union does not enjoy its full potential unless it embraces all prospective members. When some refuse to join, their interests begin to conflict with those of the union, which is apt to lead to embitterment and estrangement. Hence, the goal of having an organization alongside—and in part over against—the socialists, and persuading *all* your fellow believers to join it, is exceptionally difficult. Add to that the fact that all organization costs money, which many feel is not worth it. Attending meetings, sometimes at a fair distance from one's home, also costs precious time. Although progress has been made, we are still far from a complete organization. But no one believes that unions, so long as membership is voluntary, will ever succeed in organizing all working people. Might legislation help here?

§16 ## THE TASK OF GOVERNMENT

We have been accused of first placing all our hopes on private initiative but later switching to state socialism. This is incorrect. When I first broached the social question in Parliament, in November 1874, I argued for protecting the working classes through a labor code similar to the existing commercial code. At the time the idea was ridiculed,[11] but developments since then have vindicated me. We now have chambers of labor, an Industrial Safety Act and a Workman's Compensation Act, a Nuisance Act, an Employment Act, and so much more. [In 1903] I personally tabled in Parliament a very extensive labor law which included the regulation of apprenticeships. Since then, Minister Talma has pursued the same agenda.[12] I admit that at the outset I

---

11. See above, p. 223.

12. The Antirevolutionary Rev. Sybrandus Talma, sometimes called "the red pastor" and "the lion of Patrimonium," was minister of agriculture, industry, and commerce from 1908 till 1913 and became known for his many social legislation bills. They covered a variety of areas such as fisheries, patents, plant disease control, stonemasons, maximum hours for women and children, and health, disability, and old-age insurance for wage earners.

expected more from private initiative than could be attained, but I always thrust into the foreground that government assistance was indispensable if orderly conditions were to be achieved that would bring an acceptable solution to the social question.

From the outset I combated the Cobden school with its senseless individualism. Especially as regards the organization of the world of labor, I remain convinced that private initiative alone will never achieve its goal. There is not enough unity of vision among employers. Nor, for that matter, among the workers: badgering and harassing so-called scabs during strike actions produces only resentment and antipathy, not conviction and solidarity.

SPEECH IN PARLIAMENT §17

On November 22, 1910, I spoke in Parliament about the embitterment between organized and nonorganized workers. I raised the question whether the government could not simply order all employees without exception into workers' organizations by category or branch of industry and all employers without exception into corresponding organizations for employers; delegates from each could consult separately at the national level, draw up resolutions, and then meet together to make the decisions that the times required.[13] This proposal from the school of De Mun[14] appealed to me because it achieves completeness of organization, removes a cause of bitterness, and promises results to which both parties have contributed.

OUR STARTING POINT §18

Improvement would have to start with the apprenticeship system. Compared to workers in countries such as England, Germany, Belgium, and France, ours are poorly trained. The same holds for employers, although many a Dutch industrialist has gone to Germany to learn business economics and management. With the School of Economics in Rotterdam we have at least

---

13. *Note by the author:* See Etienne Martin Saint-Léon, *Histoire des corporations de métiers,* 2nd ed. (Paris: Felix Aden, 1909).
14. Adrien Albert Marie, Comte de Mun (1841–1914), helped organize a Society of Catholic Workers Circles, which soon covered the industrial regions of France with local clubs. Two of his most noted sayings are: "We are the irreconcilable counter-revolution," and "Socialism is the logical revolution and we are the counter-revolution; there is nothing in common between us." These notions were echoed by Pope Leo XIII in the 1891 encyclical *Rerum novarum.*

made a start, made possible once my ministry in 1904 amended the Higher Education Act, which already provided for a Polytechnical Institute in Delft. In the case of secondary schools for industrial arts, however, much work still needs to be done for which I could not get enough support at the time.

§19 ## A COHERENT PLAN

Our aim throughout was to improve people's skills at all levels. Like lawyers, doctors, and others, all people employed in business and industry should have earned a diploma, giving them the right to practice their trade or craft. This measure would make it possible to organize all the people in agriculture and industry, business, commerce, and shipping, for the purpose of defending their rights. The same would be applicable, of course, to office workers, retail personnel, and domestic servants.

§20 ## A WELL-REGULATED BODY

The entire system would have to be a well-integrated arrangement of all stakeholders. Regulation by government would not serve to restrict the freedom of business but do exactly the opposite: give full effect to its freedom.[15] At the same time, of course, such an arrangement would clear the way for having employers and employees organized according to their own convictions. Propaganda for the Christian viewpoint would not be disrupted but promoted. All members could attend the meetings, but only the delegates at the national level would consult together and be able to avoid any unpleasantries. The system would keep the government fully abreast of the needs and desires of both parties in the social movement and be able to respond with regulations harmonizing their rights and interests.[16]

§21 ## UNEMPLOYMENT

The most anxious evil for the working classes is unemployment. Does any blame rest on the government? In part, undoubtedly. Free trade and open borders, if carried too far, can put many people out of work. Imported

---

15. Note how Kuyper is careful to avoid the authoritarian nature of corporatism.
16. The arrangement here sketched in many respects anticipated the institution of the post-1945 Sociaal-Economische Raad, a tripartite advisory council in the Netherlands in which representatives from government departments, employers' organizations, and trade unions together advise the government annually on wage and price ceilings, pension indexing, and other socioeconomic parameters. It is sometimes referred as the "polder model" of central planning.

finished products that need no further processing diminish the demand for our own workers. As it is, we are a country with few natural resources and so must heavily rely on imports. Hence our negative balance of trade with countries such as Germany, France, and England. Our open borders have a similar effect. A large influx of foreign workers, who are often better trained, supplants our own people. Knowledge of foreign languages among our well-educated Dutch people only encourages this tendency.

EXCESS POPULATION §22

Increased unemployment is also caused by excess population, which finds its explanation in the absence of war, longevity due to improved hygiene, declining rates of infant mortality, earlier marriages, improved housing, and a rising standard of living. Given that our small country is already over-populated, a high birth rate can only cause poverty in the margins of the nation. One remedy would be birth control by immoral means. The other would be emigration, but the numbers who leave our country is only a tiny fraction of our growth in population, which is swelling at an increasing rate.

HOW TO INTERCEPT UNEMPLOYMENT §23

Certain measures can help reduce unemployment. A collective bargaining agreement forces a firm to deal not with one but with all its employees; unemployment insurance, forms of philanthropy, and public works projects can also be useful; and during severe but short-term crises, municipal governments can provide temporary relief. But in the end, given our growing population, these measures will not avail, and at the lower levels there will always be people who are destitute. As a nation we like to "stay at home." We have not obeyed the biblical injunction to replenish the earth (see Gen 1:28; 9:1; 11:4).

WAGES §24

The abolition of slavery and serfdom and other ties to the land have meant an incredible intellectual elevation of the lower class. But at the same time they have forced it to take on an unbelievably risky venture. When I was introduced to former slaves in Chesapeake Bay near Baltimore, what struck me was the fresh outlook they exhibited as *human* beings.[17] But

---

17. This occurred during Kuyper's visit to the United States, which spanned the final four months of 1898. See "Kuyper's Visit to the United States of America," in Peter S.

emancipation had brought cares that had been unfamiliar before. Before, the "master" took care of everything; now the responsibility rested on their own shoulders. The resulting uncertainty, having to live from hand to mouth, is the problem that wages are supposed to solve. Yet while a salary assures a steady income, wages are a payment for a specific service, mostly on a weekly basis but at times for work of only a day or even part of a day. Wage earners can be out on the street at short notice, unable to provide food for their family or even a roof over their heads.

§25 ALLEVIATION

In practice, to be sure, customs have alleviated the situation. A maid gets at least a six-week notice; others are hired for an agreed-upon period of time; and in many factories and shops wages are not suddenly cut off. Yet the question always nags: Will there be enough income, and will it be steady?

§26 MINIMAL REQUIREMENTS

The ideal would be that all workers can rely on a wage that would make it possible for them to save for sickness or old age; to spend time on other pursuits such as reading, church attendance, and recreation; and contributing to charities.

However, there are gradations in people's skills. This invites different wage levels for skilled laborers, common laborers, and those in between. In America they have carried it through with some precision, coupling wage levels to productivity. For our country, a similar differentiation would result in 12 guilders a week for a married common laborer, 16 to 17 guilders for the median category, and between 18 and 25 guilders for a skilled laborer. Of course, wages need to reflect the cost of living, which tends to be higher in urban than in rural areas. Inflation too necessitates periodic adjustments. To a small degree any income from a wife, and children from above 16 years of age, should also be part of the equation (more about that below). Still, the earnings of the head of the family should normally suffice to cover normal living costs.

Wage standards such as the above cannot be made compulsory. Yet government can lead the way, landed gentry and captains of industry can set

Heslam *Creating a Christian Worldview: Abraham Kuyper's Lectures on Calvinism* (Grand Rapids: Eerdmans, 1998), ch. 3, pp. 57–84. See also *Kuyper in America*, ed. George Harinck (Sioux Center, IA: Dordt College Press, 2012), 71.

an example, and those who agitate for reforms should not cease to point to the ideal of meeting these minimal requirements.

COOPERATION A MUST §27

Success is not possible, however, unless the laboring classes work in unison to achieve this goal. To that end, data has to be gathered about conditions throughout the country. In addition, accurate information is needed about the earnings of employers and the return on capital. It stands to reason that an entrepreneur needs the stimulus of profit to keep going; to put him on a par with workers is absurd. Nevertheless, there ought to be an equitable ratio between profit and wages. Attempts in this direction have not disappointed, but labor needs to be willing to cooperate. Distrust, loafing on the job, cheating, and pilfering have thus far prevented a rise in wage levels. Employers must take pride in their personnel if it does well and is content; but conversely, employees should take pride in the firm's success and in the ability of their employers to do well in the marketplace, knowing that their well-being depends on their employers' prosperity.

A LIVING WAGE §28

Of course it would be wonderful if every workingman could be assured of what Americans call a "living wage." But do not forget: one study puts the minimal income for a family of five at 600 dollars,[18] that is, 1,500 guilders. A fine goal, but absurdly high. If wages were raised to that level, consumer prices would immediately rise too, which would negate the raise again. If people say that socialist equality is the answer nothing would be gained: forced equality dulls productivity and would actually function regressively. Mutual trust is essential.

Some large American firms have started to open their books to their employees. In our country we lack all knowledge on that front, hence are ill equipped to promote compromise and harmony between the interests of business and labor. Workers and bosses belong together; they should be supporting and defending each other's interests. Both parties should aim for fairness and equity. And fear of God has to be the force that casts out distrust and base treatment.

---

18. *Note by the author*: See the work by John A. Ryan, *A Living Wage* (New York: Macmillan, 1906), 145.

§29

STRIKES

Had such cordial relations existed, it would never have come to today's need for work stoppages. The altered work relations and conditions of production gradually led employers to exploit their workers. The school of John Stuart Mill threw the minds off balance. The outcome was a struggle between individuals. He who lasted longest won. The "fittest" was the winner, and the less well fitted went under. This led to the evaporation of all mutual trust and the exploitation by factory owners of his workers. By the law of "the survival of the fittest" capitalists came to dominate the whole economic situation. Although many of them felt uneasy about it, they felt helpless in the face of this iron law and felt compelled to play along.

A powerful reaction was inevitable. Men of status took up the cause of the exploited working class. One fact remained: the manufacturers needed the workers. If the capitalist could be threatened with the loss of his workers, there would be hope. Thus was born the strike. At our Social Congress in 1891 we explicitly came to the conclusion that strikes are not per se to be rejected as unlawful. But strikes, many workingmen have begun to realize, are no panacea. Moreover, a strike requires an uncommon spirit of cooperation; when that is lacking the unwilling are denounced as "scabs" and treated as "traitors to the sacred cause." This has not seldom led to kangaroo courts and even murder.

§30

COUNTERMEASURES BY EMPLOYERS

What can nullify the effect of strikes are lockouts. Strikes require a good measure of moral strength as well as the habit of laying aside part of your wages to be able to ride out a lengthy strike. You need to get the baker and grocer to agree to let you buy on credit, and this will encumber your household budget long after the strike is over. If a deal is reached and work is resumed, the leaders of the strike are usually not rehired. Local strikes on a small scale can be very effective, but strikes over larger areas or even nationwide work stoppages often prove useless against the big capitalists. The latter can form trusts that are able to orchestrate lockouts everywhere. As for a general strike for political reasons, such action takes a valuable economic measure and transfers it to an area where it should have no place.

§31

BOYCOTTS

A cruel employer who grinds down his workers can be subjected to a boycott: it involves a communal agreement that no one should have dealings with him—buy from him, sell to him, or associate with him in any way whatsoever. The goal is to coerce him to give up his tyranny and institute reforms. A boycott can be very effective, but the days are past that workers are exploited so outrageously. Moreover, a boycott involves enlisting the cooperation of store owners and other suppliers, which is not always easy. And unless the grievance is downright shocking, public opinion will not support a boycott.

SABOTAGE §32

Akin to a boycott is an action of sabotage. Fueled by thirst for revenge, sabotage does not scruple to attack an employer's property, members of his family, and sometimes even his person. A notorious case was the man who after abusing young girls in his employ had his genitals cut off, stuck on a pole, and paraded around the village.[19]

The purpose of sabotage is to strike fear into other employers and so gain economic concessions. It needs no saying that, from a Christian standpoint, all violent actions are absolutely to be condemned—however understandable they may be in some circumstances.

TRADE UNIONS §33

The right way to improve conditions is still to organize a trade union. A union too can call a strike, but then it will be under more trustworthy leaders. They will not aim for general reform but solely for their specific trade which it knows inside out. They look at how the trade is doing in other regions of the country and even abroad, to assess what can be risked and what is not advisable. Moreover, a union works at improving the skills of its members and so raises their economic value, allowing them to make higher demands.

Meanwhile a more general labor federation retains its value as a unifying force. Trade unions pursue more pragmatic ends, whereas a federation serves to impart a vision and instill enthusiasm. A union arms you for the struggle; a central federation unites and inspires you.

PICKETING §34

If all workers were members of a trade union, as they should be, there would be no question of picketing. Nonmembers who are willing to work

---

19. The atrocity here mentioned could not be identified.

during a strike reduce its effectiveness, so they will be considered enemies. That can't be helped; it is only human.

Picketing is a last-minute effort to prevent nonmembers from breaking ranks. Nevertheless, the end does not justify the means. Frightening the willing by posting men at their door, hooting and jeering them, and threatening their persons, wives, and children are abominations that cannot be condemned too strongly. What is acceptable is to plead with them, persuade them, convince them. A better way is to mail them a letter in which the strike is explained and defended. The ultimate solution is to legislate workers into their corresponding trades, and picketing will be a thing of the past.

§35   ## WORKING HOURS

Wage levels should depend on a worker's productivity, which in turn is linked to the number of hours worked. A skilled laborer can deliver more work in eight hours than a slacker in twelve. Urging shorter work hours needs to be offset by greater productivity. Contributing factors are a sound apprenticeship program, a responsible trade union, effective hygiene, decent housing, proper nutrition, but also moral factors such as earnestness, a sense of duty, overcoming the sluggishness we are all prone to.

When a worker raises their productivity by, say, 10 percent, they ought either to get a 10 percent raise or else have their work hours reduced by 10 percent. A reduction in work hours is very important. A worker's life should not be totally taken up by their work. They have to take care of themselves, enrich their minds, pay attention to higher interests. They also have to be there for their spouses and children. Friendship makes demands as well, as does church membership, and attending meetings. Finally, nighttime rest should restore what has been used up during the day.

§36   ## THE COOPERATIVE WORKER

Shortening working hours should certainly be pursued. Only, the worker ought to make this possible through better training, honing his skills, and stepping up his effort. However, it must also be acknowledged that in some industries these measures make virtually no difference because production is completely done entirely by machines. But one law must always be observed: the nature of human beings is such that they can perform only so much labor as their normal health allows. If employers go over that limit when setting hours, gradually they are murdering their employees. For the worker, too, productivity is not the only goal of life.

TIME OFF

37

Time off from work is required for the Lord's Day, for the other holy days, for the Saturday afternoon, for family events, and for a short vacation in the summer. We mention these together in order to underscore that laborers are not machines but human beings. They are to enjoy these exemptions from work. In certain industries, however, it has proved to be the case that large machines cannot always be switched off and must be attended to. Only certain occupations allow for no exemptions, such as doctors, pharmacists, domestic servants, and so forth. Also worthy of mention in this context are preachers, organists, custodians, and so on.

REQUISITE LEGISLATION

38

Where a community has more than one pharmacy, closure on Sundays can alternate by mutual arrangement. However, it is the government that must step in to regulate Sunday observance for the civil service and for domestic servants. Holding elections on Sundays, as is done in France and Belgium, is a vexation we fortunately do not yet have to cope with. But government is competent to regulate working hours for firemen, utilities personnel, policemen, and so on. For public employees to take action if need be against the government, in whose service they stand, is out of the question: no one is compelled to take a government job, but once they do, they must realize in advance that if they throw in their lot with the government they cannot join issue with it.

NIGHT WORK

39

The day is for work, the night for rest. This rule even holds for the animal world, with the exception of animals of prey and poisonous insects. In the human world we make exceptions for keeping vigil with the sick, maintaining a fire brigade, and patrolling the streets against thieves and robbers. Some industries still lack guarantees against having to work at night. Journalists and bakers still suffer under this lack. Telegraph and telephone services can easily be halted, for in the past we did without these means of communication and life simply carried on. However, the press wants to inform you in the morning what transpired the day before, and that means that journalists have to work through the night. And city dwellers want to enjoy their breakfast of buns freshly baked, requiring night work from bakers. But these occupations must remain the exceptions that prove the rule. The rule is that nighttime is for sleeping. Scholars who sit behind their desks at night and students who burn the midnight oil before an exam defy nature, which soon exacts its price in insomnia, for which dangerous sleeping pills become the last resort.

§40   ANARCHY

Nihilism, syndicalism, and so much more may have made inroads in Russia, France, and Italy, but in our country they were never able to develop into forces to be reckoned with. They showed a brief sign of life during the railway strike of 1903 but were then suppressed, hopefully for good.[20] The mood is no longer for violent revolution but for patient reform.

§41   CONCLUSION

To sum up, government intervention in labor relations ought to go only so far as to leave the largest role with the workers themselves. This includes insurance schemes.[21] Modern industry and technology should prompt government to legislate the organization of both labor and management into groups defined by trade or branch of industry. These groups should be allowed to differentiate themselves according to the fundamental convictions of its members regarding the right approach to the social question. Workers of Christian persuasion must be entirely free to participate in the overall national organization of labor. Until this happens, serious conflicts should be made subject to compulsory arbitration, and both parties will have to learn to accept its decisions as binding.

We Calvinists must not let ourselves be blindsided. Professor Sombart has fulminated against Calvinists, and not without grounds. Yet as the history of Calvinism shows, the warmest defense of the working classes has always come from precisely our circles. Sombart is right in that Calvinism, as soon as it lets go of its religious ideal, leans toward capitalism.[22] Witness

---

20. The Kuyper ministry at the time countered the strike by tabling a bill to prohibit strikes by railway workers in the public interest and to commission an official inquiry into their grievances. When next the socialist movement protested by calling a general strike, the government called out the army, which, joined by men from the Protestant and Catholic labor movement, nipped the nationwide strike in the bud.

21. Kuyper deplored government-guaranteed income schemes, advocating instead insurance plans to which workers personally contributed through paying premiums. See elsewhere in this volume, pp. 245–52.

22. Kuyper refers to Werner Sombart, *Der Bourgeois* (Munich and Leipzig: Duncker & Humblot, 1913), 323.

Dutch history: the glorious period of our struggle for religious freedom was followed by the pursuit of gold and gain, which in the end killed all higher ideals. That is exactly why we never flagged in urging the maintenance of our spiritual foundation. Our hope for the future must not lie with unions and wage hikes and insurance schemes. A Christian's confidence must lie solely with God—in keeping with the words of Jesus: "After all these things do the Gentiles seek; but you with all your needs must rely solely on what you possess in your heavenly Father" [based on Matt 6:32].

WHAT NEXT?

TEXT INTRODUCTION

Kuyper's opening address to a meeting of the deputies of the Antirevolutionary Party begins by sketching the general political situation in the Netherlands and introducing the government's plans (1) to grant full parity of public funding for private primary schools and (2) to introduce universal manhood suffrage and proportional representation. He then addresses the need of the Antirevolutionary Party, in the face of the imminent general elections, to return to one of the main planks in its historic program: addressing the social question with legislation that meets the needs of the working classes.

SOURCE: Abraham Kuyper, *Wat Nu? Rede ter opening van de Deputatenvergadering gehouden te Utrecht op 2 Mei 1918* [What Next? Address at the opening of the deputies meeting held in Utrecht on 2nd May 1918] (Kampen: Kok, 1918), 13–24. Translated and abridged by Harry Van Dyke.

WHAT NEXT?

OPENING ADDRESS AT THE MEETING OF DEPUTIES
OF THE ANTIREVOLUTIONARY PARTY, UTRECHT,
MAY 2, 1918

We need not be afraid that people are feeling discouraged. The flourishing
of your own party reflects how interest in politics has grown. The number
of our local voters' clubs has for years exceeded that of the other parties.
Yet this has not stopped antirevolutionaries this year from organizing new
clubs in remote corners of the country. Meanwhile, rival parties and fac-
tions are sprouting up like mushrooms. It is as if we are entering a wholly
new electoral landscape. Our party's basis must remain, however, the same
as it always has been. "By the grace of God" must continue to animate
the life of our party. Our driving force must come from Above; otherwise
we are revolutionary. We remain Calvinists; we continue in the direction
marked out for us by Groen van Prinsterer;[1] and our leaders are to deepen
our understanding of the kind of politics we represent.

Yet all this does not answer the question *What next?* What is the foremost
political issue that should no longer have to wait for a solution? That is not
for us to choose. The facts themselves determine it. We are a political party,
but the social question pushes itself to the foreground with ever-increasing

---

1. G. Groen van Prinsterer (1801–76) was Kuyper's predecessor as leader of the anti-
    revolutionary movement.

intensity. We may separate political action and social life, but the two are increasingly intertwined. That could become dangerous if the social sphere seeks to dictate political decision making. Just look at the socialists, who turn the logical and holy order upside down.

But since the social leaders on our side insist on being called *Christian* trade unionists, there should no longer be any doubt where we stand with each other. The social component of our movement must not become a political force, and our political leaders must not underestimate the significance of that component. Our Christian people in both camps (social and political) must appreciate both their power and their mutual dependence. Both must come into their own. Our party must be on guard against every violation of social justice, and those members who work in the labor movement must be careful not to submerge their political life in the social stream. Since the most pressing question is currently about the right relationship between government and society, any further postponement of fundamental reflection on it would incur penalties.

Turning our attention to this crucial problem should not be allowed to delay the definitive solution to the schools question.[2] It would be a betrayal of our past, now that victory is within sight, to interrupt even for a moment our half century of battling for our free schools. The "free school" remains an inspiring slogan that adorns our banner in gold letters. But I dare say that before the next four years are over we may retire from that battle, and then our stalwart teachers will join the vanguard of those who are ready to tackle the social question.

***

The only thing to watch out for is a wrong starting point. We must make sure that social action remains free and independent. We must also, however, secure the backing government owes society. The former view that the state and the law have to stay out of social life has had its day. Instead, circumstances beyond its control have increasingly obliged government to enable social life to develop freely precisely by putting it under the regulation and protection of the law. The state can even be obliged to take a complete social service under its wings, such as the postal and telegraph

---

2. The struggle for educational justice was a hallmark of Kuyper's political career. For more, see *On Education*.

service, paid for from the national budget. Many more such things used to be private affairs but have gradually been devolved to local and regional governments. River banks and polder dykes are a case in point. Today's traffic is unthinkable without the vast systems of national and provincial roadways, and no one would dare enter our coastal waters without the government-sponsored pilot service. Local authorities have to take care of a fire department and street lighting. The government has to provide not only armed forces against possible enemies but also police services against rioters and criminals. In former days, no man left the house without a dagger at his side, and a society lady would not venture out without an armed chaperone.

All this fell into disuse when governments intensified law enforcement. Governments gradually accepted the obligation to provide ever more services, not because they were hungry for power but because the need was there. Reinforcing this trend was the growth of science and technology. Steam and electrical power grew to such a scale that it could endanger whole neighborhoods and protective legislation had to be introduced. The intention was not to set up state factories but to foster improved conditions for private industry. Accordingly, no one complains about all that government involvement; on the contrary, people keep asking for more of it—to such a degree, in fact, that government constantly has to take over more activities from its citizens.

In a large city, it is almost no longer possible for the water mains to be run on a private basis. Sewer pipes must be maintained along great stretches. Since the late 1700s guilds can no longer serve the needs of the working classes. The massive scale of industry makes former relationships in the workplace resemble child's play; a single employer today can have hundreds, sometimes thousands of employees. Working people became exposed to new hazards. Periodic unemployment reduced them and their family to poverty, and better-paying jobs were available only to skilled laborers. But nobler industries enriched the lives of working people, who began to insist on better housing, clothing, nutrition, and better schools for their children. Provisions against illness had to expand. All this led naturally to working people coming together to discuss their needs and interests, leading to unions and cooperatives. In industrial towns but also in rural areas, former living standards were no longer considered adequate. Primary education had to be completely overhauled and school attendance made compulsory until the age of 14. The workday had to be shortened to below 12 hours.

Wage earners gradually realized they were becoming different persons. Their experience of bondage, or at least utter dependence, had caused them to cry out for deliverance; they longed to be free people, to be on a par before God with their lords and masters. After a new period of oppression, they were able to rise in society, and when government improved the schools, they rose even higher. Today their deliverance is a fact. Compared to half a century ago, working people occupy a much higher position. Their mind is enriched, their knowledge of life in the world is greater, they possess twice the power and influence of former days. This has rapidly led, quite naturally, to the realization that there is strength in combined action. The working classes in all developed countries no longer consist of isolated individuals but have tripled their power by consorting together. Of course not everybody has shared in their rise; the majority still lag behind. But they do have their leaders, some of them of great talent. The rest of society no longer faces isolated working people; the workers' world has come together and operates as a coherent whole.

∗∗∗

Initially this development lead to inevitable yet gross one-sidedness. The newly formed groups talked only of wages, apprenticeship programs, cooperatives, emancipation, and material progress. In general they failed to raise the worker's sense of duty toward the nation as a whole and to reinforce their ties to the other classes. This was not lacking altogether; in 1903, and again recently, Christian workers showed they were all too aware that they were not free to follow the revolution-minded on their revolutionary path.[3] Hence their serious endeavor to set themselves apart in *Christian* trade unions and cling to a higher principle. But they did not yet experience their life situation as a unity. They did not sufficiently sense the need to join their struggle for improving the position of workers to their calling also to serve higher interests. Their piety ran the risk of becoming entirely separate from their class struggle. A dualism arose, from which a monism alone can save them. Godliness and the uplift of the worker should not be two ideals that run parallel, but should melt into one. Strong families, social involvement, and political action should well up from one and the

---

3. Kuyper is referring here to the railroad strike of 1903 and the anarchist riots in Amsterdam the previous summer.

same spring. That is what God's Word teaches us, what Calvin adjured us, what Groen and Elout impressed upon us.[4] Our interest must not be our only guide; our eyes should be focused on the honor of God, the future of our country, and the spiritual formation of our people.

This explains the urgent need for our political organization not to allow social action to slip, but also, conversely, for social action not to withdraw from our political struggle. The moment social developments had reached the point of united action and political aspirations, social and political groups should have entered into mutual consultation. And since that hour has come, the answer to the question *What next?* can be no other than this: after the education question has been laid to rest, our attention is drawn as a matter of course to the interest of the working classes.

I thought the hour was ripe when I was a cabinet minister at the beginning of this century. That is why I included the apprenticeship system in my bill, tried to establish a teachers' college for industrial arts, and tabled bills that included a comprehensive insurance scheme. All to no avail. And although I succeeded in opening up technical, commercial, and agricultural colleges, our fishing industry still lacks such a school. But since then the situation has ripened, and I warmly welcome what the Christian labor federation has achieved thus far. The question *What next?* can have no other answer than the unanimous declaration that our next task is to bring the social question in its entirely into harmony with our antirevolutionary politics.

Our antirevolutionary movement must be reunited; social action and political calling must be tightly knit together. Our politics must impart momentum to the social question, and conversely, the social struggle must connect with our nation's historical development. That will surely come about if the honor of God unites us in a sacred bond. That was the starting point of our movement and will have to remain our strength to the end. We may see fractures at first, but, as in the past, it will be a sign of *reculer pour mieux sauter*: go back a little, to make a better jump forward. Should the party let go of its life principle even for a moment, it will perish, never to rise again. So do not slow down and do not hang back. Let us renew our

---

4. Besides theologian and church Reformer John Calvin (1509–64), Kuyper is referring here to two predecessors as political leaders in the antirevolutionary movement: G. Groen van Prinsterer, already mentioned above, and Pieter Jacob Elout van Soeterwoude (1805–93).

vow to be faithful to God. Let us renew our strong bonds of brotherhood. May our prayers bear us up in every new struggle. And let us thank God for every new victory he sends us.

Brothers, we were always a minority and we will stay a minority. But what saved our fathers will help us too to persevere. To forsake God is to lose all, but to persevere in God will assure a future for us and our offspring—a future in God's glory.

I thank you.

MEDITATIONS

TEXT INTRODUCTION

Kuyper's devotional articles are a treasure trove. From the early 1870s until November 1920, the month he died, he wrote over 2,200. Even during his time as prime minister (1901–5) and during his trip to countries surrounding the Mediterranean (1905–6), his weekly flow of reflections continued unabated. Most of them appeared in *De Heraut*, the weekly religious newspaper Kuyper founded in 1877. Many were collected and republished in book form, both in Dutch and in English, and have been among the most widely disseminated of Kuyper's writings. They are striking for the fresh and original interpretation they bring to the Bible text that serves as the epigraph to each piece. Some appear to be inspired by a thought or idea in the Bible passage that set Kuyper's imagination alight. Others seem to be occasioned more by a topic that was first on the author's mind before he found a fitting biblical verse on which to base his reflections. Regardless of their origin, the meditations often sparkle with profound insight, both into the challenges of a Christian's faith life in general and into Kuyper's understanding of his own vocation in the world. As such, they provide not only windows into Kuyper's soul, but worked examples of the word-world integration he sought to promote. They tease out some of what Kuyper believed were the contemporary implications of biblical faith for Christian discipleship in every area of life.

The following nine meditations have been chosen to illustrate how Kuyper reflected on real-life issues in the realm of business and ethics. Among these are thrift, honesty, generosity, fairness, greed, debt, and the worship of money. While Kuyper's specific prescriptions are timebound, all these issues are timeless—helping to ensure that his reflections on them are pertinent in any age, not just the one in which Kuyper lived.

Source: For each meditation, a footnote identifies the original place of its publication as a weekly article as well as its reprint, if available, in a volume of collected meditations published under Kuyper's name. Some of these collections have appeared in English, but the following are fresh translations by Harry Van Dyke.

MEDITATIONS

DO NOT WITHHOLD GOOD FROM THOSE
TO WHOM IT IS DUE

Do not withhold good from those to whom it is
due, when it is in your power to do it.
Proverbs 3:27

Our forebears practiced strict *honesty* when it came to business dealings.[1] In every country and every marketplace, a Dutch merchant was regarded as solidity personified. Those in business or who engaged in trade in the old Dutch Republic were intent (sometimes to the point of pettiness) on prompt and scrupulous delivery of their wares and payment of their debts.

That was not due to them personally, as if they were different and better people than we are. It was due to the Word of God that was preached among them, due to the power of divine ordinances that had been impressed upon them, and due to the belief that all those who acknowledge God in their dealings would be blessed by God.

As it is written in Proverbs 3:10, "Honor the LORD with your wealth and with the firstfruits of all your harvest; *then your barns will be filled with plenty,*

---

1. "Onthoud het goed aan zijn meester niet," *De Heraut,* March 17, 1889; repr. in *Gomer voor den Sabbath* (Amsterdam: Wormser, 1889), 21–25.

and your vats will be bursting with wine." This is an instance of dying in order to live as it applies to your possessions. Those who keep what they have will become poor, and those who give of their possessions, God will make rich.

That word was made good in the case of our forebears. As a result of the powerful preaching of God's law, they had been impregnated with a deep awareness of the sin of dishonesty. It fostered strict honesty in commercial practices. It put its stamp on all trade and industry. If they were ever tempted by the prospect of dishonest profit, their very cupidity advised against it. For they firmly believed that strict honesty in the long run would drop still greater credit and thereby higher profits into their laps. Their maxim was: *honesty is the best policy.*

There were, of course, exceptions. The activities of large trading companies were sometimes disgraceful. But that did not affect the commercial norms of ordinary people. They remained solid and prompt.

Today, alas, things are different. The power of the Word is gone from our people. Instead we coast on the tranquil waters of civilization. The upshot is that on all sides we have to be on guard against fraud, deception, and swindle. We can hardly trust merchandise anymore. In all branches of commerce ugly practices have become the norm. People live in debt rather than on credit. Unrepayable debts and bankruptcies are paraded as badges of honor.

As a result, public morality and public norms have become lax. Much passes that cannot pass muster before God, nor before people who live by their conscience.

You say: "That is true about the world, but not about God's children." To say this is to forget that God's children can be infected by the evil practices of their peers.

All trade and commerce have certain norms, and you have to deal with people who have grown up with evil practices. If you want to oppose these practices, the whole market turns against you, business becomes difficult, and you suffer damage.

In that struggle most people succumb and live by two consciences: one for private life and one for business. Orthodox sermons nowadays remain stuck in a one-sided emphasis on the mysteries of faith. They are unfamiliar with a robust and penetrating proclamation of God's law as it applies to everyday life. Even the best of Christian businesspeople cave in and become complicit in shady practices, albeit from a distance.

This is an evil that must be combated—an iniquity that Scripture addresses with these words: "Do not withhold good from those to whom it is due."

The strongest application of these words is in paying one's debts. Debt is money that is not due to you but to someone else. It is theirs, not yours, and you have the God-given duty to return it to them as soon as possible.

Just as you would not keep a child that was lost but would hasten to return it to its parents, so you are to treat your debts. Debt is like a lost child that cannot stay with you but must be taken home.

This commandment should be especially sacred to you if you employ workmen. Scripture does not even allow you to keep the wages of a laborer *overnight* [Deut 24:15]. Prompt and strict payment of their wages is one of the most delicate and sacred rights of the working classes. The Lord, whose eyes range throughout the earth, pays attention to this.

The same goes for *paying one's bills*. Here again some people are unbelievably lax. They have bills outstanding that are two or more years in arrears. It has been reported that a rich man bought a chest full of silverware and boasted that the purchase was made possible from the interest he saved by deliberately paying his bills late. This is theft pure and simple. It is stolen money. It is interest that should have gone to the creditor. What makes things worse: once this bad practice becomes common, the creditor will be clever enough to inflate the bill in advance. Buyer and vendor thereby both become cheats.

Borrowing money will suffer the same fate. People used to avoid having to borrow. They knew that borrowed money must be paid back, and they would rather eat dry bread than find themselves unable to pay back the loan on time. Today other notions prevail. People who would be embarrassed to ask you for a gift now approach you for a "loan." You can hardly regard it as doing them a favor; it's purely a business transaction. They solemnly promise to pay it back, principal and interest. But their mind is elsewhere. Once the money is spent, they think that borrowed money can "sleep." This evil is so rampant that it's common for lenders to think: "Oh well, I had lost that money already!"

These practices will become a curse for our society. The divine ordinances are pushed aside. Dependability vanishes. Trust is lost. And the result is that business goes downhill, market advantage declines, and countless people file for bankruptcy. And the punishment for all this is to forfeit the blessing of the Lord that once made our nation rich.

"Do not withhold good from those to whom it is due" is the only cure for this cancer—provided you start by applying this golden rule to how you relate to the Lord. For all your possessions are God's. He only gave them to you so that you could be a steward of them, a steward who every year parts with a fixed portion to give to God and God's poor.

Whether you call this portion the firstfruits or the tithes does not matter. What matters is that a fixed portion of the wealth at your disposal is set apart for his service and his work. If in recent years our Christian people have fared somewhat better, it is because of the way God has challenged us. Through events in church and education, he has made it imperative for us, in a more generous measure than before, to no longer hold back this portion from him.

Spending your firstfruits and tithes on personal consumption or invest-ment, rather than on serving God and his poor, is nothing less than *stealing from God* the portion that he has reserved for himself. This is not permitted. It's a sin. It is an evil that meets with God's righteous judgment.

The Lord hears the cry when his church languishes in poverty and your schools have trouble meeting their budgets. He hears the cry when the blind and the sick are neglected. And he hears the cry of his poor, when poor Lazarus dies while the rich man revels in luxury.

This portion of your wealth is not yours. It is God's. The Lord is the master of that portion. Woe to you if you withhold even a fraction of this portion from its true Owner.

~~~~~~~~~~~~~~~~~~~~~~

MONEY IS THE ANSWER FOR EVERYTHING

Money answers everything.
Ecclesiastes 10:19

Of all the centuries of human history, ours has become the slave of money.[2] Money was a force in former centuries too, a force that made one person into a miser, led another to theft and murder, and moved a third to sell their body and honor. Yet money had not yet become king.

The reason for this was that money, with its inherent power to generate more money as though it were a living force, was then still in its infancy.

---

2. "Het geld verantwoordt alles," *De Heraut*, February 10, 1889; repr. in *Gomer voor den Sabbath*, 177–81.

What is now called "the power of capital" was not yet alive in the popular conscious. What mattered was hard cash.

In our time, things have changed. Money, under the name of credit, has cast its shadow on the wall. It demands that the children of our age will kneel not only before real gold but also before this shadow of gold. This has enabled money to multiply its empire tenfold. Gold and credit together now constitute the power of money. Just as you can make your shadow larger by taking steps backwards, eventually making it gargantuan, so money uses credit to expand its shadowy image to ever-larger proportions. The gigantic growth of credit has gradually reached such infinite dimensions that today it creates the impression that capital is God.

It is often said that people worship a *golden calf*. Not so. What the Israelites worshipped in the desert was definitely not the power of money. All they intended was to have a visible sign of Jehovah's presence, and to that end they made that image of gold. It brought them no money; instead, it took their money as a sacrifice.

But what has crept in today is the worship of capital, of money in its twin form of gold and credit. Almost everybody yearns after that power, and adulates whoever possesses it. No moral sacrifice seems too great to grab hold of this power and to become the priest of wealth and fortune.

God's people must take note of this. And then they must affirm that this terrible power, too, has not been created by Satan but by God. Satan creates nothing. Gold in the mine and nuggets on the river bed were made by the Lord. He created silver ore. His are all the diamonds and rubies in the world. Still more, the gift of sharp minds, resourcefulness, and keen management—the gift by means of which the money grubbers gather the sheaves from the world's fields and store them in their barns—this gift is mental power that God created and now activates and sustains in them.

In fact, you have to go a step further. The whole idea of money as a universal means of exchange, incapable by itself of furnishing pleasure yet with the capacity to provide everyone with pleasure—is not an evil human invention but came forth from the order of creation: a single standard of value for all things of worth was part of the nature of things.

Except that humans have abused this power and caused it to degenerate. Instead of putting this tremendous power in the service of justice and mercy, they have used it to sit on God's throne and play God. Big capitalists who go with the current of this world feel like gods. What could harm them!

With their money they can do anything! The whole world lies at their feet. For the sake of their money they are worshipped by all who depend on them.

Once arrogant pride entered money, it became the means for people to give free rein to their passions, to trample other people underfoot, to ride like a juggernaut over other nations, crushing them under the wheels of their victory chariot. Our century was placed on Mount Carmel to face the choice: God or gold? Who will be God? The Father of our Lord Jesus Christ, or ... this terrifying mammon?

Every child of God, when faced with this question, will of course side with Elijah and choose for Jehovah. But does that choice touch their hearts and carry over into their lives? In ancient Israel there were many who traveled every Passover to Jerusalem, only to return to the heights and the groves and there bend the knee to images of Baal. And, alas, that is how it still is. It is easier for a camel to go through the eye of a needle than for a rich person to enter the kingdom of heaven [see Matt 19:24].

It is astounding how many Christians are enslaved to their money! Forever pinching and scraping. Holding back in case it might cost money but rushing in if money can be made. This growth in sin was to be expected. It is the sin of our century, and Christians who live in this century and fail to guard the issues of their heart cannot but fall prey to much temptation. This sin, therefore, is mortally dangerous.

Dangerous, not just for big capitalists, but even more so for young men and women who have nothing. It is a sin that has so infected every social class that thirst for money has become the dominant trait of our time.

Money captivates; it stimulates the senses and fills the mind. People obsess about money and brood over money until it takes possession of their heart. Then making money becomes their goal in life and losing money puts a nail in their coffin.

I pass over lotteries, casinos, and reckless speculation. Those who are guilty of these things have taken another step along this evil road. They are people who in their feverish chase after money become delirious—until God meets them along the way, throws out of their hands everything they have scraped together, sobers them up, and brings them again on their knees before him.

God's children should see to it that they wrestle free from this sin—in all sorts of ways. They are to confront the sin of chasing after wealth and oppose it with the sharing of wealth. They ought to practice mercy for everyone in the household of faith and for all those who are needy. This is not so that they can decorate their god of gold with a halo of charity, as so many do who save 30,000 guilders a year and then throw a few guilders to the poor. On a regular basis, instead, they should consciously and deliberately break a piece off their idol and crush it on the altar of the Lord. Now that money has become Satan's tool, God's children must put money in the service of God's kingdom. To give richly, generously, copiously is to heal a wound in the heart, and to provide an escape from temptation.

That is why everyone must give. Including those who have little. For all need healing. Rich capitalists who are already swimming in money should never hoard it give their profit for each year to the service of the Lord. That is what they received it for. They are stewards of the Lord.

There is still more. A child of God should refuse to participate in the sin of those who grant honor and influence to money-grubbers merely for their money. In the eyes of Christians, someone with money but without love, without faith, should count for nothing, while a poor child of God who offers love and praise should be regarded as truly precious and truly great.

All children of God should see to it that they will never, from fear of loss, betray their Lord in the slightest thing or leave their duty before God unfulfilled. They must not rejoice overly much about financial gain, and not grieve overly much about financial loss. They should be detached from loss and gain, so as to cleave all the more to God.

Whichever way you look at it, for God's child it always comes down to this choice. Whereas the power of money is the idol of the age, the Lord our Righteousness needs to be our God. This means our money must be made subject to the power, the commandment, the service and the honor of God.

WOE TO THOSE WHO JOIN HOUSE TO HOUSE

*Woe to those who join house to house, who add field to field, until there is
no more room, and you are made to dwell alone in the midst of the land.*
Isaiah 5:8

There are six well-known "Woe to them" passages in the prophet Isaiah.[3] The first of them warns against the service of mammon, and against greed and covetousness as the beginning of national self-destruction.

---

3. "Eerste Jesaiaansche Wee U!," *De Heraut*, May 12, 1895; repr. in *Als gij in uw huis zit*, 2nd imprint (Amsterdam: Höveker & Wormser, 1899), 200–205.

People had little free capital in the days of Isaiah. Their wealth was bound up in real estate—houses and land. That colors the first *Woe to you!* as it addresses the thirst for wealth in the form of houses and fields.

This kind of sinful greed provides an argument for the perverse system of land nationalization. It also explains how God-fearing people could for a time dream that nationalization of land would save the future.[4] Although that system is to be feared rather than cheered, we frankly admit that its promoters derive strength from the kernel of truth it contains.

Overly large landholding is rooted in sin. It militates against the ordinances of God. It ends by disrupting the divinely ordained relationship between the land and the inhabitants of that land.

Long ago Calvin observed how foolish it is to want to enlarge one's house until many rooms in it stand empty, while other people barely have enough room to live in. Or how senseless it is to occupy so much land that others whom God has placed there have to evacuate it, whereas the earth was given us as a common living space.[5]

Delitzsch, a prince among the exegetes of our century, wrote in the same vein:

> "They, the insatiable, would not rest till, after every smaller piece of landed property had been swallowed by them, the whole land had come into their possession, and no one beside themselves was settled in the land" (Job 22:8). Such covetousness was all the more reprehensible, because the law of Israel provided so very stringently and carefully, that as far as possible there should be an equal distribution of the soil.[6]

Isaiah's pronouncement of *Woe to you* contains a firm and sharp condemnation of the practice of bringing large areas of land under one owner. That must not happen. Even governments should not allow it.

---

4. Probable reference to an idea circulating among the leadership of the Christian social organization Patrimonium, which was dissuaded from the idea of land nationalization at the Social Congress of 1891.

5. See CCS 7:172: "When men, swollen with ambition, make superfluous additions to their houses, only that they may live in greater luxury, and when one person alone occupies a building which might serve for the habitation of many families, this undoubtedly is empty ambition, and ought justly to be blamed."

6. Carl Friedrich Keil and Franz Delitzsch, *Commentary on the Old Testament* (Peabody, MA: Hendrickson, 1996), 7:108.

And yet, this fearsome *Woe to you!*, from which five other woes will follow, does not condemn the wrong kind of land ownership as such, but the sinful spirit it betrays.

This first *Woe to you!* curses and condemns in every human being, and in every nation, the sinful propensity to make the acquisition of a fortune—and always acquiring more possessions and more money—a goal in life.

It is a *Woe!* against the unholy fever of capitalism.

It is a *Woe!* against mammon and against all who dance around the altar of mammon the dance of greed and covetousness.

It goes without saying that this *Woe to you!* is also a protest against the sinful custom of taking over an entire street for erecting grand houses and gardens for the benefit of a few well-to-do families, while numerous families of the lower classes are put away in cellars in slums.

Calvin rightly denounced this practice as a form of ambition, vanity, and heartlessness that must be condemned. Chrysostom had earlier chastised his Byzantine listeners with the words: "Your cupidity extends so far that at last you would deprive the poor even of sunlight and free air."[7]

It has actually come to this. So the current movement to build better houses for the working classes, where those who have little can enjoy God's sweet sunlight and breathe fresh air, deserves the warmest support of every Christian.

But aside from this, in the first *Woe to you!* lies a warning to believers not to pin their faith on building large houses or palatial residences, or laying out large country estates,[8] but instead to be content with a moderate home spacious enough for normal use.

---

7. This sentiment attributed to John Chrysostom (ca. 349–407) is quoted in Calvin's commentary on Isa 5:8. See John Chrysostom, "The Homilies on the Statues," in *Saint Chrysostom: On the Priesthood, Ascetic Treatises, Select Homilies and Letters, Homilies on the Statues*, ed. Philip Schaff, trans. W. R. W. Stephens, A Select Library of the Nicene and Post-Nicene Fathers of the Christian Church 9, First Series (New York: Christian Literature, 1889), 2.19, p. 351: "God giveth all those things with liberality, which are more necessary than riches; such, for example, as the air, the water, the fire, the sun; all things of this kind. ... For if these necessaries were not common, perhaps they who are rich, practising their usual covetousness, would strangle those who were poor. For if they do this for the sake of money, much rather would they do so for the things referred to."

8. Kuyper is reflecting the real-estate terms used in Isa 5:9.

When choosing a house, the criterion should be its intended *use*, not how spacious or grand it is. Here, too, vanity can play a role, and the desire to gain advantage over others.

Is that not the root of the sin of greed, to be out to exalt oneself, and in order to reach that goal, to push back others and crowd them out?

The prophet brings this out in no uncertain terms by saying: You will join house to house and lay field to field until there is no place left for the other inhabitants and you are left to live alone. It will not come to that because their power falls short. Nevertheless, as Calvin says, as much as it depends on them they go about as though they would like to push out everyone else from their place and their property, so that the evicted will just have to live under the open sky or move elsewhere.[9]

The fever of capitalism breeds envy of neighbor.

While it is pure folly to dream of equality of property in a world where people are totally unequal in strength and talent, nevertheless there are *limits*. Rich and poor will always be with us, but that does not take away from the fact that some people are too rich, some too poor. And that is exactly the grievance that greed and covetousness are unwilling to acknowledge.

One person accumulates wealth, even though he knows that it has been skillfully and cleverly wheedled from others. Whoever can square this with their conscience will gain power. That power gives them the respect and prestige for which most people make way. This is how all that striving after money, fortune, and possessions infects the whole nation like a toxic fever. Torn away from higher ideals and higher vocations, the nation calls down the judgment *Woe to you!* from Almighty God. Even the purest thing known on earth, the love between a man and a woman and the sacredness of marriage, comes to fall under the same judgment. People choose a spouse not because they love the person, their soul, their true being, but because they love the money and the house and the land they will bring to the marriage.

Do not say that this may take place among the higher classes but that ordinary people, particularly of the lower classes, are free of this thirst for money and possessions, and for the power of wealth. The facts show otherwise.

---

9. See Calvin, *CCS* 7:172: "Such persons act as if they had a right to drive out other men, and to be the only persons that enjoyed a house or a roof, and as if other men ought to live in the open air, or must go somewhere else to find an abode."

True, among God's children in the lower classes there is a highly respectable group that lives soberly, works diligently, and earns reasonably. From those reasonable earnings this class finds greater delight in giving and distributing generously than in hoarding.

But this is not true about the general spirit in the nation.

If you listen to young people as they talk about their futures, to our merchants as they dream out loud in their leisure time, to our farmers as they plan the way ahead, and to our middle classes as they let down their nets in the currents of the economy, you will notice all too often and all too clearly that the money fever throbs in the blood of our people. Indeed, the thermometer shows some very worrisome readings. People are lusting after money, dreaming of money, chasing after money. In many circles, and in many families, people do not own their money, but their money owns them.

The reason why this is so dangerous is that the boundary between what is dutiful and legitimate on the one hand, and sinful and reprehensible on the other, is not so easy to draw.

Someone asks: Am I not allowed to be smart in my business? The answer is: You would be amiss if you neglected it. You have to be alert, and keep careful watch, in the vocation to which God has called you.

Another asks: Am I not allowed to earn money and save up for my wife and children? Again the answer is: You would be remiss if you thought only of yourself and at your death left your wife and children in dire poverty.

But now comes the difficulty.

A person lives his life, a family carries on its existence, they are all God's creatures, and none of them thinks about God. They have a soul, but they let that soul starve, dry up, wither. They are traveling to their eternal destination, but until the day they die their minds are only on houses and fields, money and possessions here on earth. They think of nothing else. They talk about nothing else. They daydream about it and dream about it in their sleep.

This is how father and mother are. Then they get children. Those children imbibe the selfsame mammon spirit. They too catch the toxic fever for money. The whole household turns into a small mammon temple.

At the next-door neighbors, left and right, the same story. Soon the spirit of the city is infected, then that that of the towns and villages. In the end, the spirit of the nation as a whole is infected. That is when the Lord sends his *Woe to you!* upon the nation and prepares it for destruction.

Only one spirit can combat the toxins and provide an antidote. That is the Spirit of Christ, the Spirit of God who speaks through his mouthpieces and witnesses, the Spirit of the Word.

That is why it is so dreadful when Christian families are infected by that insatiable, base spirit of mammon. For then all is lost. Then the abomination has penetrated the sanctuary. Then the altar of mammon is carried into the holy places, and God is provoked to his face by his own children.

Let it therefore be said to all Christian households and let it be impressed upon their hearts that they are to witness against that unholy spirit; to banish that unholy mammon; to put their highest good in God, not money; and through capacious—if needs be extravagant—generosity to lift the evil spell which, on account of money and as a result of money, still rests upon so many Christian families.

―――――――――――――

WOE TO THOSE WHO RISE EARLY IN THE MORNING

Woe to those who rise early in the morning, that they may run after strong drink, who tarry late into the evening as wine inflames them!
Isaiah 5:11

The first "Woe unto them!" turned against the growing pursuit of fortune, of goods and money—against the insatiable desire to add house to house, field to field.[10] It was directed not just at a few money-grubbers but at the lust for money that was gaining ground among the people as a whole, and eventually infected the circles of the pious.

Remember, it is always *the people of God* to whom these bitter woes are directed. "Judgment must begin with the household of God."[11]

But now hear the second "Woe to you!" This time it is not against enslavement to money, but against the opulence and to the wantonness that results from it.

"Woe to those," the prophet calls out,

---

10. "Tweede Jesaiaansche Wee U!," *De Heraut*, May 19, 1895; repr. in *Als gij in uw huis zit*, 205–9.

11. See 1 Pet 4:17. Kuyper does not quote this text but instead makes the same point with a verse from the Dutch poet Willem Bilderdijk (1756–1831), which can be translated as: "When a people must be punished for its sin / Its soul first spoils *the church within*."

> Woe to those who rise early in the morning, that they may run
> after strong drink, who tarry late into the evening as wine
> inflames them! They have lyre and harp, tambourine and flute
> and wine at their feasts, but they do not regard the deeds of
> the Lord, or see the work of his hands. [Isa 5:11–12]

This second stage of a nation's deterioration and moral demise does not begin with evil intent but is the inevitable consequence of too great an accumulation of money and the growth of personal fortunes. For those who amass money are more often hoarders than spendthrifts, adhering to the simple lifestyle in which they were raised. But when they die and the money ends up in the hands of their children, things usually take a turn for the worse. The children do not know from their parents the attachment to money, but they do feel a strong urge to enjoy that money. In it is a hidden magical power they want to uncover, as it will allow them to buy a world of luxuries and pleasures. Their parents gathered it, but their children want to show what it is really worth.

That is when the simple life goes by the wayside, when opulence begins to exert its seductive power, and wanton revelry is the ash that remains of the charred wealth.

This is how it went in Egypt and Babylon, in Samaria and Damascus, in Athens and Rome. Closer to home, this is also what happened to our country when it emerged from the war of liberation against Spain. That is when it saw the treasures of East and West glide into its harbors. Consequently, the search for God steadily declined, and the quest for gold steadily increased. Mammon gave way to wealth and luxury, and then wantonness, until in the second half of the eighteenth century, when life in our stately dwellings and old-fashioned country houses turned scandalous, God put an end to it all by letting the French confiscate our wealth, and flogging us with the scourge of Napoleon.

Today we see the same downward slide. Since the middle of the nineteenth century, money has started to flow again in or country, and before we have even arrived at the close of the century we are seeing wealth growing hand over fist. This is followed by revelry in wild drinking bouts and in books and plays that make a mockery of modesty and shame. Do not think that this is being said because here and there a few self-indulgent nabobs or conscienceless misfits can be found. Every age and every country has its scoundrels, yet that does not ruin the nation so long as the public conscience strongly protests against such practices.

No, what is being denounced here and what this *Woe to you!* addresses is the situation where prosperity has begun to infect ever-wider circles of people, including even Christians, and when the sober and solemn tone of the public square is increasingly drowned out by the drone of sensual pleasure. Then recreation and amusement become the goal of all classes in society, the prize that all chase after. Then a people has entered the second stage of its ruin, and the clarion call of the second *Woe!* repeats the urgent call to repent and come back.

This deterioration can be arrested only if God sends his judgments and replaces wealth with poverty, or else if the proclamation of the Word in no uncertain terms calls for repentance, halts the people in its headlong rush, warns against the pagan practices that are creeping in, and calls the people back to the quiet and peaceable home life that befits Christians.

Social healing will not come from attempts to "ennoble popular entertainment," nor from vain attempts to make such entertainment a form of "wholesome public utility." Such means are nothing but untempered mortar to plaster over the crack in the wall of national life to hide from view its imminent collapse. On this slippery slope a people can no longer save itself. Its constitution is too much weakened by affluence for it to find the energy and willpower. Sighing under the tyranny of fashion, to which is has become a slave, it has no choice but to go along with the trend and follow the path of opulence.

No, a people will only be saved by that core of the nation that keeps to the trusted paths, trembles before the Word, and clings to God. Jesus himself pronounced it: in that core alone is found *the salt* that can counteract the corruption. Not because those people are so much better, but because *the Word* continues to affect them and the Holy Spirit remains at work in them.

However, that arrest will not come unless the power of the Word is manifested in family life. Church attendance is a sham if the message of the Lord is not carried into homes.

That is why it is so wonderful that God teaches his people *to give*, trains them in the power of giving, makes them give ever more generously and ever more abundantly. For all that giving withdraws a lot of money from the wallet and so a lot of fuel from the furnace of luxury.

Those who give cheerfully to God have little left for luxuries. They will automatically live more soberly and more quietly and will avoid those circles, societies, and clubs where riotous revelry causes the bells on the fool's hat to jingle.

To things, therefore, should be emphasized in sermons about this *Woe to you!* First: give, give, always be giving. And second: avoid worldly circles where wealth and wantonness set the tone. Sermons should emphasize the tried and true wisdom of the old Calvinists: to eschew theater attendance, dancing, and card playing as inimical to the honor of God's people; to devote the Sabbath to God and not to the world; and to seek one's true happiness in civic virtue and quiet simplicity. This wisdom has stood the test of time and will still be effective—provided father and mother are not so self-absorbed as to think: if I just control myself, all is well.

No, discipline for life must be applied especially to our children and our young people. Families are stains on the church when parents restrain themselves but allow their children to run wild, despising their baptism and letting them grow up not as children of God but as children of the world.

God's children also knows of riches, but wholly different riches: the riches of the soul, when their hearts enjoy communion with God and when they live in fellowship with him.

After all, that is what is added to the second *Woe to you!* in the very next verse: people who allow themselves to be carried off like prey "do not regard the deeds of the LORD, or see the work of his hands" [Isa 5:12].

When the artificial light of the world blinds our eyes, the splendor of the firmament hides in darkness. Similarly, when the affluence of the world has captured our hearts, we lose our sense and taste for spiritual delights, and our vision for beholding the wondrous works of God.

That is the just punishment that comes on the heels of the splendor of wealth. It locks you up inside this world and makes invisible the horizon of eternity, the glory of God. This is the way gold draws a people away from God and earthly riches draw a people away from God's glory. A people's downward slide goes ever deeper, its delight in earthly glory fades away, its wings lose their gold dust. It must either be brought to a halt, so that it can turn back to the living God, or it will with increasingly rapid steps head straight for its ruin.

A *Woe to you!* is not just a lament or a warning. It is a flash of lightning with which God will soon set fire to a nation.

LOVERS OF MONEY

The Pharisees, who were lovers of money, heard all
these things, and they ridiculed him.
Luke 16:14

There appears to be a hidden link between piety and love of money.[12]

It happens this way. As soon as a person surrenders to the ambition to be pious, to be seen as pious, and to associate with the pious, they are asked to make a great sacrifice. From now on they are to distance themselves from all those worldly pleasures and attractions that the apostle so vividly calls the "pride of life" [1 John 2:16].

To be pious does not go together with showing delight in glamorous festivities, boisterous banquets, frivolous parties, and obscene theater productions. It is only possible to be one of these two things, not both. Whoever is attracted by the laurels of piety must turn their heart away from those sensual pleasures and give up whatever is inconsistent with their new status.

But does this make such a person a saint? Is their heart now weaned from desire for outward things, for possessions and recognition? Is a convert now rid of their sinful nature? Those who are honest with themselves know better.

If it is a work of God in them, rather than a human imitation, a complete turnabout has indeed taken place in their heart. This turnabout is not yet visible, however, in the contours of his life. To be detached from "things that are on the earth" and to "set your minds on things that are above" can only be a reality from moment to moment, through ever-renewed grace and the continually renewing work of the Holy Spirit [see Col 3:2]. Their heart still houses, therefore, the sinful desire for glamor, greatness, and glory, but it is now redirected. Their piety forbids them from spending money, but "laying it up" (as their deceitful heart now sanctimoniously calls it) is legitimate. They are not allowed to spend it, because that would be worldly; but they may "lay it up" because that comes close, comparatively speaking, to the

---

12. "Die geldgierig waren," *De Heraut*, March 17, 1878; repr. in *Honig uit den rotssteen*, 2nd imprint (Amsterdam: Wormser, 1896), 1:30–32. The Dutch word *geldgierigheid* can be translated "love of money" or "greed." In this piece, these two English terms are used interchangeably wherever the word *geldgierigheid* occurs in the original.

virtue of thrift. Their piety is expressed in not squandering but saving; not being reckless but preserving what he has.

That is the sin in its first stage.

If one does not turn away from it and by grace escape from it and made to hate it, the evil gradually turns into what Scripture calls the love of money, or greed. One's heart becomes bound to money *as money*; one begins to look upon it as god, and so commits idolatry.

If this is not thwarted by a higher intervention, such as a financial blow or a nasty bankruptcy, this at first so seemingly innocent pull of the heart will in the end degenerate into an evil demon. It dares to refuse God money when he requires it and refuses people money when they cry out in dire need. Ultimately, it deems legitimate any means that can make that money grow.

Once it has reached this stage, the unholy seed sprouts, buds, and begins to bear its unholy fruits. Every obligation and every virtue is sacrificed to the slavery and abhorrent idolatry of the god called mammon.

This is how piety can gradually and automatically develop into greed. Pious people, far more than the children of this world, are exposed to the temptation of covetousness. Extraordinary grace is required to break with the world and yet to avoid an idolatrous relationship with one's money.

This explains why the prophets in Israel had to protest no sin more vigorously, unsparingly, and persistently, than the love of money. It is also why the Lord God, knowing full well what goes on in the hearts of his people, prescribed no commandments in greater detail than the commandments of mercy, sacrifice, and generosity. They were all fatherly measures to protect Israel against the money demon.

That is why Jesus associated the Pharisees, rather than the Sadducees, with greed. That's why the apostles constantly warn against this terrible sin. That's why Jesus says that whoever bows to mammon cannot kneel before God. That's why love of money is explicitly mentioned as a barrier to ecclesiastical office [see Luke 16:14; Matt 6:24; 1 Pet 5:1]. Indeed, that's why according to Scripture the love of money is *a root of all kinds of evils* and is numbered among those flagrant sins that shut a person out of the kingdom of God [1 Tim 6:10; 1 Cor 6:10].

Alas, the history of the church demonstrates all too well the necessity of these solemn warnings. Even in her best days, also in our country, there was no more melancholy and stinging tone struck by revival preachers than their lament about people's inability to distance themselves from earthly goods. Nothing had a more deadening and vitiating effect on people than their reliance on money in the bank, rather than on God's blessing from heaven. Oh, bitter irony of God's holy judgment! Nothing has made believers visibly *poorer* than their inability to disengage themselves from their money and to let go of that which in their hymns they refer to as "worldly dross."

Of course, we are mixing two type of pious people: the pious who want people to know they are pious, and the pious who are made so by God. As for the former, nothing is more caustic than the proverb quoted by the apostle: a dog returns to his own vomit, and a sow that is washed resumes her wallowing in the mire [2 Pet 2:22].

The other type are the true children of the kingdom. For their admonition and comfort we may add that most of them feel the spur of that sin coursing through their veins. Indeed, there is not one who does not by nature succumb to it. Not a few yield to it all the way into the second stage noted above. But this is generally only temporary, as God's grace helps them overcome that temptation. That grace is wonderfully at work, even in our own time. Yet when a money-loving believer is set free from their bondage to money, they disregard the Lord's compassion if they delight in the works of mercy which *they now do* rather than in the work of mercy that *was done for them.*

~~~~~~~~~~~~~~~~~~~~~~~~

LEFTOVER FRAGMENTS

When they had eaten their fill, he told his disciples, "Gather up the leftover fragments, that nothing may be lost."
John 6:12

When Christ multiplied the loaves and the fishes, what do you think: Did he create too *much bread* so that there were leftovers, something that he never intended and that took him by surprise?[13]

Surely that can't be.

Christ's miraculous feeding of the five thousand was a work of *divine omnipotence*. It went beyond human capacity.

We humans have been given the power to multiply grain through agriculture, over several months. But it is quite beyond our power to multiply

---

13. "Overgeschoten brokken," *De Heraut*, July 7, 1895; repr. in *Als gij in uw huis zit*, 158–61.

bread on the spot, in an instant. Christ could only do this because of the divine omnipotence at work in him. This divine omnipotence does not use guesswork, because God is not only all-powerful but all-knowing.

The fact that those twelve basketfuls of leftovers were intentional suggests that they are an object lesson on what we are to do with our surplus.

The story in John shows us that Christ himself was concerned about those leftover fragments. Nothing had been kept back by the disciples; they had distributed everything. It was, instead, among *the crowd*, that the leftovers were found. The multitude that had been hungry were filled and had food left over. But the food they were unable to consume they seemed to leave carelessly behind. For there was something of a reprimand in Christ's words, "Gather up the leftover fragments, *that nothing may be lost.*"

He would not have said this if the people had picked up the remnants to eat them on the way home or once they got home. Then the remnants would not have been lost but used. What Christ said, therefore, suggests that the nonchalance of the crowd would have caused the fragments to be lost, and that is what Jesus takes exception to as something sinful. It must not be that anything is lost. That is why the disciples, and in them the church of all ages, are given the commandment of the Lord that we should always and everywhere gather up the "leftover fragments."

This has been deeply ingrained in both our fathers and our mothers in preceding generations, thanks to instruction in the Word. Even today, frugality is still practiced in good Reformed families.[14]

This is reflected in the expression "it's a sin." When it entered common speech, it lost its original meaning. But originally, on the lips of Calvinists, it meant: you may not deal carelessly with leftovers, for even food that

---

14. The association between frugality (or thrift) with Protestant faith is generally traced back to Max Weber's famous work, *The Protestant Ethic and the Spirit of Capitalism* (New York: Routledge, 2001), which has influenced generations of social scientists and historians after it was published in English in 1930. Although this book is based on series of essays Weber wrote in 1904 and 1905, Kuyper is highlighting in this piece the importance of this association several years earlier than Weber. An example of the importance attached to frugality in historic Reformed faith and practice can be found in the popular work by Puritan theologian Richard Baxter, *A Christian Directory, Or, a Body of Practical Divinity, and Cases of Conscience*, 6 vols. (London: Robert White, 1673). See also frugality as a virtue in Reformer Zacharius Ursinus (1534–83) related to the positive duties of the eighth commandment, as noted in the introduction to this volume by Jordan J. Ballor.

is left over was created by God, and to deal irreverently with what God created is a sin.

The idea here is not that some poor man could have eaten it, nor that it could have been fed to a stray dog or a hungry sparrow. Rather, the fragments that remain must not be neglected because God created them, because they are God's, and because being careless with what God made is a sin.

A child of God who has received the grace to know the will of their heavenly Father relates everything to God. That is why they call every form of carelessness or neglect a sin.

The old Calvinists were serious about this. They lived it. It is how they saw things. In their circles all waste was experienced as sinful. Like all sins, it could be reconciled only by the blood of Christ.

Even in the unbelieving world, the expression "it's a sin" is often used: "Did you have to wear your best coat in this weather? It's a sin!" But when used in this way it is nothing but a stopgap or expletive, almost a swear word. Sin is always something *in relation to God*, so using an expression that relates exclusively to God without meaning God or thinking of God is a profanity.

"Leftover fragments" remind us to respect the Creator's omnipotence, but also to honor his unmerited loving-kindness toward us.

Most families never have leftovers; everything is eaten up, and more food would have been eaten if only there had been more food. If your family, your table, your kitchen and pantry happen to have more than enough food, more than you can make proper use of, with the result that there are leftovers, then by God's grace all your needs are being met and you can eat all you want. But then you are also responsible for what you do *with the leftovers*.

The one who is responsible to God for this is the housewife.[15] She is to manage frugally, as the person in charge of the kitchen and the dinner table. Even if she delegates the work to the girls in the family or to the maids, God has given her this responsibility.

She has to ensure, in the first place, that repeated leftovers are not the result of careless housekeeping. She should normally be able to judge

---

15. Much of the rest of this piece reflects nineteenth-century norms concerning gender roles; nowadays it would be thought to apply to people regardless of gender and marital status. The anthology in which this reflection was first published as a book (see the first footnote of this reflection) was intended as a gift for newly married couples.

approximately *how much* food needs to be purchased and prepared. If she buys randomly, impulsively, and excessively, so that plates are taken away from the table every day that are still half full, she will be guilty of slovenliness and of misusing the Lord's goodness toward her household.

It is also not a matter of indifference *what* is done with the "leftover fragments," as this can betray stinginess. A housewife who carefully collects today's leftovers to reheat and serve them up the next day does the right thing if she cannot make ends meet otherwise, or if she uses the money thus saved for God's cause or for the poor. But if her household budget is adequate, or if any savings do not go to a worthy cause, then the leftovers should go to the poor. In the past this happened when the more prosperous homes that regularly had food left over would each have a designated family that came to pick up the leftovers. Sometimes the leftovers would be deliberately increased, to help that family more.

People also used to take care of the birds of the air, at least in winter. This came not from a pathological love of animals, but because birds, as God's creatures that flutter and sing for us, are not to starve while we have plenty.

This is how a housewife is to take care of her household, because God has put her in charge of it and has given her the commandment: *gather the leftover fragments, that nothing may be lost.* Food in the house that grows moldy or spoils accuses the housewife and cries out to God.

This word of Christ is not just applicable to food and drink. It also refers to clothing, furniture, jewelry, and to your leftovers of time and *money*.

Nothing is your own property; it all belongs to God, who puts it at your disposal for you to use, and who makes you accountable for what you do with it.

Christ's command to *gather up the leftover fragments, that nothing may be lost*, is the pure Christian (and therefore Calvinist) principle that contrasts with the world's mania for saving.

Saving is the watchword of our age: gather treasures for yourself here on earth, own assets, focus on getting rich—all apart from God, not concerned with God, self-seeking, culminating in a desire for material things and cultivating the deadening spirit of the mean-spirited and then of the idle person of independent means who lives off interest. With this spirit, money is made to serve people and then makes people serve money.

God's children also save, but their motive is so much higher!

They do so, not to enrich themselves, but to honor God in God's gifts. They seek to use those gifts well, including care for the poor, and to dedicate all goods entrusted to them to God's service and glory.

~~~~~~~~~~~~~~~~~~~~~~~~~~~~~~~~~~~~

DO NOT WORK FOR THE FOOD THAT PERISHES

Do not work for the food that perishes, but for the food
that endures to eternal life, which the Son of Man will give
to you. For on him God the Father has set his seal.
John 6:27

To work every day that God gives us, to accomplish something that makes up for the length of that day, indeed, to do work so well that when we retire at night the result of that day's work is finished and ready—that is a divine ordinance.[16] It applies to human being not just after the fall but also before it. To work and to be busy is our high calling as human beings.

It is true that, after the fall, God said: "by the sweat of your face you shall eat bread"; but the emphasis falls on the words "the sweat of your face." With wonderful precision, the word "work" or "labor" does not occur in this punitive judgement. Human beings do not, on account of sin, have to work but to have to work so hard it exhausts them and causes them to perspire profusely, and are forced to do so in order to feed themselves and their dependents. Work is, indeed, so little a consequence of sin that Christ glories in it: "My Father is working until now, and I am working" [John 5:17].

To be able to work, to be allowed to work, and therefore to be obliged to work, is therefore a privilege that belongs to human beings because they have been created in the image of God. With those words, Christ was speaking according to his human nature, not his divine nature. As the Father worked so he worked, as our Mediator, that is, as the man Jesus Christ.

People talk about a "right to work," and in the sense here indicated, that is correct. Since the Lord your God is a God who always works, and since you are created in his image, you can claim that right as a human being, that privilege of being allowed to work.

---

16. "Werkt niet om de spijze die vergaat" [Do not work for the food that perishes], *De Heraut*, January 28, 1894; repr. in *Als gij in uw huis zit*, 151–55.

Every Sunday you are told this in God's name. In six days the Lord made the heavens and the earth, and all that is in them; and because he was thus at work, so you shall labor and do all your work. Only in connection with this does the Sabbath have any meaning as a day of rest, lest there be any other rest in your life than in the life of your God.

Some people imagine the state of glory around God's throne as though all labor will have ended, to taste heavenly bliss in pleasant idleness. These people know neither God nor his angels nor life as it will be in heaven.

God is always *working*.

And the angels are *ministering* spirits [Heb 1:14].

And with a view to salvation Christ says to his elect: "You have been faithful over a little; I will set you over much. Enter into the joy of your master" [Matt 25:21, 23].

But this beautiful creation ordinance, too, was broken by sin.

Not working has become so attractive that often when someone dies, people find they must confess that that person had not done much all their life.

God's Word points people like that to the tiny ants, and asks: "How long will you lie there, O sluggard? When will you arise from your sleep? A little sleep, a little slumber, a little folding of the hands to rest, and poverty will come upon you like a robber, and want like an armed man" [Prov 6:9–11].

Sinners know that God gives them each day to work in, but in their heart they say: "I shall be condemned; why then do I labor in vain?" [Job 9:29]. Or after they are done with their work they are self-centered enough to declare: "A worker's appetite works for him; his mouth urges him on" [Prov 16:26].

People demand work when there is no bread in the kitchen cupboard and no money in their hand. But when hunger does not sting and our portion is sure, then idleness seems preferable and laziness seems a desirable luxury. Even in the early church such loafers tainted the life of the congregation, so that the apostle issued this command: "If anyone is not willing to work, let him not eat." And he continued: "For we hear that some among you walk in idleness, not busy at work, but busybodies. Now such persons we command and encourage in the Lord Jesus Christ to do their work quietly and to earn their own living" [2 Thess 3:10–12].

Not in paradise, not before or after the fall, but by Christ himself it was pronounced: "Are there not twelve hours in the day? We must work the works of him who sent me while it is day; night is coming, when no one can work" [see John 9:4; 11:9].

All of Scripture is opposed to the indolence in which so many, also among us, spend their days, rising and getting dressed, sauntering about and chatting a bit, eating and drinking some, staring for a spell in the hearth or through the window, and then lying down again, to return to their friend: long, sweet sleep.

God in his Word knows that work is a blessing and idleness is the Devil's workshop, and so that Word exhorts us against idleness and laziness and prods us to be diligent.

Even of the affluent housewife of Proverbs 31 it is said that "She rises while it is yet night ... and does not eat the bread of idleness" [vv. 15, 27].

Thus, it makes no difference whether you you are a believer; always to be working, here or hereafter, is our glorious human calling, because we are created in the image of a God who *always* works.

What we must rest from are our *sinful* works. We rest on the Sabbath from our slavish toil, to be more richly engaged spiritually. After we die we will also rest from our earthly labors. But always to be working is and remains the calling that we received from God in our charter as human beings. As a result, a nation, a family, a person that works is happy, while indolence destroys a nation, unhinges a family, and enervates individuals.

Yet there is a considerable difference between one who has turned to Christ and one who still wanders about without their Savior. Naturally, Christians who lead an easy life and spend their days doing nothing bear greater guilt before God. But a more significant difference is that the unbeliever labors for food that perishes, whereas the believer works, or at least *can* work, for food that endures to everlasting life.

Sinners work, and must work, to have bread to stay alive. Their lives are lives of humiliation. They realize full well that in terms of value their bodies are subordinate to their soul, yet they have to spend almost their entire lives caring for their body, to nourish and sustain it. The fact that today this is translated into money makes no difference. In virtually every household almost all the money that comes in is spent on the body: for housing, clothing, care of the body. People work for wages, for money, to buy bread and clothes; and for millions upon millions of our generation the rule of life is still: "By the sweat of your face you shall eat bread" [Gen 3:19].

That rule is God's rule for the sinner, and no one can escape it. What is said about the higher classes—that many of them do not work for their bread—is only partially true. Nonmanual work is also work—much harder work even. When a storm is brewing at sea and the ordinary seaman is ordered aloft to take in sail while the wind is howling through the rigging and the helmsman stands calmly on the bridge, surely no one will say that the seaman is working but the helmsman is not.

What of the small group of rich people who live off their laid-up treasure and have bread, and more than bread, even though they do not work? They too await the judgment of God if they have not understood their calling. Having all that wealth, they are called to be all the more preoccupied with the higher interests of other people and with the things of the kingdom of God.

But for believers God removes that humiliation of work. The believer has once again become a *child* of God. And just as a child in the family does chores without ever thinking "I am earning my keep," and works for no other reason than that mother told him to and that he enjoys helping his mother, so it has become for the Christian. Christians need have no worries about their bread. Why should they worry about their life, saying: " 'What shall I eat or what shall I put on?' Do heathens not do the same? And when they look at the birds of the air and see that they neither sow nor reap and yet are fed by God, can they then lose trust in their heavenly Father?" [see Matt 6:31-33].

We are not saying that every Christian *does* feel that way, but that they *should* feel that way. Just as children do not take care of themselves but let their parents take care of them, and because they are their parents enjoy working for them in loving obedience, so children of God leave it to God to take care of their bread and in the meantime work every hour of the day in the service of God. What they seek in their work is not wages, not money, not bread, but the *pleasure of God*. They are at home with God, in service with God, and so work all day in their God-given vocation, because God has put them there, that they may please God in it.

They do not work for their bread—not for food that perishes—but for the pleasure and favor of God—for the food that endures to everlasting life. And so the humiliation is overcome.

For Christians, life is no longer absorbed in care for the body. But the inverse also becomes true: even the most lowly and toilsome labor is taken up in the service of God and is therefore sanctified in God. Every morning, at the start of a new day, their question and prayer is: "Lord, what would you have me do?" and every evening, when the day's work is done, they lay their work as an offering before their God and give God the glory.

INCOME AND EXPENDITURE

And you Philippians yourselves know that in the beginning
of the gospel, when I left Macedonia, no church entered into
partnership with me in giving and receiving, except you only.
Philippians 4:15

Although the tone of the gospel is highly spiritual, that does not stop Scripture from also speaking of the very prosaic matter of income and expenditure.[17]

How different from the zealots! For them, writing poetry and keeping accounts are incompatible. As they see it, such mundane things as book-keeping—writing everything down, counting the cost beforehand, and calculating the cost afterward—is good for lesser souls who are absorbed in the prose of life, but it will not do for freer spirits, for men of nobler disposition who drink from the cup of poetry and eat the bread of lofty ideals.

Keeping accounts, they feel, is for shopkeepers and money-grubbers, not for those who have learned to spread their wings or for those who have scaled the mountaintop and breathed something other than the stale air of the swamps below. No, they live in higher spheres; they disdain ledgers and do not go in for keeping accounts. Or if they do, they outwit that sordid numbers game by entering any numbers that will make the books balance.

But genuinely keeping accounts, accurately, fairly and truthfully, precisely and conscientiously—that is not what such exalted spirits do. They leave that to others, to their inferiors. So long as they have money in the house, they just spend it. When there is none left, they borrow some, and only pay it back if it suits them. Or they do not borrow; they buy on credit and live off the money of their creditors. And when those creditors ask for repayment, they think it is cruel when they are sent a reminder.

That is how artists lived of old, and university students, philosophers, men of the sword, and men of the pen. Often the women in those circles joined in such careless living. Even worse, these circles were sometimes joined by Christians given to mysticism, who regarded earthly cares as too "unspiritual" to weary their souls with. History even records spiritual leaders falling into the same sin.

---

17. "Rekening van ontvangst en uitgaaf," *De Heraut*, June 23, 1895; repr. in *Als gij in uw huis zit*, 122–26.

This sin is rebuked by God's Word and afterwards is punished with financial loss if not ruin, which is the inevitable outcome of this careless handling of money.

God's Word teaches us to value money, not because it glitters like gold, or because almost anything can be bought with it, but because it is a talent *entrusted to us by God*. Primordially, it belongs *to God*, and it is entrusted to us only *for a time*. This obliges us to use it, not for serving ourselves, but for serving God, and one day to rendering an account of it to God.

This is the first foundation on which a Christian's financial building must rest.

In the second place, God's Word demands strict honesty, and it curses all dishonesty as a despicable sin. Money is to go to its master, and the Holy Scripture calls *theft* every act on your part that prevents money from going to its master. Prompt payment on specified dates, punctual redemption of loans, no keeping back wages or reneging on pledges. On these three rules hangs your right to *spend* money. Equally strict is the rule that your income should never derive from exorbitant profits, unjust actions, or fraudulent practices.

A third foundation demanded by God's Word is that you manage your expenditures not as you want but as God wills. Not for sinful use, but for what is prudent. Not just for today but for all coming days, including when your wife or child is still alive but not you. You are also to dedicate your income and expenditures, along with everything else, to loving God first, and then yourself and your neighbor [see Mark 12:30–31]. So it is not a case of: first take care of all earthly needs and then if anything is left over give a trifle to God's cause. It is rather a case of: first the gift for the Lord's cause, as a holy gift up front, and after that your own needs. Think of the poor widow: she gave of her very sustenance, and that is precisely why she won the Lord's praise [see Mark 12:41–44].

To these three foundations is added, finally, a fourth. Scripture demands *order* and *regularity* in all things. It therefore requires of you to keep your accounts so accurate that if tomorrow you should die your records will be clear and prove reliable.

This is why our Reformed forebears frequently pointed out in their practical treatises that it is not spiritual but *overspiritual*, hence *unspiritual*, when someone is careless in their accounts of income and expenditure. The soul for God and the purse for oneself—that was not to be. Soul and purse were both to be God's. The demand was for meticulousness, scrupulousness, and conscientiousness.

The intention of Scripture is not to be harsh about these things. When people lack income, the Bible challenges you to have a degree of compassion that is more tender even than what it propounds. Having to earn a living for yourself and your dependents; and then to see your expenses rise as a result of sickness, accident or inflation; and then to notice that your income is stagnant or is actually drying up in days of unemployment or a slowdown in the economy—all this can be a cause of real anguish. It can wound your heart and make you feel you cannot cope, and that your faith is sinking. You feel you are losing both your trust in the God who has counted the hairs on your head, and your confidence in the love God awakens in the hearts of your brothers and sisters in the faith. In the face of such trying situations, you will never find a single harsh word in Scripture. On the contrary, it offers words of the most moving compassion.

What Scripture does condemn is living haphazardly, squandering inheritances that have yet to fall due; spending monies that have yet to materialize; consuming emergency funds reserved for future use; robbing Peter to pay Paul, as the expression goes; spending without estimating costs; wasting money so long as it is available, and then living off other people's benevolence when the money is gone.

What is no less condemned, yet where so many slip up, is people spending over and above their earnings, not because they cannot make ends meet, but because their income does not allow them to live a life in keeping with their perceived social status or their "needs."

As food, clothing, and shelter are necessities, if income is insufficient to meet these needs, there is no shame in seeking assistance. Then others can be asked for help. Indeed, it is then God's will that you *must* be helped.

But what goes beyond such necessities is not your due if God does not give it to you, or put it at your disposal.

You cannot regulate your income according to your expenditures; you must regulate your expenses according to your income. All who learned to follow this rule since they were young have never come short, and have never felt poor. We have to live within our means.

Merchants have to keep their books in order because a human law demands it. All Christians need to do likewise because the law of God demands it, lest God's name be slandered on account of his sloppiness.

Always keep accounts and never indulge in slovenly living: that's the rule for a man as head of the family, the woman for her household, the maid in her kitchen, and the children with their small allowance. That is what you are to practice for yourself, and model it for your children, lest the next generation become even more profligate and claim even worse victims. Remember precisely that frivolous way of keeping accounts has inflicted worry and misery on many a family and in the end has ruined them.

You should also remember that keeping accounts and accountability are essentially the same.

That is why our confession and catechism repeatedly talk about the account we have with God. In contrast, spiritual laxity objects to talking about our "debt" to the Almighty and the need to "pay" for your sins. It says that God's love is far too high and his mercy too infinite to apply the vulgar image of "payment" to our relation to the Holy One. But does Scripture itself not speak of a *ransom*?

Those two things—keeping accounts and accountability—are indeed intimately connected. People who are careless about keeping accounts, and paying their debts to other people, generally do not take seriously their debt to God. They want to be pious and mystical and holy; but they have no sense of the *justice* of God and no understanding of what it means to be *justified* through faith. Our fathers, by contrast, precisely by emphasizing *justification*, reinforced and promoted justice among the people, and deepened their appreciation of it.

Do not think lightly, therefore, of your income and expenditure accounts. For either you will come to stand before your God with tenderness, in good conscience, and justified, the ransom having been paid that saves you eternally; or you will stand on account of your income and expenditure among men. In the end all is determined by one compelling question: Are you your own lord and master, or do you stand under God and therefore respect God's ordinances and owe him a final rendering of your account?

The genuinely pious keep account of their money in the first place *for God*.

THE LOVE OF MONEY IS A ROOT OF ALL KINDS OF EVILS

The love of money is a root of all kinds of evils. It is through this craving that some have wandered away from the faith and pierced themselves with many pangs.
1 Timothy 6:10

When reading the apostle's warning about love of money in 1 Timothy 6:10, many people will say to themselves, quite correctly: "That's not me, I don't love money, I don't covet it."[18] Indeed, such people can be quite generous and occasionally waste money. When they hear Scripture say that the love of money is the root of all evil, they get a good feeling about themselves, thinking: "At least I don't have the root of *all* evil in me."

Yet they are mistaken. The apostle's solemn warning about the love of money is not meant only for misers or cheapskates. Coveting money is passionately longing for it, craving it, desiring it above all else.

Just listen to what Paul writes in the preceding verse: "Those who desire to be rich fall into temptation, into a snare, into many senseless and harmful desires that plunge people into ruin and destruction." Then follows the text: "The love of money is a root of all kinds of evils." In other words, the love of money is not the root of all kinds of sin, but of all kinds of *misery*, *calamity*, and *ruin* (although it is also true that love of money is the mother of all sins, since money can buy just about any kind of sin).

Thus, the apostle's admonition is directed not just at the miser but also at the spendthrift, in fact at all sinners for whom money has a powerful attraction and who find themselves wishing, "If only I had more money!"

What is it about money that makes it so attractive? It is that money is a god on earth. Just as God is almighty, so money irresistibly impresses itself on our sinful and corrupted heart as giving us *power* to do almost anything.

To be sure, believers know better, and deep down in their conscience unbelievers know it too. But if appearances are allowed to fool us, there is every reason to call money almost omnipotent. For, what indeed cannot be bought for money? What does not succumb to the magical power of money? If you lose everything except money, you can still create a new world for yourself.

Without money you are almost nothing—helpless, alone, without respect, not counting for anything. While for someone with money, all doors open, for people without money every door stays shut.

The terrible thing about money is not only that it is a power in the marketplace of the world and in the circles of pleasure and sin, but also that in the absence of money things that are pure, noble, and lofty cannot flourish.

---

18. "De geldgierigheid is een wortel van alle kwaad" [The love of money is a root of all kinds of evil], *De Heraut*, July 8, 1883.

Even in the small circle around Jesus there had to be a purse, and money had to change hands. That shrill contrast—Jesus and the money purse—could only lead to the character of a Judas. Among Jesus' closest friends, money made a thief.

Likewise today, is there anything that can operate without money, including in Christ's kingdom? Without money no charity. Without money no schools. Without money no missions. Without money no worship services. Without money no preaching of the Word. Money diffuses its awesome power into literally everything.

This is where mammon enters the picture. The name *mammon* does not refer so much to an idol as to a person who puts *faith in money*.

Faith is what ties you to your God. If your faith is in the living God, you are safe. Not so if you put your faith in money, so that you come to rely on it. Then you are bowing to mammon, whether or not you will it or are aware of it.

The rich do this when they bask in their riches. But the poor do so too—if only they had such riches, they would boast of them just like the wealthy! In fact, even the child that is always out to ask for a penny or beg for a dime is just as much worshipping mammon as the speculator in financial markets. The feverish chase after money dominates the whole world. To become rich is a dream that everybody has had. To make a fortune is an adventure everyone has pined for. Just look at the popularity of lotteries: millions of people, just to have one chance to make a fortune, throw away their saved pennies. It is a fever that stops at nothing. The other day, an exorbitant lawsuit in Rotterdam showed how thirst for gold has reached unprecedented levels.

For this reason alone, to *become a Christian* is a wonderful thing. For as soon as it is known that you have become a Christian, you will be approached for donations. You will be asked to give to the church, to charities, to Christian schools, and so forth. Money, always more money.

And that is your salvation. That is a blessing brought by your faith. For, always having to give relieves you of one of the chains that cause the most pain. It sets you free again to live for something higher and to serve God.

The fact that so much pluck and honorable attitude can be found among Christians flows naturally from all that *giving* and always more *giving*.

Oh, the benefit of this is so great! For the God of heaven is a God of compassion, but the money-god on earth is a god of boundless cruelty. Love of money abases you, dishonors you, robs you of spirit and backbone, and extinguishes in your soul the impulse for high and holy things. Money deprives you of your dignity, even when it gilds your life, your status, your position in society. It is not *you* that are rich, but it is money that *makes* you rich. If tomorrow your money is gone, gone is your glory. That is the lie that enters the world through love of money, corrupting everything. Since everything can be bought for money, the love of money won't stop until it has corrupted everything—through family feuds, usury practices, theft and robbery, breach of trust and deception, and in the end through suicide.

What a frightful contrast! Those who choose the Lord as their God receive all lasting good for eternity; but those who put their faith in the god of money are heading for all manner of sorrows.

Poor century! This then is your glory, that you have unleashed love of money. You promised us freedom, yet you shackle us in the chains of contempt.

APPENDIX

COMMON GRACE AND COMMERCE[1]

For he is rightly instructed; his God teaches him.

ISAIAH 28:26

Another factor of social life stems from the need for food, shelter, and cloth- §1
ing —needs that vary widely depending on times, places, and circumstances.
Consider those tropical and subtropical regions, where the warm climate
stimulates hunger less and at the same time mightily boosts crop production; where the same climate does not require any clothing other than what
covers the loins; and where one's dwelling consists of little else than a hut
made of reeds, brush, or wood. In our regions, by contrast, good nourishment, warm clothing, and a cozy dwelling are indispensable. In fact, this
need has even increased among us over time. Our ancestors were satisfied
with what to us would no longer be considered living. And even today the
needs in cities and in rural areas differ widely, as they do among people
of varying income levels, albeit for different reasons. But no matter how
different and diverse the need for food, shelter, and clothing may be, it is

---

1. Chapter 59 of Abraham Kuyper, *Common Grace*, vol. 3, edited by Jordan J. Ballor
    and J. Daryl Charles, translated by Nelson D. Kloosterman and Ed M. van der Maas
    (Bellingham, WA: Lexham Press, 2020).

a need that calls for emphatic and urgent satisfaction and that must be acknowledged as the chief motivational force behind the dynamic of human society. From God comes the *counsel* and from God comes the *wisdom* for all of this [see Isa 28:29]. That is to say, God has laid out for us the many ways in which human needs might be satisfied. It is God who has shown and taught human beings what is necessary for life, and it is God who provides the strength for it, blessing human efforts and making them succeed.

Where the need for food is concerned, this is readily apparent in *agriculture*. Isaiah asks how the farmer gets his varied knowledge of plowing, harrowing, sowing, and threshing and, more specifically, how he knows that one seed must be threshed differently from another. The prophet gives this summary answer: "He is rightly instructed; his God teaches him" (Isa 28:26). The whole section reads,

> Does he who plows for sowing plow continually?
>> Does he continually open and harrow his ground?
> When he has leveled its surface,
>> does he not scatter dill, sow cumin,
> and put in wheat in rows
>> and barley in its proper place,
>> and emmer as the border?
> For he is rightly instructed;
>> his God teaches him.
> Dill is not threshed with a threshing sledge,
>> nor is a cart wheel rolled over cumin,
> but dill is beaten out with a stick,
>> and cumin with a rod.
> Does one crush grain for bread?
>> No, he does not thresh it forever;
> when he drives his cart wheel over it
>> with his horses, he does not crush it. [Isa 28:24–28]

Isaiah finishes with the observation that, in this respect, *all* knowledge concerning agriculture comes from the *counsel* of the Lord and that all application in practice comes from his *wisdom*. This is stated in verse 29: "This also comes from the LORD of hosts; he is wonderful in counsel and excellent in wisdom." These words contain in effect the basis of all of social life. We must keep in mind, however, that Isaiah did not limit this to his own time; rather, this *counsel* and *wisdom* of God with regard to agriculture still continue. This extends not only to the fact that God gives rain and sunshine but also to the very different sense that he continually expands man's *knowledge* with regard to agricultural matters. Every new invention to make the soil fertile, to improve the livestock, to refine dairy production, or to reduce the amount of work through implements by the application of steam energy—all this comes to us from God. Thus, if the farmer were to refuse to have anything to do with this progress, or even resisted it instead of gratefully accepting this new *counsel of God*, that would amount to an *unwillingness* to be taught by God.

This process is nothing other than common grace. None of us can say §2 what social conditions would have developed if the pure life of paradise had continued. But we may suspect that man's nourishment would have been very different. Eating bread "by the sweat of your face" was instituted as a result of sin, and God's omnipotence would not have fallen short had he wished to let food spring from the soil by itself like in paradise, even without our agriculture. Palms and dates still are proof of this. But when man no longer stood in paradise but on the cursed earth, the task of cultivating the soil was imposed on him. It was a task that reflected both *punishment* and *grace*, for it is precisely through this necessity of providing for his own needs that the great development of the human race has occurred. This explains why the richest progress of the human race has not come from the warmer regions of the globe, where the needs are limited, but rather in the cooler regions, where much more has been needed to satisfy human needs. The common grace at work here thus included three realities: (1) that the soil of the earth delivered up a treasure for our human life; (2) that human beings, through instinct and experience, became capable of bringing this treasure up from the soil; and (3) that God, as the Noahic covenant says, would not disturb the seasons of sowing or harvest or fruitfulness [see Gen 8:22], yet at the same time transfers from one generation to the next the knowledge that has been acquired. God himself has used the needs that came about to guide humankind to an ever-higher level, and in that guidance toward a higher level he displayed his own *counsel* and *wisdom* for the glorification of his name.

Agriculture and mining teach us that our treasure comes from the soil of the earth. Not only do we derive from the earth our basic foods and the materials for our clothing, we also derive beef from cattle, fleece from various animals, and material from the silkworm that feeds on the products of the earth, just as we derive from the soil fertilizer, coal, and all sorts of minerals. We need to remember that the earth produces of its own accord all that is necessary to feed animal life, and that only human nourishment requires cultivating the soil. This process occurs even to the extent that animals that find no food in the winter hibernate at the end of autumn, only to wake up again in the spring to begin feeding again. The fact that food is grown today specifically for animals does not contradict this fact. This is done so that more cattle can be kept in a limited area; it does not occur in open regions where the herd nevertheless maintains itself.

Clothing shows the same pattern. God himself clothes the animals—for example, four-footed animals with fur, and birds with feathers—while fish, being cold-blooded, have no need of clothing at all. Human beings, on the other hand, must clothe themselves through the work of their own hands, whether by taking the fur or fleece from animals, processing wool and silk, or getting cotton and linen from agriculture. It is only somewhat different with respect to human dwellings. Some animals choose their lair in holes, while other animals—the elephant, for example—have no need of a dwelling at all. Yet others such as ants, bees, and beavers built a type of nest, as do almost all birds. The swallow even does it with special artistry. But human beings are much more dependent in this respect, and when we see a richly appointed royal palace and compare it with the simplicity of the swallow's nest, we are amazed at all that God has provided for human beings in terms of perfecting a suitable dwelling.

Here, then, we observe not only agriculture but *industry* as well, with its goal of processing and fashioning the treasure that has been acquired either from the earth, from the plant kingdom, or from the animal kingdom. Precisely this is what comprises all industry, including all trades. The goal is always to *process* what the soil gives us in terms of food or a mineral or what has been acquired from the plant or animal kingdom. The result is all types of clothing, all types of dwelling, all types of household goods, all types of tools, and all types of ornaments. And here even Holy Scripture points us to the fact that all of this involves an art that God shows and teaches us—an art that he transmits from generation to generation. Consider alone what is written about Bezalel and Oholiab when the tabernacle was to be built:

> Then Moses said to the people of Israel, "See, the LORD has
> called by name Bezalel the son of Uri, son of Hur, of the tribe
> of Judah; and he has filled him with the Spirit of God, with skill,
> with intelligence, with knowledge, and with all craftsmanship,

to devise artistic designs, to work in gold and silver and bronze, in cutting stones for setting, and in carving wood, for work in every skilled craft. And he has inspired him to teach, both him and Oholiab the son of Ahisamach of the tribe of Dan. He has filled them with skill to do every sort of work done by an engraver or by a designer or by an embroiderer in blue and purple and scarlet yarns and fine twined linen, or by a weaver—by any sort of workman or skilled designer. [Exod 35:30-35]

In all of this craftwork we observe, then, a *wisdom* that humans receive from their God, and it is because of God's providential care that the knowledge and skill once acquired do not get lost again but rather are transmitted from generation to generation.

Initially, human civilization was limited to two phases. There was a §3 tilling of the soil and there was the processing of acquired materials for clothing, dwellings, household goods, tools, and ornaments for the body. But as yet there was no distribution; that is, the trader had not yet come on the scene. There was as yet no store, no trade, no commerce or shipping. In addition to agriculture there was small-scale fishing and hunting, but this is a category of its own. The reason that commerce as yet was lacking was that each family still provided for its own needs. Each family cultivated its own plot of land. Each family had a cow and drank its own milk. Each family had its own sheep and warmed itself with its own wool. Similarly, each family planted hemp or cotton and spun silk from its silkworms. In short, people took care of all of their own needs. They built their own dwellings with the help of a neighbor. They constructed their own plows and their own tools. In short, people still lived entirely from the work of their own hands. As long as this condition continued, neither commerce nor trade could emerge. Not only did such conditions exist in the past, they still exist in some parts of the world today. This primitive condition persists among isolated tribes in continental Africa or among the inhabitants of the steppes of Asia, which is why no social life as we understand it emerges among these tribes and on these steppes. There is family life and tribal life, but not what we call social life.

Social life began only when people began to *exchange* things. This was originally still very primitive in nature. One person was more involved in cattle raising, another more in agriculture, and the one with cattle exchanged milk for agricultural products from the other. Particularly in the manufacturing of metals, a similar need arose, though with a much stronger effect. Working with metals takes much effort and skill, and since each farmer needs new tools only now and then, it is not worth his effort to acquire an anvil and hammer only for the purpose of making these tools. Hence, the custom soon arose that one person did the work as a blacksmith for the whole village, and in exchange the villagers provided him with grain, fruits, meat, milk, eggs, and so forth. Once this system of distributing labor in exchange for the products of labor had begun, it could only spread in an almost automatic fashion. This explains the birth of individual trades, shops, small businesses, and then retail trade. But the process could not stop there. There existed a significant difference between the products of one region and those of another. Fleece could be found everywhere, but fur was present only in regions where animals roamed freely. Wood was to be found everywhere, but certain kinds of wood were much more suitable for making fine furniture than others. Iron was not found everywhere, let alone silver and gold. Spices such as myrrh, aloe, and incense were found in only a few regions. Sugar, coffee, and spices had to be obtained from the Far East. As a result, the more that inhabitants of one part of the world were exposed to products from another part of the world, the more the desire and inclination developed to offer the products for sale in another region. This is how trade by caravans emerged, by which one group of merchants traveled with a large number of camels to bring goods from their own country to another, distant land. When such a caravan arrived, the "market" opened; local merchants, as well as those from outside the region, joined in, and in this way wholesale business gradually emerged.

In this way, goods are produced through agriculture and mining, processed through crafts and trading, and transferred and distributed through commerce and shipping. Shipping as such was originally nothing but the transferring of goods across the sea instead of over land. But herein was lodged a new grace. God created water and wood in such a way that the sea could carry the ship. What initially was discovered as a result of hollowing out a tree trunk soon developed into shipbuilding. Once begun, shipbuilding evolved from coastal trade to seafaring and crossing the ocean. This brought about the advantage of bringing into contact with one another various regions that had no contact over land. This delivered islands from their isolation and reduced the cost of transportation enormously. And more importantly, it gave human beings courage to brave the elements, and because of this new outlook, a heightened sense of awareness was awakened in humans that led to greater levels of human freedom. It can be argued that it was the seafaring nations that have contributed the most to our freedoms. Consider, first, the Phoenicians, then the Greeks, after that the Venetians, then the Dutch, and soon England and America. Viewed thusly, all of the commerce and shipping on the high seas is not a mere human invention but something that God ordained. If the ratio of the specific weight of water to the specific weight of wood and to the buoyancy of a hollow metal hull had been different, shipping could never have come about. These realities were already lodged in creation from the beginning, prepared by God.

On this basis, it simply could not have been otherwise: when man's knowledge of these things and their usage increased, they were ordained to develop in a logical manner, as indeed they have. Agriculture, animal husbandry, hunting, fishing, mining, crafts, shops, retail business, markets, annual fairs, wholesale business, inland shipping, international shipping, and so forth—all this necessarily had to develop, given what lay in creation and what God, despite the curse, has preserved and perpetuated for us. Discoveries and inventions belong to this as well. They have not brought to light—nor could they bring to light—anything other than what resided in creation. The remarkable thing here is only that very important discoveries waited to appear for many centuries and that we owe them to what we could almost call an accident. And yet, every Christian believes that we owe them to God's providence. And particularly the fact that these discoveries were not made at a much earlier time but emerged only centuries later shows poignantly how it is God himself who guides all of human affairs, giving human civilization an entirely new impulse only when, in his counsel, it was destined to happen. Steam power, to cite but one example, was discovered virtually by accident. There was no human reason as such why steam power could not have been discovered centuries earlier, but this did not happen. Only in the last century did this new source of power become known in human existence, changing it entirely.

We should consider money in the same way. Only in the previous century §4 did money become a dominant force in the world. While it also exerted influence in earlier centuries, this did not occur in such huge proportions. Money initially served only to facilitate bartered trade, but in time this exchange proved to be too cumbersome. As a rule, one came to the market with one's own products; however, all too often it was virtually impossible to measure fairly the value of what one bought and the value of what one wanted to sell. Especially in trade with those traveling by caravan, which involved great volumes and occurred only a few times per year, the challenge was to find a caravan merchant who simply wanted to buy what another had to offer. On his far-flung journeys, the caravan merchant could not accept whatever was perishable, and the precious things he sought were in the possession of only a few. Thus, in a very natural way, "money" became a solution, for which precious metals were a ready alternative. Only through money did commerce take off in terms of a means of payment. Initially, however, paying with money remained the exception, and in fact in many regions of the world it still is. What Jesus describes in the parable of the lost coin is not an image drawn from life as we know it today. To illustrate, no contemporary housewife who loses a coin and then finds it again will call her neighbors together to celebrate. The imagery illustrates how extremely rare money still was in the ancient world and how much value was placed on a single coin. By contrast, especially in our cities today, we are used to everything being paid for with money. At the same time, even in our own nation there still exist remote regions in which a reasonably good farmer will see no more than a hundred guilders pass through his hands in an entire year and barter still exists on some sort of scale.

Such exceptions notwithstanding, money has gradually become an independent force in the marketplace, bringing blessing but also a curse. Only by becoming a legitimate force in its own right has sufficient capital been gathered to create large enterprises, which in turn have led to the expansion of commerce, shipping, diverse inventions, and human enrichment as a result of our mastery over the material world. But it is equally true that the appetite for money has become a form of idolatry, that the amassing of goods has resulted in an unhealthy ascendancy of capitalism, and that so-called credit resulting in the accumulation of wealth in a few hands has led to such extraordinary influence that it becomes a threat to society and to the peace of the nations. What Cecil Rhodes and his people have perpetrated in England with an eye to South Africa provides the most graphic example of this.[2] And yet we are only standing at the beginning of the development of money's influence. What the trusts or syndicates in America seek is aimed at controlling the fate of the whole world through

---

2. Cecil Rhodes (1853–1902) served as prime minister of the Cape Colony in South Africa from 1890 to 1896, advancing British imperial economic and political interests through the British South Africa Company.

one mighty conglomeration of money. At least in Europe, anti-Semitism is nothing but a reaction against perceived money-grubbers of Semitic blood.[3]

The ease with which large sums of money can create credit, doubling and multiplying over a short time without any effort, is the downside of money insofar as it ceases to be merely a *means of exchange* but now becomes its own object of commerce, with the result being that the so-called banking business has come into being. Social democracy seeks in part to be a reaction against this by arresting the momentum of this "banking business" by means of lowering interest rates and taking away credit. But this downside of money does not remove the fact that, taken as a means of exchange, money is a means provided by God by which we can develop social life. Of course, sin seeks to usurp all of this. The saying that everyone acts as a thief in his own business, which is to say that everyone seeks unfair advantage in his business, is a reflection of this reality. Indeed, there is sin involved with shipping, and sea ports are notorious for their immorality. Sin is involved in business, and not everyone can remain honest at the stock exchange, where speculation intrigues the mind in a sinful manner. People sin in our factories. Quite simply, there is *no part* of our human life where sin does *not* find a point of contact. But this does not abolish the truth that *abuse does not cancel out use* and that, as Christians, we must be prepared to counteract the festering of sin in *all* areas of life by means of our example.

We must never say, therefore, that the production, processing, and distribution of earthly goods would be a realm that is prohibited for Christians. On the contrary, only Christians can develop social life by contributing to these areas, thereby honoring the reality of common grace. These realms of human existence do not lie outside the divine providence; to the contrary, they belong to it in the sense that we find in them a manifestation of human life that we share in common with all of our fellow citizens. We participate with all in them, rather than separating ourselves in our narrower circles. We therefore must reject the attitude of those who consider agriculture,

---

3. The historic association rooted in specific social contexts of Jews with money has been the occasion for anti-Semitic discrimination. The origins of this phenomenon and the stereotypically negative assessment of Jews by many Christians are to be found in the long history of Christian Europe. When combined with the legal prohibition against Jewish participation in many other professions, "the economic forces pushing Jews out of other occupations were matched by others pulling them into the money trade." See Derek J. Penslar, *Shylock's Children: Economics and Jewish Identity in Modern Europe* (Berkeley: University of California Press, 2001), 17.

retail business, industry, and commerce as areas that are less important and for which we have no calling. Contrarily, as applies to church life or education or charity, it is absolutely necessary that Christians, too, know how to make a profit in business, in order that our common Christian life might be maintained. And even apart from this, it is precisely the children of God who should pride themselves in their ability not to do second-rate work in these realms. For precisely in these areas of life, it is God himself who gives us wisdom, it is God himself who prepares the means for us, and it is God himself who guides the development of human social life through his common grace. In the days of our own national flowering and historical greatness, it was the Calvinists who outstripped the others. The reverend Petrus Plancius continues to stand out in history as a devout Christian who preached with great passion and at the same time showed our merchants and sea captains the way across the high seas through his geographical study.[4] The inclination to view agriculture, industry, and commerce as "worldly" side issues and then to insulate fellow believers—a mindset that is not uncommon today—stands diametrically opposed to this. Bringing the best goods to the market, being the best craftsmen, and working in commerce with utter integrity—this manner of living, as was once demonstrated empirically, was, and still *remains*, the path to prosperity in our present world, a reality that applies to Christians as well.

---

4. Petrus Plancius (1552–1662) was a leading Reformed theologian from the Low Countries and a scholar of a variety of subjects, including geography and astronomy.

AFTERWORD

As a successor to Abraham Kuyper as prime minister of the Netherlands, I feel deeply indebted to him. I was a student and then a professor at the VU University Amsterdam he founded. I led the Christian Democratic Appeal, a party formed from a merger involving the Antirevolutionary Party, which Kuyper also founded. I was honored, in addition, to receive the prestigious Kuyper Prize at Princeton in 2004. More importantly, I've been inspired throughout my adult life by his vision of Christianity offering a worldview that engages with every area of life.

Against this background, I am delighted that Peter Heslam has produced this fascinating and important anthology. Peter's book *Creating a Christian Worldview: Abraham Kuyper's Lectures on Calvinism* (Grand Rapids: Eerdmans, 1998) established him as a Kuyper scholar. He is, however, also an authority on the interface between faith, business, and development. He brings all these fields of expertise together in assembling, editing, and introducing this fine collection of Kuyper's reflections on business and economics. Although much attention has been given to Kuyper's writings on other issues, his engagement with the commercial sphere has been largely overlooked. Now we have a book that shows Kuyper rising above such polarizations as left-right and conservative-progressive, to offer fresh and inspiring perspectives that are deeply grounded in central tenets of the Christian faith.

This makes the book very timely. There is an urgent need for deliberate and thorough reflection on current socioeconomic, financial, and environmental developments. In Kuyper's terminology, we need an "architectonic" critique of contemporary society. Some elements of such a critique are starting to emerge. The United Nations' Sustainable Development Goals hold up a moral mirror to countries and economies and call for action. The papal encyclical *Laudato Si* expresses fundamental concerns about production and consumption processes. Concerns about inequality are mounting.

Debate is flourishing about new market models: moral capitalism, inclusive capitalism, conscious capitalism, and stakeholder capitalism. Demand is growing that businesses should generate social value, not merely economic value. The crisis precipitated by the coronavirus in 2020 has spurred questions about how a more socially and ecologically responsible economy can be built.

All these discussions have a strong moral content. The "moral sentiments" are back. Peter Heslam's publication of Kuyper's ideas is therefore of great contemporary relevance. I commend it wholeheartedly to leaders in business, economics, theology, and public policy.

Jan Peter Balkenende

BIBLIOGRAPHY

Adler, Georg. *Rodbertus, der Begründer des wissenschaftlichen Sozialismus.* Leipzig: Duncker & Humblot, 1884.

———. *Zur Erkenntnis unsrer staatswirthschaftlichen Zustände.* Neubrandenburg: Barnewitz, 1842.

———. *Zur Erklärung und Abhülfe der heutigen Creditnoth des Grundbesitzes.* 2 vols. Jena: Mauke, 1876.

Ahuvia, Aaron, and Elif Izberk-Bilgin. "Well-Being in Consumer Societies." Pages 482–97 in *The Oxford Handbook of Happiness*, edited by Susan A. David, Ilona Boniwell, and Amanda Conley Ayers. Oxford: Oxford University Press, 2013.

Baart, J. F. *Adam Smith en zijn onderzoek naar den rijkdom der volken.* Leiden: Van Der Hoek, 1858.

Ballor, Jordan J. "The Economies of Divine and Human Love." *Research in the History of Economic Thought & Methodology* 31, no. 1 (2013): 157–64.

———. "Interdisciplinary Dialogue and Scarcity in Economic Terminology." *Journal of Markets & Morality* 23, no. 1 (Spring 2020): 131–37.

———. "Theology and Economics: A Match Made in Heaven?" *Journal of Interdisciplinary Studies* 26 (2014): 115–34.

Ballor, Jordan J., and Victor V. Claar. "Creativity, Innovation, and the Historicity of Entrepreneurship." *Journal of Entrepreneurship & Public Policy* 8, no. 4 (2019): 512–22.

———. "Envy in the Market Economy: Sin, Fairness, and Spontaneous (Dis) Order." *Faith & Economics* 61–62 (Spring/Fall 2013): 33–53.

———. "The Soul of the Entrepreneur: A Christian Anthropology of Creativity, Innovation, and Liberty." *Journal of Ethics & Entrepreneurship* 6, no. 1 (Spring 2016): 115–29.

Barine, Arvède. *L'Oeuvre de Jésus-ouvrier*. Paris: Fischbacher, 1879.

Bartholomew, Craig G. *Contours of the Kuyperian Tradition: A Systematic Introduction*. Downers Grove, IL: IVP Academic, 2017.

Bartholomew, J. G. *Atlas of the World's Commerce*. London: G. Newnes, 1907.

Bastingius, Jeremias. *In Catechesin Religionis Christianae*. Dordrecht: Canin, 1588.

———. *An Exposition or Commentarie Upon the Catechisme of Christian Religion*. Cambridge: Legatt, 1589.

———. *Verclaringe op den catechisme der Christelicker religie*. Dordrecht: Canin, 1591; Amsterdam: J. A. Wormser, 1893.

Bavinck, Herman. *Christelijke wereldbeschouwing*. Kampen: Kok, 1904.

———. *Christelijke wetenschap*. Kampen: Kok, 1904.

———. *The Christian Family*. Edited by Stephen J. Grabill. Translated by Nelson D. Kloosterman. Grand Rapids: Christian's Library Press, 2012.

———. *Christian Worldview*. Translated and edited by Nathaniel Gray Sutanto, James Eglinton, and Cory C. Brock. Wheaton, IL: Crossway, 2019.

———. *Essays on Religion, Science, and Society*. Edited by John Bolt. Translated by Harry Boonstra and Gerrit Sheeres. Grand Rapids: Baker Academic, 2008.

———. *Magnalia Dei: Onderwijzing in de christelijke religie naar Gereformeerde Belijdenis*. Kampen: Kok, 1909.

———. *Philosophy of Revelation: A New Annotated Edition*. Translated and edited by Cory Brock and Nathaniel Gray Sutanto. Peabody, MA: Hendrickson, 2018.

———. *Reformed Dogmatics*. 4 vols. Edited by John Bolt. Grand Rapids: Baker Academic, 2003–8.

———. *Wijsbegeerte der Openbaring*. Kampen: Kok, 1908.

Baxter, Richard. *A Christian Directory, Or, a Body of Practical Divinity, & Cases of Conscience*. 6 vols. London: Robert White, 1673.

———. *How to Do Good to Many: The Public Good Is the Christian's Life*. Edited by Jordan J. Ballor. Grand Rapids: Christian's Library Press, 2018.

Beets, Nicolaas. *Brokkelvloer van rijmspreuken*. The Hague: M. M. Couvée, 1891.

Bell, Daniel M., Jr. *The Economy of Desire: Christianity & Capitalism in a Postmodern World*. Grand Rapids: Brazos, 2012.

Bellamy, Edward. *Looking Backward 2000–1887*. Boston: Ticknor, 1888.

Bergsma, E. *Het pensioeneeren van werklieden*. Rotterdam: H. A. Kramers & Zoon, 1882.

Bierma, Lyle D. *An Introduction to the Heidelberg Catechism: Sources, History, & Theology*. Grand Rapids: Baker Academic, 2005.

———. "Remembering the Sabbath Day: Ursinus's Exposition of Exodus 20:8–11." Pages 272–91 in *Biblical Interpretation in the Era of the Reformation*, edited by Richard A. Muller and John L. Thompson. Grand Rapids: Eerdmans, 1996.

Bilderdijk, Willem. *Briefwisseling met Tydeman*. 2 vols. Sneek: Van Druten &
      Bleeker, 1866–67.
———. *Nieuwe Oprakeling*. Dordrecht: J. de Vos, 1827.
———. *Vermaking*. Rotterdam: A. F. H. Smit, 1828.
Birks, Thomas Rawson. *First Principles of Moral Science: A Course of Lectures
      Delivered in the University of Cambridge*. London: Macmillan, 1873.
Block, Maurice. *Les progrès de la science économique depuis Adam Smith*. 2 vols.
      Paris: Guillaumin, 1890.
Blondel, Jules Edouard. *La question sociale et sa solution scientifique*. Paris:
      Guillaumin, 1887.
Bluhm, Richard, Denis de Crombrugghe, and Adam Szirmai. "Poor
      Trends: The Pace of Poverty Reduction after the Millennium
      Development Agenda." UNU-MERIT working paper series, IPD WP19,
      February 2014.
Bornhak, Conrad. *Die deutsche Sozialgesetzgebung*. Freiburg: Mohr, 1890.
Bratt, James D., ed. *Abraham Kuyper: A Centennial Reader*. Grand Rapids:
      Eerdmans, 1998.
———. *Abraham Kuyper: Modern Calvinist, Christian Democrat*. Grand Rapids:
      Eerdmans, 2013.
———. "Passionate about the Poor: The Social Attitudes of Abraham Kuyper."
      Journal of Markets & Morality 5, no. 1 (Spring 2002): 35–44.
Bruni, Luigino, and Robert Sugden. "Reclaiming Virtue Ethics for
      Economics." *Journal of Economic Perspectives* 27, no. 4 (Fall 2013): 141–
      64.
Chafuen, Alejandro A. *Faith & Liberty: The Economic Thought of the Late
      Scholastics*. Lanham, MD: Lexington, 2003.
Christian Society of Social Economics. *Quatre écoles d'économie sociale,
      conférences données à l'Aula de l'université de Genève* [Four socio-
      economic schools: Lectures delivered in the auditorium of the
      University of Geneva]. Paris: Fischbacher, 1890.
Chrysostom, John. "The Homilies on the Statues." In *Saint Chrysostom: On
      the Priesthood, Ascetic Treatises, Select Homilies & Letters, Homilies
      on the Statues*. Edited by Philip Schaff. Translated by W. R. W.
      Stephens. A Select Library of the Nicene and Post-Nicene Fathers
      of the Christian Church, First Series, 9. New York: Christian
      Literature, 1889.
Claar, Victor V., and Greg Forster. *The Keynesian Revolution & Our Empty
      Economy: We're All Dead*. New York: Palgrave Macmillan, 2019.
Congrès international du repos hebdomadaire. Paris: Guillaumin and
      Fischbacher, 1890.
Cooper, Thomas. *Lectures on the Elements of Political Economy*. Columbia:
      Telescope, 1826.
Da Costa, Isaac. *Bezwaren tegen den geest der eeuw*. Leiden: L. Herdingh, 1823.

————. *Da Costa's kompleete dichtwerken*. 3 vols. Haarlem: A. C. Kruseman, 1861–63.

DeKoster, Lester. *Work: The Meaning of Your Life—A Christian Perspective*. Grand Rapids: Christian's Library Press, 2015.

Dennison, James T., Jr., ed. *Reformed Confessions of the 16th & 17th Centuries in English Translation: 1523–1693*. 4 vols. Grand Rapids: Reformation Heritage Books, 2008–2014.

Deville, Gabriel. *Le Capital de Karl Marx, résumé et accompagné d'un aperçu sur le socialisme scientifique*. Paris: H. Oriol, 1883.

Douma, J. *The Ten Commandments: Manual for the Christian Life*. Translated by Nelson D. Kloosterman. Phillipsburg: P&R, 1996.

Dyke, Harry Van. "Abraham Kuyper and the Continuing Social Question." *Journal of Markets & Morality* 14, no. 2 (Fall 2011): 641–46.

————. "How Abraham Kuyper Became a Christian Democrat." *Calvin Theological Journal* 33, no. 2 (November 1998): 420–35.

————. "Kuyper's Early Critique of Unchecked Capitalism." *Philosophia Reformata* 78, no. 2 (2013): 115–23.

Easterlin, Richard A. "Paradox Lost?" IZA discussion paper series no. 9676 (January 2016).

Eckersley, Richard. "Is Modern Western Culture a Health Hazard." *International Journal of Epidemiology* 35 (2006): 252–58.

Effertz, O. *Arbeit und Boden: Grundlinien einer Ponophysiocratie*. Berlin: Puttkammer & Mühlbrecht, 1889.

Eglinton, James. *Trinity & Organism: Towards a New Reading of Herman Bavinck's Organic Motif*. London: T&T Clark, 2012.

Elbogen, Friedrich. *Die Erlösung: sociale studien*. Zurich: Schröter & Meyer, 1889.

Ely, Richard T. *Recent American Socialism*. Baltimore: Johns Hopkins University Press, 1885.

————. "Socialism in America." *North American Review* 142, no. 355 (June 1886): 519–25.

Endemann, Wilhelm. *Jahrbücher für Nationalökonomie und Statistik*. Vol. 1, *Die national-ökonomischen Grundsätze der canonistische Lehre*. Edited by B. Hildebrand. Jena: Friedrich Mauke, 1863.

Fabius, D. P. D. *Mozaïsch en Romeinsch recht*. Amsterdam: J. A. Wormser, 1890.

Falkenberg, Paul. "Der Eigentumserwerb von dem veräußernden Nichteigentümer nach Handelsrecht." Diss., University of Leipzig, 1891.

Fikkert, Brian, and Kelly M. Kapic. *Becoming Whole: Why the Opposite of Poverty Isn't the American Dream*. Chicago: Moody, 2019.

Fikkert, Brian, and Michael Rhodes. "Homo Economicus vs. Homo Imago Dei." *Journal of Markets & Morality* 20, no. 1 (Spring 2017): 101–40.

Flipse, Ab. *Christelijke wetenschap: Nederlandse rooms-katholieken en gereformeerden over de natuurwetenschap, 1880-1940*. Hilversum: Verloren, 2014.

Flürscheim, Michael. *De nationalisatie van den bodem*. Haarlem: Met & Meylink, 1883.

Fouillée, Alfred. *Propriété sociale et la démocratie*. Paris: Hachette, 1884.

Frey, Bruno S. *Happiness: A Revolution in Economics*. Cambridge, MA: MIT Press, 2010.

George, Henry. *Progress & Poverty: An Inquiry into the Cause of Industrial Depressions & of Increase of Want with Increase of Wealth*. New York: Doubleday, 1879.

———. *Sociale vraagstukken*. Translated by J. Stoffel. Deventer: W. Hulscher, 1884.

Gilon, Ernest. *Maatschappelijke nooden*. Translated by G. Keller Jr. Amsterdam: H. Gerlings, 1889.

Goheen, Michael W., and Craig G. Bartholomew. *Living at the Crossroads: An Introduction to Christian Worldview*. Grand Rapids: Baker Academic, 2008.

Goheen, Michael W., and Erin Glanville, eds. *The Gospel & Globalization: Exploring the Religious Roots of a Globalized World*. Vancouver, BC: Regent College Publishing, 2009.

Gonzáles, Justo L. *A Brief History of Sunday: From the New Testament to the New Creation*. Grand Rapids: Eerdmans, 2017.

Gootjes, Nicolaas H. "Man as God's Steward." Translated by S. Carl Van Dam. Pages 249-55 in *Teaching & Preaching the Word: Studies in Dogmatics & Homiletics*, edited by Cornelis Van Dam. Winnipeg: Premier, 2010.

———. "De mens als Gods rentmeester." *Radix* 6 (1980): 20-26.

Goudzwaard, Bob, Mark Vander Vennen, and David Van Heemst. *Hope in Troubled Times: A New Vision for Confronting Global Crisis*. Grand Rapids: Baker Academic, 2007.

Graham, Carol. *Happiness around the World: The Paradox of Happy Peasants & Miserable Millionaires*. New York: Oxford University Press, 2009.

Graham, Carol, Shaojie Zhou, and Junyi Zhang. "Happiness and Health in China: The Paradox of Progress." Working paper 89, Brookings Institution, Washington, DC, June 2015.

Guillard, Edmond. *Protection et organisation du travail*. Paris: Guillaumin, 1887.

Harinck, George, ed. *Kuyper in America*. Sioux Center, IA: Dordt College Press, 2012.

Haun, F. J. *Das Recht auf Arbeit*. Berlin: Puttkammer & Mühlbrecht, 1889.

Hengstmengel, Joost W. "Dooyeweerd's Philosophy of Economics." *Journal of Markets & Morality* 15, no. 2 (Fall 2012): 415-29.

———. "The Reformation of Economic Thought: Dutch Calvinist Economics, 1880-1948." *Philosophia Reformata* 78, no. 2 (2013): 124-43.

Hertzka, Theodor. *Die Gesetzen der sozialen Entwicklung*. Leipzig: Duncker & Humblot, 1886.

———. *Freiland: ein soziales Zukunftsbild*. Dresden: E. Pierson, 1890.

Heslam, Peter S. "Christianity and the Prospects for Development in the Global South." Pages 359–83 in *The Oxford Handbook of Christianity & Economics*, edited by Paul Oslington. Oxford: Oxford University Press, 2014.

———. *Creating a Christian Worldview: Abraham Kuyper's Lectures on Calvinism*. Grand Rapids: Eerdmans, 1998.

———. "Prophet of a Third Way: The Shape of Kuyper's Socio-political Vision." *Journal of Markets & Morality* 5, no. 1 (Spring 2002): 11–33.

———. "The Role of Business in the Fight against Poverty." Pages 164–80 in *Christian Theology & Market Economics*, edited by Ian R. Harper and Samuel Gregg. Cheltenham: Edward Elgar, 2008.

———. "The Spirit of Enterprise: Abraham Kuyper and Common Grace in Business." *Journal of Markets & Morality* 18, no. 1 (Spring 2015): 7–20.

Heslam, Peter S., and Eric A. S. Wood. "Faith and Business Practice amongst Christian Entrepreneurs in Developing and Emerging Markets." *Koers: Bulletin for Christian Scholarship* 79, no. 2 (2014): 1–7.

Himes, Brant M. *For a Better Worldliness: Abraham Kuyper, Dietrich Bonhoeffer, & Discipleship for the Common Good*. Eugene, OR: Pickwick, 2018.

Howell, A. G. Ferrers. *S. Bernardino of Siena*. London: Methuen, 1913.

Jacoby, P. *Etude sur la sélection*. Paris: Baillière, 1881.

Jäger, Adolf. *Die soziale Frage im Licht der Offenbarung*. 2 vols. Neu-Ruppin: Rud. Betrenz., 1891.

Jäger, Eugen. *Die Französische Revolution und die Soziale Bewegung*. Berlin: Puttkammer, 1890.

Karlowitsch, Nicolai. *Die Entwicklung des Nihilismus*. 3rd ed. Berlin: Behr, 1880.

Kasser, Tim. *The High Price of Materialism*. Cambridge, MA: MIT Press, 2002.

Kasser, Tim, et al. "Changes in Materialism, Changes in Psychological Well-Being: Evidence from Three Longitudinal Studies and an Intervention Experiment." *Motivation & Emotion* 38 (2014): 1–22.

Keil, Friedrich, and Franz Delitzsch. *Commentary on the Old Testament*. Vol. 7. Peabody, MA: Hendrickson, 1996.

Keynes, John Maynard. *A Tract on Monetary Reform*. London: Macmillan, 1923.

Knowlton, Charles. *An Essay on the Population Question*. Rotterdam: Van der Hoeven & Buys, 1878.

Kollewijn, R. A. *Bilderdijk, zijn leven en werken*. 2 vols. Amsterdam: Van Holkema and Warendorf, 1891.

Kossman, E. H. *The Low Countries, 1780–1940*. Oxford: Clarendon, 1978.

Kraay, Aart. "When Is Growth Pro-Poor? Evidence from a Panel of Countries." *Journal of Development Economics* 80, no. 1 (June 2006): 198–227.

Kuyper, Abraham. *Als gij in uw huis zit*. 2nd imprint. Amsterdam: Höveker & Wormser, 1899.

———. "Christ and the Needy." In *On Charity & Justice*, Edited by Matthew J. Tuininga. Bellingham, WA: Lexham Press, forthcoming.

———. *Common Grace: God's Gifts for a Fallen World*. Translated by Nelson D. Kloosterman and Ed M. van der Maas. Edited by Jordan J. Ballor, Stephen J. Grabill, and J. Daryl Charles. 3 vols. Bellingham, WA: Lexham Press, 2016–2020.

———. *De Christus en de Sociale nooden en Democratische Klippen*. Amsterdam: J. A. Wormser, 1895.

———. *Eenige Kameradviezen uit de jaren 1874 en 1875*. Amsterdam: J. A. Wormser, 1890.

———. *Gomer voor den Sabbath*. Amsterdam: J. A. Wormser, 1889.

———. *Honig uit den rotssteen*. 2 vols. 2nd imprint. Amsterdam: J. A. Wormser, 1896.

———. *Lectures on Calvinism*. Grand Rapids: Eerdmans, 1931.

———. *Ons Program*. Amsterdam: Kruyt, 1879.

———. "The Reefs of Democracy." In *On Charity & Justice*, edited by Matthew J. Tuininga. Bellingham, WA: Lexham Press, forthcoming.

———. *Het Sociale Vraagstuk en de Christelijke Religie: Rede bij de opening van het Sociaal Congres op 9 November 1891 gehouden*. Amsterdam: J. A. Wormser, 1891.

———. *Souvereiniteit in eigen kring: rede ter inwijding van de vrije Universiteit, den 20sten October 1880 gehouden, in het Koor der Nieuwe Kerk te Amsterdam*. Amsterdam: Kruyt, 1880.

———. *Tractaat van den sabbath. Historische dogmatische studie*. Amsterdam: J. A. Wormser, 1890.

———. *Verslag der Handelingen van de Tweede Kamer der Staten-Generaal gedurende het zittings-jaar 1910–1911*. The Hague: Algemene Landsdrukkerij, 1911.

———. *E Voto Dordraceno: Toelichting op den Heidelbergschen Catechismus*. 4 vols. Amsterdam: J. A. Wormser, 1892–95.

———. *Vrijheid: Rede, ter bevestiging van Dr Ph.S. van Ronkel, gehouden den 23 maart 1873, in de Nieuwe Kerk te Amsterdam*. Amsterdam: De Hoog, 1873.

———. *The Work of the Holy Spirit*. New York: Funk & Wagnalls, 1900.

Laspeyres, Étienne. *Geschichte der Niederländischen National-Oeconomie*. Leipzig: S. Hirzel, 1863.

Laveleye, Emile de. *Lehr-und Handbuch der politischen Oekonomie*. Vol. 1, *Grundlegung*. 2nd ed. Leipzig: C. F. Winter, 1879.

———. *Lehr-und Handbuch der politischen Oekonomie*. Vol. 5, *Finanzwissenschaft*. 3rd ed. Leipzig: C. F. Winter, 1884.

———. *Lehr-und Handbuch der politischen Oekonomie*. Vol. 6, *Fortsetzung*. Leipzig: C. F. Winter, 1880.

Le Play, Pierre. *La Réforme sociale en France*. 2 vols. Paris: E. Dentu, 1866.

———. *L'Organisation dutravail*. Tours: A. Mame, 1870.

———. *L'Organisation de la famille*. Paris: Téqui, 1871.

Lestrade, Gaëtan Combes de. *Eléments de sociologie*. Paris: F. Alcan, 1889.

Letourneau, Charles. *L'Evolution de la propriété*. Paris: Vigot Frères, 1889.

Lilienfeld, Paul von. *Gedanken über die Socialwissenschaft der Zukunft*. 4 vols. Hamburg: E. Behre, 1873.

List, Friedrich. *Gesammelte Schriften*. 3 vols. Stuttgart: Cotta, 1850–51.

———. *The National System of Political Economy*. Translated by Sampson S. Lloyd. London: Longmans, Green, 1885.

Long, D. Stephen. *Divine Economy: Theology & the Market*. New York: Routledge, 2000.

Malthus, Thomas Robert. *Essay on the Principle of Population*. 7th ed. London: Reeves and Turner, 1872.

Marglin, Stephen A. *The Dismal Science: How Thinking like an Economist Undermines Community*. Cambridge: Harvard University Press, 2008.

Marlo, Karl [Karl Georg Winkelblech]. *Untersuchungen über die Organisation der Arbeit, oder System der Weltöconomie*. 3 vols. Kassel: Wilhelm Appel, 1853.

Martensen, Hans Lassen. *Socialismus und Christenthum*. Gotha: Rudolf Besser, 1875.

Martineau, Louis. *La prostitution clandestine*. Paris: Delahaye, 1885.

Martyr, Justin. "The Second Apology of Justin." Pages 188–93 in *The Apostolic Fathers with Justin Martyr & Irenaeus*, edited by Alexander Roberts, James Donaldson, and A. Cleveland Coxe, vol. 1 of *The Ante-Nicene Fathers*. Buffalo, NY: Christian Literature, 1885.

Marx, Karl. *Das Kapital. Kritik der politischen Oeconomie*. Hamburg: Meissner, 1871.

Maurice, F. D. *Social Morality: Twenty-One Lectures Delivered in the University of Cambridge*. London: Macmillan, 1890.

Mellink, Bram. "Towards the Centre: Early Neoliberals in the Netherlands and the Rise of the Welfare State, 1945-1958." *Contemporary European History* 29, no. 1 (February 2020): 30–43.

Meyer, Rudolf. *Der Emancipationskampf des vierten Standes in Deutschland*. 2 vols. Berlin: Aug. Schindler, 1874–75.

Meyer, Rudolf, and F. Ardent. *La question agraire*. Paris: Retaux-Bray, 1887.

Miaskowski, A. von. *Das Problem der Grundbesitzvertheilung in Entwicklung*. Leipzig: Duncker & Humblot, 1890.

Michaels, F. S. *Monoculture: How One Story Is Changing Everything*. Kamloops, BC: Red Clover, 2011.

Mill, John Stuart. *Principles of Political Economy*. 2 vols. London: John W. Parker, 1848.

Montgomery, David, and Marcel van der Linden, eds. *The Workers' Movement in The United States, 1879-1885*. Translated by Harry Drost. New York: Cambridge University Press, 1998.

Moreau-Christophe, Louis-Mathurin. *Du problème de la misère et de sa solution, chez les peuples anciens et modernes.* 3 vols. Paris: Guillaumin, 1851.

Morosti, Louis. *Les problèmes du paupérisme; la vérité sur la propriété et le travail.* 2nd ed. Paris: A. Ghio, 1887.

Mueller, John D. *Redeeming Economics: Rediscovering the Missing Element.* Wilmington, DE: ISI Books, 2010.

Naquet, A. *Socialisme collectiviste et socialisme libéral.* Paris: E. Dentu, 1890.

Naugle, David K., Jr. *Worldview: The History of a Concept.* Grand Rapids: Eerdmans, 2002.

O'Flaherty, Edwards, and Rodney L. Peterson with Timothy A. Norton, eds. *Sunday, Sabbath, & the Weekend: Managing Time in a Global Culture.* Grand Rapids: Eerdmans, 2010.

Orr, James. *The Christian View of God & the World.* 2nd ed. Edinburgh: Andrew Elliot, 1893.

Oslington, Paul. "The Kuyperian Dream: Reconstructing Economics on Christian Foundations." *Faith & Economics* 75 (Spring 2020): 7–36.

———. *Political Economy as Natural Theology: Smith, Malthus & Their Followers.* London: Routledge, 2018.

Passy, Frédéric. "L'École de la liberté." Pages 155–231 in *Quatre écoles d'économie sociale, conférences données à l'Aula de l'université de Genève* [Four socio-economic schools: Lectures delivered in the auditorium of the University of Geneva]. Paris: Fischbacher, 1890.

———. "The School of Liberty (1890)." *Journal of Markets & Morality* 20, no. 2 (Fall 2017): 413–69.

Penslar, Derek J. *Shylock's Children: Economics & Jewish Identity in Modern Europe.* Berkeley: University of California Press, 2001.

Périn, Charles. *De la richesse dans les sociétés chrétiennes.* Paris: Victor Lecoffre, 1861.

Personal & Social Evolution with the Key of the Science of History. London: Fisher Unwin, 1890.

Pierson, N. G. *Grondbeginselen der staathuishoudkunde.* 3rd ed. Haarlem: Bohn, 1891.

Poulin, P. *Religion et socialisme.* Paris: Lacroix, Verboeckhoven, 1867.

Prinsterer, G. Groen van. *Adviezen in de Tweede Kamer der Staten-Generaal.* 2 vols. Utrecht: Kemink en Zoon, 1856–57.

———. *Adviezen in de Tweede Kamer der Staten-Generaal, zitting van 1849–1850.* 2 vols. Amsterdam: Johannes Müller, 1851.

———. *Handelingen van de Staten-Generaal, 1853–1854.* Den Haag: Algemeene Lands-Drukkerij, 1854.

———. *Nederlandsche Gedachten.* Second series. 6 vols. Amsterdam: H. Höveker, 1869–76.

———. *Vrijheid, Gelijkheid, Broederschap; toelichting op de spreuk der Revolutie.* The Hague: L. van Nifterik, 1848.

Proudhon, Pierre-Joseph. *What Is Property? An Inquiry into the Principle of Right & of Government*. Translated by Benjamin R. Tucker. New York: Humboldt, 1890.

Quack, H. P. G. *De Socialisten: person en en stelsels*. 3 vols. Amsterdam: P. N. Van Kampen & Zoon, 1875–92.

Raalte, Ersnt van, ed. *Troonredes, Openingsredes, Inhuldigingsredes 1814–1963*. 's-Gravenhage: Staatsuitgeverij, 1964.

Reuss, Louis. *La prostitution au point de vue de l'hygiène*. Paris: J.-B. Baillière, 1889.

Ricardo, David. *Rente, salaires et profits*. Paris: Guillaumin, 1888.

Richard, Emile. *La prostitution à Paris*. Paris: J.-B. Baillière, 1890.

Rienzi [Henri Hubert van Kol]. *Christendom en socialisme*. The Hague: Rh. W. Raadgeep, 1882.

Rodbertus, Karl. *Das Kapital. Vierter sozialen Brief an Von Kirchmann*. Edited by Theophil Kozak. Berlin: Putttkammer & Mühlbrecht, 1884.

Rogers, James E. Thornold. *Work & Wages*. London: Swan Sonnenschein, 1890.

Rosburg, Britney, Terry W. Griffin, and Brian Coffey. "The Cost of Being Faithful: What Do Farmers Give Up to Keep the Sabbath?" *Faith & Economics* 73 (Spring 2019): 25–45.

Roscher, Wilhelm. *Geschichte der National-Oekonomik in Deutschland*. 2 vols. Munich: R. Oldenbourg, 1874.

Rossbach, Johann Joseph. *Geschichte der Gesellschaft*. 8 vols. Wurzburg: Stuber, 1868–75.

Rullman, J. C. *Kuyper-bibliografie*. 3 vols. Kampen: Kok, 1923–40.

Ryan, John A. *A Living Wage*. New York: Macmillan, 1906.

Saint-Léon, Etienne Martin. *Histoire des corporations de métiers*. 2nd ed. Paris: Felix Aden, 1909.

Sandel, Michael. *What Money Can't Buy: The Moral Limits of Markets*. New York: Farrar, Straus and Giroux, 2012.

Say, Léon. *Le socialisme d'Etat*. Paris: Calmann Lévy, 1890.

Schaeffle, Albert Eberhard Friedrich. *Das gesellschaftliche System der menschlichen Wirthschaft*. 2 vols. Tübingen: Laupp, 1873.

———. *The Quintessence of Socialism*. London: Swan Sonnenschein, 1889.

Schauenburg, Karl Hermann. *Hygieinische Studien über die Sonntagsruhe*. Berlin: Theobald Grieben, 1876.

Schönberg, M. *Die Ziele und Bestrebungen der Sozialdemokratie*. 10th ed. Leipzig: Levien, 1890.

Secrétan, Charles. *Etudes sociales*. Paris: F. Alcan, 1889.

Slotemaker de Bruïne, J. R. *Christelijk-sociale Studiën* [Christian social studies]. 3 vols. Utrecht: Ruys, 1908.

Smeenk, C. *Voor het sociale leven. Handboek ten dienste van de christelijke vakorganisatie en de algem. arbeidersbeweging* [For social life: Manual for Christian trade unions and the labor movement in general]. Rotterdam: Libertas, 1914.

Smith, Adam. *An Inquiry into the Nature & Causes of The Wealth of Nations*. 3 vols. London: Cadell and Davies, 1812.

Smith, L. *Les coalitions et les grèves*. Paris: Guillaumin, 1885.

Sombart, Werner. *Der Bourgeois*. Munich and Leipzig: Duncker & Humblot, 1913.

Stephen, James Fitzjames. *Liberty, Equality, Fraternity*. London: Smith, Elder, 1873.

Stoffel, J. *De oplossing der sociale kwestie door opheffing van het privaat grondbezit*. Deventer: A. W. Hovenaar Rutering, 1889.

Stöpel, Franz. *Das Geld in der gegenwärtige Wirtschaft*. Minden: Bruns, 1885.

Svensson, Manfred. "Aristotelian Practical Philosophy from Melanchthon to Eisenhart: Protestant Commentaries on the *Nicomachean Ethics* 1529–1682." *Reformation & Renaissance Review* 21, no. 3 (2019): 218–38.

Tang, Zhilin. "They Are Richer, but Are They Happier: Subjective Well-Being of Chinese Citizens across the Reform Era." *Social Indicators Research* 117, no. 1 (2014): 145–64.

Tertullian. "The Prescription against Heretics." Pages 243–67 in *Latin Christianity: Its Founder, Tertullian*, translated by Peter Holmes, edited by Alexander Roberts, James Donaldson, and A. Cleveland Coxe, vol. 3 of *The Ante-Nicene Fathers*. Buffalo, NY: Christian Literature, 1885.

Thiusen, Ismar [pseud.]. *Looking Forward; or The Diothas*. London: G. P. Putnam's Sons, 1890.

Thun, Alphons. *Die Geschichte der revolutionären Bewegungen in Russland*. Leipzig: Duncker & Humblot, 1883.

Thünen, J. H. von. *Der isolirte Staat in Beziehung auf Landwirthschaft und Nationalöconomie*. 3 vols. Rostock: G. B. Leopold, 1842.

Tov, William, and Evelyn W. M. Au. "Comparing Well-Being across Nations: Conceptual and Empirical Issues." Pages 448–64 in *The Oxford Handbook of Happiness*, edited by Susan A. David, Ilona Boniwell, and Amanda Conley Ayers. Oxford: Oxford University Press, 2013.

Troost, A. "Property Rights and the Eighth Commandment." *International Reformed Bulletin* 24/25 (1966): 31.

United Nations. *The Millennium Development Goals Report 2015*. New York: United Nations, 2015.

———. *Sustainable Development Goals*. New York: United Nations.

Ursinus, Zacharius. *The Commentary of Dr. Zacharias Ursinus, on the Heidelberg Catechism*. Translated by G. W. Willard. Cincinnati: Elm Street, 1888.

———. *Explicationum Catecheticarum D. Zachariae Ursini*. Heidelberg: Johannis Halbey, 1607.

Vijf en twintig jaren middenstandsbeweging: gedenkboek van de Nederlandse Middenstandsbond, uitgegeven ter gelegenheid van zijn 25-jarig bestaan. Bewerked door A Ingenool. 's Gravenhage: Vereeniging De Nederlandse Middenstandsbond, 1927.

Villard, Amédée. *Le Socialisme moderne; son dernier état.* Paris: Guillaumin, 1889.

Voetius, Gisbertus. *Catechisatie; dat is, een grondige ende eenvoudige onderwijsinge over de leere des Christelicken Catechismi.* Edited by C. Poudroyen. Dordt: Abraham Andriessz, 1662.

Votsch, Wilhelm. *Die Vertheilung der Menschen über die Erde.* Berlin: Habel, 1884.

Vries, Tiemen de. *Overheid en Zondagsviering.* Leyden: Sijthoff, 1899.

Wagenman, Michael P. *Engaging the World with Abraham Kuyper.* Bellingham, WA: Lexham Press, 2019.

Waltershausen, August Sartorius von. *Der Moderne Sozialismus in den Vereinigten Staaten von Amerika.* Berlin: H. Bahr, 1900.

Weber, Max. *The Protestant Ethic & the Spirit of Capitalism.* New York: Routledge, 2001.

Wendel, H. von. *Die landwirthschaftliche Ankaufs- und Verkaufs-Genossenschaften.* Berlin: Parey, 1886.

Winterer, Landelin. *Le socialisme international; Coup d'oeil sur le mouvement socialiste de 1885 à 1890.* Paris: Lecoffre, Mühlhausen: Gangloff, 1890.

Wittelshöfer, Otto. *Untersuchungen über das Kapital, seine Natur und Function.* Tübingen: Laupp, 1890.

Wolterstorff, Nicholas. *Until Justice & Peace Embrace.* Grand Rapids: Eerdmans, 1983.

Woude, Rolf van der. *Geloof in de brouwerij: Opkomst, bloei en ondergang van bierbrouwerij De Gekroonde Valk.* Amsterdam: Lubberhuizen, 2009.

———. "Taming the Beast: The Long and Hard Road to the Christian Social Conference of 1952." *Journal of Markets & Morality* 14, no. 2 (Fall 2011): 419–44.

———. "Willem Hovy (1840–1915): Bewogen christelijk-sociaal ondernemer." Pages 129–60 in *Geloof in eigen zaak: Markante protestantse werkgevers in de negentiende en twintigste eeuw,* edited by Paul Werkman and Rolf van der Woude. Hilversum: Verloren, 2006.

Zacharias, Otto. *Die Bevölkerungs-Frage in ihrer Beziehung zu den sociale Nothständen der Gegenwart.* 4th ed. Jena: Mauke, 1883.

Zeegers, A. *Van Kuyper tot Keynes: De A.R.-partij op de dirigistische doolweg.* Amsterdam: Stichting Johannes Althusius, 1958.

Zeller, Eduard. *Die Philosophie der Griechen.* 3 vols. Leipzig: Fues, 1875.

Zhang, Jia Wei, Ryan T. Howell, and Colleen J. Howell. "Living in Wealthy Neighborhoods Increases Material Desires and Maladaptive Consumption." *Journal of Consumer Culture* 16, no. 1 (2016): 297–316.

ABOUT ABRAHAM KUYPER (1837–1920)

Abraham Kuyper's life began in the small Dutch village of Maassluis on October 29, 1837. During his first pastorate, he developed a deep devotion to Jesus Christ and a strong commitment to Reformed theology that profoundly influenced his later careers. He labored tirelessly, publishing two newspapers, leading a reform movement out of the state church, founding the Free University of Amsterdam, and serving as prime minister of the Netherlands. He died on November 8, 1920, after relentlessly endeavoring to integrate his faith and life. Kuyper's emphasis on worldview formation has had a transforming influence upon evangelicalism, both through the diaspora of the Dutch Reformed churches, and those they have inspired.

In the mid-nineteenth-century Dutch political arena, the increasing sympathy for the "No God, no master!" dictum of the French Revolution greatly concerned Kuyper. To desire freedom from an oppressive government or heretical religion was one thing, but to eradicate religion from politics as spheres of mutual influence was, for Kuyper, unthinkable. Because man is sinful, he reasoned, a state that derives its power from men cannot avoid the vices of fallen human impulses. True limited government flourishes best when people recognize their sinful condition and acknowledge God's divine authority. In Kuyper's words, "The sovereignty of the state as the power that protects the individual and that defines the mutual relationships among the visible spheres, rises high above them by its right to command and compel. But within these spheres ... another authority rules, an authority that descends directly from God apart from the state. This authority the state does not confer but acknowledges."

ABOUT THE
CONTRIBUTORS

Jan Peter Balkenende (Ph.D., VU University Amsterdam) is former prime minister of the Netherlands and former president of the European Council. He is currently professor of governance, institutions, and internationalization at the Erasmus University Rotterdam, chairman of the Dutch Sustainable Growth Coalition, and adviser to corporations and nonprofits.

Jordan J. Ballor (Dr. Theol., University of Zurich; Ph.D., Calvin Theological Seminary) is a senior research fellow at the Acton Institute for the Study of Religion & Liberty and a postdoctoral researcher with the Moral Markets project at the VU University Amsterdam. He serves as a general editor of the Abraham Kuyper Collected Works in Public Theology series and a coeditor of the three volumes on *Common Grace*.

Kenneth Barnes (D.Min., Reformed Theological Seminary/Highland Theological College) is Mockler-Phillips Professor of Workplace Theology and Business Ethics and Director of the Mockler Center for Faith and Ethics in the Workplace at Gordon-Conwell Theological Seminary. He has decades of experience as a corporate executive, university chaplain, researcher, and teacher, and is author most recently of *Redeeming Capitalism* (Eerdmans).

Brian Fikkert (Ph.D., Yale University) is professor of economics and community development and the founder and president of the Chalmers Center for Economic Development at Covenant College. He is coauthor of books, including *When Helping Hurts: How to Alleviate Poverty Without Hurting the Poor ... and Yourself* (Moody) and *Becoming Whole: Why the Opposite of Poverty Isn't the American Dream* (Moody).

Peter S. Heslam (D.Phil., University of Oxford) is director of Transforming Business and a senior member of Trinity College, University of Cambridge. Previously he was director of the Entrepreneurial Leadership Initiative, University of Oxford. He has published widely on business, economics, and religion and is the author of *Creating a Christian Worldview: Abraham Kuyper's Lectures on Calvinism* (Eerdmans).

Paul Oslington (Ph.D., University of Sydney; D.Theol., University of Divinity) is professor of economics at Alphacrucis College in Sydney, Australia. He is also an honorary research professor at Australian Centre for Christianity and Charles Sturt University in Canberra, Australia. He is a resident member at the Center of Theological Inquiry at Princeton in 2020, and author and editor of a number of works, including *Political Economy as Natural Theology: Smith, Malthus and Their Followers* (Routledge), *The Oxford Handbook of Christianity and Economics* (Oxford), and *Adam Smith as Theologian* (Routledge).

SUBJECT INDEX

SCRIPTURE INDEX

Old Testament

New Testament